WORLD GEOGRAPHY OF TRAVEL AND TOURISM

A REGIONAL APPROACH

Alan A. Lew, C. Michael Hall and
Dallen J. Timothy

ELSEVIER

AMSTERDAM • BOSTON • HEIDELBERG • LONDON • NEW YORK • OXFORD
PARIS • SAN DIEGO • SAN FRANCISCO • SINGAPORE • SYDNEY • TOKYO
Butterworth-Heinemann is an imprint of Elsevier

Butterworth-Heinemann is an imprint of Elsevier
Linacre House, Jordan Hill, Oxford OX2 8DP, UK
30 Corporate Drive, Suite 400, Burlington, MA 01803, USA

First edition 2008

British Library Cataloguing in Publication Data
A catalogue record for this book is available from the British Library

Library of Congress Cataloging-in-Publication Data
A catalog record for this book is available from the Library of Congress

ISBN: 978-0-7506-7978-7

For information on all Butterworth-Heinemann publications
visit our website at books.elsevier.com

Typeset by Charon Tec Ltd (A Macmillan Company), Chennai, India
www.charontec.com

Printed and bound in Canada

10 11 12   10 9 8 7 6 5 4 3

Contents

INTRODUCTION 1

1.1   GEOGRAPHY AND THE STUDY OF TOURISM

The old adage of *needing a vacation to recover from a vacation trip* reflects the often strenuous nature of holiday travels, as we try to squeeze in as many activities as possible within the short period that we are free from work. Travel and tourism, therefore, are typically considered leisure activities and a form of recreation that takes place away from the home place. The fact that tourism involves travel from one place to another, and occurs in places that are often shaped intentionally by the tourism industry, also make it very geographical.

Leisure as Non-Work

Most people have an inherent sense of what they consider to be a *leisure* activity. We generally know that it is not *work* and not something that you *must* do. In fact, it is easier to define what leisure is not than what it is. In part, this is because leisure is very subjective – what one person considers a leisure activity, another person may not consider leisure at all. A hike in the woods might be considered leisure by some, and work by someone else. Furthermore, the same person can hold these divergent views from one day to the next, depending on the social context and an individual's attitude. Despite the subjective complexities of leisure, we can generally say that leisure occurs when an individual is undertaking an activity that he or she wants to do and enjoys doing.

Leisure, therefore, can be defined as time spent free of obligation and necessity, when one is in control of one's own destiny. During pure leisure, there are no overt outside factors or forces that determine what we do and how we spend our time. While we have each been socialized to consider some forms of leisure activities more acceptable than others, we feel that during our leisure time we are free from society's expectations and demands of us.

This definition of leisure raises some intriguing questions about free will and social expectations. However, it is also limited in that it is not easily quantifiable because it does not specifically address different types of leisure (for counting purposes), nor does it describe to what extent one is free from social obligation (such as when a business trip becomes a tourist holiday). Because defining leisure as the opposite of work and obligation is so vague, we will move on to a second definition of leisure that focuses on activities.

Leisure Activities

Leisure can also be defined as a specific activity that results in the physical or mental relaxation and rejuvenation of an individual. Some popular activities that are normally associated with these results include watching television, participating in sports and other outdoor recreation activities, reading books and magazines, going to the movies, and listening to music. These activities bring relaxation to the mind, body and soul – for most people. As mentioned above, individuals can vary a lot in the types of activities they find relaxing and stressful. For some, work may actually be considered a leisure activity, while for others a leisure activity may be considered work. Defining leisure as a set of specific activities makes leisure quantifiable, but may not address an individual's motivations and goals for leisure. Therefore, a third definition has also been proposed.

Leisure as a State of Mind

Leisure can also be defined as a state of mind. This idea was expounded by the Greek philosopher Aristotle (384–322 BCE), who saw leisure as a form a self-meditation and self-improvement. He saw leisure as the most essential element of humankind because it allows for self-development, creativity and self-actualization. It enables us to step back from the constant struggles of daily life to consider what is really important in life. Only then will we know what areas of our life need improvement. While this view of leisure offers many avenues for humanistic understanding, it shares the challenges of the non-work time definition by leaving a lot of room for subjective interpretation.

While each of these views has its flaws, a combination of these views offers a fuller definition of leisure. Leisure is, therefore, an activity that spans a period of time and which is chosen of one's own free will instead of a work or social obligation, and which allows for personal relaxation, contemplation and rejuvenation.

Geography and Leisure

Almost every aspect of life is interwoven with leisure (including both recreation and tourism), either as a leisure activity or as its opposite. Because of this, the study of leisure is undertaken from a wide range of disciplinary perspectives, the most prominent being sociology and economics. Geographers have also made major contributions to leisure studies, especially in the area of tourism, because of their interests in the nature and development of places, how people use and behave in places, and the varied relationships that exist between places. The study of geography is distinct in that it encompasses both the physical sciences (physical geography) and social sciences (human or cultural geography).

Tourism, Mobility and Migration

Another way of conceptualizing tourism is as a form of voluntary temporary mobility by which people travel to another location – often for leisure or visiting friends and relations (VFR). This way of thinking about tourism helps differentiate it from forced mobility, as in the case of political or environmental refugees, for example, people having to move because of a major flood, or permanent migration. The concept of temporary mobility therefore includes a wide range of tourism-related phenomenon such as leisure travel, health tourism, volunteer tourism, educational travel, travel to second homes, working holidays and business travel.

Tourism Geography

Geography may be defined as the study of the structure and interaction of two major systems: (1) the ecological and social systems that link humans to each other and to their environment and (2) the spatial system that links one area of the earth's surface with another. From a geographical point of view, tourism studies requires an understanding of the places of tourist origin (or tourist generating areas), tourist destinations, and the relationship between the place of origin and the destination, which includes transportation routes, business and marketing relationships, and traveler motivations.

This chapter introduces many of the essential concepts of tourism geography. The remaining chapters primarily focus on a geographic understanding of tourism regions and destinations. The geographic approach to understanding regions and places is approached from two basic perspectives: physical geography and human geography.

Physical geography is divided into three areas of study: climatology, geomorphology and biogeography. *Climate* is the annual pattern of weather in a place. By contrast, *weather* is the day-to-day condition of the atmosphere. Climate has a major impact in shaping the seasonal distribution of tourist travel to destinations, and the activities they participate in when they are there. Global climate change will have major impacts on the world's tourism industry as many of the most tourism-dependent economies are located in coastal areas (where sea levels are rising) and in mountain regions (where snow is becoming more rare).

Geomorphology is the study of the shape of the earth's land surfaces and the spatial distribution of continents and islands. This includes plate tectonics, mountain building processes and surface erosion processes. These geologic processes are constantly, albeit slowly, changing the surface of the planet, creating some of the most spectacular scenic and recreation destinations in the world. Biogeography is the study of the geographic distribution of plants and animals. Climate and geomorphology define the type of vegetation that would be endemic to a place, although humans have often changed the natural vegetation over time. An understanding of biogeography is essential for the management of most ecotourism destinations and outdoor recreation resources.

Sedimentary, Igneous and Metamorphic Rock

The surface physiography of a region is shaped by its underlying rock structure. The three main types of rock are sedimentary, igneous and metamorphic. Sedimentary rock consists of successive layers of wind or waterborne materials. Under pressure, these deposits turn into rock such as sandstone, shale, limestone and coal. Sedimentary rocks are the most common type found in the United States.

PHOTO 1.1
Rural Landscape in the KwaZulu Natal province of South Africa

Source: Alan A. Lew

Igneous rock originates deep within the surface of the earth. High temperatures in the center of the earth cause rock to melt. Molten magma *plutons* push their way up through the earth's crust. If the pluton solidifies before it reaches the earth's surface, it is known as an *intrusive igneous formation*. A batholith is a massive intrusive feature. Batholiths exposed through the erosion of upper rock layers, such as California's Sierra Nevada Range, are usually composed of granite. Plutons that reach the surface of the earth extrude as lava.

Metamorphic rocks were once either sedimentary or igneous but have been changed through intense heat and pressure. This often happens where there is folding and crumpling of the earth's crust. Marble is a metamorphosed form of sedimentary limestone, while diamonds are a metamorphosed form of sedimentary coal.

Continental Drift and the Emergence of Life

Although the planet earth seems to be a solid, it is actually much more of a liquid. The very core of the earth is believed to be comprised of solid iron, measuring some 780 miles (1250 km) from the center to its edge. The next 3,000 miles (4800 km) out is all liquid. The first 1,380 miles (2200 km) is liquid iron and nickel, while the remaining 1,550–1,750 miles (2500–2800 km), varying in different locations, is a mixture of molten and solid rocks known as the mantel. The outermost 5–40 miles (8 to 65 km) is the solid crust which we stand on and feel so secure about. In fact, the molten iron ore and rock beneath us is in constant motion, churning upwards in the same way the bubbles boil from the bottom of a boiling pot of water. This churning motion causes the hard crust to crack and shake (earthquakes). The mantel material pushes its way to the surface through volcanoes and undersea oceanic rift zones. The lightest material in the earth's crust has gradually come together to form the continents, which literally float on top of the heavier crustal material. The churning molten rock below pushes the continents around in a process known as continental drift. In addition to the continents, large blocks of heavier ocean floor are also being pushed about the surface of the earth. The study of this process is known as *plate tectonics*. Some 20 ocean and continent plates have been identified on the surface of the earth today.

It is believed that the earth solidified as a planet approximately 4.7 billion years ago. For the first 1.5 billion years of its existence, there was no life on the planet. While some areas of the planet have exposed rock that dates back some 4 billion years, most of the surface rock is much younger. The first plant life, algae, probably came into existence 3.2 billion years ago. Two billion years of plant development passed before the first waterborne animal life came into existence. Trilobites dominated the seas 600 million years ago, and the first fish came into existence 100 million years later. About 440 million years ago the first surface life appeared in the form of plants. Fish began to crawl from the sea 400 million years ago, leading to the development of the first amphibians.

About 360 million years ago, all of the continental land masses moved together to form a single land mass call Pangaea (meaning *all lands*). Many large mountain chains were created from the collision of the continents. After some 75 million years of evolution, the reptiles became what we now call dinosaurs and dominated animal life over the entire planet. Trilobites finally became extinct at this same time (225 million years ago). Geologic evidence indicates that starting approximately 200 million years ago,

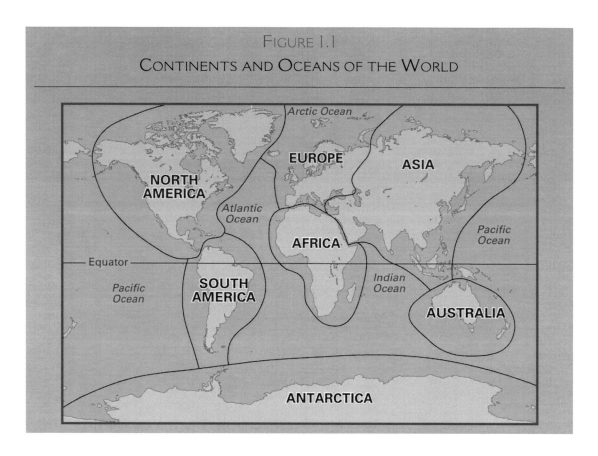

FIGURE 1.1

CONTINENTS AND OCEANS OF THE WORLD

Pangaea started to break up into separate continents that would eventually become what we know today. The mountains also stopped growing at this time and have been eroding ever since, forming some of the lower mountain systems of the world today, including the Appalachians in North America and the Urals in Russia.

The first birds came into existence some 160 million years ago. Most dinosaurs suddenly died out 90 million years later. It was at this time that the tallest mountains today first started forming, including the Himalayas (Asia), the Alps (Europe), the Andes (South America) and the Rocky Mountains (North America). All of these mountain systems were created from the collision of continental and ocean plates. Current evidence indicates that the first primates were also coming into existence some 65 million years ago, as mammals replaced the dinosaurs as the dominant species on all the continents, except Australia. Elephants appeared 45 million years ago. After over 60 million years of evolution, primates eventually evolved into humans – a mere 2 million years ago (in the form of the Homo habilis species). Modern humans (Homo sapiens) evolved 40,000 years ago, at about the same time the earliest crossing of humans into North America from Asia may have occurred. (Most scholars accept that humans crossed into North America 12,000 years ago – evidence of crossing prior to that is somewhat controversial.) The earliest recorded history of any civilization dates back 5,000 years. Our modern calendar dates back 2,000 years. The modern period of European settlement in North America is only 500 years old. If the 110-story Sears Tower in Chicago were to represent the entire history of the planet earth, the top 12 inches would be the part in which the various human species have been present (Figure 1.1).

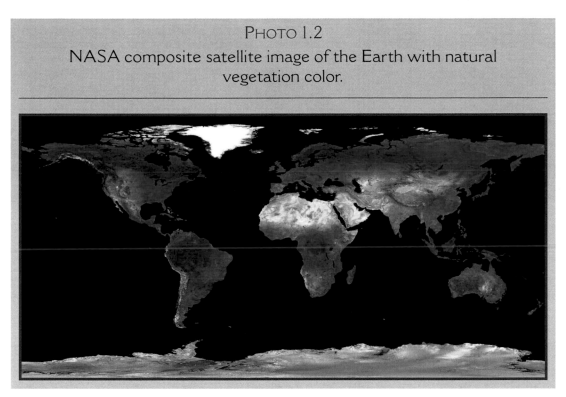

PHOTO 1.2

NASA composite satellite image of the Earth with natural vegetation color.

Source: NASA Visible Earth

Factors in Weather and Climate

Weather refers to the day-to-day changes in the atmosphere of a place. Climate, on the other hand, refers to the annual pattern of atmospheric conditions in a place. Climate classifications are primarily based on (1) the seasonal variations in temperature and (2) the annual rainfall amount and seasonality. The major factors that influence climate are (1) latitude, (2) continentality, (3) air masses and (4) surface physiography.

Because the earth moves around the sun on a tilted axis, the northern hemisphere is closest to the sun in June and farthest from the sun in December. These extremes become most pronounced as one gets closer to the poles. North of the Arctic Circle, Alaska's summer days have 24 hours of sun, while winter days have 24 hours of cold darkness. At the other extreme, the length of Florida's days stays about the same all year round, and average winter temperatures are only 10°F less than average summer temperatures. Higher latitudes (closer to the poles), therefore, have greater annual temperature extremes and especially cold winters.

Continentality and Maritime Climates

Land (rocks and dirt) heats and cools faster than does water. Climatically, this means that the large continents of the world are warmer than the oceans in their summer months and colder than the oceans in their winter months. This further contributes to the intense winter cold experienced by the interior of the continents. Conversely, summer temperatures are as much as 50°F hotter in the interior of the continent than in coastal areas. Along the edges of most continents, the moderating influence of the oceans keeps summer temperatures down and winter temperatures relatively high. The onshore ocean winds hitting San Francisco, for example, give it almost the same temperature all year round. The maritime climate of San Francisco is the opposite of the continentality found in Denver in the interior of North America.

High and Low Pressure Air Masses

Large movements of air over the surface of the earth generally have either rising or falling patterns. Air that is rising from the earth's surface forms low pressure air masses. When the rising air falls, it forms a high pressure air mass (because the air is pushing down on the earth's surface). Rings of predominantly high and low pressure encircle the earth. Low pressure on the equator brings year-round rainfall, creating tropical rain forests. Descending dry air creates high pressure north and south of the equator. These are where the large deserts of the world are located. Humid low pressure systems ring the globe north of here, creating cool weather rain forests on the coasts of Washington and British Columbia in North America and the British Isles in Europe. Finally, a dry high pressure system is situated over the North and South Poles, turning the north coast of Alaska and central Antarctica into a frozen desert (Figures 1.2 and 1.3.)

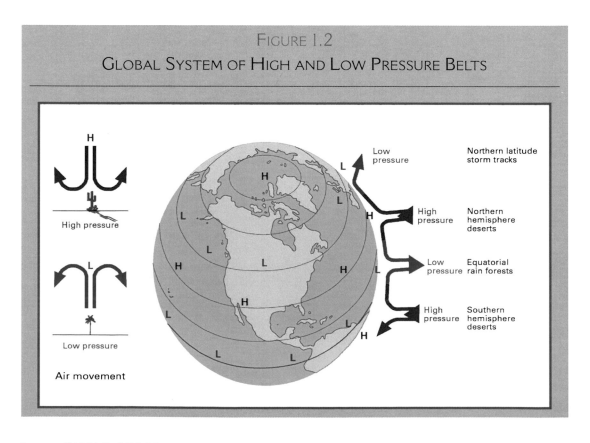

FIGURE 1.2

GLOBAL SYSTEM OF HIGH AND LOW PRESSURE BELTS

FIGURE 1.3

WORLD CLIMATES, WIND DIRECTIONS AND OCEAN CIRCULATIONS

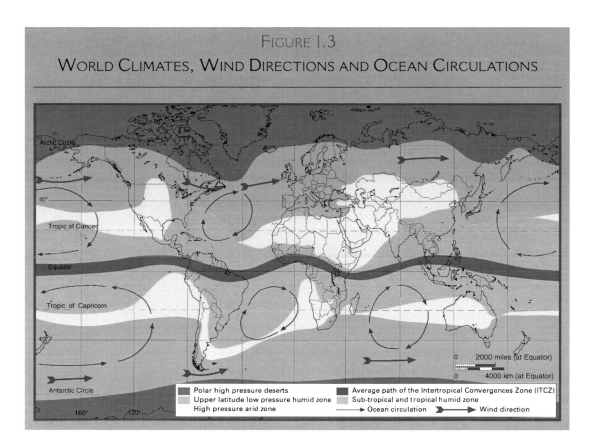

Polar high pressure deserts	Average path of the Intertropical Convergences Zone (ITCZ)
Upper latitude low pressure humid zone	Sub-tropical and tropical humid zone
High pressure arid zone	Ocean circulation / Wind direction

PHOTO 1.3

NASA composite satellite image of the Earth with cloud cover. The Intertropical Convergence Zone can be seen along the equator, high and low pressure desert areas can be seen with little cloud cover, and upper latitude storm tracks can be seen over northern North America and Eurasia and below Australia and South America

Source: NASA Visible Earth

Surface Physiography: Altitudinal Zonation and Rainshadows

One of the two ways that surface physiography influences climate is through altitudinal zonation. *Altitudinal zonation* results from the fact that higher elevations are colder than lower elevations. As one moves up a high mountain slope, the climate and resulting vegetation change from warmer to colder weather types. The effect is similar to moving from lower to higher latitudes (i.e., from the equator to the poles). Altitudinal zonation is most pronounced in arid regions, like the southwestern United States, where mountain peaks stand out as lush islands in a sea of desert.

The second way that physiography influences climate is through the creation of a *rainshadow*. Water molecules slow down when the air gets colder, allowing condensation and clouds to form. When the temperature is warmer, the molecules warm up and move faster, and the clouds dissipate. As a mass of warm air rises into an area of colder air, it will eventually cool to a temperature at which condensation will occur and a cloud will form. This is known as the *dew point* temperature. If the air mass continues to rise and cool, condensation increases until precipitation (rain, snow, hail, etc.) occurs.

This process takes place regularly in mountain areas throughout the world. Air masses are pushed up the windward side of the mountains in a process known as *orographic uplift*. This cools the air and typically results in precipitation (rain or snow). By the time the air mass reaches the top of these ranges, it has lost much of its original moisture. The air mass then starts down the back side of the mountain. This causes the air to warm up and the molecules to speed up, with the result that the clouds disappear

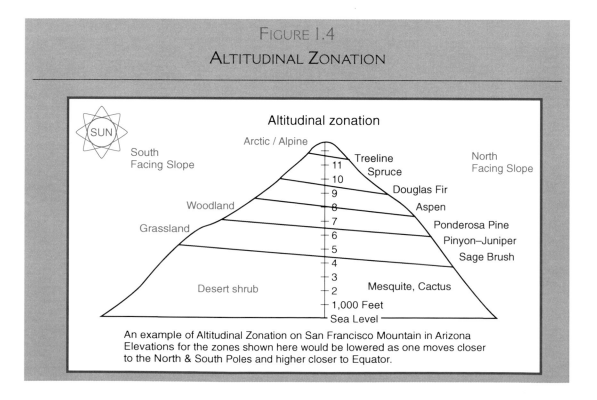

FIGURE 1.4

ALTITUDINAL ZONATION

An example of Altitudinal Zonation on San Francisco Mountain in Arizona
Elevations for the zones shown here would be lowered as one moves closer
to the North & South Poles and higher closer to Equator.

and the little moisture that is left is now spread out over a wider area. The downwind (or *leeward*) side is in the *rainshadow* of the mountain (Figure 1.4).

Climate and Biogeography

Climate has a direct impact on the biogeographic distribution of the natural vegetation in a region. In fact, the two are often inseparable. The major factors of climate that affect vegetation patterns are humidity (precipitation) and temperature. High humidity and high temperature are associated with lush, green vegetation, such as that found in tropical rain forests. High temperature and low humidity are associated with arid, desert vegetation. Humidity becomes less important as temperatures decrease. The lowest temperature regions are associated with spruce coniferous trees (found in most of Siberia and Canada) and tundra (a treeless type of grass and moss found in the northern extremes of the continents). Between these three extremes (1: high temperature and humidity, 2: high temperature and low humidity, and 3: low temperature) is a mixture of evergreen trees, deciduous trees (those that lose their leaves in winter) and grasslands.

1.3   HUMAN GEOGRAPHY

Human geography is not as easily broken down into subdisciplinary areas as is physical geography. In very general terms, however, it is possible to identify an economic geography branch (including population, urban, transportation and other related geographies) and a cultural geography branch (including historical geography, environmental perception and human ecology). In all areas of geography, there is considerable crossover with other disciplines (such as economics, history and biology). However, geographers tend to maintain a unique perspective in their emphasis on *space*, *place* and *regional* phenomena.

Place and Space

Geography deals with two basic areas of inquiry about the world around us: place and space. Geography seeks to portray accurately the character of places. Place location (where is it?) is fundamental to understanding a place's characteristics. Place description (what is it like?) is part of the art of geography. These are the types of questions that most people would readily identify with geography. Geographers attempt to develop an awareness and understanding of the qualities of a place that make it special. We say that places that exhibit these special qualities have a strong sense of place; they are places that have a personality and significance and are often remembered long after we have left them.

Places are points of presence. A place exists and has a location. Geographic places exist in geographic space – typically some location on the surface of the earth. Other, non-geographic places also exist. These are mostly fictional places, but can also be virtual

Source: Dallen J. Timothy

places. In this book, the word place always refers to geographic places. All places, whether geographic or not, share in common (1) some means of distinguishing one place from another (for geographic places, this may simply be a location address, but typically also includes physical and cultural landscape features such as mountains and buildings) and (2) a relationship with other places within its spatial realm (for geographic places, you can at least measure a distance between any two places on the planet, although many other types of relationships also exist, such as economic and cultural).

Geographic Space

Space is another central or transcendent theme of geography. Besides knowing where a place is and what it is like, geography seeks to determine the reason places are located where they are and why they develop the characteristics that they have. The answer often involves understanding how places relate to one another over space. Examples of spatial relationships between places include transportation routes and communication linkages (both of which have changed over time with technological developments), ethnic ties (as people migrate from one place to another), and political associations (which often involve complex historical processes). The distribution of something over an area is called its spatial pattern or spatial organization. The word spatial here refers to geographic space, rather than outer space. Geographic space is the three-dimensional space that encompasses the livable surface of the earth.

Geography is sometimes called a spatial science because of the importance of spatial relationships in a geographic understanding of the world. This spatial aspect of geography is most easily seen and perhaps understood in the production of maps and map-like diagrams – most of which show the distribution of one or more variables over space. Maps are also identified by the general public as being a fundamental aspect of geography. How these patterns came to be and how they function are key questions in geography. Geography is essentially the study of the spatial organization of the world in which we all live.

Regional Geography and Regions

All of these various aspects of geography are brought together in the study of places and regions. For this reason, regional geography has been referred to as a *virtuoso performance* – it requires familiarity with the breadth of geography and competence in pulling together the diverse strands of knowledge to create a sense of place or regional character. The difference between a *region* and a *place* is dependent on scale and perception. A metropolitan area (comprising many cities that grow into one another) can be considered a place, at a national or international scale, or a region, at a local scale.

Another definition of a region is an area of land that is larger than a place and which contains a common characteristic, such as the growing of a particular crop or the market area of a product. There are many ways in which space can be regionalized in this way. Examples include political regions, economic regions, physical regions and cultural regions. Most regions are single, contiguous areas, although there are exceptions to this, such as the separation of Alaska from the rest of the United States by the country of Canada. Regions can be divided into smaller units, or subregions, if appropriate for analysis. Each region or unit, however, contains some collection of shared characteristics. Sometimes, these are more physical in nature; at other times, they are more social.

The geographic regions of the world, around which the chapters of this book are constructed, include both physical and human characteristics. For some regions, the human characteristics are emphasized more, while other regions are based more on physical characteristics. There is no fixed rule regarding this, and regional definitions can and do change through time as people's image and perception of them change. In general, regions with sparse populations are more likely to be defined in terms of their physical geographic features, while those with high population densities, such as the northeastern Atlantic seaboard, are characterized more by their cultural and economic characteristics.

Core Area and Transition Zone

Most of the discussion of different regions in this text focuses on core area characteristics. The core area is the place where the shared characteristics that are used to define a region are most predominant. The core area of one region is distinctly different from the core area of a neighboring region. Transition zones are areas between two regions that share characteristics of both to some extent. The characteristic(s) that defines each region are generally weaker in the transition zone. For example, the Mediterranean Sea clearly marks a distinct boundary between Europe and Africa, with almost no transition zone. You are either in Europe or you are on Africa. On the other hand, the boundary between the Europe and Asia is a broad transition zone. Though the Ural Mountains provide a convenient demarcation between the two continents, there is actually nothing especially noticeable about the Urals that separates the European physical and cultural realm from that of Asia. Similarly, the division between the United States South, the United States Midwest, and the United States Great Plains subregions is not easily defined. The state of Missouri, for example, is included in the south by some authors, although it could justifiably be included in the Midwest or the Great Plains, because it shares core area characteristics with all three of these regions.

Homogeneous Regions

Homogeneous regions contain a common characteristic that is found throughout an area in equal degree. Island nations, such as Japan, tend to be more homogeneous than continent-based nations, though exceptions exist. The common characteristic may be one or a group of characteristics. A political entity, such as a country or state, which by definition encompasses its own citizens within its boundaries, is a homogeneous region. Also known as *uniform* and *formal* regions, homogeneous regions have more clearly defined boundaries (i.e., more narrow transition zones) than do nodal regions.

Nodal Regions

Also known as *functional* and *focal* regions, nodal regions have a central point at which the characteristic defining the region is most predominant. The farther away from this central point, the less predominant is the characteristic. A city's area of economic and social influence is usually nodal. The farther one moves away from a major metropolitan city, such as Sydney, Australia, the less is its economic influence, until one moves into the influence area of another major city, such a Melbourne, Australia. The area within the sphere of influence of a nodal center is known as its hinterland or periphery. Nodal regions have well-defined core areas and poorly defined boundaries, with broad transition zones. The *core-periphery* model of economic development, which assumes that the development of peripheral locations is controlled by decision makers in core locations, is fundamentally the description of a nodal region.

PHOTO 1.5
NASA simulation of night time light distribution over the surface of the earth, based on population density and level or economic activity. In this image, large areas with the same light level, such as much of India, would be homogenous regions. Those with bright lights that quickly fade to dim lights, such as the west coast of the United States, are examples of nodal regions

Source: NASA Visible Earth

A *Priori* Regions

An *a priori* region is one that is arbitrarily drawn on the surface of the earth. Political units, such as states, provinces and countries, are the most common type of a priori region. Sometimes, the political boundary separating one country from another is not related to any natural or human geographical boundary but is instead decided by negotiation or expedience. Almost every straight line on a map is a sign of a prior negotiation that ignores cultures, mountains, valleys and other terrain features. Many of the political boundaries in Africa and the Southwest Asia (the Middle East), are the result of political processes that, either intentionally or out of ignorance, divide major cultural groups into more than one country.

A *Sense of Place*

Geographer Yi-Fu Tuan has suggested that a place comes into existence when humans give meaning to a part of the larger geographic space. Anytime we give a name to a location, we separate it from the undefined space around it. Some places, however, have more social meaning, or stronger definitions and names, than others. For geographers, and others, these places are said to have a strong *Sense of Place*.

Geographers are interested in why certain places hold special meaning to particular people. Places that have a strong *sense of place* have a strong identity and character that is deeply felt by both its inhabitants and visitors. It is a social phenomenon that exists independent of any one individual's perceptions or experiences. This feeling may be derived from the natural environment, but is more often made up of a mix of natural and cultural features in the landscape, including the people who occupy the landscape.

Places that lack a *sense of place* are referred to as *placeless*. Placeless landscapes are those that have no special relationship to the place in which they are located – they could be anywhere. Roadside strip shopping malls, gas stations and convenience stores, fast food chains, and national department stores are examples of placeless landscape elements.

Sense of Place Tourism Examples

Can you think of a place that has a strong sense of place? How about a *placeless* place? Most communities have examples of both; and leisure landscapes can be of both types, as well. Have you ever heard of Paris as being a romantic place to visit? Does Paris have some magical air or water that transforms people into romantics? What Paris has developed is a *sense of place* that includes love and romance. The environment provides an *atmosphere of love* based on its history, architecture, culture and mythology.

Many tourists are attracted to specific places because of an established sense of place expectation. For example, certain older retail districts provide particular fascination for visitors by offering experiences of the past or of other places. Thematic retail districts include historic preservation districts, waterfront *fisherman's wharf* districts, and more playful cowboy towns and Scandinavian or German communities.

The importance of sense of place and tourism is clear. Tourists travel to places for specific reasons. Many of those reasons are because the destination has a known sense of place. Whether the *sense of place* is based on religion, art, romance, food, or just for cultural information, people travel for the experience. Places all over the globe provide those experiences for different meanings and at different degrees of personal significance.

Individual Sense of Place

Individuals also have a personal sense of place, which creates special existential relationships between them and places that they feel most attached to. The place where one lives often has this special meaning, even though most outsiders might not feel such a strong sense of place there. Places that have served as significant settings in one's life also may have a strong sense of place for an individual. Ancestral homelands are often like this. Examples include Israel for Jewish people everywhere, China for overseas ethnic Chinese, and Ireland for Irish-Americans. These special places often attract us again and again, as tourists, recreationists, and sometimes as genealogists.

People tend to remember places by their feelings. Sight, sound, smell, taste and hearing are all methods that we use to remember particular places. Geographers, psychologists and other social scientists have only recently begun to explore the multiple ways that we experience and remember places we have visited.

Environmental Perception and Behavior

Environmental perception is an area of study that overlaps geography and psychology, and sometimes philosophy. It deals with how people perceive and, as a result, behave in the environment where they live. For example, the northern Europeans initially perceived the Great Plains as a useless environment, referring to it as the *Great American Desert*. Alternatively, the Spanish coming from Mexico recognized the region as having great potential for cattle raising, similar to what they were used to in central Spain. In another example, many more traditional societies today consider communal ownership of land as far more appropriate than private land ownership, which has long been predominant among those originally from European and East Asian cultures. The way people perceive and behave in the world reflects many aspects of their culture, experiences, socioeconomic background, and value system and has a lot to tell us about the cultural landscapes they create.

Globalization and Localization

The world has become a much smaller place in recent decades due to advances in technology and the opening up of global trade, both of which have contributed to an increase in placelessness worldwide. Through television and movies, values and experiences are shared across cultures and continents. Through the Internet, people today are able to communicate closely with friends and colleagues on opposite sides of the globe just as if they were in the building next door. Transnational corporations (TNCs, producing in two or three countries) and multinational companies (MNCs, with offices in three or more countries) are often cited as the new force bringing about this global transformation by operating beyond the political and geographic confines of traditional countries. While there is some truth to this, it is also true that states are as important as they have ever been, and a trend that is directly opposed to globalization seems to have become particularly significant in recent years. Increasing localization is emerging at the same time as globalization, as communities seek to express their individuality and local autonomy. In some places, this has resulted in demands for greater political autonomy or even independence. In other cases, it can be seen in such things as the rapid rise in local micro-breweries across North America in the 1990s.

Postindustrial and Post-Fordist Society

The trend toward localization has been attributed to a fundamental change in North American European society – the transition from an industrial economy (in which more people work in industries than any other economic sector) to a postindustrial economy (with the majority of people employed in service jobs). Accompanying this economic transition there has been a shift from an emphasis on assembly-line, mass-produced merchandise (which Henry Ford first perfected in building the model-T automobile, and known as *Fordism*) to one on products that are more personalized and individualized, known as *post-Fordist*. This is reflected in an increasingly diverse array of products (including landscape experiences) designed to match the interests of smaller niche markets of people who are willing to pay more for personal and customized services. Specialty travel, such a culinary and bicycle tours, are examples of post-Fordist tourism.

Postmodernism and Historic Preservation

Another concept that is related to these economic trends is *postmodernism*, which came out of architecture but has since been expanded to encompass a broad realm of values in contemporary society. Architecture plays a major role in shaping the visual landscape. Modernism was the total rejection of historical approaches to architectural

PHOTO 1.6

Creek street in Ketchikan, Alaska. Historic creek street is within easy walking distance of the large cruise ships that ply the inside passage to Glacier Bay National Park

Source: Alan A. Lew

design and was an architectural trend that dominated much of the late 19th and early 20th century building construction in North America. Skyscrapers are typical of the modernist approach. Postmodernism is a rejection of modernism and is sometimes viewed as a return to, or an embracing of, more historical approaches to building design, as well as social values. This is most clearly seen in the historic preservation movements that first became popular in North America in the 1960s.

At a broader social scale, a postmodern world is also more relativist (everything can and should be judged on its own merit, rather than based on universal moral values), and thus we can select from not only the past, but also from an eclectic and diverse realm of elements of different cultures around the world. Thus, postmodernism brings together both the local and the global and, hopefully, does not create something that is placeless in the process.

McDisneyfication

McDisneyfication is a postmodern opposite of Sense of Place. This term was coined by George Ritzer and Allan Liska to describe the *McDonaldization* (another Ritzer term) of service industries (fast and mass produced) and the Disneyfication of tourism (the epitome of which includes Disneyland and Las Vegas). McDonalds restaurants and the Disney theme parks are considered *hypermodern* models of:

1. *Efficiency*: Getting the most for one's money, which usually means seeing, doing and eating as much as possible
2. *Predictability*: Safety, known cleanliness and service standards, plus the ability to communicate in a common language
3. *Calculability*: Precisely defined itineraries, with no unexpected costs or other surprises
4. *Control*: Service employees whose behavior is tightly controlled by scripts (telling them what to say and how to react), and the preferred use of advanced technologies to control employees and clients/guests

These models now influence many aspects of the contemporary modern landscape and lifestyle. Examples of McDisneyfied places include: theme amusement parks, cruise ships, Las Vegas hotels and casinos, themed shopping malls and strip malls, some chain restaurants (e.g., the Rainforest Cafes), and a variety of public entertainment spaces. The very success of these environments seems to indicate that this is what people want. The holiday lifestyle is becoming omnipresent in the American (and global) landscape. Yet, these McDisneyfied places are as placeless as the less entertaining mass shopping and work environments that are even more widespread in the globalizing international urban landscapes.

Environmental Impacts

Globalization encompasses many of the major economic and social impacts that international tourism has on destinations. Tourism, however, also impacts the physical environment. For many places the natural environment is the destination's major attraction. Ocean beaches, high mountains, and tropical and temperate forests, are all popular tourist environments. Many of these natural environments, however, are sensitive to over-use and mis-use. In Northern Arizona the major tourist attraction is the Grand Canyon, which is also one of the best known international attractions in the United States. However, with some 4 million tourists a year, mostly concentrated in the summer months and mostly arriving by private automobile, the Grand Canyon National Park has experienced significant urban-like congestion and pollution. Haze has increased in the canyon, and photographers are finding it more difficult to get a good picture because of a decrease in the number of very clear days. While tourists themselves contribute to the haze problem, it mostly comes from urban air pollution from the metropolitan areas of Las Vegas and Los Angeles. Will people want to continue visiting the Grand Canyon if its beauty and magnificence are masked by air

TOURISM ISSUES AND INSIGHTS
GLOBAL ENVIRONMENTAL CHANGE

Although we often recognize change at a local level it is becoming increasingly apparent that environmental change is occurring at a global scale and that tourism is involved in these change processes in various ways. Human impacts on the environment can have a global nature in two ways. First, global refers to the spatial scale, e.g., the climate and the oceans have the characteristic of a global system and both influence and are influenced by tourism production and consumption. A second kind of global environmental change (GEC) occurs if a change, occurs on a worldwide scale, or represents a significant fraction of the total global resource, for example, biodiversity loss and urbanization. Tourism is significant for both types of change which encompass several different areas of environmental impact:

- Climate change
- Land use change
- Mobility of diseases, pests and weeds
- Water availability
- Urbanization
- Biodiversity loss

The media focus is often on climate change, but it is important to recognize that this is only one, albeit extremely important, area of GEC. Furthermore, it must also be recognized that these changes are interrelated although change is never uniform across time and space. Therefore, the changes you see in your neighborhood will often be different from those occurring in other parts of the world. How we react to those changes though will depend on such factors as our knowledge level, political institutions, culture and how we rank environmental risk in relation to the other factors that affect our lives and decision making.

Sources

Gössling, S. and Hall, C.M. (eds) (2006) *Tourism and Global Environmental Change*, Routledge, London.
Hall, C.M. (2006) New Zealand tourism entrepreneur attitudes and behaviours with respect to climate change adaption and mitigation, *International Journal of Innovation and Sustainable Development*, 1(3): 229–237.

pollution? What would the Grand Canyon experience be if visitors could not see it or if most of their experience was traffic congestion?

Sustainable Tourism

Sustainable development is defined as development that meets the needs of the present without compromising the ability of future generations to meet their own needs. The application of sustainable development to tourism is known as *sustainable tourism*, which has become an important part of planning for the conservation and development of natural and cultural resources. Sustainable tourism often includes an emphasis on mass transit, renewable resources, leave-no-trace activities and community development. The challenge of the *sustainable development* concept is how to balance environmental conservation (the *sustainable* part) with economic development (the *development* part). This is typically simplified into a political dichotomy between the environmental *Left* and the pro-development *Right*. Successful sustainable development efforts have overcome these political divisions to find and work toward a common future.

In recent years the United States National Park Service (NPS) and other government authorities have been trying to address the environmental degradation of the Grand Canyon by limiting the impact of sightseeing helicopters and airplanes, reducing the number of motorized boats on the Colorado River, working to adopt a mass transit system that would replace the use of private automobiles within the park, and increasing pollution controls on regional power plants. The NPS also requires the private vendors who manage the hotels and restaurants in the park to practice resource conservation and renewable energy in their operations.

Interpretation

Interpretation, or education, about the natural environment is a key component of any tourism experience. Without it, tourists might not be inspired to engage in an activity, might not be able to find their way to locations, and might not understand the full significance of the area they are visiting. Subliminal forms of interpretation tell us about places in indirect ways, such as through music, news stories, fiction, movies and architectural design. More direct and intentional forms of interpretation include maps, information boards and human guides. How places are interpreted in these many different ways influences people's perception and experience of places and environments. Interpretation serves as a key variable in creating satisfactory visitor experiences, though many places are subject to different and conflicting interpretations that represent divergent views within a society. Interpretation is also related to the concept of *sense of place* and how people interpret places and place experiences.

Summary

Geography is important to the study of tourism because tourism is geographical in nature. It occurs in places, it involves movement and activities across space (between places), and includes activities in which place character and personal self-identities are formed through the relationships created among places, landscapes and people. Physical geography provides the essential background against which tourism places are created. Environmental impacts and concerns are major issues that must be considered in managing the development of tourism places. Human geography provides an understanding of the social and economic relationships that exist in providing tourism opportunities and activities, as well as the special meaning that these places have to individuals. An area's sense of place, in many circumstances, is the driving force behind tourism development. After all, without the uniqueness of places, tourism would be mundane and uninteresting. Through an understanding of the physical and human geography of the earth, a goal of this book is to provide that sense of place for destinations around the globe.

1.4   THE TOURISM INDUSTRY

Tourism is a global phenomenon that includes a multitude of different types of businesses and government entities. It is a source of substantial economic and social consequence and requires objective and scientific understanding. However, just as the definition of leisure presents a challenge, so too does the definition of the *tourism industry*.

PHOTO 1.7
The Geographer Cafe in the historic port city of Melaka, Malaysia

Source: Alan A. Lew

Defining Tourists

Without tourists there would be no tourism industry. Tourists travel to attractions and find new attractions even when developers and locals have not yet found or promoted them. It is more common, though, that the tourist (or potential tourist) is the one who is bombarded with advertisements and hawkers trying to get them to spend their money.

We usually think of a tourist as someone who is vacationing somewhere that is far from home. But the technical definition of a tourist is a little more specific. Most of the definitions that are used for statistical purposes consider a tourist as anyone who travels to a place outside of their usual residential environment and stays away for at least one night, but no more than one year. The motivation for the trip is irrelevant – the trip could be for business reasons, to visit friends and family (known as VFR travel), for education, or simply for pleasure. This definition is used to compare tourist arrivals among countries internationally, by organizations such as the World Tourism Organization (UNWTO).

Different definitions are sometimes used within a country and within local destinations. China, for example, counts day visitors (not staying overnight) in its total tourist numbers, although they also provide standardized numbers to the UNWTO. Many countries separate business travelers from leisure travelers. For international travel overall, leisure travelers generally outnumber business travelers two to one. This, however, varies considerably among destinations. Business travelers tend to pay more for their airline tickets and hotels than do vacation travelers, but their stay at a destination is usually shorter.

Recreationists

At the opposite end of the tourist trip is the recreation activity. The clearest form of a non-tourism recreation activity is any leisure activity that occurs within someone's residential home place. (The exception would be planning a vacation trip.) As recreationists travels further away from home, the same activity might be transformed into tourism. In general, recreation activities become *tourists activities* (or *tourism products*) when they are provided by private sector companies who mostly service non-resident visitors. They are considered recreation products when visiting tourists comprise a minority of the clients served.

Day Trippers

Day trips (also known as *excursions*) are trips that take someone away from their home, but do not involve an overnight stay. A day excursion can be considered a recreation activity, though because it normally occurs well beyond the home place, the activities and services that are used are normally the same as those provided to tourists by the tourism industry. In many tourist destinations, separating those who are tourists from those who are day-tripping recreationists is difficult. One way of doing this is to compare overnight tourist numbers estimated from hotel taxes and total visitor numbers estimated from attraction receipts. The methodology is not perfect, but can be an important first step in segmenting visitors into major types for marketing purposes.

Market Segmentation

Geography, including distance traveled and place of origin, is one of the most widely used forms of visitor market segmentation. It is generally the easiest form of visitor data to obtain because it requires only one simple question of the visitors, and can be obtained from hotel and motel registration records (with appropriate privacy measures). Advertising and promotional campaigns can then be tailored for use in each of the major places from which visitors and users originate. The second most important form of data for market segmentation is visitor or user motivation. Though more difficult to obtain, a lot of research has been done to define the varied motivation of tourists.

Defining Industries

An industry is defined as a set of businesses that share in the production of a common product. For example, the auto industry consists of businesses that manufacture, sell and service automobiles; the gaming industry includes businesses that are associated with the activity of gambling. A set of businesses must meet three criteria to be considered an industry:

1. They produce essentially the same product
2. They use essentially the same technology
3. The product output is large enough to warrant data collection and reporting

Tourism is one of the largest service industries in the world. International tourism expenditures and receipt account for 30 percent of all international trade in services (2002 data, World Tourism Organization). This definition of tourism includes a large part of the recreation activities that occur on the planet, especially anything that is considered an *attraction*, as well almost all of the hospitality industry (hotels, restaurants and related businesses), and a good chunk of the transportation industry (especially airplanes, intercity buses and trains). However, international definitions of what constitutes particular sectors is important in determining estimates of their relative size.

Demand for travel and tourism continues to increase, despite terrorist threats, and especially as leisure time and economic well being increase in the newly developing economies of Asia, Latin America, Eastern Europe and elsewhere. In fact, according to the UNWTO and aircraft manufacturers, such as Airbus and Boeing, the number of international travelers and installed seats in aircraft are both expected to double between 2000 and 2020. As a result of growth in the number of aircraft worldwide and demand for travel the overall distances of flights are predicted to increase, with the average distance flown growing from 1,437 km in 2002 to 1,516 km in 2022.

International Standards

Some accounts claim that tourism is the world's largest industry overall, not just the largest service industry. These claims are subject to debate. More conservative estimates place tourism as the world's fourth largest industry when compared to heavy industrial sectors, accounting for 7 percent of global trade, and behind chemicals, automobiles and oil.

For such a claim to be made, tourism must be defined and measured in a way that is consistent with the conventions and tools used in macroeconomics. These include the International Standard Industrial Classification (ISIC), the Central Product Classification (CPC) and Systems of National Accounts (SNA is the analytical framework used by most countries to collect, order and analyze macroeconomic performance).

Tourism Industry Elements

However tourism is defined, most people would include the elements of movement (transportation), of remaining temporarily in one place (accommodations), consuming food and drink (which could be an attraction), and participating in activities (attractions). The transportation sector generally includes airlines and airports, trains, buses, taxis, private automobiles, boats and ferries, the servicing and repair of these transportation modes, and travel agents and tour companies that facilitate transportation. The accommodations sector can include hotels, motels, resorts, campgrounds, the homes of friends and relatives, cruise ships, accommodation booking agencies and businesses that service these different accommodations.

Food and Beverage

Food and beverage consumption is often closely related to accommodations, though not always. The food and beverage industry includes all forms of restaurants and eateries (including those in hotels and at attraction sites), other providers of food and drink to tourists (including grocery stores), wholesalers who sell food and drink to restaurants, and businesses that provide other services to restaurants and food providers. Food and beverage, as a sector of the tourism industry, is especially challenging to measure because most of these businesses serve local residents as much, or more, than tourists. The balance between tourists served and residents served varies considerably from one establishment to the next.

Attractions

Attractions are extremely diverse, varying by scale and interest. The city of San Francisco is considered an attraction, as is the city's Fisherman's Wharf district, and the Ghirardelli (Napa Valley), and accommodation (e.g., all-inclusive resorts). Attraction types can be categorized based on their form (e.g., a famous building, mountain or theme park) and their experience (e.g., recreation, relaxation, entertainment and education). The challenge in identifying the attraction sector further complicates definitions of the *tourism industry*.

These four sectors (transportation, accommodations, food and beverage and attractions) contribute to providing a product called *tourism*. They are all service industries, which they market to a common clientele (tourists). Even though they are among the largest industries in the world, there is no clear and simple way to meaningfully aggregate their diverse products into a single generic product that can be compared to more traditional industries. This is because tourism is not a material product, but an experience that is purchased and kept more in your memory than in your living room.

Tourism Expenditures

Anything that can be purchased is a *commodity*. By creating tourist attractions, the tourism industry tends to commodify almost all aspects of the contemporary world. This is known as *commodification*. The UNWTO has defined a *tourism commodity* as any good or service for which a significant portion of demand comes from persons engaged in tourism as consumers. *Significant portion* is not defined, however, if we assume that this is more than 50 percent, then a tourism commodity is any product or service for which at least 50 percent of the buyers are tourists. (Depending on the product, service and place, the tourist demand could be less than 50 percent.) Furthermore, almost anything can become a tourist attraction, with the right marketing. Attractions can include forms of transportation (e.g., San Francisco's Cable Cars), food and beverage (e.g., wine tourism in California).

The magnitude of tourism as an economic activity in a destination is usually measured primarily by estimating the total expenditures made by visitors in the course of a trip (or on behalf of a visitor, such as contracts with a hotel made by a tour operator in assembling a tour for sale). A few purchases before and after a trip can be considered part of the trip's expenses, such as the purchase of consumables made immediately before departure, such as gas for the car, and expenditures such as the dry cleaning of travel clothes immediately after the trip.

Tourism and Non-Tourism Commodities

The major challenge in measuring the economic magnitude of tourism can be summed up as four dilemmas:

1. Visitors consume both tourism and non-tourism commodities
2. Residents consume both tourism and non-tourism commodities
3. Tourism industries produce tourism and non-tourism commodities
4. Non-tourism industries produce tourism and non-tourism commodities

Many commodities that are purchased by tourists are also purchased by non-tourists. Food and drink, for example, is a product that is widely used by both tourists and local residents. They are a tourism commodity, they are a recreation–leisure–entertainment commodity and they are a basic needs commodity. In addition, the balance in the proportion of tourist and non-tourist consumption of food and drink will often vary among communities and neighborhoods, from one season to another, and on different days of the week.

Input–Output Models

In general, only a small number of commodities account for the bulk of tourism spending. Identifying the portion of demand for a commodity that is directly attributable to tourism requires significant data about tourism supply and demand. In the past this was done with extremely complicated and time consuming input–output models. These models measure the monetary flows into and out of a community, and between every business and business sector within a local economy, including both tourism and non-tourism businesses.

While the resulting model provides a comprehensive snapshot of a local economy, they are too difficult to apply to regional and national economies. Measuring tourism's contribution to a nation's economy is a particular challenge because, for reasons noted earlier, tourism is not an industry in the SNA.

Tourism Satellite Accounts

National accountants in France were the first to explore ways to analyze aspects of a nation's economy that are not adequately represented within the SNA. To do this they developed a concept called comptes satellites (satellite accounts), which is known as Tourism Satellite Accounts (TSAs) when applied to the tourism industry. The TSA approach identifies the tourism percentage of each traditional industry (account) in a country's overall economy (SNA). (For example, tourism may account for 15 percent of Food and Beverage industry profits in one country, but 50 percent in another.) The tourism portions can then be added up to determine tourism's total contribution to a country's economic performance.

TSAs are usually constructed for a national economy, so national averages guide the selection of commodities that are included in the analysis. The identification of tourism commodities will, however, vary among nations. The arts, textiles, agricultural products, and transportation products may receive a significant portion of their demand from visitors to some countries, but much less in others.

1.5 TOURIST DEMAND

A common approach to studying of tourism is to divide it into the broad areas of demand and supply, and then examine each separately. The demand-side is the market for tourism attractions and facilities. It includes the reasons why people choose to travel, and why they prefer some activities over others. Looking at it from a particular destination's point of view, it is knowing who the client or market is for a place. The supply-side of tourism refers to the destination resources that are available for the tourist and recreationist. These include facilities and attractions of all kinds (such as

PHOTO 1.8

The Golden Triangle is where Myanmar, Thailand and Laos meet on the Mekong River. In this photo, the tourists are in Thailand, Myanmar is seen below the sign, separated from Thailand by a small river, and a sandbar in the Mekong River is in Laos to the right. Unique geographic locations like this can be significant tourist attractions

Source: Alan A. Lew

sports fields, parks, beaches and entertainment), as well as supporting infrastructure (such as transportation, hotels and restaurants) and services (such as travel agents, and recreation programs and activities).

Migration studies have long categorized the reasons for choosing to move from one place to another into *push factors* and *pull factors*. Push factors encourage an individual to leave a place (or to take a trip away from home), while pull factors affect where an individual goes after the desire to leave has been established. This is similar to tourism demand. A traveler is pulled to the amenities advertised for a given resort after a propensity toward travel has been established by push factors (such as stress at one's work). This is similar to tourism supply.

Demand can create supply. In a liberal market economy, commodities will be produced to meet a market demand. When people want to consume something (including recreation and tourism), the market will respond by creating more goods for them. Economic success comes to those who are best able to meet a market demand.

Knowing the motivations and needs that drive people to consume (participate in) a leisure activity is essential to understanding patterns of demand for a leisure product. Motivations must be understood to successfully design, develop and promote a product. The location, design, amenities, and special features of a development must be attractive to clients and visitors who comprise its principal markets. And because markets are constantly changing, adjustments need to be made to address new desires and expectations. To market effectively, the needs of the consumer must be identified.

In a demand-driven model, tourist motivations influence the development of a destination. Conversely, a supply-driven model creates its own market demand. Some natural features (such as the Grand Canyon, the Himalayas and Ayres Rock) and some special cultural sites (such as the Taj Mahal, the Pyramids at Giza and the city of Venice) are seen by most people to be of inherent interest to recreationists and tourists. While there may be a natural market for a site, growing that market will also require knowledge of tourist motivations and market segments.

It has been argued that the supply and demand dualism is superficial and that supply and demand are actually different perspectives on the same leisure phenomenon. What we know of as *tourism*, for example, would not exist if we did not have both tourists and destinations or attractions. The tourist shapes the destination (even in the case of the Grand Canyon) because the destination must respond to the tourist's presence in some way. And the destination is shaping the tourist by generating expectations, motivations and experiences that would not exist if that particular destination, and its interpreters, did not exist.

Tourist Motivation

There is no one approach or model that is widely accepted as the standard for assessing tourist motivation. This is due to the diverse combination of products and experiences that comprises the tourism industry, and the associated wide range of tourist interests and needs. Motivations and needs also change over time, such as over the course of a lifetime, from one trip to the next, and from one activity to the next on the same trip. In addition, many tourists are not aware of what motivates them to take a certain trip or visit a particular attraction, except in the most general of terms which typically include recreation, relaxation, education and escape from their work-a-day world.

One example of a tourist motivation model that incorporates significant elements of supply is that suggested by Mayo and Jarvis (1981). They proposed that travel motivation can be divided into the following four types, based on what the tourists most wish to gain, see or experience in the trip. More than one of these can occur at the same time, though one tends to be more prominent than the others for any single trip.

1. *Physical Motivators*: The desire for physical rest, sports participation, beach recreation, relaxing entertainment and health considerations
2. *Cultural Motivators*: The desire for knowledge of other countries, including their music, art, folklore, dances, paintings and religion.
3. *Interpersonal Motivators*: The desire to meet new people; to visit friends or relatives; to escape from routine, family, or neighbors; or to make new friendships

away from the home setting; to experience *anomie* (which refers to social interactions in an anonymous setting).

4. *Status and Prestige Motivators*: The desire for recognition, attention, appreciation and a good reputation among family, friends and acquaintances in the home setting. (This is also referred to as ego enhancement.)

Source: Mayo, E.J. and Jarvis, L.P. (1981) *The Psychology of Leisure Travel, Effective Marketing and Selling of Travel Services*, CBI Publishing, Boston.

The advantage of this approach is that participation in specific activities can be used to classify motivations. Visitation to a museum is, therefore, an indication of a cultural motivation, while going to a beach would be a type of physical motivation. The attachment of motivation to activities facilitates the easy collection of data on tourist behavior at its most apparent level, making this approach preferred by local and national tourism boards.

Maslow's Hierarchy of Needs and the Leisure Ladder

The psychologist Abraham Maslow proposed a Hierarchy of Needs (1954) that is widely used in explaining motivations for human behavior (Figure 1.5). According to the original model, individuals first and foremost focus on satisfying their physiological needs for survival. Once these have been satisfactorily met, then the next level becomes the primary motivation of behavior. Belonging and love are generally achieved through the family unit, while esteem is typically achieved through work accomplishments. The ultimate goal of human existence is the top level need of self-actualization, where

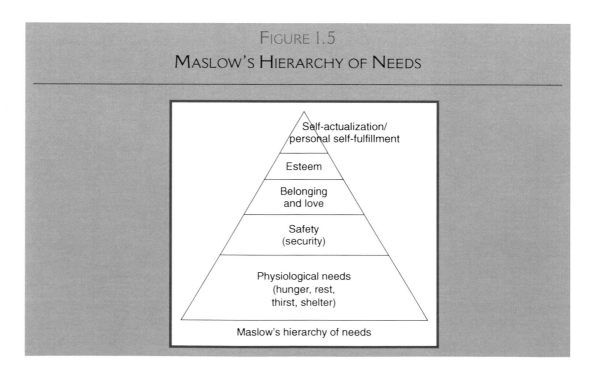

FIGURE 1.5
MASLOW'S HIERARCHY OF NEEDS

Self-actualization/
personal self-fulfillment

Esteem

Belonging
and love

Safety
(security)

Physiological needs
(hunger, rest,
thirst, shelter)

Maslow's hierarchy of needs

one takes part in activities or a lifestyle that is rewarding, fulfilling and allows for the full expression of a person's individuality, creativity and purpose for living. This is similar to Aristotle's definition of leisure. Many see tourism as a way of achieving some degree of this level of need – if only for a transitory period, and via a commodified and packaged product.

The major criticism of Maslow's hierarchy is that human needs occur simultaneously, and research indicates that even those who are struggling to meet basic physiological needs are looking for opportunities for self-actualization at the same time. Such a mix of motivations is also common in tourism and recreation. Maslow added several additional layers to the pyramid in later years, including a *Need to Understand* and an *Aesthetic Need* above the *Esteem* level, and a *Transcendence* level above the Self-Actualization Need. All have considerable implications for tourism and recreation. Maslow further identified deficiency or tension-reduction motivations (push factors) and inductive or arousal-seeking motives (pull factors) as supplements to his hierarchy of needs model.

Building on Maslow's hierarchy, Philip Pearce proposed a Leisure Ladder, with five motivational levels. The Leisure Ladder exists entirely within the realm of recreation and tourism, and defines the most basic level as relaxation and bodily comfort, which is probably somewhere above Maslow's basic need of food and shelter for survival. At this level, recreation and tourism are a recuperative therapy for dealing with the stress of work. The second level is leisure as *stimulation* and play, which can be physically and mentally as hard as work. The third level is leisure as a social experience where interpersonal relationships are a key component, while the fourth level is leisure as a mastery of skills and educational experience. The highest level is similar to Maslow's self-actualization peak fulfillment experience. According to Pearce, one of these levels dominates the motivation for any leisure activity, lower levels must occur before one can experience a higher level, and lower levels can occur simultaneously with higher levels. Increased age and life experiences is associated with higher levels of leisure.

Plog created a model in 1972 to analyze destination choices made by different types of tourists. He did this by classifying Northeastern United States travelers on a scale of psychological types and then determining the destination that each type of tourist tended to choose. Travelers ranged on a continuum from *psychocentrism* (a focus on one's self) to *allocentrism* (a focus on other people). Psychocentrics are characterized as being conservative, inhibited, and more safety conscious when they travel. They usually spend less money and travel to familiar places. Allocentrics are more outgoing, willing to take risks, open to new experiences, and interested in travel to exotic places. He suggests that allocentrics would more likely travel to Africa or Asia, while psychocentrics would prefer travel to nearby destinations and theme parks (Table 1.1).

Geographer have suggested that destinations evolve and change in the types of tourists they attract. New destinations tend to be *discovered* by adventurous allocentrics, with near-allocentrics soon following them. Over time, it may become a psychocentric destination. Palma de Mallorca (Spain) was a near-allocentric or midcentric destination for British tourists in the 1950s and today it is considered a purely psychocentric destination. Phuket Island, off the Indian Ocean coast of Thailand, was an allocentric destination in the early 1970s, visited by alternative Western backpackers and *hippies*. It became a midcentric destination by the 1990s, and is probably a near-psychocentric destination today (at least for Europeans and Australians).

Table 1.1

Plog's Psychocentric-Allocentric Motivation Model

Psychocentric and Near-Psychocentric Motivations = 0 ns = urn:schemas-microsoft-com:office:office/>

- Travel for acceptance within a social group
- Ego enhancement and an increase in social status
- Travel as a cultural norm, including paid vacations required by law (more common in European countries)
- Visits to places seen or read about in the news, especially travel news
- Visits to amusement parks
- Pleasure, fun, enjoyment, parties

Mid-centric Motivations

- Rest and relaxation
- Visiting close friends and relatives
- Health, including a change in climate, search for sunshine, visits to spas and medical treatment
- Change of pace or 'escape' for a short period of time
- Perceived glamour or prestige of a destination
- Appreciation of nature, including trips to national and state parks, forests, lakes, canoe trips, ocean coasts
- Sensual indulgence, including food (gourmet meals, buffets), comforts and luxuries for the body, romance
- Shopping for souvenirs, gifts, luxury and specialty products, jewelry, art, cars, antiques
- Transportation experiences, including cruise ships, comfortable trains, buses, airplanes and cars
- Pre- and post-travel experiences, including trip planning (anticipation, learning, dreaming) and sharing pictures and describing the trip upon return
- Family or personal matters

Near-Allocentric Motivations

- Religious pilgrimage or inspiration
- Gaming, including casinos and horse races
- Participation in sports events and sports activities
- Travel as a challenge or test of endurance, such as rock climbing, mountaineering, sky and underwater diving
- Business travel, conferences, meetings, conventions
- Theater and special entertainment
- Temporarily trying out a new lifestyle or home

Allocentric Motivations

- Educational and cultural motives, including learning and appreciation; scientific or purposeful trips with expert leaders
- Genealogy research, study and exploration
- Search for the exotic (from a Western perspective, major destinations include the Pacific islands, Southeast Asia, and = stl? ns = urn:schemas-microsoft-com:office:smarttags/>West Africa)
- Satisfaction from a sense freedom, including anonymity through travel; air and sea experiences; fast trains and cars
- Meeting people and making friendships in foreign places
- Sharpening perspectives, such as an awakening of senses or a heighten awareness of the world

Source: Plog, S. (1987) Understanding psychographics in tourism research, In Ritchie J. and Goelder C. (eds) *Travel Tourism and Hospitality Research*, New York: Wiley

A *model* is a simplification of reality that tries to eliminate all but the most important factors to explain how something works. Because human behavior is so complex, no single model will ever be able to address all of the variation in tourist motivations. The psychographic model does not consider the fact that people travel with different motivations on different occasions, and even at different times on a single trip.

A wealthy allocentric may travel to Africa on an annual vacation, but may also take weekend trips for a psychocentric experience. Life cycle changes, changes in health, and changes in financial resources can all lead to fluctuations in travel behavior and psychographic levels. Finally, just as individuals are complex, so are destinations. Any large metropolitan area, for example, contains a full range of psychocentric to allocentric neighborhoods and attractions.

Market Segmentation

Once a tourist's motivation has been established, then the potential to match that person with an appropriate destination is increased. Such a match will most likely maximize satisfaction by producing the kind of experience the traveler seeks. This can be used by travel agents, tour wholesalers, destination marketers, and tourism product developers. Understanding the tourist's desire provides a basis for decisions on the types of environments and services that should be provided at a destination now and in the future, and dictates the message content of promotional campaigns. Advertising can be more effective in targeting interested consumers. Advertising campaigns can be designed to dispel potential visitor worries, create or confirm a desired image of a destination, or simply create an awareness of a destination for a new, potential market population.

As mentioned above, most destinations offer a range of different types of accommodations and attractions that are suited to the interests of different types of tourists. Market segmentation is the process of identifying the range of different tourist markets that are most suited to the range of sites and experiences available in a destination. Rather than dissipating promotional resources by trying to attract all potential travelers, or a very narrow portion of them, efforts can be specifically aimed towards the most likely prospects.

Understanding motivations for leisure, travel and recreation is essential to the tourism industry. To understand tourist motivations, researchers have created numerous models to simplify the complexity of travel behaviors. Several examples have been described above. With a better understanding of leisure motivations, services can be better catered to meet user needs and advertising campaigns can be directed to the highest potential market. Travel agents can also better direct travelers to destinations and experiences that suit their wishes and temperament. The tourism industry, in general, can be strengthened with a fuller understanding of tourist motivations and destination offerings.

Barriers and Constraints to Travel

As much as people want to travel, they often do not realize that most of the time and cost involved in touring is devoted to finding food and drinks, getting to lodging and restrooms, and sitting on some form of uncomfortable transportation. Many destinations are much dirtier, and involve more hassling with local business people, than their promotional literature makes out. Poor ground transportation systems are the leading cause of death for tourists around the world. Concern over the comfort and safety of a destination's facilities and accommodations, along with the distance required to get to a destination, will keep some people from taking a trip. In addition to these comfort concerns there are a lot of other barriers to travel in general, as well as travel to specific destinations, including:

- Lack of personal time can prevent travel, including a lack of adequate free time and vacation time, and need to stay home to care for children, elderly or ill.
- Institutional barriers, including legal restrictions on travel within one's own country (such as United States restrictions on travel to Cuba), visa restrictions that limit the amount of time a person can visit a country, or the general difficulty of obtaining a passport and visa in a timely manner.
- Personal health and disability-related issues can prevent participation in some or all forms of travel and recreation activities.
- Crime concerns, including fear of financial scams and concern over being injured, robbed, or kidnapped will prevent people from traveling to some destinations.
- Civil unrest, terrorism, and war are very strong barriers to travel, due to the threat of being captured, injured or killed.
- Disease concerns can have a major impact on travel, including fear of infection from a specific disease (such as the SARS (severe acute respiratory syndrome) outbreak in 2003–2004, which temporarily decimated travel to and within Asia), or a more general concern, such as traveler's diarrhea from unhygienic food, which has become an increasing problem on Caribbean cruise ships.
- Personal phobias, with fear of flying (aerophobia) being a common affliction, prevent many people from traveling to some types of destinations.
- Weather and disaster concerns will keep people away from some destinations, including undesirable weather, such as hurricanes, or natural disasters, such as earthquakes and fires.
- Negative local attitudes toward tourists and other outsiders can reduce travel to a destination, and especially prevent repeat visits (people visiting more than once).
- Lack of money to pay for travel expenses keeps some people from traveling, although there are many forms of travel that cost very little.
- Lack of information about a destination will keep people from going there.

Travel Advisories

Many countries issue official government advisories which they use to keep their citizens from getting into trouble overseas. In addition, many other organizations post-travel warnings and other information to raise tourist awareness about the challenges of travel to certain destinations. No country is totally absent of warnings, and nowhere are tourists completely immune to predators. On any given week, civil unrest in many countries results in advisories urging people to not travel to certain countries. In some cases those who are in a country are urged to leave, if they can do so safely. Official advisories can have a major impact on travel to a destination. Government advisories related the SARS (severe acute respiratory syndrome) outbreak in China and Southeast Asia in 2003 contributed in a huge decline in travel (2.8 million tourism-related jobs were lost in China alone), and were highly criticized by governments and industry representatives in the region.

One of the most significant issues facing tourism is the increased costs of energy and issues of availability. According to the Energy Committee at the Royal Swedish Academy of Sciences (2005: 1) *It is very likely that the world is now entering a challenging period for energy supply, due to the limited resources and production problems now facing conventional (easily accessible) oil. Nearly 40 percent of the world's energy is provided by oil, and over 50 percent of the latter is used in the transport sector.* According to the Committee mitigation measures must be initiated in the next few years in order to secure a continued adequate supply of liquid fuels, especially for the transport sector. Aviation will be more fuel efficient in the future as a result of technological innovations but possibilities are limited and although energy use per person per km will fall the overall predicted increase in the number and distance of people flying will mean that overall fuel use and amount of emissions will continue to grow.

However, over the longer term, completely new energy solutions are required given the decline of cheap oil. Key issues with respect to oil supply are outlined below.

Shortage of oil

The global demand for oil is presently growing by almost 2 percent per year with consumption at the end of 2005 set at 84 million barrels per day (1 barrel = 159 liters) or 30 billion barrels per year. Finding additional supplies is increasingly problematical since most major oil fields are well matured. Already 54 of the 65 most important oil-producing countries have declining production and the rate of discoveries of new reserves is less than a third of the rate of consumption as of the end of 2005.

Reserves of conventional oil

Since 1990 two-thirds of the increases in reserves of conventional oil have been based on increased estimates of recovery from existing fields and only one-third on discovery of new fields. A conservative estimate of discovered oil reserves and undiscovered recoverable oil resources is about 1200 billion barrels, according to the United States Geological Survey; this includes 300 billion barrels in the world's, as yet unexplored, sedimentary basins.

The key role of the Middle East

Only in the Middle East and possibly the countries of the former Soviet Union is there potential (proven reserves of 130 billion barrels) to significantly increase production rates to compensate for decreasing rates in other countries. As of the end of 2005 Saudi Arabia provided 9.5 million barrels per day (11 percent of the current global production rate).

Unconventional oil reserves

There are very large hydrocarbon resources, so-called unconventional oil, including gas (c. 1,000 billion barrels of oil equivalent, much of which could be converted to liquid fuels), heavy oil and tar sands (c. 800 billion barrels), oil shales (c. 2,700 billion barrels); and coal. Problems with unconventional resources include long lead times in development, environmental impacts and the availability of water and natural gas for the production process.

Continued

Immediate action on supplies

Improvements in the search for and recovery of conventional oil as well as the production rate of unconventional oil are required to avoid price spikes, which would lead to instability of the world economy over the next few decades.

Liquid fuels and the transport system

Oil supply is a severe liquid fuels problem and less of a general energy supply problem; 57 percent of the world's oil is consumed in the transport sector. Alternatives need to be developed to oil in the transport sector otherwise not only will there be increased oil prices but also increased competition between transport and other oil users.

Economic considerations

In the long run, the price of crude oil will be determined by the price of substitutes. Continued high oil prices are anticipated as long as the pressure from the expanding Asian economies such as China and India is maintained.

Environmental concerns

Unconventional oil will significantly extend the length of the hydrocarbon era and its subsequent contributions to greenhouse gas (GHG) emissions. Constraints similar to those imposed on other fossil fuels (e.g., emission controls and CO_2 sequestration) will be necessary and provide major challenges for industry. From a global point of view, transport is the most relevant sector in terms of the long-term environmental sustainability of tourism, accounting for an estimated 75–90 percent of all GHG emissions caused by tourism. Within tourism transport, the share of aviation-related GHG emissions corresponds to about 75 percent of all transport emissions. However, the contribution of GHG emissions from aviation is obviously not spread evenly across the world and instead is concentrated in the wealthier countries from where the vast majority of tourists actually come from.

Sources

Gössling, S. and Hall, C.M. (2006) Uncertainties in predicting tourist flows under scenarios of climate change, *Climatic Change*, 79(3–4): 163–173.
Royal Swedish Academy of Sciences (Energy Committee) (2005) *Statements on Oil*, Royal Swedish Academy of Sciences, Stockholm.

Conclusions

The desire to participate in tourism and recreation is strong and deeply rooted in the human psyche. For any one individual, however, motivations can vary considerably. How people participate in travel and tourism, in particular, is largely guided by social norms and the large socioeconomic context of the travel industry. Numerous individual and societal barriers and limitations further shape the pattern of participation in tourism. Why people travel and what they seek from travel has major implications for people in local destinations, as well as for the global economy.

1.6   TOURISM SUPPLY

One way of looking at tourism supply is to focus on tourist attractions. Tourist attractions are fundamental to the very existence of tourism. Without attractions there would be no tourism. Without tourism there would be no tourist attractions. But what is a tourist attraction? Several definitions have been proposed, including:

- An exploitable *resource*
- A marketable *product* and *image*
- A place *attribute* or *feature*

All of these definitions are simple and beg for additional definitions of what is a resource, a product, an image, an attribute and a feature. Another definition of tourist attractions is all those sites in a *non-home* place that are of interest to tourists. There are three essential elements in this definition:

1. a tourist
2. a sight or site in a *non-home* place
3. an interest or reason for the tourist to want to view the sight or experience the site

These three elements comprise a model of tourist attractions that was first suggested by MacCannell (1976), and later defined by Leiper (1990) as the *tourist attraction system*. Their argument is that you cannot have a tourist attraction unless all three of these features are present. If there is a site and a tourist, but no reason for the tourist to take an interest in the site, then the site cannot be considered an attraction. It is like Yi-fu Tuan's difference between Space and Place – the attraction emerges as a special place from the surrounding undifferentiated space through the meaning that is given to it by the tourist (or the tourism industry).

Similarly, if there is a site and a reason for tourists to be interested in it, but there are no tourists, then the site is not a functioning tourist attraction. And finally, if there is a tourist who has a motivating interest to see or experiences a certain type of attraction, but there is no site that offers that experience, then there is no tourist attraction.

In practice, however, the tourist attraction system has some limitations. The first limitation is the problem that almost anything can become a tourist attraction. Historic sites, amusement parks and spectacular scenery are almost always attractions. Food is often an attraction, accommodations (resorts) can be an attraction, and sometimes transportation (cruise ships) and the tourists themselves (Spring Break parties) are attractions. The diversity of potential tourist attractions is phenomenal. For example, alternative tours have been developed to take people into sewer systems, to homeless neighborhoods, to cemeteries and into working mines.

The second problem is that the tourist attraction system is not how most people think about tourist attractions. For most people tourist attractions include landscapes to be observed, activities to participate in, and experiences to remember. The role of the *tourist* is seldom considered because he or she is visually separated from the attraction. The tourist is, therefore, taken-for-granted in a more common definition of attractions. The meaning or purpose of the attraction is less taken-for-granted by most people. But instead of meaning, most people view this as the attraction's importance. Attractions are perceived by tourists to be ranked above or below each other in importance. The hierarchy of attractions will vary from one person to the next based on the set of available attractions that a tourist is aware of, depth of knowledge that the tourist has of each attraction, and the tourist's personal interests.

The Tourist Attraction Site

It is the attraction site that most people think of when they hear the word *tourist attraction*. Lew (1987) examined the different ways that researchers defined attractions when they conduct attraction inventories and found three distinct approaches. Although they were often mixed together in a single list of attractions, each is actually a characteristic that all attractions share. These characteristics are:

1. a form, identity or name
2. an organizational and developmental structure
3. a perceived experience

At their most basic level, attractions are identified by their individual name. Lists of attractions by name are most often used in inventories of small areas, such as towns or small cities. At the other end of the form approach is the use of Standard Industrial Codes (SICs, such as accommodations, restaurants, retail stores) to identify general types of attractions. SIC-based attractions can be useful to determine monetary flows because governments use them to summarize economic census data. Schmidt (1979) suggested that attractions are best divided into geographical, social, cultural, technological and religious. Schmidt's approach is typical of that used in attraction inventories to assess the tourism supply in a destination, though these vary considerably in details from one place to the next. Tourist guide books usually classify attractions under a combination of both specific names for the most important sites, and more general categories. Guidebook categories vary from one destination to another, though they typically include the general categories of retail stores, restaurants, accommodations, museums, amusements, sports and recreation.

The two basic types of formal attractions are nature-based attractions and human-based attractions, although there is a transition between them, which results in a third type of attractions. Examples of these are shown in Table 1.2. In practice these types of forma attractions are divided up among categories that are most relevant to a specific destination.

Tourist Attraction Structure

The structural approach to tourist attractions does not examine the individual attraction's form or identity, but instead focuses on its spatial, capacity and temporal nature. Geographic size is the simplest basis for categorizing the spatial character of

TABLE 1.2
TYPES OF FORMAL ATTRACTIONS

Nature-based Attractions
- Panoramas: mountains, sea coast, plains and valleys, arid lands, islands
- Ecosystems: climate, sanctuaries (national parks nature reserve)
- Landmarks: geological; biological (flora and fauna), hydrological

Mixed Nature-based and Human-based Attractions
- Oservational Nature: rural and agriculture landscapes, scientific gardens (animals zoos, arboretums rocks), and archeology
- Participatory Nature: mountain activities (summer and winter), water activities, other outdoor activities
- Leisure Nature: trails, parks (beach, urban, other), resorts

Human-Based Attractions
- Settlement Infrastructure: utilities (e.g., dams), settlement activities and morphology (retaining, finance, government, education and science, religion), people (way of life, ethnicity)
- Tourist Infrastructure: forms of access (to and from a destination, tour routes), information and reception (welcome centers), basic needs (accommodations, meals)
- Leisure Infrastructure: recreation and entertainment (performances, sports related, amusements), culture, history and art (museums, monuments, performances, festivals, cuisine)

Source: Lew, A.A. (1987)

an attraction. A spatial hierarchy of attraction scale would progress from the smallest specific object of interest in a site, then to cities, then regions, then an entire country and continent. Asia, for example, is a destination, as is China, and Beijing, and Tienanmen Square. Scale considerations can provide insights into the geographic grouping or clustering of attractions, which is important in the planning and marketing of tourism. Tourism marketers promote the images of specific, small-scale attractions (which are easier to sell) to create identifiers for larger attraction complexes. An example of this is the Eiffel Tower as a marketing icon for France. Planners, however, are then faced with the problem of an over-concentration of demand at some tourist sites and under-utilization of others.

In addition to the spatial structure of an attraction (or group of attractions), the temporal or time nature of attractions is important. Special events (such as the Olympic Games) can be huge attractions, but only for short periods of time. Outdoor recreation activities (such as snow skiing) are similarly time dependent. This can have a major impact on the seasonality of visitors to a destination, which must find ways to attract visitors during off-season periods. A third type of structural characteristic is capacity. This is similar to spatial scale, but is internal to the attraction. Some attractions can hold a lot more visitors at one time than others can. This, also, presents challenges to tourism and recreation planners.

In describing attractions based on their structural characteristics, some of the terminology that has been used by tourism researchers include:

- Attractions Nucleus, Inviolate Belt, and Zone of Enclosure (around the attraction)
- Remote or Isolated Attractions
- Structured or Unstructured Development
- Planned or Unplanned Infrastructure

- Accessible or Inaccessible Location
- Touring, Clustered or Destination Attractions
- Rural, Suburban or Urban
- Local, Regional, National or International scale
- Craft or Industrial Tourism
- Slow or Rapid Growth
- Small, Medium or Large Capacity
- Event, Transitory, Seasonal or Permanent Attraction
- Single or Multiple visitation

Tourist Attraction Perception

Studies of tourist perceptions and experiences of attractions comprise the third major approach to the study of tourist attractions. Pearce defined a tourist place as "any place that fosters the feeling of being a tourist" (1982: 98). One way this experience is felt is in the degree of *outsideness* and *insideness* that one feels when visiting a destination. Some have argued that a major goal of the tourist is to penetrate into the *inside* (or *back region*) of the attraction to experience its authenticity. For the tourist, some risk is required to take this leap into authenticity.

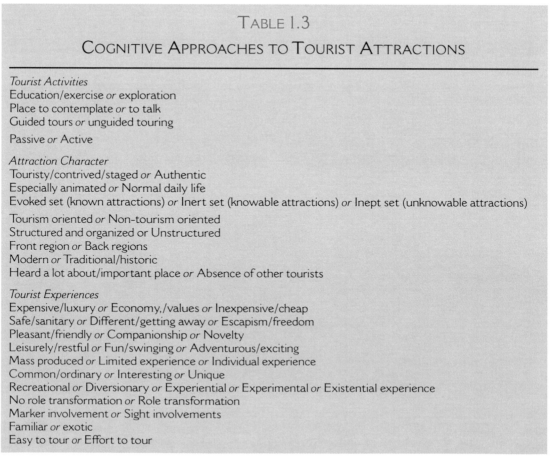

TABLE 1.3

COGNITIVE APPROACHES TO TOURIST ATTRACTIONS

Tourist Activities
Education/exercise *or* exploration
Place to contemplate *or* to talk
Guided tours *or* unguided touring

Passive *or* Active

Attraction Character
Touristy/contrived/staged *or* Authentic
Especially animated *or* Normal daily life
Evoked set (known attractions) *or* Inert set (knowable attractions) *or* Inept set (unknowable attractions)

Tourism oriented *or* Non-tourism oriented
Structured and organized or Unstructured
Front region *or* Back regions
Modern *or* Traditional/historic
Heard a lot about/important place *or* Absence of other tourists

Tourist Experiences
Expensive/luxury *or* Economy,/values *or* Inexpensive/cheap
Safe/sanitary *or* Different/getting away *or* Escapism/freedom
Pleasant/friendly *or* Companionship *or* Novelty
Leisurely/restful *or* Fun/swinging *or* Adventurous/exciting
Mass produced *or* Limited experience *or* Individual experience
Common/ordinary *or* Interesting *or* Unique
Recreational *or* Diversionary *or* Experiential *or* Experimental *or* Existential experience
No role transformation *or* Role transformation
Marker involvement *or* Sight involvements
Familiar *or* exotic
Easy to tour *or* Effort to tour

Source: Lew, A.A. (1987)

Approaches to tourist attraction perceptions and experiences are shown in Table 1.3 and are closely related to tourist motivation, as discussed above. This reflects the inseparable relationship between the site and the visitor in the tourist attraction system. Because most tourists are outsiders and newcomers to a place, many studies of attractions perception focus on security and the minimization of risk. To do this, they typically take place in staged, inauthentic and highly structured environments.

Tourists also mostly interact with the advertised images, rather than a direct and unmediated experience of a site. MacCannell (1976) referred to this as *marker involvement* because the tourist is more focused on the label that is attached to the attraction than the attraction itself. Most historic sites, such as empty battlefields, are marker involvement attractions, as opposed to *sight involvement* attractions that would not require any interpretation. Outstanding natural landscapes and culturally unique places are examples where sight involvement often predominates over marker involvement.

The perceptual or cognitive approaches can be applied to any of the formal attraction types in Table 1.3. In fact, many researchers freely mix formal, structural and perceptual approaches in their attraction inventories, without thinking about the differences. For example, one study of attractions in Greece classified them into three formal types (Ancient Greece, Picturesque villages, and Sun and sea), two structural types (Clustered–isolated and Accessible–inaccessible), and one perceptual type (Unique–common). In general, the selection of one or more approach depends on the goals of the research. A comprehensive study would want to use all three major approaches, whereas a more narrowly focused study might only use one approach.

1.7   TOURISM LANDSCAPES

Places are a major focus of geographic study because they are the focal point of relationships among local residents, outside visitors, economic processes, the physical environment and culture. The visual landscapes of places are readily accessible for anyone to experience. Landscapes have strong representational and symbolic meaning, and they form a veritable stage for play and recreation. Landscapes are often used to promote a destination, through television and print advertisements, and through these media landscape become the first and most basic setting for the tourist experience. Landscapes are also captured by tourists through photographs that become lasting memories. However, because they are so omnipresent, forming the basis for everyday life, landscapes can be challenging to interpret and understand.

Landscapes are often an integral part of the image of a destination. The New York City skyline and Hong Kong's harbor are among the more recognized landscape icons. Tourism marketers turn landscapes into representations of destinations. Tourists use these representations to decide whether or not to visit a place, and then once there, to assess and validate their experiences. At the same time, the destination manages its landscape to meet the needs of both locals (hosts) and visitors (guests). Some elements of the landscape are either transformed or intentionally preserved for the guest, while others are oriented more toward local needs. As tourism and leisure become more pervasive elements in daily life, it is becoming more difficult to separate host and guest landscape elements.

PHOTO 1.9

Yorktown, Virginia battlefield where United States and French forces defeated the British in 1781. The importance of many historic sites is often not apparent in their physical landscape alone

Source: Alan A. Lew

Tourism Landscape Studies

Geography and other social sciences have developed an increasing interest in tourism landscapes since the 1990s when the tourism economy became a dominant global service industry. This interest reflected a widespread realization of the degree to which tourism has been responsible for modifications to many landscapes around the world, from revitalization of older retail districts and building of suburban mega-malls (the Mall of America in Minnesota is one of the top attractions in the United States), to the conservation of nature areas and the rise in ecotourism. The bigger the alterations in land use and the larger the visitor flows, the more such development can result in environmental degradation, incompatible construction, carrying capacity issues and social change to the pre-existing landscape.

At the same time, there has been a growing interest in the landscape in general, including landscape policy, landscape values and landscape assessment. New analytical methods, some using geographic information systems (GIS), have skyrocketed. Many have had a focus on evaluating, protecting and enhancing the quality and use of the landscape at the local, regional, national and international levels.

Classifying Landscapes

The earliest approach the geographic study of leisure and tourism landscapes was the classification of scenic quality and land use. This approach was most popular in the first half of the 20th century, though is still widely used today. It involves classifying landscapes into different types (such as retail districts, public parks, open space, amusement parks and wilderness) and then assessing and evaluating the condition of each landscape type, as well as the overall situation. The major tools used in this approach are land use maps and demographic and other social and economic data that lend themselves to quantitative and spatial analysis. This approach to landscape research continues to be dominant in environmental studies and in the design professions (urban planning and landscape architecture). They reflect an assumption that tourism and leisure management involve hard facts and clear typologies, and follow predictable economic models – which is not always the case.

Resort Morphology

Geographers have long been interested in the distribution of land use in a community and what that can tell us about the past and future development of a place. Standard land uses include industrial, retail, residential and open space, although these are often further divided into many additional types. *Urban morphology* refers to the shape or pattern of land use in a community – which types of land uses are located where. This approach is also quantitative in nature, but is more interpretative in application. When applied to tourism and recreation, it has mostly been used in the study of resort communities, and island and coastal landscapes. How retail, attractions, accommodations, and residential land uses have changed over time in these areas has given rise to the concept of the *Recreation Business District* (also known as the *Tourism Business District*) as a distinct land use type in many coastal resort communities.

Structuralism

Another way that social scientists study tourism landscapes is from the perspective of structuralism. Structuralism focuses on larger social norms, belief systems, and societal practices that shape and force certain forms of behavior and decision making (and resulting landscapes) on society. Economic, social and environmental policies established by national governments, as well as decisions made by multinational corporations, are examined as the primary actors in local landscape modification.

Structuralists have focused on the nationalization and globalization of cultural and social norms, through mediums such as Hollywood movies and pop music videos, and how they have contributed to a homogenization of landscapes (placelessness). They examine how big money interests override local small money interests, commodifying local uniqueness, and making destination landscapes more alike than different. For the structuralists (of which there are several different approaches, including Marxism), the principle struggle is between the individual and society, and between local culture and the dominant political and economic structure.

In tourism this is often seen in stories of the struggle between *authentic* villagers and multinational hotel developers, or between local mom and pop hotel and restaurant owners and outsider fast food and chain store companies. In most places the latter groups have been gaining ground over time, with changes in the landscape that are both quantifiable and visible.

Cultural Landscapes

More recently, geographic research on tourism landscapes has shifted in scope and scale from the macro-analysis of symbolic landscapes to the micro-analysis of town and resort landscapes. This is somewhat of a return to classification and morphology studies, but with a greater emphasis on the symbolic nature of place features in the local communities. This cultural perspective stresses the distinctive physical and material nature of places, along with their social and cultural meaning and symbolism. One outcome of this shift is that many of the new landscape geography studies in recent years have discovered the unexpected importance of leisure and tourism in the everyday landscape.

Cultural meanings are inherent in the landscapes of our built environments, and in how we value and treat our natural surroundings. They visually illustrate the relationships between social structures and local cultures and between the larger society and the individual. Various approaches have been used to interpret tourism development, tourism economics and tourism psychology through their imprint on the landscape. There is no question that the landscapes of tourism in any place will change as tourist markets change, creating new opportunities for entrepreneurs to pursue, and for students of tourism to study. The speed and form of how local communities respond, and how they manage their political-economy and long-term cultural interests, are a major focus of interdisciplinary research on the landscapes of tourism, recreation and leisure.

1.8 OVERVIEW OF THIS BOOK

This chapter introduced basic geography and tourism concepts and themes that relate to discussions of the regional sections. The remainder of the book is divided into four chapters, each of which includes several regional and subregional sections. The traditional approach to regional geography begins with physical geography (geomorphology, climatology and biogeography) and then covers human geography (historical, cultural, economic and political).

This book takes this basic regional geography approach, beginning each region's section by describing the natural features and their geographic variations. These discussions form the basis for describing the supply of nature-based tourist attractions and considerations, including opportunities and challenges, for their development and visitation. The same approach is taken with the human geography of each region. Each region section identifies major cultural subregions, their historical development and their contemporary development issues, particularly as these are relate to tourism. This discussion includes development of the cultural tourism supply in each region and its subregions.

In addition to the basic foundations of physical and human geography and nature-based and culture-based tourism supply, special issue topics are discussed in each of the sections. These topics are related to the major tourist attractions and tourism issues that the regions face. The approach used in this book provides readers with a fundamental understanding of the diversity of our contemporary world, the uniqueness of the landscapes and tourist experiences of different regions and places in the world, and the important role of tourism and travel around the world.

World Regions

Traditionally, the continents of the world include: Europe, Asia, Africa, North America, South America, Australia and Antarctica. With the exception of Europe, each of these is a large land mass that is completely surrounded by oceans and seas. Europe is actually a peninsula of the Eurasian land mass, and is treated separately from the rest of Asia because of its cultural difference and economic importance. However, the importance of those differences is changing, which creates increasing challenges for geographers trying to divide the world into major geographic regions. The problem is that, while geographic regionalization requires a broad, holistic view of both physical and cultural phenomena, at some point a decision must be made to emphasize one basic characteristic over another. This decision is sometimes easy, and other times not. Different decisions made by different geographers result in different regionalizations (Figure 1.6).

In this book, the regions of the world are grouped into four larger chapters. The chapters and their contents include:

Chapter 2 – Europe and Eurasia

In terms of international travel, Europe is the most visited and most important region in the world. For these reasons all of Chapter 1 is devoted to Europe and its

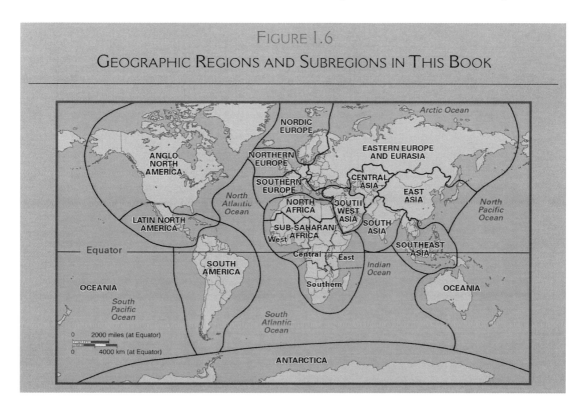

FIGURE 1.6

GEOGRAPHIC REGIONS AND SUBREGIONS IN THIS BOOK

subregions. The major subregions in Europe are Western Europe and Eastern Europe. These are sometimes treated as two separate world regions, though the transition between the two is increasingly difficult to define. Western Europe is further divided into the Nordic countries, the Northern European countries (excluding Scandinavia), and the Southern European countries. In addition, in recent years, the European Union (EU) has become a major political and social force in the countries that are members of the EU. Because of this, EU and non-EU countries are discussed separately in Chapter 1. The most important non-EU country is Russia, which extends to the Pacific Ocean and includes areas that are sometimes considered part of Asia instead of Europe.

Chapter 3 – The Old World: Central Asia Through Africa

This chapter covers a vast territory that includes three traditional world regions: Central Asia, Southwest Asia and North Africa (which includes the *Middle East*), and Sub-Saharan Africa. In contrast to Europe, the regions and countries of Chapter 2 are among the least visited in the world. They include two major cultural realms. Central Asia through North Africa is a predominantly Muslim area. A major difference is that Central Asia was formerly part of the Soviet Union, while Southwest Asia and North Africa were more influenced by Western European colonial powers. Sub-Saharan Africa, which is all of Africa south of the Sahara Desert, is comprised of mostly Black racial groups.

Chapter 4 – Asia and Oceania

In terms of total population and the total surface area of the globe, Asia and Oceania is the largest of the four chapters of this book. It includes four major global subregions: South Asia, Southeast Asia, East Asia and Oceania. Asia is the fastest developing region of the world, both in terms of average incomes level and in travel and tourism development. Oceania is the least populated of these, though it includes three very different subregions: Australia, the South Pacific Islands and the continent of Antarctica.

Chapter 5 – The Americas

The *New World* of the Americas are one of the easier regions to define, since it is relatively isolated from the Old World of Africa and Asia. The subregions of the Americas are also widely accepted. These include South America, the Caribbean Islands, Central America (including Mexico), and North America (Canada and the United States, sometimes referred to as Anglo North America). North America has the most international visitors, with the United States borders with Mexico and Canada being among the most crossed in the world. The countries of the Caribbean Sea, however, are among the most dependent on tourism in world.

	Chapter	Population 2006 (1,000)	World population share 2006 (%)	International tourist arrivals (1,000)		Change since 1990 (%)	World market share 2004 (%)
				1990*	2004		
WORLD		**6525170**	**100.0**	**436757**	**776837**	**77.9**	**100.0**
Europe and Eurasia	**2**	**737666**	**11.3**	**257964**	**410718**	**59.2**	**52.9**
Old World: Central Asia to Africa	3	1272166	19.5	32698	94281	188.3	12.1
Asia and Oceania	4	3690063	56.6	53292	147150	176.1	18.9
The Americas	5	892411	13.7	92803	124688	34.4	16.1
Most Visited Subregions							
1 Southern Europe	2	152098	2.3	132907	204901	54.2	26.4
2 Northern Europe	2	190189	2.9	77563	98379	26.8	12.7
3 Eastern Europe– Eurasia*	2	370487	5.7	37549	92504	146.4	11.9
4 East Asia	4	1546659	23.7	23367	79412	239.8	10.2
5 Southwest Asia and North Africa	3	432342	6.6	24006	72683	202.8	9.4
6 Anglo North America	5	331672	5.1	54572	65237	19.5	8.4
7 Southeast Asia	4	581909	8.9	21469	48309	125.0	6.2
8 Latin North America	5	185294	2.8	30509	43397	42.2	5.6
9 Sub- Saharan Africa	3	748649	11.5	6871	17643	156.8	2.3
10 South America	5	375445	5.8	7722	16054	107.9	2.1
11 Nordic Europe	2	24891	0.4	9945	14934	50.2	1.9
12 South Asia	4	1528357	23.4	3304	9272	180.6	1.2
13 Central Asia	3	91175	1.4	1821	3955	117.2	0.5

Reference Cited

Lew, A.A. (1987). A Framework of Tourist Attraction Research. *Annals of Tourism Research* 14(4): 553–575.

Leiper, N. (1990). Tourist attraction systems. *Annals of Tourism Research* 17(3): 367–384.

MaClannel, D. (1976). *The tourist: a new theory of the leisure class.* New York: Schocken Books.

Pearce, P. (1982). *The Social Psychology of Tourist Behavior.* Oxford: Pergamon.

Schmidt, C.J. (1979). The Guided Tour, Insulated Adventure. *Urban Life* 7: 441–466.

EUROPE AND EURASIA

2.1. The Geography of Europe

2.2. Tourism in Western Europe

2.3. Tourism in Eastern Europe

In terms of international tourist arrivals, Western Europe is the most visited region in the world. France and Spain are the two most visited countries in the world, while Italy, the United Kingdom, Germany and Russia are also in the top 10 most visited. For this reason, this section is devoted entirely to Europe, along with its eastern and southeastern extensions into the Asian continent. Section 2.1 covers the basic physical geography and human geography of Europe. Section 2.2 discusses tourism in Western Europe, while Section 2.3 covers Eastern Europe. The division between Eastern and Western Europe is based on overlaying. In both of these sections, the emphasis is initially on European Union (EU) countries, and then on non-EU countries.

FIGURE 2.1
THE EURASIAN LAND MASS AND ITS SUBREGIONS

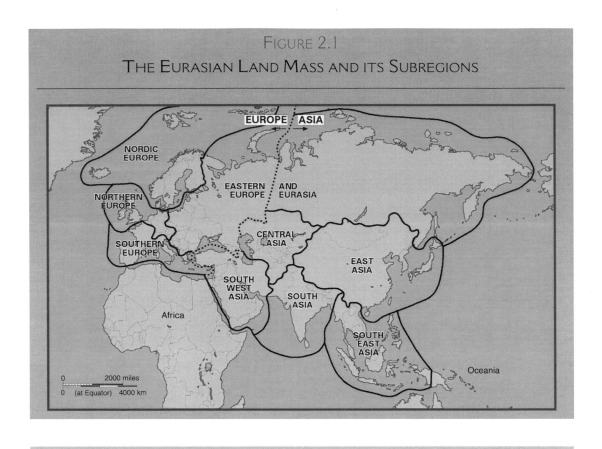

PHOTO 2.1
Europe from Space – Composite image of Europe, the North Pole and Northern Africa

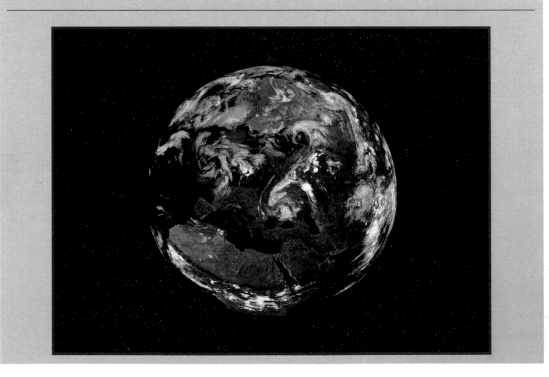

Europe is typically considered one of the world's continents. However, it is unlike the other continents in that it is not completely surrounded by water. Instead, Europe is really a peninsula, jutting out from the much larger Eurasian land mass. Just where this peninsula begins and ends is not obvious on a map. For the most part we accept the Arctic Ocean, the Atlantic Ocean, and the Mediterranean Sea as the northern, western and southern sides of the European continent. The eastern edge of the continent is typically defined by the Ural Mountains in Russia.

The large Eurasian continent has several other peninsula-type regions that are equally as deserving as Europe of the status of a continent (including South Asia and Southeast Asia). We will be discussing each of these later. However, only Europe is regularly designated as a separate continent. The reason for this is purely due to cultural perceptions. One of those cultural perceptions relates back to the ancient Greeks. Greek geographers divided the world into three continents: Europe, Asia and Africa (which they called Libya). Greece was part of Europe. Africa was on the other side of the Mediterranean Sea, and Asia was on the other side of the Aegean Sea. Being culturally different from Asia and Africa has been one of major factors in Europe's aspiration to be a separate continent.

Another reason for Europe's special status is that for most of the past 500 Years, Europe has been one of the most important regions of the world economically, politically and militarily. Starting in the 15th century, European explorers ventured out to other parts of the world seeking to expand their economic influence. They established colonies in Asia, the Americas, Africa and elsewhere. Through their colonies, they introduced new models of economic and political development. Today, those colonial ties still have influences in the form of special trade relationships, as tourist destinations for Europeans, and as sources of immigrants to European countries.

For all these cultural and historical reasons, most geographers consider Europe a separate continent. It is also the most popular tourist destination in the world, and the most important source of tourists to other parts of the world.

Today, much of Europe is encompassed by the European Union (EU) it is sometimes colloquially referred to the United States of Europe, although this description is not completely accurate. Like the United States, travel between most EU countries does not require a separate visa and seldom requires a stop at a border. This is quite an achievement for a continent that was the home of both World War I and World War II, two of the most devastating conflicts of the 20th century. However, the member nations of the EU hold considerable more power than the United States with only a limited amount of authority having been passed on to the EU and the European Parliament.

Despite the creation of the EU, Europe remains one of the most diverse regions in the world both culturally and physically. Europe has one of the world's highest population densities, squeezed into one of the smallest major geographic realms that we will be discussing. Within the small land area of Europe, numerous languages and cultural traditions exists, as does a great variety of landform and climatic conditions, all of which serve to enhance its tourism attractiveness.

Major Regions of Europe

The major geographic regions of Europe are based on a combination of culture and language; political boundaries and alliances; and climatic and terrain. They include the following, though keep in mind that there is some overlap in these definitions.

Western Europe consists of:

- France; the Benelux countries of Belgium, the Netherlands and Luxembourg; and the German-speaking countries of Germany; Switzerland; and Austria.
- The British Isles consists of the United Kingdom (England, Scotland, Wales and Northern Ireland) and the Ireland, and is typically considered part of Western Europe, though they are sometimes treated as a separate region.
- Switzerland, Liechtenstein and Austria are sometimes broken out to form a separate Alpine Europe region.
- Nordic Europe consists of Denmark, Greenland, Norway, Sweden, Finland and Iceland. Greenland (in North America) and the Faeroe Islands are autonomous territories of Denmark that are part of the Nordic Group. The Åland Islands situated between Sweden and Finland are the other territory recognized as part of the Nordic grouping. Although a part of Finland, this Swedish-speaking territory has considerable political independence. Denmark, Norway and Sweden are collectively referred to as Scandinavia.
- Mediterranean or Southern Europe consists of the Iberian Peninsula, which is Andorra, Spain and Portugal; Italy; the Vatican City; Vatican City San Marino; Greece; and the island states of Malta and Cyprus. France and Turkey are sometimes considered part of Southern Europe, as well. Southern Europe and Scandinavia are considered separate from Western Europe in some definitions.

Eastern Europe is generally divided into two political and geographical groupings. EU Accession States, those countries of the region that have either joined the EU since 2000 or which have applied to join, and EU Non-Accession States – countries of the region that have not applied to join or which are only at the very earliest stages of discussion with the EU.

- The *EU Accession States* consist of Bulgaria, the Czech Republic, Hungary, Poland, Romania, Slovakia and Slovenia, as well as the three BALTIC states of Latvia, Lithuania and Estonia. The Baltic countries regained their independence in 1991, after the formal collapse of the Soviet Union in 1990. Estonia, which has strong cultural, language and economic ties to Finland, has also attempted to portray itself as a Nordic country, although it is not formally a part of the Nordic group. The Czech Republic and Slovakia were formerly the country of Czechoslovakia but separated peacefully in 1993. Historically, the accession countries have had closer ties to Western Europe than have other Eastern European countries.

  Bulgaria, Romania and Slovenia are also a part of the *Balkan Peninsula*, along with Albania, Serbia, Montenegro, Croatia, the Republic of Macedonia and Bosnia-Herzegovina. These countries comprise the Southern part of Eastern Europe. Greece is also physically part of the Balkans but was never a Communist-ruled country as were the others. So for cultural and political reasons, including

FIGURE 2.2

THE COUNTRIES OF EUROPE, CAPITALS AND MAJOR CITIES

its earlier membership of the EU, Greece is normally discussed separate from the other Balkan countries.

- THE *EU Non-Accession States* consists of Albania, Armenia, Belarus, Bosnia and Herzegovina, Croatia, Georgia, the Republic of Macedonia, Moldova, Montenegro, Russia, Serbia and Ukraine. These countries were either formerly a part of the Soviet Union or the Republic of Yugoslavia, which fell apart in the early 1990s after the fall of Communism.

Physical Geography

The Greek geographer Strabo (63 BC to 24 CE), described Europe as *a very irregular peninsula.* He was referring to the interpenetration of land and sea on three sides of the European continent. Europe is a peninsula, but it also has many smaller peninsulas and islands extending out from its coastline. Conversely, Europe has many small seas and bays that extend between these land extensions.

One way of conceptualizing the physical form of the landscape was proposed by the geographer William Morse Davis (1850–1934). Although a simplification, his approach does help in understanding Europe's diversity. Davis suggested that landforms can be divided into the categories of youth, maturity and old age. Youthful landscapes are areas of recent and new mountain building, and mostly consists of high mountains and deep valleys (Southern Europe). Mature landscapes usually have lower hills that long ago stopped growing and have since eroded considerably (Central Europe). Old age landscapes consist of flat, low-lying plains that were once high mountain systems, but have since been completely eroded (Northern Europe).

Waterways

The two largest rivers of Europe are the Rhine and the Danube. If Europe were extended to include all of the land area to the Ural Mountains, then the Volga River in Russia is also one of the largest rivers of Europe. (Russia will be discussed in more detail later.) Smaller rivers that are also very important include: the Maine River in Germany, the major tributary of the Rhine; the Po River in Italy; the Seine River in northern France and the Rhone River in Southern France; the Elbe River in former East Germany; and Vistula River in Poland.

PHOTO 2.2

Budapest, Hungary. A tourist boat makes its way on the Danube river through Budapest, the capital of Hungary

Source: Jarkko Saarinen

Europe also has several very important canals. The Mittelland Canal cuts across the North Europe Plain from east to west. The Rhine-Maine-Danube Canal is an 80 mile-long (130 km) canal in southeast Germany that connects the Rhine River system to the Danube River system, allowing ships to travel from the Black Sea to the North Sea. The Emperor Charlemagne (742–814 CE) first attempted to construct this Canal in 793 CE, but it was not opened until July 31, 1992. The combined water system traverses the length of 2170 miles (3500 km), which is about 175 miles (280 km) longer than the Mississippi River in the United States. It travels through 10 different countries and provides a significant route for tour boats of various types, from upscale canal barges to small cruise ships and day ferries.

Climates of Europe

Climate refers to the average annual pattern of weather in a place or region. There are two primary factors that influence the climate of a place. The first is its land features, including the place's location relative to oceans and other large bodies of water. The other major factor that influences climate is the atmosphere, primarily the high and low air masses that circulate around the globe.

The major terrestrial features of Europe that affect its climates include:

1. Europe is located in a temperate zone. This means that Europe is located between the Tropic of Cancer and the Arctic Circle. It receives sunlight all year

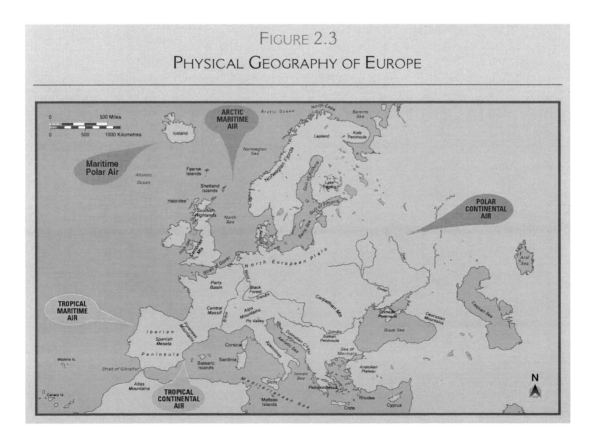

FIGURE 2.3

PHYSICAL GEOGRAPHY OF EUROPE

because it is mostly below the Arctic Circle. However the sun is never directly ahead because it is north of the Tropic of Cancer. The very northernmost part of Europe is subarctic, while the southernmost part of Europe is subtropical.

2. Europe is located on the eastern side of the Atlantic Ocean and also has large bodies of water on its north and south sides. Because the temperature of large bodies of water changes little from one season to the next, the Atlantic Ocean, the North Sea and the Mediterranean Sea have a moderating influence on the climate of most of Europe. In addition the northern Atlantic Ocean contains the Gulf Stream, which is also known as the North Atlantic Drift. The Gulf Stream brings warm water from the Gulf of Mexico across the Atlantic directly into the English Channel and the North Sea. This warm water keeps these water bodies ice free most of the time, which is unusual at such a northerly latitude.

3. Europe is mostly influenced by winds and air masses that flow from west to east. In the temperate zones of the earth air masses and winds move from west to east. For Europe, this pattern brings moist and relatively warm (from the Gulf Stream) ocean air to most of the European continent, north of the Alps. This results in higher land temperatures in the winter than one would normally find this far north.

4. Europe is located on the western edge of the world's largest land mass, the Eurasian continent. Large land masses (i.e., continents) gain heat in the summer and lose heat in the winter at a much faster rate than do large water bodies, such as oceans. In the winter the north-central portion of the Eurasian landmass is the coldest place on earth. In winter, bitterly cold and dry continental air comes out from this area and dominates the climate of Russia. It also extends into Eastern Europe and occasionally into Western Europe.

5. Europe does not have a continuous North South mountain range. Unlike North America and South America, air masses coming off the Atlantic Ocean do not come up against a large north–south trending mountain range that both slows them down and changes their moisture content. Instead, air masses can extend considerably far inland before their ocean influences dissipate. When the Atlantic Ocean air systems weaken, dry continental air masses (hot in summer, cold in winter) from Russia can similarly extend west into northern Europe.

6. Europe has an almost unbroken east to west mountain chain in its south-central region. The mountain ranges, starting with the Pyrenees in the west and extending through the Alps and the Carpathians, forms a sharp divide between the climate zones of northern and southern Europe. The mountains prevent large scale interchanges between the tropical air masses to the south and the polar air masses to the north.

Air Masses

Air masses from the far north pole are either *arctic* (from the Arctic Ocean) or *polar* (from the far north). Air masses from areas to the south of Europe are *tropical* and very warm. Air masses that pass over an ocean before reaching Europe are *maritime* and generally bring humidity and precipitation. Those that originate over land before reaching Europe are *continental* and tend to be very dry. There are five major air masses that affect the climate of Europe.

The principal air mass affecting most of Europe is the polar maritime air mass which originates over the North Atlantic Ocean and brings cold moist air to northern and central Europe through much of the year. This air mass affects central Europe more in the summer than the winter. In the winter, it can sometimes migrate south of the Alps into the Mediterranean region. In the winter, an arctic maritime air mass that is very cold and dry (because it is so cold) moves southward, mostly affecting the northern portions of Europe, but occasionally extending much further south. Eastern Europe is mostly affected by a polar continental air mass from the interior Eurasian continent. This dry air mass is very cold in the winter, and relatively warm in the summer. It can sometimes move further westward into central Europe.

Mediterranean Europe is mostly affected by two air masses. The first is a tropical maritime air mass that originates over the Atlantic Ocean and is warm and moist, mostly affecting Portugal and the Atlantic coast of France. The second is a tropical continental air mass that originates over Africa and brings hot and dry air to the Mediterranean region in the summer, especially its eastern portions.

In the winter, all of the air masses move southward, while in the summer they all move northward. In the winter, the difference in temperature between northern and southern Europe becomes quite extreme.

In the summer the Arctic and maritime polar air masses move northward and the temperature differences between northern and southern Europe are more moderate. Winds from the tropical maritime and tropical continental air masses come to dominate southern Europe and occasionally areas north of the Alps. Southern Europe exhibits a *Mediterranean Climate*, in which rainfall occurs in the winter, and summers are hot and dry. The only other large area in the world that has this type of climate is the state of California in the United States.

Climate Regions

The result of the seasonal changes in these air masses is that Europe has three major climate regions. The climate of Northern Europe is a maritime *Marine West Coast* climate (which is also found in the Pacific Northwest of the United States and in British Columbia in Canada). It is mostly affected by low-pressure systems (cold fronts) bringing storms off the Atlantic Ocean. The precipitation occurs all year round, with the higher amount in winter. Northern Europe receives over 30 in. of rain a year, and snow is relatively rare at sea level, though it can be quite considerable at higher elevations. The region has high humidity, a lot of clouds, and considerable fog in the winter.

Southern Europe has a subtropical and *Mediterranean* climate. In the summer, the region is dominated by a high pressure air system (from Africa), which is dry and hot. In the winter, low-pressure systems from the North Atlantic occasionally migrate south below the Alps. Summers are hot, with an average above 80°F. Winters are cool to cold, but almost always above 32°F. Because air masses tend to move from the west to the east, coastlines that face the west are much more humid than coastlines on the eastern side of peninsulas and islands. The mild and warm year round temperatures of southern Europe have made it one of the most attractive beach destinations in the world.

Eastern Europe is dominated by a *Continental* climate, consisting of air masses that originate over the interior of the Eurasian continent. Summers tend to be warm and dry, though maritime air masses from the North Atlantic and moisture from the Mediterranean Sea and Black Sea can also bring rainfall during the summer months. In the winter the region is dominated by a very cold and dry air, which often results in a permanent snow cover throughout the winter months. Eastern Europe is often colder in winter than Scandinavia, which is much closer to the North Pole. Continental climates are characterized by large seasonal fluctuations in temperature, and Eastern Europe is no exception to this. Low temperatures in winter are often 0°F, while summer highs can reach over 90°F.

In between these three climate zones are transition areas. In these areas weather is often unpredictable and changeable, as they can sometimes be affected by the Continental climate to the east, the Marine West Coast climate to the west or the Mediterranean climate to the south.

TOURISM ISSUES AND INSIGHTS
THE THREAT OF CLIMATE CHANGE AND GEEGEES

Climate change has become a major contemporary environmental concern. The Fourth Assessment Report of the Intergovernmental Panel on Climate Change, indicates that:

- The frequency of hurricanes and storms will increase dramatically.
- Snow will disappear from all but the highest mountains.
- Deserts will spread.
- Oceans will become acidic, leading to the destruction of coral reefs and atolls; and
- Deadly heat waves will become more prevalent.
- Sea levels will rise over the century by around half a meter.

Climate change issues and there significance will be noted throughout the book. Sea level change will have a significant impact on low-lying areas – such as those of the Netherlands, northern Belgium, eastern Denmark and the east of England. Just a 3.3 ft (1 m) rise would threaten one-third of the world's agricultural land, 6.6 ft (2 m) would make the Thames flood barrier that protects London redundant and 13 ft (4 m) would drown the city of Miami, leaving it 37 miles (60 km) off the United States coast. A worst-case scenario would see a return to conditions that existed about 14,000 years ago, when sea levels rose 45 ft (3.5 m) the height of a three-storey house – in the space of about 300 years. Such scenarios would have enormous implications for coastal tourism.

However, recent research indicates that climate change may have other effects on the environment and human-beings in ways that were not previously recognized or thought related including an increase in volcanic activity, earthquakes, submarine landslides and tsunamis. For example, following the retreat of the glaciers around 18,000 years ago, after which sea levels jumped back up to where they are today, a 300 percent increase in volcanic activity occurred in the Mediterranean.

Even small changes in sea level can make a difference. For example, eruptions of Pavlof volcano in Alaska tend to occur during the winter months when, for meteorological reasons, the regional sea level is barely 12 in (30 cm) higher than during the summer. If other volcanic systems are similarly sensitive then there would be a burst of volcanic activity as anthropogenic climate change drives sea levels upwards.

Continued

The Human Geography of Europe

Europe is a major center of culture, education and history that has had global influence through colonial ties, migration, education systems and the media. Because of this, much of the tourism in Europe is culture-based. Knowledge of the cultural and historical geography of Europe is necessary to appreciate fully the experience that Europe has to offer.

The Influence of Ancient Greece

The first major European civilization that is usually recognized was that of the Greeks. Early Greek civilization was composed of independent city states (cities that were also countries) scattered throughout the Mediterranean Sea and Black Sea area, but centered on Greece. They were tied together by their culture and history. Greek culture rose about 1000 BC, and peaked in about 500 BC. The Greeks were conquered by the Romans in 147 BC. Greek civilization laid the philosophical foundations for Europe. Socrates (469 to 399 BCE, which was also about the same time as Confucius in China) was a proponent of the idea that wisdom could be taught to anyone. He founded the *Academy* in 387 BCE, which could be considered the first university in the Western world. To the Greeks, man was the measure of all things. Morality was based on decisions made by humans, not the gods. Greek gods were essentially mortals with superpowers – they were to be worshiped, but they were not of moral values. Socrates was put to death in 399 BC for *corrupting the young*, which basically meant *asking too many questions*.

In the Greek city states, *citizens* were considered free individuals, although they were also all males and most Greek city states had more slaves then citizens. The Greek city states experimented with different forms of government including: tyranny, which is a dictatorship government; aristocracy, which is rule by the elite; oligarchy, which is rule by the few; and democracy, which is rule by the people (citizens). The Greeks also contributed major advances in geometry, which was used for navigating the Mediterranean Sea, and medicine, from which doctors today still adhere to the Hippocratic Oath. And Greeks also introduce the idea of the professional athlete, supported by city state governments, in their Olympic competitions. Other contributions were made in the arts, architecture and education.

PHOTO 2.3
The Acropolis in Athens, Greece

The Romans

Roman civilization lasted from about 500 BCE to about 500 CE. The Romans were the first to gain a true awareness of Europe as an entire continent. Through conquest they integrated much of Northern Europe into the existing civilization of southern Europe often destroying much of the existing regional cultures and religions, such as the Druidic traditions in much of Britain and France. They built a unifying road network throughout their European empire, which saw the blossoming of a major period of tourism and travel during the height of the Roman Empire. The Romans admired Greek philosophy and ideas, which they spread throughout Europe in the way they built their cities, laying out their streets in a grid pattern with a central plaza and public buildings. Greece was also a major tourist destination for the Romans, who purchased souvenir statues of Greek gods and models of the Acropolis to take back with them to Rome, much as tourists do today.

The Romans made major contributions to European traditions of law, public administration (including the concept of a Senate), military organization, and communications. During the Roman period different parts of Europe came to specialize in different economic activities and trade flourished along the Roman roads. North Africa was the major grain producing region for the empire. The Mediterranean islands focused on the mining of iron ore. Spain was a major center for silver and lead mines, while Cornwall in south-west England was a source of tin. Further north, agriculture was the main industry. All roads from these regions led to Rome, which was the central marketplace for goods from throughout the empire.

Latin became the lingua franca throughout Europe. This was the first and only time that most of Europe spoke the same language, although the use of Latin was primarily among intellectuals and the upper classes. The Latin influence today is primarily seen among the Romance languages, including French, Italian (and Sardinian), Spanish (and Catalan), Portuguese and Romanian. All Romance languages descend from Vulgar Latin, which was the language of the soldiers and merchants of the Roman Empire, which was somewhat different from the Latin of the Roman elite. (In fact the Roman legacy for language is such that in 1954 the Latin Union was established as an international association of nations that use a Romance language). Toward the end of the Empire the Roman Emperors also helped spread Christianity often through force, throughout much of their empire the limits of which at its greatest extent were as far north as Hadrian's Wall near the border of England and Scotland, but did not cross the Rhine River, on the other side of which were located the Germanic tribes. Nevertheless, Roman influence extended beyond those borders through trading relations.

The decline of the Roman Empire began about 200 CE. A period of hyperinflation led to a collapse of the Roman currency and people returned to a barter society, which meant that Rome was unable to collect taxes. Necessary reforms did take place in the eastern Roman Empire, centered in Constantinople (modern-day Istanbul), that saved it from the collapse of the Rome-based empire during the 5th century AD. The latest date given for the end of the Western Roman Empire is 610 when the Emperor Heraclius based in Constantinople readopted Greek as the language of Imperial administration. The Eastern Roman Empire, also referred to as the Byzantine Empire, survived until 1453 when Constantinople fell to the Ottoman Turks under Mehmed II.

Ancient Tourism

Although tourism is often claimed as a new industry, dating either from the advent of the railway or the jumbo jet, domestic and international leisure travel has in fact been going on for thousands of years. In August 2007, archeologists at a site in south-central Turkey found a huge (4–5 m in height), carved statue of the Roman Emperor Hadrian who ruled Rome from 117 AD to 138AD, about 5 m below ground, among the buried ruins of a bath house at Sagalassos, an ancient mountaintop town in southern Turkey. The bath house in which the statue was found was destroyed by a major earthquake sometime between the late 6th and early 7th centuries AD. It is believed that the statue was likely erected to honor Hadrian in thanks to him for officially recognizing Sagalassos as the *first city* of the Roman province of Pisidia and therefore made it the regional center for worship of the emperor. This status would have meant that the city attracted thousands of visitors during imperial festivals thereby boosting trade and making the town prosperous.

Sagalassos was by no means the only Roman tourism destination in present-day Turkey. A present-day major heritage destination is that of Troy which in Roman times was the city of Ilium. Homer's Iliad provided the basis not only for contemporary cultural understandings of Troy as portrayed in books and film but in an historical context was part of the founding myths of a number of different European nations and their rulers. The Roman poet Virgil in the *Aeneid*, traced the ancestry of the founders of Rome to the Trojan prince Aeneas. Therefore, Troy became a significant travel destination for the Roman aristocracy and wealthy middle classes, particularly from the time of Augustus (27BC) until 200–300AD. They could be taken by tour guides to see the locations at which particular battles or scenes took place in exactly the same way that some present-day visitors are.

The Great Migration

Starting in the 5th century was a period known as the great migration. During this time the Germanic-speaking tribes crossed the Rhine River and spread throughout Europe. The Saxons settled in northern France and later migrated to England along with the Angles. The Franks settled in France and Belgium. The Lombards settled in the Po Valley of Northern Italy. The Alemanni settled in northern Germany. The Burgundii settled in the upper Rhone River Valley. The Goths and the Visigoths migrated to the Iberian Peninsula, and the Vandals migrated to northern Africa. In 410 CE the Goths and Vandals sacked Rome, marking the beginning of the end of the Roman Empire. Various theories have been provided about the reason for these migrations, but the most likely explanation appears to be a combination of the decline of the military and political strength of the Roman Empire and environmental change.

As these Germanic tribes moved north, west and south, Slavic-speaking people from further east moved into modern-day Eastern Europe. Slavic languages today dominate the region from the Balkan Peninsula in the south to Poland in the north, and east to Russia.

Each of these tribes established a mini-state of its own. Europe thus entered the Middle Ages, which lasted from approximately 500 CE to about 1500, with 1492, when Columbus sailed to the New World, often seen as a critical date. During this time, Europe was divided, wars were frequent, and feudalism prevailed. Most of Roman high culture was lost within Europe, as travel in Europe was difficult and learning was suppressed, with its legacy being maintained during this period by Christian scholars. However, three distinct periods are usually identified by contemporary scholars: the early (500–1000 AD), high (1000–1300 AD) and late Middle Ages (1300–1500 AD).

The Early Middle Ages is also often described as the Dark Ages or the Viking Ages because of the extent to which Roman territory was invaded by various tribes early in the period and the Scandinavian Vikings began to exert their influence from 700 AD on in a series of invasions and raids throughout Europe. Trading links broke down and famine was common as a result of the Dark Ages cold period, which was associated with a decline in agricultural production. This period also saw the emergence of a new challenge to European culture with the emergence of Islam in Arabia and the growth of the Arabian Empire with most of the Iberian Peninsula of Spain and Portugal coming under Islamic control in the 8th century and leaving a legacy that lasts to this day in southern Spanish culture.

The High Middle Ages from 1000 CE onward marks the period at which the last of the great migrations had been undertaken, although war and invasion were still commonplace, for example, the Norman invasion of Anglo-Saxon England in 1066 and Ireland in 1169. This was also the time of the Catholic Inquisitions, which are associated with the period in the public imagination. Although inquisitors had existed in the Church since Roman times, the Episcopal (1184–1230s), Papal (1230s) and Spanish Inquisitions (established 1478) used particularly terrifying methods to find and destroy what were judged by the Church as heretic mass movements. For example, the Cathars and Waldensians in France and the Jews in Spain were often subject to the acts of the inquisition with many being massacred. Ironically, such events have served as tourist attractions in recent times with the Cathars being featured in tourism promotions for Carcassonne in France and profiled in a number of publications and television programs that focus on the Knights Templar and the Holy Grail.

The Late Middle Ages began with the Great Famine of 1315–1317 and the Black Death, which dramatically reduced the population of Europe. Although the period was marked by great scientific achievements, it was also characterized by crises within the Catholic Church including the Papal schism of 1378–1417 when there were multiple claimants to the papacy as well as the reform movements associated with John Wyclif (in England), Jun Hus (Czech) and Martin Luther (Germany). A number of other church related aspects of the High and Late Middle Ages also serve as tourism attractions to the present-day. Many of the great cathedrals of Europe date from this period while a number of pilgrimage routes remain in use and are arguably more popular than ever as heritage trails. Also significant are the many walled towns of Europe, art and the writing of some of the first travel accounts such as the works of Marco Polo and William of Rubruck.

The Byzantine Empire

The cultural contributions of the Greeks and Romans, however, was preserved in the eastern Roman Empire, which was also known as the Byzantine Empire. It was also preserved in the Arab Empire, which was centered in Baghdad, and was possibly the world's largest and most advanced civilization of that time period. (The Arab Empire will be discussed in more detail later.)

The Roman emperor, Flavius Valerius Aurelius Constantinus, or Constantine I (c. 274 CE to 337), made Byzantium the center of the Roman Empire in 330 CE, changing its name to Constantinople. The Byzantine Empire lasted until 1453 AD, when it was conquered by the Turks, who changed the name of Constantinople to Istanbul. During the Dark Ages, Constantinople was the foremost city of trade and culture in Europe. The people of the Byzantine Empire called themselves Romans, and called territory the Romani Empire. They copied Roman and Greek art and literature, and Constantine made Christianity the state religion (in 324 CE). They brought orthodox Christianity to the Slavic peoples to the north and introduced the Cyrillic alphabet throughout their territory. They also transmitted Latin and Greek cultural traditions to the new Germanic rulers of Western Europe. While the rulers of Byzantium sought to replace Rome as the center of the old Roman Empire, they were never able to hold on to the more distant territories of Europe and Africa.

Unlike the Roman Empire, where church and state were largely separate, in the Byzantine Empire the emperor came to be considered God's representative on Earth. The defeat of the emperor would only occur by the will of God. Extremely elaborate palaces were built to impress visiting barbarians of the Byzantine wealth and power.

PHOTO 2.4

Alexander Nevsky Cathedral, Sofia, Bulgaria. This 19th century Neo-Byzantine building is one of the largest eastern orthodox cathedrals in the world, capable of holding up to 5,000 worshippers

Today, Byzantine architecture can be found throughout Europe. The city of Venice, for example, is architecturally a Byzantine city.

The Byzantine Empire protected Eastern Europe from mostly Muslim invaders during the Dark Ages, allowing a new Europe to develop from the ruins of the Roman Empire. The fact that Europe faced a powerful Muslim empire to its south and east contributed to a sense of Europe as a separate territory from the rest of the world. This was especially true after Christianity was also adopted by the Germanic tribes starting with Charlemagne, the King of the Franks, in the 8th century.

The Nation State

The concept of the nation state gradually developed in Europe during the Dark Ages. Different from the idea of a country, a nation is a territory that shares a common language, history, politics and culture. The word state refers to a politically independent and sovereign territory. As cultural-based nationalistic identities increased in Europe, the anarchy of the great migration, and the subsequent divisions of feudalism, gradually came to an end. Feudal lords lost their power and independence as nation state kings came to dominate. Prior to this the king was just another feudal lord who ruled his own domain and had a slightly different title than the other feudal lords.

The rise of the nation state took several centuries and was the result of several different processes. One was the rise of a new merchant class. These were basically landless (and therefore homeless) peasants who became traders and crafts-people and migrated from one village to the next. As their numbers grew, merchant towns with artisans and crafts-people began to appear, especially along the major rivers. The mercantile class formed a middle-class between the lords and the peasants. The mercantile towns also served as centers for the sale of excess agricultural products. The sale of these products provided surplus wealth which enabled peasants to purchase crafts that were produced in the towns, as well as imported goods from other places. Some of these mercantile towns became university towns, signaling a revival in learning.

An increase in the ability of people to travel in Europe also signaled the decline of feudalism. This began with The Crusades (1095–1270), which introduce people to different parts of Europe and to places beyond Europe. New ideas and new products were brought back to Europe as a result of The Crusades.

Townspeople lived outside of the feudal lord system. As such, they looked to the regional king for their security. The king gained his wealth from taxing the townspeople, so the wealthier the townspeople became, the wealthier and more powerful the king became. With time, the king's military became much stronger than that of the lords. The 100 Years War between France and England (1338–1454) resulted in even stronger kings seeking to expand their territory, as well as the rise of national heroes and symbols. Joan of Arc was one such hero. She fought against the British in the 100 Years War and was burned at the stake after her capture in 1430. The 100 Years War also led to the unification of France (and the final collapse of feudalism) for the first time in the later 1400s.

France is often cited as the best example of the nation state. It was a political territory that shared a common language, history and culture. Spain became a nation state in 1469 when the marriage of Ferdinand and Isabella united the Spanish-speaking territory of Iberia. England was united in 1485 after the War of the Roses was fought among feudal lords. Similar processes occurred in the Netherlands and Portugal. Italy and Germany, however, were not unified as nation states until the 1860s.

Another state in the political development of Europe occurred when nation state leadership changed from a strong monarchy to a constitutional monarchy and direct democracy. The earliest constitutional monarchy form of government appeared in England in 1215 with the signing of the Magna Carta. The first democracy in Europe was formed in France after the 1789 revolution that overthrew the French monarchy. For Eastern Europe, limitations on absolute monarchy rule did not occur until after World War I (1914–1918). However, Iceland was the first European country to have a parliament with the Alþing (Althing in English) established in 930.

1492 is often used to mark the end of the Dark Ages. This was the year that Columbus sailed to the Americas, and the Muslim Moors were pushed out of Spain. And it was the middle of the European Renaissance (14th to 16th centuries). With the growth of an increasingly more powerful mercantile class of traders and sailors, economic nationalism came to be the predominant policy of the nation states in Europe. What was good for the traders and merchants was good for the country and the king. The military power of the king was therefore used to control or dominate trade, often by directly conquering and colonizing distant lands. The growing economic wealth of Europe resulted in rising standards of living and advances in education. But Europe was still largely an agricultural society, with some large cities based primarily on foreign trade. The only industrial activities were craft guilds, not factories.

The European Renaissance began in Southern Europe in the 14th century. This was the time of Michelangelo, Raphael and Leonardo da Vinci. By the end of the 15th century, European explorers were crossing the Atlantic to the Americas and rounding the Horn of Africa to Asia. Much of this period of overseas colonization was dominated by Spain and Portugal. By the 16th century, the center of European culture and economic dominance had shifted to northern Europe, especially France, Belgium, the Netherlands and England. In England, this was the time of William Shakespeare, Sir Francis Bacon, and Thomas Moore and also a period in which travel became more commonplace for the young men of the aristocracy as the Grand Tour through Europe came to be seen as an important part of the education process.

The Industrial Revolution

1869 was another important year of change for the European continent. That was the year in which the Suez Canal opened, giving European ships access to Asia without having to circle the entire continent of Africa. This was also a time when the Industrial Revolution had reached its peak in Europe. (The Industrial Revolution began in England in the late 1700s and was soon exported to northern Europe.) The result of these changes was a huge expansion in Asian and African colonization by European countries after 1869.

With the Industrial Revolution, the steam engine freed small-scale industries from river locations, and enabled the building and use of increasingly larger machinery. The mass production of large-scale iron products and machinery, and of finished goods that were created from raw materials shipped from colonies, made Europe the wealthiest region in the world. Europe's population exploded at this time, as birthrates increased and death rates declined despite the high health hazards in the industrial cities of Europe. Large machinery enabled fewer people to work larger tracts of farm, which resulted in huge migrations from the countryside to the cities. By 1800 England had the largest cities in the world. However, those cities were also badly overcrowded, with poor housing and sanitation, child labor and slavery, and dangerous working conditions. Nevertheless, this period marked the beginning of modern tourism in several ways. First, the invention of the steam engine allowed for the development of the railway and the steam ship, which revolutionized travel. Second, the industrial revolution provided for the emergence of a new middle class who had income and the desire for travel, while higher levels of education and improvements to the printing press meant that it was much easier to promote leisure travel. Third, the transport system and time became standardized, thereby allowing for scheduling and, along with the invention of the telegraph, dramatically improved the commercialization of transport. Finally, as a reaction to the conditions of many of the industrial cities the Romantic movement grew, led by Poets such as Coleridge and Wordsworth, which meant that mountainous and wild countryside became a desired place to visit for the first time ever in European culture, thereby making places such as Switzerland, Scotland and Norway attractive to visitors from industrial Europe.

England used its vast colonial territories, including Australia, North America and countries of the developing world, as source of raw materials and as an outlet for immigration out of England to relieve the population pressures there. Many Americans can trace their ancestry to the 1800s when large numbers of Europeans migrated to the United States. This migration began with immigrants from the British Isles at the start of the Industrial Revolution. Subsequent immigrants to the United States came from areas of Europe as they came under the influence the Industrial Revolution. Northern Europeans from the Netherlands and Germany migrated to the United States in large numbers in the mid-1800s, while southern and eastern Europeans migrated in the late 1800s and early 1900s. (After World War I, Europeans accounted for only a small percentage of immigrants to the United States.) The flow of migrants as well as the mercantile connections of empires also provided a basis for international travel and tourism, and by 1872 Thomas Cook was promoting his first World Tour.

Demographic Changes and Tourism Impacts

Higher European standards of living have led to smaller families as birthrates have decreased to match death rates. Many European countries today are experiencing negative population growth because birthrates are much lower than death rates. However as a result of their past colonial ties, most European countries today also have large immigrant populations, whose growth rates are higher than those of the native Europeans. Turks went to Germany, Algerians went to France, immigrants from Suriname and Indonesia went to the Netherlands, and England welcomed large numbers of immigrants from India, Hong Kong, South Africa and other former British colonies. In such changes the legacy of European history can clearly be seen and a new stage of travel patterns and connections are now being formed as migrant groups seek to stay in contact with one another as they have done for hundreds of years.

In addition to migration the other major demographic factor that will affect tourism is the aging of the world's population. This substantial demographic shift has occurred because of dramatic improvements in health care and a decline in the birth rate in the developed world and this is predicted to continue well into the coming centuries so long as the world's resources are able to support the increases in population. The United Nations Population Division estimated that at the end of the 20th Century 11 percent of the world's population was aged 60 and above. By 2050, it is estimated that

20 percent will be 60 years or older; and by 2150, approximately one-third will be 60 years or older. Just as significantly the older population itself is aging. The increase in the number of very old people (aged 80+ years) between 1950 and 2050 in the world is projected to increase by a factor of between 8 and 10 times the present amount. As well a general aging of the world's population there are also substantial regional differences in the aged population. For example, currently 20 percent of Europeans are 60 years or older, but only 5 percent of Africans.

Given that the majority of the world's international tourists come from developed countries, an aging population will clearly have substantial implications for the tourism industry. Not only may particular types of tourism favored by older travelers such as cruising, continue to grow in popularity, but second homes and retirement homes and the provision of health facilities for retirees will likely become increasingly important in the development strategies of some destinations. For example, areas of Mediterranean Europe (Italy, Greece, Cyprus) and the Iberian Peninsula (Portugal, Spain) and in North America, the south-west United States, Florida and some parts of coastal Mexico are already subject to substantial seasonal and permanent retirement migration, much of which is international.

A further influential factor with respect to demographic change and tourism is that it is estimated that among the major industrialized countries only the United States is estimated to have significant population growth by 2050. The United States is expected to have reached a population of 420 million by 2050, an increase of 43 percent. But Europe is expected to have 60 million fewer people than today and some countries could lose more than a third of their populations. Japan may have shrink in size to approximately 100 million people by 2050. Over the same period Eastern Europe is also predicted to experience major population loss. Bulgaria is expected to lose 38 percent of its people, while Romania could have 27 percent fewer and Russia 25 million fewer people. Germany and Italy are expected to shrink by approximately 10 percent.

Although the world's developed countries are expected to grow in total population by about 4 percent to over 1.2 billion, the population in developing countries is predicted to grow by up to 55 percent to more than 8 billion. Under this scenario Western Asian nations are expected to gain about 186 million people by 2050 and Sub-Saharan African countries more than one billion people. By 2050, India will be the largest country in the world, having long passed China.

2.2   TOURISM IN WESTERN EUROPE

The European Union

Tourism is an area of great economic significance to the EU. About 900 million holiday trips, almost evenly distributed between short (1–3 nights) and long holidays (4 and more nights) were made by EU tourists in 2005. Tourism expenditures and receipts were nearly in balance for the EU as a whole. Expenditures stood at €235.6 billion, while receipts from tourism stood at €232.6 billion. Although Europe's market share, in terms of both arrivals and revenue, of international tourism is tending to diminish in relation to other world regions, notably the Asia-Pacific, Europe is still a major force in world tourism, with increased ease of travel between the EU member countries encouraging greater integration and therefore continued tourism growth. In 2005, 87.5 percent of all nights spent in collective accommodation were spent by either residents of the country (59.1 percent) or by residents of other EU member states (28.4 percent). Tourism comprises more than 4 percent of the EU's GDP, with about two million businesses employing about 4 percent of the total labor force, representing approximately eight million jobs. If the links to other sectors are taken into account, the contribution of tourism to gross domestic product (GDP) is estimated to be around 11 percent and provides employment to more than 12 percent of the labor force (24 million jobs).

The EU is comprised of 27 European countries and the combined economy of its members is the largest in the world. The EU has a single economic market between its members, a common trade policy, a common agricultural and fisheries policy, and an extensive series of regional development policies. Although the EU has many of the trappings of a country, such as the European Parliament, the European Court of Justice and the European Central Bank, it is important to recognize that the EU is a supranational body with control only over a number of policy areas that its member states have acceded to. For example, although the Euro is a common European currency it has only been adopted by 13 member states. Accordingly, a number of member states, such as the United Kingdom, have retained their own central bank.

The formation of the EU has taken several decades and reflects the desire of European countries to work together in economic and political goals. Established in 1957 the founding members were Belgium, France, Germany, Italy, Luxembourg and the Netherlands. In 1973 it was expanded to include Denmark, Ireland and the United Kingdom. Greece joined in 1981 and Portugal and Spain in 1986. Other Western European nations to join included Austria, Finland and Sweden in 1995. After the fall of the Soviet Union in 1991, most Eastern European countries sought entry into the EU. The EU offered a large, affluent market and development subsidies to poorer regions. The prospect of membership has provided a stimulus to democratic reforms and market economic policies in Eastern Europe, which must be achieved prior to admission to the EU. EU expansion took a major leap on May 1, 2004 when 10 Eastern and Southern European countries joined: Latvia, Lithuania, Estonia, Poland, Hungary, the Czech Republic, Slovakia, Slovenia, Malta and Cyprus. Together, they increased the EU's population by 20 percent to 450 million. Bulgaria and Romania were admitted in 2007 although their admission was delayed because of the greater challenges that they still faced in tackling post-communism economic, political and social issues. Turkey had applied to join the EU with the other 10 countries admitted in 2004. Turkey has issues related to human rights and the treatment of its Kurdish minority that must be addressed. In addition, Turkey is a very large and poor country, with a predominantly Muslim population, all of which raises new issues for the EU. The number of countries that are members, its economic and political significance, and its role as a market means that the history and development of the EU is important to understanding European tourism.

The Development of the European Union

Shortly after the end of the World War II Belgium, Luxembourg and the Netherlands formed an alliance (BENELUX) that was meant to help each of these small countries recover from the socio-economic devastation of the war. The primary goal of the

BENELUX agreement was to bring down the trade barriers that existed between the three countries and allow freer flow of goods and people across their common borders. In this way, each of the member states could focus more on what it produced best and could more freely import what its neighbors specialized in. At the same time the European Coal and Steel Community was founded with France, West Germany, Italy, and BENELUX, in order to pool their steel and coal resources and create a common market for those products as part of post-war reconstruction.

As part of this pan-European movement of the 1950s two further organizations were created in 1957 by what is known as the Treaties of Rome: The European Economic Community (EEC), which established a Customs Union to eliminate or lessen trade barriers and tariffs between member countries in Western Europe, and the European Atomic Energy Community (EAEC or Euratom), which was established for reasons of cooperation in the area of nuclear energy. The EASC was later merged into the EEC in 1967 in what was known as the Merger Treaty, which developed a single membership with a combined set of treaties and institutions. This new collectivity was originally referred to as the European Communities, although now just the European Community and is one of the three *pillars* of the EU with the others being Common Foreign and Security Policy, and Police and Judicial Co-operation in Criminal Matters. However, in many diplomatic areas the term European Community is often used instead of EU.

Supranationalism is strongest in the first pillar. Its function generally corresponded at first to the three European Communities (European Coal and Steel Community , EEC and Euratom). In the other two areas the powers of the European Parliament (elected every 5 years), the Commission and European Court of Justice are much more limited with many countries holding on to their national authorities and institutions. The relative powers of the EU and its member states are a hotly debated issue. The signed but unratified European Constitution signed by representatives of the member states in 2004 proposed the merger of the European Community with the other two pillars of the EU, making the EU the legal successor of both the European Community and the EU in its current form. However, the proposed Constitution was not approved by its members as a result of it being rejected by French and Dutch voters who disagreed with several of its tenets. Substantial opposition to the Constitution also existed in the United Kingdom as a result of further concerns over the loss of national sovereignty over a number of issues. A *Draft Treaty Amending the Treaty on EU and the Treaty Establishing the European Community* better known as the Reform Treaty or the Lisbon Treaty due to being proposed to be signed in Lisbon in October 2007 will replace the proposed European Constitution but retain a number of its elements.

The debate over EU and national authority has been integral to the development and history of the EU, and the areas over which the EU system has authority has slowly grown since the 1950s. Since its foundation the union has expanded its goals to include citizenship issues, foreign policy and security arrangements. In an effort to create a completely border restriction-free zone in Western Europe, the Netherlands, Belgium, Luxembourg, Germany and France signed the Schengen Agreement in 1990, followed later by Spain, Portugal, Italy and Several other Countries. While the goals of the treaty were many, its primary purpose was to abolish immigration and customs controls at border-crossing points inside *Schengenland* and to initiate negotiations on establishing a common visa. Even though the Schengen Agreement was meant to create a borderless region of contiguous states, it took several years for the complete removal of border controls between member nations. The 1992 Maastricht Treaty reinforced the Schengen goals and changed the alliance's name to the EU on January 01, 1993. The birth of this union officially eliminated immigration, customs and trade barriers between member states and created a single market, which in theory at least guaranteed the free movement of products, people, services and capital within the EU.

The European Commission has worked to promote social and economic solidarity and reduce regional disparities. Many of their efforts in recent years have included tourism. The industry was solidly positioned in EU policy with its recognition as a separate economic entity in the 1992 Maastricht Treaty. Perhaps owing to its status as the most truly integrated of all supranational alliances, the EU has demonstrated the greatest emphasis on developing pan-European tourism policies. Many studies and development projects have been commissioned and policies formulated by the EU Commission, and billions of euros have been devoted to community development through tourism in the peripheral regions of Europe through structural funding programs, such as Interreg (Interregional) and Leader.

In the EU, the elimination of border formalities and the creation of a common EU/ Schengen visa have created a freer flow of Europeans and non-Europeans alike, which some observers believe will have the long-term effect of increasing intra-European tourism and tourist arrivals to the continent from the rest of the world. The extent of intra-EU travel is indicated in Tables 2.1 and 2.2 which show the three main inbound and outbound markets per country in the EU in 2005.

Tourism Development

A major goal of the EU is to reduce regional socio-economic disparities among member states and improve the standards of living in the less affluent areas of Europe. Financial assistance is provided in various forms throughout the EU, as well as to non-member neighboring countries through various *structural funds*, namely the European Social Fund (ESF), the European Regional Development Fund (ERDF), the Financial Instrument for Fisheries Guidance (FIFG) and the European Agricultural Guidance and Guarantee Fund Section (EAGGF). Perhaps the most influential of these for tourism, the ERDF, was established in 1975 to create economic balance in the EC by helping to develop areas that fell behind the normal standard. This is especially the case in declining industrial regions and peripheral rural regions where tourism has come to be regarded as a potential mechanism for economic development and employment generation.

While tourism itself has been a fairly minor focus of the EU's overall economic development goals until quite recently, the industry has received considerably much more attention in recent years and many projects that include tourism have been funded through the ERDF. In addition, the EU Commission has established ERDF-based policies for tourism that aim to utilize the industry as a course for economic development and to assist tourism-dependent regions in diversifying their economies to offset the effects of seasonality and outside forces that cause other shifts in demand. The EU has initiated several programs through the ERDF and other structural funds that are targeted at strengthening social, economic and ecological balance, including tourism. Programs such as Interreg, Leader and Envireg are especially important in the context of tourism. The main focus of the Interreg program was the creation of jobs through cooperation between EU states in anticipating a decline in employment

TABLE 2.1

THREE MAIN INBOUND MARKETS PER COUNTRY IN THE EU-25, 2005

Country	First market country	%	Second market country	%	Third market country	%	Top three markets (%)
EU-25	**DE**	**23.8**	**UK**	**17.3**	**NL**	**8.0**	**49.1**
Belgium	NL	31.7	UK	14.1	DE	12.6	58.4
Czech Republic	DE	30.0	UK	9.2	IT	6.0	45.2
Denmark	DE	29.5	SE	16.6	NO	16.4	62.5
Germany	NL	17.5	US	9.2	UK	8.2	34.9
Estonia	FI	53.0	SE	7.9	DE	7.2	68.1
Greece	DE	22.9	UK	18.8	IT	7.4	49.1
Spain	UK	33.0	DE	26.1	NL	5.7	64.8
France	UK	20.8	NL	16.2	DE	12.1	49.1
Ireland	—	—	—	—	—	—	—
Italy	DE	30.0	UK	8.6	US	7.7	46.3
Cyprus	UK	55.8	DE	10.5	RU	5.1	71.4
Latvia	DE	15.8	FI	11.0	UK	8.2	35.0
Lithuania	DE	18.7	PL	13.1	RU	8.3	40.1
Luxembourg	NL	40.3	BE	19.5	DE	10.5	70.3
Hungary	DE	30.7	UK	7.6	AT	6.6	44.9
Malta*	UK	40.5	DE	12.1	IT	6.6	59.2
Netherlands	DE	39.8	UK	14.5	BE	9.5	63.8
Austria	DE	55.1	NL	9.3	UK	4.8	69.2
Poland	DE	44.8	UK	5.9	US	4.4	55.1
Portugal*	UK	29.6	DE	16.3	ES	10.7	56.6
Slovenia	IT	19.6	AT	15.5	DE	15.5	50.6
Slovakia	CZ	28.0	DE	20.9	PL	12.1	61.0
Finland	SE	13.3	DE	12.1	RU	11.1	36.5
Sweden	NO	24.5	DE	19.3	DK	9.7	53.5
UK*	US	20.2	DE	9.3	FR	7.1	36.6
Iceland	DE	17.5	UK	13.5	US	10.2	41.2
Norway	DE	22.8	DK	13.9	SE	11.4	48.1

Notes
*2004 figures; Iceland and Norway are not members of the EU-25, but are members of the Schengen Agreement and are included in official EU travel statistics.
— data not available

in border-related activities with the finalization of the single market. Tourism was seen as a key industry for new jobs. Cooperation in tourism development between EU states and non-member states along the EU periphery was another important element of Interreg. These efforts were especially important along the borders of eastern and western Europe and between Switzerland and its EU neighbors. Leader began in 1991 as a way of funding integrated rural development projects conceived and initiated by community action groups. Tourism was treated as a fundamental component of this program as it provided a wider range of linkages to rural and countryside tourism and recreation and assisted with improvements in technology and equipment provision, service quality and information. Communities and tourism benefited from Envireg through the project's efforts to reduce the ecological impacts of tourism and other industries in coastal regions and other sensitive areas.

Although the European Parliament has been relatively slow in establishing policies for tourism relative to other economic, social and environmental areas of interest,

TABLE 2.2

THREE MAIN OUTBOUND MARKETS PER COUNTRY IN THE EU-25 FOR TRIPS ABROAD OF HOLIDAYS OF FOUR NIGHTS AND MORE, 2005

Country	First market country	%	Second market country	%	Third market country	%	Top three markets (%)
EU-25	**ES**	**16.7**	**IT**	**9.8**	**FR**	**8.3**	**34.8**
Belgium	FR	30.8	ES	13.4	IT	8.2	52.4
Czech Republic	SK	18.2	IT	12.9	EL	6.6	37.7
Denmark	ES	12.8	FR	10.2	IT	7.7	30.7
Germany	ES	15.9	IT	14.4	AT	14.4	44.7
Estonia	—	—	—	—	—	—	—
Greece*	IT	11.4	DE	9.7	UK	9.0	30.1
Spain*	FR	18.0	IT	9.3	PT	8.1	35.4
France*	ES	15.3	IT	9.8	UK	3.9	29.0
Ireland*	ES	28.9	UK	15.4	US	10.8	55.1
Italy*	FR	13.6	ES	13.4	EL	7.2	34.2
Cyprus	EL	40.9	UK	15.2	FR	2.7	58.8
Latvia	DE	10.4	TR	7.6	AT	5.7	23.7
Lithuania	DE	14.0	SE	7.5	TR	5.5	27.0
Luxembourg	FR	20.8	ES	11.1	IT	10.0	41.9
Hungary	DE	14.7	AT	12.4	IT	9.6	36.7
Malta	—	—	—	—	—	—	—
Netherlands	FR	14.6	ES	11.8	DE	11.7	38.1
Poland	DE	22.9	IT	9.0	UK	6.7	38.6
Portugal*	ES	35.7	FR	11.0	UK	9.5	56.2
Slovenia	—	—	—	—	—	—	—
Slovakia	CZ	11.5	EL	10.3	IT	7.6	29.4
Finland	ES	16.6	EE	9.4	EL/SE	6.5	32.5
Sweden	ES	19.0	EL	8.1	IT	7.2	34.3
UK*	ES	31.8	FR	11.5	US	7.4	50.7
Iceland	—	—	—	—	—	—	—
Norway	ES	15.9	AT	14.5	IT	14.4	44.8

Country abbreviations:

BE	Belgium	LU	Luxembourg
CZ	Czech Republic	HU	Hungary
DK	Denmark	MT	Malta
DE	Germany	NL	Netherlands
EE	Estonia	AT	Austria
EL	Greece	PL	Poland
ES	Spain	PT	Portugal
FR	France	SI	Slovenia
IE	Ireland	SK	Slovakia
IT	Italy	FI	Finland
CY	Cyprus	SE	Sweden
LV	Latvia	UK	United Kingdom
LT	Lithuania	NO	Norway

Notes

* 2004 figures; Iceland and Norway are not members of the EU-25, but are members of the Schengen Agreement and are included in official EU travel statistics.

— data not available

Source: Eurostat (2007) Inbound and Outbound tourism in Europe, Statistics in Focus, Industry, Trade and Services, Population and Social Conditions, 52/2007, European Communities.

TOURISM ISSUES AND INSIGHTS
SUPRANATIONALISM

International trade unions, economic blocs or economic communities, as they are variously known, such as the EU are manifestations of *supranationalism*, which refers to national governments or organizations working together to achieve common goals at an extra-national level, usually in areas of trade and economic development. In addition to the EU other examples of such organizations include the OAS (Organization of American States), ASEAN (Association of South East Asian Nations) and SADC (South African Development Community). The notion of a supranational organization is often used interchangeably with international organizations but there are differences. A supranational organization is a multilateral organization consisting of three or more members plus although international in scope they are often not global organizations in the sense that almost every country is a member, for example such as the United Nations. Many supranationalist alliances exist throughout all parts of the world and will be discussed in more depth in various other sections in this book. Usually, a major goal of most supranational alliances is to facilitate the flow of products and services, capital and investment, and people. In the context of tourism, the people most affected by a decrease in the barrier effects of border are tourists who reside in the trading bloc countries, tourists from outside the alliance, and tourism employees from member countries. The 1985 Schengen Agreement among European states allows for the abolition of systematic border controls between participating countries; includes provisions on common a common policy on the temporary entry of persons (including visas), the harmonization of external border controls, and cross-border police cooperation. Citizens of non-EU (or non-European Economic Area) countries who wish to visit Europe as tourists can obtain a common Schengen visa on arrival at a border and then not require further visas within the Schengen area.

Because supranational organizations and agreements tend to increase the flow of tourists they tend to be seen very favorably by the tourism industry. However, passports and IDs are still usually required to for tourism movement from one country to another while the movement of a person as a tourist may also be much easier than moving as a worker or migrant. Heightened concerns over national security since 2001 have also often made it more difficult for nationals of some countries to enter supranational areas as well as national boundaries and a major challenge for members of such regions is to balance the rights of tourists, economic interests of the tourism industry and security needs.

partly as a result of not being included in considerations of the first European Treaties, the extent of EU involvement in tourism is considerable. The official recognition of tourism's importance by the European Commission in the 1992 Maastricht Treaty elevated the industry in the Union's administrative structure and paved the way for new endeavors in the areas of education, culture, transportation, environmental protection and job training. The responsibility for tourism policy in the European Commission lies with the Tourism Unit of the Directorate General Enterprise. The European Parliament has a Committee for Tourism and Transport and there is also a European Parliament inter-group for tourism, which brings together members of the European Parliament who share an interest in tourism issues. Attention in EU tourism policy has recently focused on establishing a Tourism Division within the European Commission, upholding the principles of sustainable tourism by balancing conservation and growth, supporting the diversification of tourism products, and examining closely trends in tourism demand to support improvements in quality tourism experiences. Yet in one sense the relative lack of *official* recognition of tourism has not meant that the EU has been without significant influence. The representative body of the hotel, restaurants and café sector in Europe, HOTREC, identified over 250 EU measures that directly impact on the hospitality and tourism industry. These measures have been developed in a number of Directorate-Generals of the European Commission, including Agriculture (farm and rural tourism), Environment (impact assessment, climate), Transport (Single European Sky) and Enterprise (entrepreneurship and innovation policy).

A Common Currency

One of the highest priorities of the EU fairly early on was to establish a common currency among its member countries. Finally, in 1990, the Economic and Monetary Union (EMU) was established within the EU, with all but Sweden, Denmark and the United Kingdom signing the accord – these three countries choosing instead to keep their own currencies, at least for an extended time. In 1995 the euro was established as the EMU's new currency among its 12 members, and the European Central Bank was established in 1998 to oversee the union's finances and creation of the

PHOTO 2.5
Tourism at a traditional farm house in Norway

Source: C. Michael Hall

euro. While the euro has been operating as a recognized currency on world markets Since 1999, it was only introduced physically in January 2002, when euro notes and coins replaced the currencies of the EMU's 12 member states. Some observer groups believed that the adoption of the euro by most of the EU's member states would have a positive result on tourism in the future by making the industry more competitive and standardizing prices better throughout the region. However, perhaps the most notable benefit has been for tour operators, hotel companies and other service providers who operate in a trans-European market, who no longer need to deal with foreign exchange regulations, or exchange currencies each time a border is crossed or when more than one country is involved.

Western Europe: The Nordic Countries

Northern Europe Landscape

Northern Europe, is an old age landscape. This is the region between the highlands of Central Europe and the Western Uplands of Scandinavia, and is known as the North European Plain. Here the European landscape flattens out into a broad coastal plain. Elevations seldom reach over 500 ft (152 m) and the continental shelf extends under the relatively shallow Baltic Sea and North Sea. In fact, these seas become exposed land whenever ocean levels are lower than they are today, and most of the North European Plain is covered with water when sea levels are higher than they are today. The British Isles are continental *shelf islands*.

The oldest exposed rock in Europe (over 1 billion years old) is on the Baltic shield, which extends under the Baltic Sea. The Baltic shield is related to the Canadian shield and the Siberian shield. All of these contain exposed rocks that are over one billion years old and were part of Laurasia, the supercontinent that formed 300 million years ago out of North America and Eurasia. These massive rock shields also contain large areas of fossil fuels in the form of oil and natural gas. These fossil fuels were formed by dense vegetation that grew on the edge of the shallow seas that once covered large areas of these rock shields. In Europe this can be seen in the large oilfields found in the North Sea that have mostly benefited Norway and the United Kingdom.

The Nordic Cultural Landscape

The Nordic countries of Northern Europe comprise five states, Denmark, Finland, Iceland, Norway and Sweden, and three autonomous territories: the Åland Islands, the Faroe Islands and Greenland. The term Nordic refers to *the northern lands* and characterizes the countries not only in terms of location but other aspects of their geography, culture and history that lead to substantial political and societal commonalities to the present-day. During the early and high middle ages Denmark, Iceland, Norway and Sweden shared a common language (Norse), cultural behaviors and shared belief systems that are often described as *Viking*. From the Late Middle Ages onward Finland also became increasingly drawn into Norse culture as a result of Swedish settlement and its becoming a part of Kingdom of Sweden. At the same time Greenland, the Shetland and Orkney Islands (now part of Scotland) and much of mainland Scotland and Ireland were also parts of the Danish Kingdom. For much of the following 600 years Denmark and Sweden would contest for political supremacy in the region with substantial shifts in borders over that period. However, the structure of the present-day Nordic countries started to emerge when Sweden ceded Finland to Russia in 1809 under the Treaty of Fredrikshamn. Finland emerged as a fully independent nation in 1917, although Finnish nationalism, particularly through the promotion of Finnish language and culture, had been expressed well before this. In 1905 the union of Norway and Sweden was dissolved, while Iceland declared its independence from Denmark in 1944.

The Nordic countries are also a supranational political entity with a cooperation forum in the form of the Nordic Council and the Nordic Council of Ministers. The Council was formed in 1953 with Finland joining in 1956. The formation of the Council has had a number of significant implications for tourism including a common labor market and free movement across borders for the countries citizens. In addition, the Nordic Council has supported a number of initiatives to support tourism between the countries, promote the region and encourage tourism as a form of regional development. Although the region includes countries and regions both inside (Denmark, Finland and Sweden) and outside (Iceland, Norway, the Åland Islands, the Faroe Islands and Greenland) the EU, the region can still be considered a distinct geographical and political unit, particularly as a result of the ease of travel without passports between the countries.

A significant feature of the Nordic region is the presence of indigenous peoples. On the European mainland the north of the Scandinavian Peninsula and northern Finland and Russia is often described as Lapland in reference to the presence of the Lapps, or Sami, who traditionally herded reindeer, but for whom cultural tourism is now a major activity. The population of Greenland is primarily Inuit (sometimes referred to as Eskimo).

Denmark

Denmark is the southernmost of the Nordic countries and is located north of Germany on the Jutland Peninsula. In addition to the mainland there are also well over 400 islands that are part of the country, many of which, such as Bornholm, are significant tourism areas. The capital, Copenhagen, is on the island of Sjaelland in the western part of the country. It is also the smallest Nordic country (just over 16,600mi^2; 43,000km^2), if the autonomous regions of Greenland and the Faroe Islands are excluded, although it is the largest if they are included! The population of Denmark is approximately 5.5 million people.

Denmark is a constitutional monarchy and became a member of the EEC, a forerunner to the EU, in 1973. However, in a 2000 referendum, monetary union with the EU was rejected. Therefore, the currency remains the Danish krone. Greenland and the Faroe Islands are outside of the EU, including the customs zone. Like many of the Nordic countries, Denmark has a strong welfare system and is highly unionised. However, it also has a strong developed economy with high-technology industries as well as a very strong agricultural sector, with Danish ham and butter being a premium food product.

Copenhagen is a major transport hub for Scandinavia, as well as a significant tourist destination in its own right. Copenhagen is one of the major hubs for SAS (Scandinavian Airline Systems) airlines, which is jointly owned by the governments

PHOTO 2.6
The little Mermaid statue, with a tourist boat in water, in Copenhagen, Denmark

Source: C. Michael Hall

of Denmark, Norway and Sweden. Copenhagen is also a major rail hub with a direct rail link to Malmö, Sweden. However, possibly the most obvious form of transport is the enormous number of people riding bicycles in the city along the extensive series of bicycle paths. The city also provides bicycles for hire.

The city has long been an urban tourism destination of international renown. The Tivoli Gardens amusement park and pleasure garden was opened in 1843 and was one of the inspiration behind Disneyland. It has one of the oldest wooden roller coasters in the world as well as the world's tallest carousel. Although open year-round the Gardens attracts the greatest number of people in the summer months when it also hosts concerts and other events. The Capital Copenhagen also hosts a number of museums and galleries, as well as royal places, and centers of Danish design. Some of the most popular attractions also include the Carlsberg Brewery and the iconic Little Mermaid, which is on a rock in Copenhagen harbor. Erected in 1913 the statue commemorates the fairytale of the Little Mermaid written by Hans Christian Andersen who is probably Denmark's most well-known writer and an important factor in the international image of the country and of *Wonderful Copenhagen.*

In addition to specific attractions Copenhagen also has a number of distinct shopping areas as well as a vibrant restaurant and café scene. One of the significant features of Copenhagen is the extent to which the old waterfront areas have been redeveloped for tourism/entertainment/heritage purposes, while also including housing. The former naval dockyards area is growing in importance with respect to heritage tourism while the Copenhagen Opera House that opened on the island of Holmen is also part of the dockland redevelopment.

Although Copenhagen is a focal point for international tourism, there are a number of other significant tourism sites in the country, especially in relation to the country's historic military and naval rivalry with its neighbor Sweden as well, at other times, with Germany and Great Britain. There are numerous historic castles in Denmark but possibly the most famous is Kronborg castle, known by many as Elsinore the setting of Shakespeare's *Hamlet.* The Castle is located in the town of Helsingør at the extreme northern tip of Zealand and at the narrowest point of the Øresund, the narrow sound of 2.5 mi (4 km) that separates Denmark and Sweden. There are ferry services approximately every 20 minutes across the sound to Helsingborg on the Swedish side. The castle is regarded as one of the most significant Renaissance castles in Northern Europe, although the site also includes a series of interesting battlements and military barracks. The site was made a World Heritage Site in 2000.

One of the other significant tourism features, and one common throughout the Nordic countries, is the importance of second homes or summer cottages for domestic tourism. Many of these are located in coastal areas and on some of the islands, such as Bornholm, the eastern-most island of Denmark located in the Baltic Sea between Sweden and Poland, for which summer visitation is a very important part of the economy. As with many of Denmark's coastal areas its strategic significance has meant that it has a number of important historical sites, most well known of which is probably Hammershus Castle—northern Europe's largest medieval fortification.

Finland

The Republic of Finland is a modern country in more ways than one, having only achieved full independence in 1917. Until then it had been a part of Russia and Sweden. Finland is the most sparsely populated country in the EU, which it joined in 1995. It has a population of 5.3 million people and an area of over 130,500 mi^2 (338,000 km^2). Finnish is one of the few official languages of the EU that is not Indo-European in origin, but instead is a member of the Finno-Ugric group of languages (including Estonian and Hungarian). Finnish is also an official minority language of Norway and Sweden, while Swedish is an official language of Finland, although it is spoken by only about 6 percent of the population as their native tongue.

Like all of the Nordic countries, Finland is noted for its low corruption levels, substantial gender equality (it was the second country in the world to have universal suffrage), freedom of the press and civil liberties, as well as a strong state welfare system. Finland is these days probably best known internationally for its design, shipbuilding (many of the world's largest cruise ships are Finnish), forest products (wood and paper) and Nokia. However, the latter is only the best known of a number of electronic companies that are based in Sweden. The importance of Nokia to the national economy is substantial; it accounts for about a third of the capitalization of the Finnish stock exchange, some 20 percent of exports, and in 2006 Nokia generated more revenue than the government budget. It is therefore not surprising that Finland is sometimes jokingly referred to as *Nokialand*. The northern position of Finland and the effects of ice age glaciation mean that agricultural production is limited by climatic factors and poor quality arable land. Notwithstanding, rye is grown far to the north, while forest foods such as berries and mushrooms are also important traditional foods. Fish, such as herring and salmon, have also been important culturally and economically, but the pollution of the Baltic Sea and over-fishing have severely damaged some of the commercial fisheries.

Helsinki is the capital and largest city of Finland with a population of 570,000, although the capital region, which also includes Vantaa, Espoo and Kauniainen, has well over a million people. Helsinki-Vantaa Airport is the international gateway to Finland along with ferry services that connect Helsinki with Rostock (Germany), Tallinn (Estonia) and Stockholm. The city has an impressive architectural heritage ranging from neoclassical buildings of the 19th century, such as the Helsinki Cathedral, through to the Art Nouveau buildings of the early 20th century and the modernist and functionalist architecture of the latter parts of the 20th century, perhaps best represented in the architecture of Alvar Aalto. As with many capital cities, there is also an assemblage of museums and art galleries that give full expression to Finland's rich cultural heritage, perhaps most unusual for many international visitors, yet most representative of Finnish culture is the museum of the sauna.

Saunas are integral to Finnish lifestyle and are unusually integrated into domestic bathrooms. Yet the tradition of having a sauna available at lakeside summer cottages also remains strong. The second home is an extremely important part of domestic tourism and is often waterside, simply by virtue of the immense numbers of lakes in the country; some 9.4 percent of the country's area is actually water. According to Statistics Finland, there are 187,888 lakes larger than $500\,m^2$ and 179,584 islands. Therefore, it is perhaps not surprising that lakes are an important element of the promotion of Finland internationally, while another important element of the landscape are the forests that cover about 75 percent of the country. The forests, which are comparable to the northern forests of Norway, Russia and Canada, are categorized as Taiga and common tree species include conifers such as larch, spruce, fir and pine and deciduous species such as birch and willow. In addition to being harvested, the forests are also important in cultural and ecological terms, with an extensive system of national parks now established to conserve significant species, such as the brown bear. In the south-east of the country the Saimaa Lake system is home to the endangered Saimaa Ringed Seal, the emblem of the Finnish Association for Nature Conservation, and one of only three lake seal species in the world.

Iceland

The Republic of Iceland is home to the world's northern-most capital city, Reykjavík, and has been very much influenced by its landscape. Iceland has an area of a little over $38,600\,mi^2$ ($100,000\,km^2$) and a population of approximately 310,000 people. Although the country's government strongly encourages decentralization, the population is concentrated in the capital. Iceland is built upon a strong tradition of self-sufficiency,

TOURISM ISSUES AND INSIGHTS
PLANNING FOR TOURISM IN NATIONAL PARKS: THE EXAMPLE OF FINLAND

As well as being extremely important for domestic tourism nature is an extremely important part of Finland's international tourism promotion. As of 2005 there were 35 parks in Finland and the total number of visits in Finnish national parks is approaching 1.5 million. The average number of visits in Finnish National Parks has almost doubled since the 1990s and in remote areas such as Northern Finland the national park related tourism development has been even stronger. Such has been the recognized tourism significance of national parks that regional and local stakeholders and policy actors usually support the plans for opening parks, for the national park status as they believe it increases the attractiveness of the area and promotes nature-based tourism. Consequently, national parks have become a significant tool for regional economic development.

However, while tourism is obviously important for national parks in Finland it is not the sole rationale for their establishment with biodiversity and landscape conservation obviously also significant. As in other national park jurisdictions, the original Finnish legislation included provision for both conservation and visitation, a balance that has become increasingly difficult given the growth in tourism numbers in recent decades. The 1923 Nature Conservation Act had an aim to preserve untouched nature although, as in the United States, it also stated that national parks were meant for pleasure and enjoyment for all citizens, that they should have value as an attraction and that be easily reached by people. Metsähallitus, the Finnish Forest and Park Service, reports that the role of the Finnish network of protected areas form a varied network intended to preserve for present and future generations a suitable number of representatives and ecologically viable areas of all the ecosystems and natural habitat types occurring in Finland, taking into account geographical variations and the various stages of natural succession.

As part of the aims of protected are conservation, the following should be preserved:

- Natural gene pools and ecosystem diversity.
- Species, geological and geomorphological features, especially species and features which are either naturally rare or threatened or declining as a consequence of human activity.
- Landscapes and habitats shaped by previous generations, including the cultural heritage associated with the Finnish countryside, along with endangered domesticated plant and animal breeds.
- The natural succession of ecosystems and other natural processes at various stages.
- Areas of outstanding natural beauty.
- Wild areas.

The growth of ecotourism and an increase in the number of visitors to protected areas is regarded as indicating a more favorable attitude toward nature conservation. Yet tourism is regarded as only one out of ten different uses of the Finnish protected area system that require a policy statement (the others being everyman's right to access, fishing and hunting, photography, local residents, traffic, forestry, mineral prospecting and mining and leasing land). These different use demands are usually managed via a master plan for a given protected area. The Finnish experience mirrors the approaches of the Nordic countries and other national park agencies in the developed world with respect to the relationship between tourism and national park and protected area planning. The difficult task of balancing conservation aims while still encouraging visitation is one that is almost universal at destinations that are either national parks or have a significant area set aside as protected area.

Continued

The Finnish approach of land use zoning with particular zones providing for specific activities and visitor experiences is an extremely common strategy. However, they also promote attempt the perspectives of local communities, tourism industry and other government bodies as well as an understanding of the market in the planning process.

Sources

Gössling, S. and Hultman, J. (Eds.) (2006) *Ecotourism in Scandinavia*. Wallingford, CAB International.
Metsähallitus (Forest and Park Service) (2000) *The Principles of Protected Area Management in Finland: Guidelines on the Aims*, Function and *Management of State-owned Protected Areas*. Metsähallituksen luonnonsuojelulkaisuja Sarja B No.54. Vantaa: Metsähallitus – Forest and Park Service, Natural Heritage Services.
Saarinen, J. and Hall, C.M. (Eds.) (2004) *Nature-based Tourism Research in Finland: Local Contexts, Global Issues*. Finnish Forest Research Institute, Research Papers 916. Rovaneimi, Rovaneimi Research Station, Finnish Forest Research Institute.

but it is also extremely international in outlook. The economy is strongly connected to natural resources in various ways either through thermal and hydroelectric energy or via its fishing industry. The country is not a member of the EU, primarily because it wishes to maintain control of its fisheries, and the currency is the Icelandic Króna. However, some debate exists over whether the euro could be adopted without joining the EU.

Rural areas with grasslands do still produce niche products such as lamb and mutton, and milk products. But the rural economy is increasingly connected to tourism, particularly for fishing, wilderness hiking (approximately 11 percent of the country is glaciated while the country has an extensive set of volcanic features), and horseriding on Icelandic ponies – an activity geared to American and European tourists. The volcanism for which the country is famous has also generated another set of tourist attractions in the form of hot springs. It is also possible to undertake a leisurely drive around Iceland on the country's ring road (Route 1), which is just under 1870 miles (1,400 km) long. This journey has long been popular with domestic tourists but is also increasingly attractive to international arrivals.

Keflavík near the capital is the international gateway, while its trans-Atlantic position has also made it a stopover point and a weekend getaway destination from both New York and London. Reykjavík has the reputation of being one of the world's best clubbing destinations but also has a number of cultural institutions and provides easy access to Iceland's natural landscape.

Norway

Norway is the westernmost country of the Scandinavian Peninsula and has an elongated shape with the easternmost part on the border with Russia and Finland being as far east as Istanbul. However, the vast majority of the land border is shared with Sweden and runs through various mountain ranges. Physical geography has played an enormous role in shaping the history of the country. Dominated by heavily glaciated mountainous terrain with substantial valleys and deep fjords, transport linkages between settlements have either been via the sea or along the valleys, with many valleys historically being quite isolated in winter. However, much of the country is made habitable, as with Iceland, by the presence of the Gulf Stream, which warms the country. The coastline is extensive and stretches over 15,500 mi (25,000 km). However, the coast is also an important marine tourism resource and location of second homes, particular in the south. Another important influence of the Gulf Stream is its contribution to coastal precipitation and snowfall further inland. Bergen, the country's second city, has the nickname of Regnbyen, which means city of rain.

The country is extremely well off economically as a result of its substantial oil and gas wealth and a relatively small population of approximately 4.7 million. However, the relative current wealth belies the fact that for most of its history Norway has been one of the poorer countries in Europe with fishing and shipping being some of the most important industries, a tradition that continues to the present-day, with Norwegian cruise ships being an important part of the cruise industry throughout the world.

The strength of the Norwegian currency, the krone, and a high rate of taxation means that Norway is regarded as an expensive tourist destination compared to other Nordic countries, particularly its neighbor Sweden. However, its nature-based tourism with respect to coastal cruising and visits to the fjords, as well as travel to the northernmost point of mainland Europe the North Cape (which because of the Gulf Stream is often shrouded in mist) means that international tourism is still a significant part of the economy. Ecotourism promotion in Norway faces difficult promotional obstacles, as while activities such as whale watching or observing reindeer and moose are attractive to many visitors, eating them may not be, although they are a traditional food. Furthermore, the independent spirit of the Norwegian people is such that external pressure from conservation groups in other countries may well be counterproductive, particularly as these foodstuffs have a long tradition together with wild berries and mushrooms from the forests.

Also important in Norway for domestic tourism is the summer house or cottage, which has become a feature of leisure and holiday activity. Originally, such houses were often very primitive and associated with summer work, such as grazing cattle or sheep in the mountains or fishing along the coast, to prepare for winter and earn extra money. However, over time the summer houses came to be regarded more as a cheap form of holiday and weekend leisure to allow activities such as fishing or skiing. Even though many Norwegians could afford to buy holiday homes in the Mediterranean (and some do), the traditional cottage in the mountains or along the coast continues to play an important part in Norwegian life and travel.

Sweden

At almost 174,000 mi^2 (450,000 km^2), Sweden is the third largest country in Europe and, excluding Greenland, the largest Nordic country. It is therefore perhaps not surprising that the country has a very low population density outside of the major urban centers of Stockholm (the capital), Gothenburg and Malmö. The Laponia region of northern Sweden, for example, is one of the largest areas of relatively unmodified natural environment in the world and primarily populated by Sami. The majority of people live in the south of the country where the climate is more benign, therefore also allowing better agriculture and better access to markets. Although an empire in the 17th century, Sweden, like many of the Nordic countries, has historically been relatively poor for much of its history. However from the second half of the 17th century on the industrial development of Sweden particularly as a result of its large iron ore reserves and engineering expertise, helped provide a substantial boost to the economy giving it one of the best standards of living in the world. Although it should be noted that criticism is often made of the extent to which Sweden's neutrality during World War II helped provide the framework for subsequent developments.

The imperial and mercantile heritage of Sweden is a focus for much of the urban tourism in Sweden. Stockholm, sometimes described as the *Venice of the North* because of its location on a number of islands, has a range of old districts, royal buildings and palaces (the changing of the guards at the royal palace is a significant attraction), and historic waterfronts. Although the Vasa Museum on the island of Djurgården, which displays the Vasa, an almost fully intact 17th century 64 gun warship that sank on her maiden voyage in 1628, as well as other features of Sweden's maritime history, is probably one of the best-known heritage attractions in all of Scandinavia. Gothenburg on the west coast of Sweden also has a strong maritime influence as it has been a major trading port and industry center for hundreds of years, which also make it a major center for business travel. Although more recently its university has served to give the city a sense of vibrancy and contemporary culture that has made it a popular urban attraction.

Malmö and the province of Skåne, which includes cities such as Lund and Helsingborg, also had a substantial industrial legacy that continues to the present-day. However, tourism has become increasingly important for the area particularly following the completion of the Øresund Bridge linking Sweden with Denmark and allowing even greater mobility between the two countries. For example, it is estimated that 10 percent of the Malmö population works in the Copenhagen area.

In common with other Nordic countries, one of the most notable features of tourism in Sweden is the importance of summer houses or cottages (second homes), which are integral to Swedish domestic holiday making and which are found in all areas of the country. Since Sweden joined the EU in 1995 there has also been substantial second home purchase by Germans in the south of the country. Other major non-Swedish second home owners include the Norwegians, particularly in some of the mountain areas near the Norwegian border.

Second homes are particularly important for tourism and the economy in the north of Sweden, which is otherwise marked by its dependence on forest products and mining, though in recent years new forms of tourism are developing. For example, the city of Umeå, the gateway to the north, is a prominent university town and business center, which also has a nearby cheese (Västerbotten – named after the county) factory that is being developed as a tourist attraction. Perhaps more famously Kiruna in Norrbotten County in the far north is home to the *ice hotel* every winter and the site of a European space tourism center being developed in conjunction with Virgin Galactic.

Western Europe: The Northern Countries

The countries of Northern Europe have significant cultural and historical commonalities that have been brought back together in recent years following the expansion of

Trans-territorial organizations are organizations that have area boundaries that include the territories of constituent members. A number of trans-border regional agencies have been established within Europe with the support of the EU and national and regional governments. One of the most recognized is that of Øresund.

The Øresund region links the region of Skåne in south-western Sweden with Zealand in Denmark. The most concrete as well as symbolic example of the Øresund region was the construction of the cross-border Øresund bridge, across the Øresund Strait, between Denmark and Sweden which connects the cities of Malmö (Sweden) and Copenhagen (Denmark) by road and train. Although a physical connection between Denmark and Sweden had been suggested since the 19th century, a new cross-border regional governance structure did not emerge until the 1950s. Various economic and political factors delayed both the physical and political connectivity of the cross-border region until the convergence of a number of interests in the late 1980s. These interests were expressed in a number of institutions that promoted the Øresund concept. Foremost among these is the region's governing body the Øresund Committee (Øresundskomiteen) which is a forum for local and regional politicians and authorities from both side of the Øresund Strait. Also of great importance are a number of other organizations that contributed to the development of the Øresund Region concept. These include:

- Scandinavian Academy of Management (a business and economics think tank).
- Medicon Valley Academy (a network organization that facilitates the collaboration of educational institutions and biomedical, biotechnological and pharmaceutical firms).
- Copenhagen Capacity (a marketing organization aimed at attracting and retain firms and industries).
- Wonderful Copenhagen (a tourism marketing organization, Copenhagen has the region's international airport hub).
- Øresund University (a network composed of universities in the region).
- Øresund Science Park (a network of the various science parks in the region).

The development of new organizational networks and structures has practical implications for tourism as they encourage greater movement of people within the region both directly through requirements for business travel and meetings but also as a justification for further transport provision. In addition, running parallel to the organizational and political development of the Øresund regional concept was the development of place marketing and promotional strategies that aim to reinforce an Øresund brand and identity both within the region and externally to potential visitors and investors.

Source

Hall, C.M. (2008) *Tourism Planning*, 2nd edn., Prentice Hall, Harlow.

the EU. Although Rome did influence the region through occupation of some areas and by trade, the cultural heritage was primarily Celtic and Gothic in origin and marked by the Druidic faith until Christianized. In the early Middle Ages, as the influence of the Norse was also extremely significant and while Roman language has been influential,

PHOTO 2.7

Bruges, Belgium. Leisure tour boats are a popular way of touring the historic cities of Europe

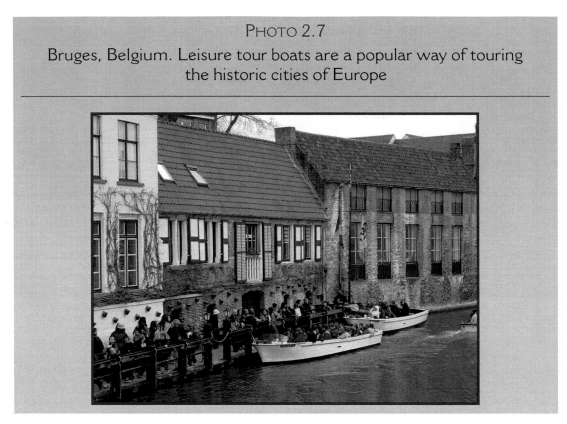

Source: Alan A. Lew

PHOTO 2.8

The beach at Budleigh Salterton in Devon, England. Southwest England is the warmest part of the country due to relatively warm waters of the gulf stream

Source: C. Michael Hall

PHOTO 2.9
Souvenir shop in London, England

Source: C. Michael Hall

PHOTO 2.10
St. Andrews, Scotland, the *Home of Golf*. St. Andrews is known at the home of golf because of its world famous golf courses, and its royal and ancient golf club, which establishes golfing rules worldwide (Except for the United States and Mexico)

Source: C. Michael Hall

Photo 2.11

Glacier-Carved Tundra Landscape of the Scottish Highlands. This part of the United Kingdom is sparsely settled, but is a very popular tourist destination in the summer months

Source: Alan A. Lew

it is the Germanic language forms which dominate, providing a linguistic as well as geographical divide between northern and southern Europe.

The Benelux Countries

The term Benelux refers to the customs and economic union between Belgium, the Netherlands (Holland) and Luxembourg that entered into force in 1947, although Belgium and Luxembourg had established an economic union as early as 1921. The Benelux union was an important precursor to the creation of the EU with all three countries being founding members, along with West Germany, France and Italy. The three countries are also sometimes referred to as the Low Countries, which is an historical reference to the lands around the delta of the Rhine, Scheldt and Meuse rivers, although a number of other cultural, linguistic and political similarities also contributed to the region's identification. The three countries have been united several times, although the most recent was after the Napoleonic Wars. Belgium and the Netherlands became separate kingdoms in 1830, while the Grand Duchy of

PHOTO 2.12

Road warning sign in Scotland. While most of Europe, drives on the right side of the road, the United Kingdom and Ireland drives on the left side. This sign reminds toursts in rural Scotland to stay on the left side.

Source: Alan A. Lew

Luxembourg left its union with the Netherlands in 1890. Luxembourg is the world's only sovereign Grand Duchy.

As befits the term *Low Countries* the outstanding geographical feature of much of the region, but particularly the Netherlands, is how flat and low-lying the land is. Much of it has been reclaimed with the lowest point being almost 7 m below sea level. The romantic image of the Netherlands with a windmill beside a dyke (a canal or channel used for draining land) was very much based on the reality of wind power being used to drain low-lying areas of farmland. These days such images still remain with many modern windmills to be seen in the Dutch countryside, although they are as important for power generation as they are for drainage.

The rich Rhine delta soil has provided the foundations of a strong agricultural economy with the Netherlands being world famous for cheese production (Edam, Gouda) and wooden clogs worn by agricultural workers in former times. But the extensive network of waterways also means that sailing, riverboats and other forms of water-based tourism are extremely popular in the countryside. In addition, the flat country means that the bicycle is a very important form of transport for shorter journeys, while an extensive railway network is also a very important part of tourist transport.

Amsterdam, the Dutch business capital, is a major center for international tourists and is based on a curious mixture of heritage attractions and contemporary culture. Amsterdam's Schipol Airport is also a major aviation hub and one of the busiest airports in the world, being one of the hubs of Air France-KLM. Historic cultural attractions are found in both Amsterdam and the seat of government in The Hague (Den Haag) (somewhat bizarrely the Dutch constitution states that the official capital is Amsterdam even though government has been based at The Hague since 1584). Amsterdam is extremely popular as an attraction because of the large number of major art galleries, including the Van Gogh and Rembrandt museums, and the attraction of the old-town area and the canals. More contemporary cultural attractions include Anne Frank House; de Wallen, the city's red-light district; the availability of hash cookies in many of the city's excellent coffee shops; and the sex museum.

Brussels, the capital of Belgium, and Luxembourg, the capital of Luxembourg, are also major business and diplomatic centers, but primarily with respect to their roles within the EU system. Luxembourg is the seat of several key EU institutions, including the European Court of Justice, the European Court of Auditors, and the European Investment Bank. Brussels is home to the European Parliament (along with Strasbourg), the European Commission and the Council of the EU, the North Atlantic Treaty Organization (NATO), and the European Organization for the Safety of Air Navigation (EUROCONTROL).

A significant cultural feature of Belgium is that it straddles the divide between the Germanic languages of Northern Europe and the Romantic languages of the south. The two largest regions are Dutch-speaking Flanders in the north and French-speaking region of Wallonia in the south. The Brussels-Capital Region, with a population of over a million people is an officially bilingual enclave. There is also a small German-speaking community in eastern Wallonia near the German border. Belgium's linguistic diversity has contributed to the development of a complex system of federal government based along linguistic lines, while the linguistic divisions also contribute to differences in culture.

Belgium is a heavily industrialized country, which has contributed to poor water and environmental quality in some regions. However, many of the old industrial regions are now being restructured and industrial heritage tourism is being developed as a response. Belgium is also known for the quality of its chocolate, a product that developed from its colonial empire, although another famous product is beer, of which there are over 500 varieties, many of them fruit beers. The brewing traditions in Belgium have meant that in the same way countries with vineyards have wines associated with regions, so in Belgium regions and towns are associated with particular types of beer.

Germany and Austria

Although Germany is a modern economic superpower – it is the world's third largest economy and the largest exporter of goods – it comes as a surprise to many people that it is a country that only achieved the status of a nation-state in 1871. However, it has already been divided and reunified since that time. In fact the history of the area occupied by present-day Germany and much of Austria has been one of shifting political boundaries made up of different amalgamations of political sub-units of independent duchies or kingdoms. It should therefore be of no surprise that befitting its political heritage, Germany is currently a federal republic consisting of 16 different states. Although, in German political tradition, states are called Länder (countries), with the concept of Germany referring to the alliance or confederation of these independent Länder. The relative independence of the states holds to the present-day with the Länder retaining the right to act independently at an international level under Articles 23, 24, and 32 of the German Federal Constitution (The Basic Law of the Federal Republic of Germany). Such political traditions also underlie Germany's historical enthusiasm for the EU of which it was a founding member.

The notion of a German identity in a broader sense exists from 900AD and was often associated with the Holy Roman Empire, which in its heyday was an amalgamation of hundreds of political entities such as duchies, kingdoms, principalities and cities covering most of Europe. The emperor could be elected from throughout the realm of the empire, but by the beginning in the 15th century, emperors were elected nearly exclusively from the Austrian Habsburg Dynasty. A critical point in German history was the effect of the Reformation, which by 1530 resulted in a separate Protestant Lutheran church, which came to be acknowledged as the official religion in many German states although significant religious conflict between Protestants and Catholics lasted for many years culminating in what was known as the Thirty Years' War (1618–1648). The War is regarded as one of the bloodiest periods of German and European history with Germany's population being reduced by almost a third through military actions and associated famines and diseases.

The Peace of Westphalia (1648) ended religious warfare among the German states. However, it had the long-term effect of dividing the various principalities and territories of the empire along political and religious lines with the Austrian Habsburg monarchy dominating the southeastern German states and what became modern-day Austria and Hungary; the Kingdom of Prussia dominated much of what is now modern Germany. The German Confederation, a loose alliance of 39 states was created in 1814 following the Congress of Vienna, which convened to redraw the map of Europe after the defeat of Napoleon Bonaparte. A tariff union developed at the time also helped encourage German integration. However, the most critical feature of the period was the growing power of the state of Prussia (much of which is now in present-day Poland and the Kaliningrad exclave of Russia on the Baltic Sea). Prussian victory in the Austro-Prussian War of 1866 enabled the creation of the North German Federation (Norddeutscher Bund) of 22 states and excluded Austria, formerly the leading German state, from the affairs of the remaining German states and cementing the political and, to an extent, cultural divide between the two countries that exists to the present-day.

The nation-state of Germany can be identified with the creation of the German Empire in 1871 and the height of German power with the acquisition of a number of colonies around the world. Yet despite close family ties between the royal families of Europe, German military and colonial ambitions contributed substantially to World War I. Defeat meant the loss of large portions of German territory. The loss of territory combined with the conditions imposed on Germany following the Great War helped provide fertile ground for Adolf Hitler and the Nazi movement, but defeat in World War II led to a further loss of territory and the forced migration of many Germans from territories that had come under Soviet control. Division of Germany along the lines of military occupation of different sectors led to the sectors controlled by France, the United Kingdom and the United States merging in May 1949 to form the Federal Republic of Germany (commonly referred to as West Germany), and the Soviet Zone becoming the German Democratic Republic (East Germany) later that year. Berlin was also divided into West Berlin and East Berlin. The East–West division ended in 1989 with the collapse of the Berlin Wall and mass migration to the west from East Germany. Germany was officially reunified in 1990, although some of the social, economic and political divisions from that time can still be seen.

Germany is better known for outbound travel than inbound tourism, with German tourists being extremely important for the coastal areas of the Mediterranean and destinations throughout the world. Nevertheless, there is a significant inbound tourism market for which business travel is extremely important, and a substantial cultural tourism market that comes to see many of the palaces and castles of the various states and art galleries and museums that contain works from those periods. Many of the most prominent castles are found in the mountains of southern Germany and along the banks of the Rhine, the latter also attracting visitors to the vineyards located along the river valley.

World War II internment, concentration and extermination camps are also a significant feature with continued interest in the holocaust as well as other aspects of the war. Other sites of significant World War II events have become tourist attractions. Berchtesgaden in the Bavarian Alps near the border with Austria is famous as Hitler's mountain residence, the Berghof, which was situated there. An Intercontinental Hotel has also been built on Herman Goering's former property in the area. However, like much of alpine southern Germany the mountains also serve to attract visitors to present-day national parks and skiing opportunities.

Another form of heritage tourism is the growth of interest in tourism provided by the former East Germany. The sense of nostalgia created by the elapse of time since the fall of the Berlin Wall has allowed the development of hotels that recreate the accommodation experience of East Germany, while some of the former workers hotels and camps on the Baltic Sea have been converted into backpackers (youth hostels), second homes or hotels.

Austria shares language and cultural ties with Germany, but apart from the time Austria was incorporated into Nazi Germany, it has been politically separate from Germany since the beginning of the 19th century. Like Germany, Austria is a former imperial monarchy but is now a parliamentary representative democracy consisting of nine federal states. Along with Finland, Ireland, Sweden and neighboring Switzerland and Liechtenstein, Austria has declared permanent neutrality, although since joining the EU in 1995, the interpretation of neutrality has come to be reassessed as a result of EU security commitments. Nevertheless, such a position along with Vienna's status as a meeting place between Western and Eastern Europe has allowed Austria to host a number of major international organizations including the secretariat of the Organization for Security and Cooperation in Europe and the headquarters of the International Atomic Energy Agency, the United Nations Industrial Development Organization, the United Nations Drug Control Program, the Organization of Petroleum Exporting Countries and the Comprehensive Test Ban Treaty Organization.

Austria's imperial past provides a substantial cultural heritage to be explored, particularly in the capital of Vienna which has an impressive array of cathedrals, galleries, museums and many heritage buildings from a range historical periods. Vienna is a noted cultural and education center which means that the city is blessed with an impressive range of art galleries and performance centers for both classical and contemporary music. The Danube River flows through the city and is a significant focal point for visitor and local recreational activities and provides opportunities for international travel via cruise ships that travel up and down the river.

Austria has a long tourist tradition dating from the 16th century, when some of the first health and spa resorts were developed for the aristocracy. More recently, summer

TOURISM ISSUES AND INSIGHTS
DARK TOURISM

Dark tourism is travel to sites of human tragedy, such as the sites of the holocaust or the killing fields of Cambodia or even taking a walking tour in London of Jack the Ripper. Dark tourism is not a new phenomenon. In the Middle Ages Christians used to go on pilgrimages to Rome and be shown the catacombs in which the early Christians were tortured and imprisoned. More recently, Ground Zero in New York has become an essential part of the tourism itinerary for many visitors. However, media and transport now puts the places shown on the History Channel or of the history books on to the tourist itinerary. To some visiting such locations may be an act of reverence or even atonement while to others it is probably voyeurism.

Over half a million people visit the Auschwitz Birkenau German Nazi Concentration and Extermination Camp (1940–1945) in Poland each year. The camp commandant, Rudolf Höss, testifed at the Nuremberg Trials that up to 2.5 million people had died at Auschwitz. This figure was revised in 1990 by the Auschwitz-Birkenau State Museum which put the figure at between 1.1 and 1.6 million. It is estimated that 90 percent of them were Jews. Large numbers of Poles, Gypsies and homosexuals were also killed. A July 2, 1947 Act of the Polish Parliament established the Auschwitz-Birkenau State Museum on the grounds of the two extant parts of the camp, Auschwitz I and Auschwitz II-Birkenau. The site was given World Heritage status in 1979. In 1996, Germany made January 27, the day of the liberation of Auschwitz-Birkenau, the official day for the commemoration of the victims of *National Socialism*.

The standard guided tour of Auschwitz-Birkenau lasts for two-and-a-half-hours. However, given the history of the place and the significance of the events that took place there the question can be asked as to whether this is sufficient enough or whether tourism in such a place is appropriate at all. Alternatively, it could be argued that even this time may be sufficient to convey significant interpretive messages. Of course another issue is that such places are interpreted through present-day eyes. In fact the passage of time may be important in even enabling dark tourism locations to be promoted to visitors otherwise their transformation to a tourism attraction may conflict with the values of those affected by them. Regardless of the arguments it is apparent that dark tourism sites will continue to be a significant part of the tourism experience. The challenge got the attraction managers is to be able to handle the conflicting stakeholder values and interests that surround such sites.

and winter alpine tourism has been developed with the country hosting a range of ski runs to suit a range of different markets, as well as opportunities for summer hiking in the cool of the mountains, which is enjoyed by many Austrians and central Europeans seeking to avoid the heat of summers on the plains.

Another growing aspect of rural tourism in Austria, like Germany, is the development of food and wine tourism. These are primarily found along the Danube Valley and the southeast of the country near Lake Neusidl near the Austria-Hungary border, an area famous for sweet wines. The lake, which is about 22 mi (36 km long), and between 3.5 and 7.5 miles (6 km and 12 km) wide, is extremely shallow with a depth of no more than 6 ft (1.8 m); some of its surrounds have been declared a World Heritage Site, and it is a significant tourist attraction for fishing, sailing and windsurfing. It is also the site of an annual crossing of the lake from Mörbisch, Hungary, to Illmitz, Austria.

The British Isles: Ireland and the United Kingdom of Great Britain and Northern Ireland

The British Isles comprise more than 6,000 islands off the northwest coast of continental Europe, including the countries of the United Kingdom of Great Britain (England, Scotland and Wales) and Northern Ireland, and the Republic of Ireland. The group also includes the United Kingdom crown dependencies of the Isle of Man, and by tradition, the Channel Islands (the Bailiwicks of Guernsey and Jersey), even though these islands are strictly speaking an archipelago immediately off the coast of Normandy (France) rather than part of the British Isles. It should be noted that the term British Isles is unpopular among many people in Ireland as a result of that country's succession from the United Kingdom in 1922 and the continued differences over control of Northern Ireland. No branch of the government of the Ireland officially uses the term in a way that includes the Republic. However, the term is widely used in the international setting, often without realizing the political offense it may cause the Irish.

Despite Ireland's independence, there are still several areas of political cooperation between the countries. Most notably for tourism, this includes what is known as the *common travel area* between all the countries and dependencies in the British Isles. This allows passport-free travel between them with only minimal or no border controls.

Nevertheless, the various nations that have occupied the Isles since Roman times have had a close-knit set of relations that remains the basis not only for the development of the British Empire and the consequent spread of English as a language around the world but also the history which is a major factor for tourism in the region.

Following the end of Roman rule in Britain, numerous kingdoms came to be formed throughout much of Britain. These added to the existing kingdoms of Scotland and Ireland that had never been under Roman control. The seven major kingdoms of southeast and central Britain, Northumbria, Mercia, East Anglia, Essex, Kent, Sussex and Wessex, along with minor kingdoms, eventually came to form the nation of England, although this process was not completed until the 10th century when King Alfred of Wessex united the various kingdoms against a common Danish (Viking) enemy.

By the end of the 13th century, the British Isles were dominated by the four major kingdoms of England, Wales, Scotland and Ireland, although Norse areas such as the Kingdom of Mann and the Isles of Orkney and the Shetland Islands remained independent until 1266 and 1472 respectively. The Norman invasion of England in 1066 not only served to bring England under one clear government authority but also provided impetus to bringing Wales, Scotland and Ireland under the English Crown. Many of the cathedrals built in the high to late Middle Ages have become major focal points for tourism, such as Canterbury Cathedral in southeast England, which is the seat of the head of the Anglican Church. In addition, the conflicts that occurred in this period led to the development of another piece of infrastructure that is now a significant attraction for tourists in the form of many castles in major towns and throughout the countryside. Although they became obsolete with the development of artillery, many castles were converted into country grand houses and have become an important part of the tourism promotion of Ireland and the United Kingdom.

The religious conflicts that affected the European mainland and Germany with respect to the Reformation also had tremendous impacts in the British Isles. Apart from conflict over the throne itself, James I encouraged the settlement of Scottish and English Protestants in Ireland on land confiscated from Irish Catholic landowners in what was known as the Plantation of Ulster. This was done in an attempt to prevent further Irish rebellion against the English colonists. This colonialism has a substantial historical legacy, as the present-day partition of Ireland into the Ireland and Northern Ireland is primarily a result of the settlement patterns of the plantations of the early and late 17th century with the Protestant descendants of settlers in the north favoring linkages with Britain. In Northern Ireland, the Catholic-Protestant divide was a major contributor to the troubles, the term used to describe the communal violence involving Irish Republican (loyal to Ireland) and Loyalist paramilitary organizations (loyal to the United Kingdom), and the British Army for which the peace process is still underway, although a ceasefire was enacted officially in 1998.

Religiously inspired conflicts and wars often tied to competition for the throne were also significant in England and Scotland for much of the 17th century and did not finally subside until the late 18th century. England did have a republican government for a brief period of time (1649–1660) following the English Civil War, but the monarchy has long had a central place in English political life and is often regarded as a source of stability. Today the monarchy is also a very important tourist attraction with palaces and royal events being a major draw card. The Queen's residence in London, Buckingham Palace, is invariably one of the *must see* attractions particularly if it coincides with the changing of the Royal Guard.

The end of civil wars and fighting between the various kingdoms also saw the development of British colonialism and the growth of the empire. Even though America was lost in the 18th century, the rise of the industrial revolution, mercantile trade and the power of the British navy all contributed to the expansion of the empire and reinforce the importance of London, the capital, as a political and economic center. The imperial legacy remains important to London even today. London has long been a cosmopolitan city with a rich built heritage. Many of the monuments to the empire and government buildings remain despite bombings during World War II. It is home to many museums and key historic sites. Some of the most visited attractions include the reconstruction of The Globe Theatre of William Shakespeare, the Tower of London (which served as a royal prison and is the home of the British Crown Jewels), the Tate Gallery, the National Portrait Gallery and the Victoria and

Albert Museum. More recently developed attractions include the home grounds of English soccer clubs, such as Chelsea's Stamford Bridge, which are followed by supporters all around the world, and shopping. For example, Harrods in Knightsbridge is possibly the most famous department store in the world and is commonly visited by tourists, although Fortnum and Mason, often shortened to just *Fortnum's*, in Piccadilly, is often regarded by locals as higher quality and is famed for teas and luxury meals.

Like the days of the British Empire, London is today a major European transport hub, although now it is aviation rather than passenger ships. Heathrow airport is one of the world's busiest airports and getting through United Kingdom customs or through security and gate control on departure is a memorable experience for many visitors in its own right. Even with the completion of a new terminal (Terminal 5) it is likely that the airport will still remain congested. Therefore, there are proposals to expand Heathrow and build more runways and airports in the south of England.

Although cities are the focal point for tourism, the countryside is often a key factor in the attractiveness of the British Isles. The rural landscape developed from a combination of physical and human factors. Key physical factors include the Gulf Stream that passes the west coast of Ireland and Scotland and helps keep the climate warmer than equivalent latitudes in North America by several degrees. The warm ocean current also ensures that there is plenty of moisture in the air, thereby ensuring plenty of rain, which has had the consequence, for example, of ensuring good grass growth and contributing to Ireland's *green fields* image. Another important item is islandness. By being islands since the Ice Age there is actually a relatively low number of indigenous species, with most species being introduced from Europe and elsewhere and becoming acclimatized. Glaciers covered most of the British Isles during the Ice Ages which has also meant the loss of previous species.

Physical factors notwithstanding, the human influence on the rural landscape has been remarkable. Much of the countryside with its fields of hedgerows and farm holdings has only existed in its present form since the enclosures at the time of the Industrial Revolution. Landholdings were amalgamated, and tenants, who had often been on the land for generations, were forcibly removed to provide more efficient farming. Many went to the industrializing cities while others became part of the great migrations to North America, Australia and New Zealand to find a better life and land they could call their own. However, the landscape had been changing significantly before this time. For example, many of the areas of grassland or moorland that have become national parks or scenic areas were formerly forests. However, the combination of grazing and tree-cutting, often for mining or for charcoal, as in Dartmoor in southwest England, has meant that the uplands became denuded of trees with constant grazing keeping it that way. Although there is a *wilding* movement in the United Kingdom to return such sites to forest land many people oppose such changes because of their landscape preferences.

Little remains of the extensive original forests of the Isles. Even the famous New Forest of Hampshire was a combination of extant and planted woodlands that were protected for royal hunting since the 13th century. Nevertheless, despite being highly developed, the countryside remains a very important part of the attractiveness of the United Kingdom and Ireland.

Western Europe: The Southern Countries

Southern Europe Landscape

Southern Europe has a youthful landscape. It consists of steep mountains with peaks reaching over 10,000 ft (3000 m) and separated by deep river valleys. Coastal plains are narrow, if they exist at all, because the mountains extend vertically from the oceans and seas. The mountain systems of Southern Europe were created during the most recent geologic time period, the Alpine Orogeny, which started 136 million years before present (m.y.B.P.). *Orogeny* refers to a geologic time period of mountain uplifting. During the Alpine Orogeny, not only were the Alps formed, but so were the Himalayas in Asia, the Rocky Mountains in North America and the Andes in

PHOTO 2.13
Tourism in the Italian Alps

Source: Jarkko Saarinen

PHOTO 2.14
Fishing Boat at Naxos on the Island of Sicily, Italy

PHOTO 2.15

Lindos Bay on the Island of Rhodes in Greece. Rhodes is one of the larger Islands of Greece that is located off the Coast of Turkey in the Aegean Sea

South America. The major mountain ranges of Southern Europe include the Pyrenees in Spain and France; the Alps; the Carpathian Mountains in Eastern Europe; the Apennines in Italy; the Dinaric Alps in Croatia and Bosnia-Herzegovina; and the Anatolian Plateau of Turkey.

About 136 million years ago, the Alps started to rise, and the Mediterranean Sea started to sink. The Alps pushed up land that was formerly the bottom of the Tethys Sea between the ancient continents of Gondwana and Laurasia. Today, the Ionian Sea, part of the Mediterranean Sea, is 15,000 ft (4600 m) deep. Other portions of the Mediterranean are over 10,000 ft (3000 m) deep. The Appenine Mountains, which form the spine of the Italian Peninsula, used to be part of a mountain chain that connected the Alps to the Atlas Mountains in northwest Africa. The island of Crete is a remnant of the land bridge that once connected Turkey and Greece, but which has since been pushed down below sea level.

Human Geography

The human geography of Southern Europe is saliently affected by the Mediterranean, which has for many years provided trade routes between countries of the region, North Africa and Asia Minor, and allowed the development of ancient civilizations to spread their influence throughout all parts of the region. These included the Phoenicians, Greeks and Romans. The Roman legacy is still felt over most of the western Mediterranean because of the dominant Romance languages that are rooted in Latin.

The Mediterranean is also a focal point for human settlement. Over a third of Europe's total population lives within 30 miles (50 km) of the coasts, and that figure is growing. By 2025, the percentage of the population of Spain, France, Greece, Italy and Croatia living in coastal cities is projected to be more than 85 percent on average, and as high as 96 percent in Spain. Coastal populations are also growing not only as a result of internal migration, but also because of international retirement migration and second home purchases within the EU. All countries in Southern Europe are major tourism destinations and rank among the largest international tourist destinations in the world. The Mediterranean region, therefore, accounts for about 30 percent of all international tourist arrivals, and estimates suggest this figure is growing. This has contributed to significant urbanization in the most popular coastal resort areas on the Mediterranean Sea.

Another common characteristic of the southern countries is the role of food and wine in the region's cultural geography and tourism. Such synergies should not be surprising, for wine, food and tourism are all products differentiated on the basis of regional identity. Wine is often identified by its geographical origin (e.g., Burgundy, Champagne, Porto, Rioja), which in many cases, has been formalized through a series of appellation controls, in turn founded on certain geographical characteristics of place. Foods (e.g., cheese such as Parmesan) are also identified by their place of origin. Within the region and other parts of the EU, such geographical place designations have been given special legal protection, which is also significant for tourism as the cuisine of a country can be a source of attraction in its own right with respect to consuming the authentic article, while place name protection is also useful for marketing and branding.

France

France is usually identified as the world's top tourist destination with respect to numbers of international visits. In many ways metropolitan France provides a geographical link between northern and southern Europe, although culturally it is very much a part of southern Europe. France also has a number of overseas departments in the Americas, the Indian Ocean and the South Pacific.

France has been a separate political entity since 843 and the division of Charlemagne's Carolingian Empire. The name France originates from the Franks (Francs), a Germanic tribe that occupied the northern border of the Rhine in a region called Francia. After the fall of the Roman Empire, the Western Franks moved westward, gradually becoming the Kingdom of France, while the Eastern Frankish Kingdom evolved into what it is now Germany.

The language of the Franks was Germanic. Contemporary French has primarily evolved from Vulgar Latin, although some Frank words were incorporated into the language as it developed. In addition, the influence of the Vikings (Norse) on French has also been substantial, although more recently French has become notable for its lack of capacity to absorb new words from other languages, which is perhaps a reason for its replacement by English as the language of international trade and business.

Since the French Revolution in 1789, when King Louis XVI and his wife, Marie Antoinette, were executed, France has been politically organized as a series of republics, the exception being the First French Empire under Napoleon Bonaparte (1804–1814), the July Monarch (1830–1848) of Louis-Philippe, and the Second French Empire of Napoleon III (1852–1870). The core of the various French republics has been one of the fundamental documents of the French Revolution *The Declaration of the Rights of Man and of the Citizen* (La Déclaration des droits de l'Homme et du citoyen), which defined a set of individual rights and collective rights of all of the three estates (clergy, aristocracy and the general populace) as one. *Men are born and remain free and equal in rights. Social distinctions can be founded only on the common utility* (Article 1), which is often simplified to the words *Liberty, equality, fraternity*. However, while laudable sentiments and extremely important to the broader growth of the concept of political rights, the extent to which they have been achieved in French society has been highly variable. In fact, France, like many EU countries, is grappling with issues of the growth of large immigrant populations and their relative rights, particular with respect to religion and culture. Although, some sets of beliefs, such as Scientology, are not recognized as religions and are instead regarded as cults.

Although France has an estimated population of over 64 million people and is the largest country in the EU with considerable natural population growth (unlike many other European countries), population growth is occurring in urban areas such as Paris, Marseille, Lyon, Nice, Nantes and Toulouse. Rural areas are suffering from substantial depopulation. Partly in response to this, but also in light of the place that rural and peasant culture has in French society, the French agricultural sector remains highly protected from foreign competition –an issue that causes international trade negotiation difficulties not only in the EU but also with other agricultural nations. Nevertheless, some French agricultural products, such as wine, cheese, truffles, escargot (snails), frog's legs and *foie gras*, as well as French cuisine are appreciated around the world.

The culinary diversity of France is also reflected in its cultural diversity which is reflected in the differences between the provinces and regions, although for many visitors Paris remains the central expression of French culture and lifestyle. In part this is because of its gateway function and center of government over many centuries. Because Paris has been the capital for many years and center of various French Empires and Kingdoms, it has an incredible concentration of built heritage ranging from religious edifices, such as Notre Dame Cathedral, to secular sites, as in world-class art galleries (e.g., the Louvre). In addition, its long tradition for political and cultural tolerance means that Paris is exceptionally cosmopolitan; as an international fashion center, style is also equated with the city as well. Nevertheless, in recent years the development of new attractions, such as EuroDisney, has led to a significant change in the profile of visitors to the city, including day-trippers from southern England who travel to EuroDisney and Paris itself on trains through the Channel Tunnel.

Other significant areas of France for international tourism include the wine regions of Alsace, Champagne, Bordeaux and Burgundy, as well as Provence, which has become a heavily romanticized region owing to various films and novels, and the growth of holiday homes. Southern France is also featured strongly in tourism promotions, largely because of its climate and association with glamour and the film industry, most famously the international Cannes Film Festival, which is held there each year.

Greece

Greece is often regarded as the home of European civilization, and the sites of ancient Greece and Greek mythology have historically provided a major reason to visit. However, in more recent years, Greece has become a mass destination particularly for sun and climate, although there are some mountainous areas that offer winter skiing. The landscape of Greece is often considered in terms of the Aegean islands, coastal peninsulas and rugged inland terrain. The mountains and uplands of Greece were once well wooded, but deforestation, resulting from agricultural practices, particularly sheep and goat farming, has led to soil erosion. Agriculture is significant in the fertile plains and valleys, with olives, olive oil and grapes being significant crops and exports.

Greek identity is substantially shaped by the legacy of ancient Greece and by many years of occupation by the Ottoman Empire, with Greece only gaining its independence in 1831. In the modern historical period Greece has been one of Europe's poorer countries and has often experienced periods of authoritarian leadership, most recently being a military coup d'etat against the elected government and King Constantine II on April 21, 1967. Between 1967 and 1974, a United States-supported military junta, known as *The Junta* or the *Regime of the Colonels*, was established. As in Spain and Portugal at the same time, tourism was encouraged by an authoritarian government to attract foreign exchange, create employment and help provide a positive image to the rest of the world. The role played by tourism continues to the present-day, with the service sector being the largest sector in the Greek economy, including banking services. On many of Greece's islands, tourism is the primary economic sector, and tourism in the overall Greek economy is extremely important, more so than in many other European countries.

Italy

Although Italy is usually associated with the Roman Empire and its unifying forces, for most of its history since Roman times Italy has been a series of different kingdoms and states fighting among themselves for territory and being subject to foreign intervention. Unification of Italy began in 1861 with the Venetian region being added in 1866 from the Austrians, and Rome in 1870 from the French. Following the period of fascist dictatorship under Mussolini and the end of World War II, Italy became a republic after a popular referendum held on June 2, 1946, a day celebrated since as Republic Day. The period from 1946 to 1992, known as *The First Republic*, was characterized by its highly unstable national governments, although economic growth was still being achieved in part because of Italian membership of the EU. The period from 1992 to present, known as *The Second Republic*, has had a slightly more stable government, although in the 1990s there was considerable voter disenchantment with politics as a result of corruption, an accusation that continued to plague the then Prime Minister Silvio Berlusconi, who is Italy's richest person and owner of three of the seven national television channels. In 2006, he was narrowly defeated in elections by Romano Prodi, who served as President of the European Commission from 1999 to 2004.

Because of their relatively recent unification, Italians think of themselves as much in provincial and regional terms as they do with respect to being Italian. There are also substantial historical north–south divides with respect to economics and politics, with industry and most of the population being concentrated in the wealthy north where industrialization and modernization began in the 19th century and the south, which is poorer and more agriculture-based. As in France, this divide is also partly reflected in what people eat with dairy products such as butter being associated more with the mountainous north and olive oil with the south.

Although Italy is the world's sixth-largest exporter of manufactured goods, the country is often perceived in rural terms. Indeed, one interpretation of the origin of the term Italy derives from the Greek word meaning *land of cattle*. In great part this is because of the international success of Italian cuisine and various books and films that focus on the region of Tuscany. Undoubtedly, the rural areas of Italy are important in terms of their agricultural production, especially olive oil, cheeses and wine. However, in recent years many rural areas of Italy have started to focus on tourism as a means of economic development, and like other parts of the Mediterranean such as Spain and Portugal, there has been substantial retirement and second-home development. Such processes have also been encouraged as Italy has one of the lowest birthrates in Europe, and many rural communities have therefore had difficulties in maintaining their population bases.

Italy is regularly ranked as the fifth major tourist destination in the world with over 40 million international visitors each year. Many of these, and domestic tourists, concentrate in areas with high amenity values, particularly the coast. However, there are increasing concerns over the environmental sustainability of coastal tourism development. In Italy over 43 percent of the coastline is completely urbanized, 28 percent is partly urbanized, and less than 29 percent is still free of construction. There are only six stretches of coast over 12 miles (20 km) long that are free of construction and only 33 stretches between 6 and 12 miles (10 and 20 km) long without construction.

In addition to its coastal and mountainous regions, Italian cities also host many heritage attractions. In addition to Roman sites, the art and architecture of the Renaissance is extremely important, with sites in Milan, Rome, Venice and Florence being major draw cards. Rome is also significant as the seat of the Vatican (see below), which therefore is a site of significant religious importance for many Catholics and culturally significant in its own right. The role of heritage in Italy is evidenced by the fact that it has 41 World Heritage Sites, more than any other nation.

The Iberian Peninsula: Portugal and Spain

The Iberian Peninsula or Iberia, includes Portugal, Spain, Andorra and the British Overseas Territory of Gibraltar. Iberia has been occupied by humans for thousands of years as evidenced by prehistoric remains. In historic times Iberia was successively settled by waves of colonists and invaders, including the Phoenicians, Greeks, Carthaginians, Romans, Germanic tribes and the Moors. The Muslim Moors ruled parts of the peninsula for 700 years with Seville and Granada being their last strongholds. The Moors left an architectural and culinary presence that lasts to the present-day. Following the defeat of the Moors in 1492, the various small states gradually amalgamated, although the only time the entire peninsula was united as a single political unit was from 1580 to 1640 in a period referred to as the Iberian Union. Since then Portugal and Spain have remained independent states. Spain has called for the return of Gibraltar, a small but strategic British territory near the Strait of Gibraltar, known colloquially as *The Rock* or *Gib*, which was ceded by Spain to Britain in perpetuity in 1713 under the Treaty of Utrecht, helping end the War of Spanish Succession. However, in referendums held with respect to the future of the territory, the majority of Gibraltarians have rejected unification with Spain or even co-sovereignty. Tourism is important in Gibraltar, although it was hurt by the unilateral closure of its border with Spain (by Spain) between 1969 and 1985, when it was reopened. Since 1985 traffic has flowed consistently across the border in both directions.

Portugal and Spain had significant overseas empires as a result of maritime expansion and exploration in the 15th and 16th centuries. Both countries controlled large territories of the Americas, while Portugal also had possessions in Africa and Asia. Spain had minor holdings in Africa and more in Asia. The colonial territories were important sources of wealth for the metropolitan powers and provided income vis a vis gold, silver, spices and slaves. The loss of the American territories was a major financial blow to both countries, but their empires had been in decline long before then, partly as a result of European wars, but also because of the rise of the French and British Empires. However, civil wars and disastrous international wars served to lead both countries into relative decline.

Modern Portugal and Spain have also been marked by periods of autocratic dictatorship. In Spain, General Miguel Primo de Rivera ruled between 1923 and 1931, and following the bitter Spanish Civil War (1936–1939), which ended the Second Spanish Republic, General Francisco Franco ruled until 1975. Franco won the civil war with the support of Italy and Germany, but from the mid-1950s Franco reentered the international arena as a result of the United States desire to base forces in Spain during the Cold War. In Portugal a revolution deposed the monarchy in 1910, but following considerable economic problems a military coup d'état occurred 1926 leading eventually to the establishment of a right-wing dictatorship by António de Oliveira Salazar. The Salazar regime was based on Catholic social doctrine and corporativism, in which power is given to civic assemblies that represent particular economic, industrial, agrarian, social, cultural and professional groups. The Portuguese authoritarian government was overthrown in 1974, and Franco died in 1975, and even that revived the deposed Spanish. Both Spain and Portugal made extensive use of secret police and repression to remove opposition. However, the political stability provided by dictatorship and the need for foreign currency and economic development provided the impetus for tourism growth in the two countries in the late 1960s and early 1970s.

Spain and Portugal both joined the EU in 1986, which proved to be immensely beneficial to their economies both in terms of EU assistance to marginal regions, as well as encouraging second home ownership in the countries' coastal areas. Such developments led to substantial capital investment and employment generation, particularly in the Spanish construction industry. However, the environmental impacts of these coastal developments are increasingly being questioned, particularly as there are increased concerns over competition for scarce water supplies between agricultural users and tourism and leisure industries, especially golf courses.

Winegrowing (viticulture) is a major agricultural sector in Portugal and Spain. Spain is well-known for the production of sherry and a variety of white and red wines. Rioja in northern Spain is probably the most famous wine region internationally, but other areas are becoming better known especially as a result of large numbers of tourists traveling to Spain and drinking local wines. Portugal, by virtue of its long trade links with Britain, has long used wine as a means to link wine regions with tourism. The city of Oporto in northern Portugal uses the port wine connection extensively in its promotions and in hosting events and festivals. From the perspective of local politicians and government officials, such relationships create opportunities for long-term loyalty from visitors to the region in terms of their wine purchasing behavior. However, while port has a high profile in the British market, it has diminished in popularity as consumers have begun to focus on lighter, fruitier styles of wine for immediate drinking. Nevertheless, market awareness of port has provided an opportunity for Portugal to promote its other red and white wines. The Alto Minho region in northern Portugal, which is best known in wine terms as producers of vinho verde, has also been attempting to develop linkages between wine and tourism. The Vinho Verde DOC region is Portugal's largest demarcated wine region. The area has received substantial EU funding through various regional and rural development programs to improve tourism product development and promotion, including wine tourism. Interestingly, the region's wine tourism has mainly targeted international and domestic tourists who have already arrived in the region to see culture and heritage, rather than specifically using the region's wine as a branding tool to attract tourists. Wine tourism-related development has included the founding of wine routes, home-stay accommodations and guides to the region's gastronomic opportunities.

The imperial legacies of both countries, the role of the church and the presence of many different colonists have provided a wide range of heritage attractions, including very important Catholic pilgrimage sites (Santiago de Compostella, Spain, and Fatima, Portugal). Spain has the second highest number of UNESCO World Heritage Sites in the world (40). Portugal has 13 World Heritage Sites with three of them (Torre de Belem, Sintra, Mosteiro dos Jeronimos) located near to the capital, Lisbon. Both Spain and Portugal have also sought to promote tourism and urban redevelopment via the hosting of mega events such as World Expos and Olympic Games with Barcelona in particular focusing on events as a means of promoting its culture.

The Island States of the Mediterranean: Malta and Cyprus

Malta and Cyprus are the southernmost parts of the EU, becoming member states in 2004. Even though extremely densely populated (almost 3300 people per mi^2 (1300 people per km^2)), Malta is the smallest country in the EU in terms of population and area. An archipelago of seven islands situated in the Mediterranean Sea between Italy in the north, Libya in the south and Tunisia to the west, Malta's strategic location has long been fodder for fighting between other countries to control the Maltese islands. The United Kingdom was the last colonial power until independence was declared in 1964. Malta became an independent republic in 1974. For much of the 19th and 20th centuries, Malta was primarily economically dependent on the presence of the British navy and other military postings. The economy is presently based on tourism, freight (as a transshipment point from the Suez Canal), and manufacturing. The country is also seeking to develop its economy by investing heavily in education and developing a knowledge-based economy. However, a significant constraint to the island's development, including tourism, is the lack of freshwater supplies in summer and the need to import nearly all of its energy.

The divided island of Cyprus in the eastern Mediterranean Sea provides an interesting case study of political unrest and its effects on tourism in a popular seaside destination. In response to a coup d'état against the government of Cyprus by revolutionaries who desired unification with Greece, Turkish armed forces arrived on the island in July 1974, and in an effort to protect Cyprus' Turkish population from annexation by Greece, occupied the northern third of the island. This was an unwelcome advance in the eyes of Greece and among the island's Greek population. Fierce fighting ensued between the Greek and Turkish populations of the island, resulting in thousands of lives lost on both fronts. A ceasefire was eventually declared in August 1974, and a de facto boundary was drawn across the island, separating the northern third of the territory from the southern two-thirds. By the end of 1975, some 185,000 Greek Cypriots had migrated from the northern portion of the island to the Greek-controlled south (Republic of Cyprus), and approximately 45,000 Turkish Cypriots moved northward into the Turkish zone. The new political landscape of division, dominated by the scar (ceasefire line) known as the Green Line, was a stark reminder of the conflict and its effects on everyday life, including tourism.

This conflict and the new border became major barriers to tourism, which had already begun to flourish and provided a major source of foreign exchange earnings. In 1970, the number of international tourist arrivals to Cyprus was approximately 140,000. Three years later, in 1973, the number had grown to nearly 300,000. However, this figure fell drastically with the July 1974 Turkish invasion/intervention on the island. Visitor arrivals dropped to 150,000 in 1974, most of which arrived before July, and in 1975, only 47,100 visitors arrived on the island. This sliding trend lasted only a few years, however. Since 1975, the Republic of Cyprus (the Greek south) has seen considerable tourism growth in both arrival numbers and infrastructure development. The industry has in fact recovered fully in the south, while the north's (Turkish Republic of Northern Cyprus – TRNC) tourism industry has been beleaguered by slow growth in arrivals, a sluggish tourism economy, and minimal investment in tourism infrastructure and services. The sluggish growth of tourism in the north is a result of several factors: (1) the Turks were seen as the aggressors in the conflict, which has affected the international image of the Turkish-controlled north; (2) international economic sanctions against the TRNC has severely curtailed visitor arrivals and foreign investments; and (3) in response to the world community's embargo, the government of the north has opted to focus on economic development through agriculture, food processing and textiles, rather than tourism, although it is growing in importance.

Following the 1974 incident, non-Cypriots visiting the island were permitted to cross from the south to the north during daylight hours, but they were not permitted to purchase any products north of the border, and entry to the island in the north was strictly prohibited by the government of the south. For the island's residents, the Green Line became a very significant barrier. Greek Cypriots were forbidden from crossing into the north, and the Turkish population was not allowed south of the border. Thus, travel between the north and south and vice versa for Cypriots was almost impossible, until 2003. On April 23, 2003, the situation changed as the border opened up in both directions, thereby allowing Greek Cypriots to visit the North and Turkish Cypriots to visit the South. At the time of writing, the situation had begun to normalize, and hundreds of Cypriots from both sides were crossing the border in both directions each day for shopping, work, gambling (in the north) and various other activities. However, outsiders are still not permitted to enter the island through the North.

Western Europe – The Non-EU Countries

The non-EU countries of Western Europe (excluding the Nordic countries of Iceland and Norway) are Switzerland, San Marino, Vatican City, Andorra, Monaco

PHOTO 2.16
Picturesque village in the Switzerland's Alps

Source: Jarkko Saarinen

and Liechtenstein. With the exception of Switzerland, the non-EU countries of Western Europe are all microstates. The term *microstate* generally refers to countries and islands with populations of less than one million people. However, in the context of Europe, the term has additional meaning and often refers to the smallest of the microstates, in that they are both physically and demographically very small, albeit independent, countries that function legally and in practical terms as sovereign nations. The microstates are discussed in more detail below.

Switzerland

Switzerland is a land-locked country bordered by Germany to the north and Italy to the south, France to the west and Austria and Liechtenstein to the east. Switzerland has a population of 7.5 million people and occupies an area of $15,940\,mi^2$ ($41,285\,km^2$). The history of Switzerland has been strongly influenced by its geography, which is primarily alpine, with many glacial valleys and even the northern

PHOTO 2.17

Liechtenstein. Most of the micro state of Liechtenstein is visible here on the left (east) side of the Rhine River Valley in the Swiss Alps

Source: Dallen J. Timothy

part of the country where most of the population resides and the largest cities, such as Geneva, Bern, Basel and Zürich, are located, remains quite hilly and is also characterized by numerous lakes.

The country's official name is the Swiss Confederation. Politically it is a federal republic with a direct democracy based on 26 cantons that are the equivalent of states or provinces. The cantons have their origins in geographically determining features such as urban areas, forests and valley systems. The position of the country in Europe and the relative isolation of the various cantons from each other for much of Swiss history with few transport connections, and the difficulty of travel in winter, have resulted in Switzerland's being a multilingual country with different language groups being concentrated in different regions. The official languages are French, German, Italian and Romansh (a Romance language that developed from Vulgar Latin). The range of languages spoken in the country has become an important factor in Switzerland's international orientation as has its long history of neutrality.

Switzerland has not been involved in a foreign war since 1815, although a civil war in 1845 primarily between Catholics and Protestants, was a pivotal point in national history as it provided impetus for revision of federal relations, as well as the development of direct democracy which is a prominent feature of the Swiss political system. As a result of Switzerland's position of neutrality and democratic and political orientation, it has long been the headquarters of international institutions. The International Committee of the Red Cross was founded in Switzerland in 1863 and the International Federation of Red Cross and Red Crescent Societies (IFRC), founded in 1919, is based in Geneva. The United Nations also has several institutions in Geneva, although Switzerland did not join the UN itself until 2002. The location of numerous international bodies in the country along with Switzerland's substantial business community, including internationally branded companies, such as Nestle, Credit Suisse, Novartis and Swatch, means that business travel is an important element of tourism.

Switzerland's economy is regarded as one of the most competitive in the world. Key industries include banking and finance, pharmaceuticals and biomedical research, chemicals and engineering, with Swiss watch-making being world famous. There is also significant agriculture and food production with Swiss wine having a growing international presence, although cheese and chocolate probably remain its most famous international food items. Tourism is an important industry particularly in rural areas that have otherwise been affected by global agricultural restructuring.

International tourism in Switzerland dates from the Romantic period of the late 18th and early 19th centuries. Prior to this time the country was generally passed through rather than sought after as a destination in its own right. However, the massive shift in attitudes toward natural and rural landscapes (see the previous discussion with respect to the industrial revolution in Europe) helped create a favorable perception of mountain landscapes for the first time. This became extremely important for Switzerland as the development of positive aspects toward the mountains saw the country come to be regarded as a sports destination for mountain climbing, a health destination because of the clear air and a location for sightseeing. The development and promotion of skiing saw a new stage in Swiss tourism development with the establishment of many ski resorts, which in summer are also used for alpine walking.

One of the features of Switzerland and the Swiss tourism industry has been its environmental emphasis with considerable attention being given to recycling and anti-littering. Considerable effort is also given to conserve landscapes and moderate the effects of skifield development. However, in recent years considerable concerns have been raised about the potential impacts of climate change in the country's alpine areas, which have affected the financial viability of ski resorts, especially with low altitude runs, because of the loss of guaranteed snow. Yet climate change and pressure from visitors and overgrazing is also impacting alpine ecologies with treelines and alpine grasslands and herbfields shifting in response. In addition, there is increased concern over the long-term future of alpine glaciers which have an important tourism role as landscape features and for recreation as well as a significant source of water supply.

The European Alps and Climate Change

The European Alps are regarded as being particularly sensitive to climate change with recent warming being approximately three times the global average. The years 1994, 2000, 2002 and 2003 were the warmest on record in the Alps in the last 500 years, but climate model projections show even greater changes in the coming decades, predicting less snow at low altitudes and receding glaciers and melting permafrost higher up. From 1850 to 1980, glaciers in the region lost 30–40 percent of their area. Since 1980 a further 20 percent of the ice has been lost. The summer of 2003 led to the loss of a further 10 percent. By 2050 about 75 percent of the glaciers in the Swiss Alps are likely to have disappeared, rising to 100 percent in 2100.

Andermatt, a popular ski resort in central Switzerland, has decided to act on the threat to winter sports tourism that climate change represents and has started to experiment with a high-technology protective blanket to stop the Gurschen glacier from melting away. Yet the amount of area that can be covered remains limited. Changing the terrain by grading the slopes and rerouting natural streams also carries risks to the natural environment and increases chances of natural hazards such as flash floods and rockslides.

The European Microstates

There are five mini microstates in Europe, namely San Marino, Vatican City, Andorra, Monaco and Liechtenstein, ranging in size from $180\,mi^2$ ($468\,km^2$) for Andorra to $0.17\,mi^2$($0.44\,km^2$) for the Vatican City. Tourism is a very important part of the economies of all five of the European microstates. In fact their smallness and novelty value is something that makes them attractive to many visitors.

Located in the Pyrenees mountains between Spain and France, Andorra is popular as a major duty-free shopping, skiing and hiking destination and has several major ski resorts, such as Soldeu/El Tarter and Pal/Arinsal. Tourism is an important part of the economy although its tax-haven status means that the banking sector is also significant. Andorra has a population of just over 70,000 people, and the official language is Catalan.

Surrounded completely by Italy, San Marino is famous for its archery festivals, historic buildings and smallness. Founded in 301 CE, it is regarded as the oldest constitutional republic in the world. The country has an area of $23\,mi^2$ ($61\,km^2$) and a population of just below 30,000 people. Although not a member of the EU, it has been allowed to use the euro as its official currency. The language of San Marino is Italian.

Monaco is a major seaside destination known for yachting, gambling (it has a major casino) and hosting a Formula 1 Grand Prix on its street circuit. One of the most expensive places in the world, it is often regarded as one of the *playgrounds of the rich* as there is no income tax on individuals, something which has proven attractive to many sports stars and business people. However, the tax-haven status has raised concerns over control of money laundering and other criminal activities. Monaco's currency is the euro, although it is not a member of the EU, because it has a close relationship with France, including a customs union, with whom it shares its land border. Monaco has a population of approximately 32,000 people and an area of .75 mi² (1.95 km²), although this is expanding as a result of reclamation activities that will see a new ward, Le Portier, constructed by 2014. The language of Monaco is French.

Liechtenstein is a land-locked country of alpine Europe bordered by Switzerland to the west and Austria to the East. It is most commonly visited for skiing, mountain scenery, shopping, museums and hiking. Leichenstein is a constitutional monarchy with a population of approximately 35,000 people and an area of $61\,mi^2$ ($160\,km^2$). However, a notable feature of its history is that even though the lands that make up present-day Liechtenstein were purchased by the Liechtenstein dynasty in 1699 and 1712 no member of the family visited the principality until 1818. As with many other microstates, the country is a tax haven with advantageous business tax rates and is unusual in that it has more registered companies than citizens. The official language is German and the currency is the Swiss Franc because of a customs union with Switzerland.

The Vatican City, the smallest sovereign country in the world, is best known as the center of the Roman Catholic Church and a major pilgrimage center for Catholics from around the world. An argument could be for the Vatican to be the most visited country in the world as well, based on the assumption that nearly all tourists in Rome also visit the Vatican, and that the thousands of Italians who visit the country each day for religious purposes, are technically, international day visitors. The Vatican is the last widely recognized state without full UN membership.

Many people consider the Vatican City (located in Rome) to be the smallest country. However, there are some who argue that the smallest sovereign state in the world is the Sovereign Military Hospitaller Order of Saint John of Jerusalem, of Rhodes and of Malta (often referred to as the Order or Knights of Malta or SMOM, for short), which consists of several buildings located in the Palazzo Malta in Rome. The Order issues passports and has diplomatic relations with over 95 other countries and other international bodies, such as the EU and the International Committee of the Red Cross. The Order has observer status at the UN and is a Catholic charitable and social service organization, membership of which includes many of the wealthy and elite from around the world. Another candidate for the world's smallest country is the Principality of Sealand, which is an abandoned World War II military fortress in the North Sea, whose current owners declared its independence in 1967, although no other countries recognize its independence. Several other potential microstates states exist in Europe, including Seborga, a small town in the Ligurian region of Italy, near the French border and in sight of Monaco. This appears to have the most legitimate claims to sovereignty of any other owing to errors and oversights in the treaties that created the Italian Republic. In the early 1960s Giorgio Carbone, head of the local flower-growers cooperative, began promoting the idea that the town regain its historic status as a principality similar to Monaco. In 1963 he assumed the title of Prince and declared himself head of state with the publicity surrounding the *principality* helping to boost tourism. In the mid-1990s the town's citizens voted in an informal referendum for a constitution and independence from Italy, although this has never been acknowledged by the Italian government to whom the citizens still pay their taxes.

The Value of Being Different

The microstates of Europe have been able to use their non-membership of the EU as a source of differentiation in the international marketplace. Because they are not members of the EU and therefore subject to its laws, they can use differences in taxation and regulation to attract investors or provide products to visitors. For example, Andorra is able to sell a wide range of duty-free products, much cheaper than in France or Spain. Nevertheless, the microstates in one sense can have the best of both worlds by still being included in various agreements with the EU, particular in terms of trade and customs. Tax-haven status, in the form of low-cost company registration and minimal business tax rates, is also important for tourism as it often encourages significant flows of business travel.

Eastern Europe – EU Countries

Central Europe Landscape

In contrast to the mountains of the south, Central Europe is a mature landscape. Central Europe has low-lying hills and plateaus that generally range from 500 to 2000 ft (150 to 600 m) in height. A few of the peaks in this region reach 4000 ft (1200 m). The mountain ranges are interspersed with major basins, where considerable settlement has taken place. These mountains are older than those of Southern Europe, being created between 570 and 136 million years ago, during the Caledonia and Hercynian Orogenies. At that time, these mountains were as high as the Alps. Subsequently, they were eroded and mostly submerged below sea level, along with most of Europe and Russia. As Europe began to rise from the sea during the Alpine Orogeny, these older mountains were again exposed. Depositions in the basins in this area became sites of major coal deposits that contributed to Europe's Industrial Revolution.

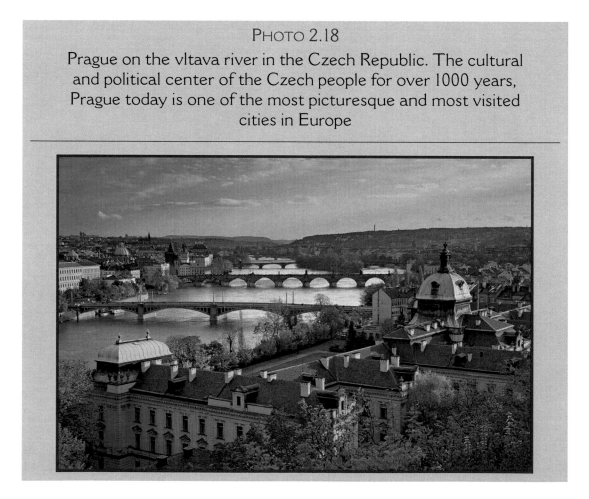

PHOTO 2.18

Prague on the vltava river in the Czech Republic. The cultural and political center of the Czech people for over 1000 years, Prague today is one of the most picturesque and most visited cities in Europe

The major mountain systems of Central Europe are heavily forested and include the Central massive in France; the Central German Uplands; the Jura Mountains, which include the Black Forest in Germany; and the Bohemian massive in the Czech Republic. The Western Uplands of Scandinavia, Ireland and Scotland, as well as the Ural Mountains in Russia, were also created during this geologic orogeny. The Appalachian Mountains in the United States and the mountains of eastern Australia are of the same geologic time period.

The Fall of Communism

Perhaps the most remarkable socio-political event to have occurred in Europe during the past 20 years was the collapse of communism/state socialism in Eastern Europe in the early 1990s, which dominated the region since the 1940s and functioned as one of the most repressive forms of government in the world. Under communist control food and fuel were scarce, health care was rudimentary, and few citizens were permitted

PHOTO 2.19

Tallinn, Estonia. Tallinn is the capital and largest city in Estonia, and is situated on the Gulf of Finland, part of the Baltic sea

Source: Jaarko Saarinen

to travel outside their own countries – at best they were allowed periodic holidays in other socialist states of Central and Eastern Europe, Cuba and the Soviet Union. The exceptions to this rule were Hungarians and Yugoslavs, who enjoyed the most freedom to travel among all the citizens of the Eastern Bloc countries, and were occasionally permitted to travel to Western Europe on their annual vacations. Nonetheless, in most cases, considerable efforts were made by the various eastern regimes to curtail contact between the people of the west and those in the east. In many cases, eastward travel by citizens of Western Europe, North America and other parts of the capitalist world was made difficult by strict government regulations, including difficult visa requirements, and mandatory minimum per diem currency exchange rules.

Among the earliest events to bring about change in the communist east was the establishment of workers' *solidarity* unions, which began working for more rights and freedoms for blue-collar employees. Many people were imprisoned for their efforts in these movements, but the efforts had the intended effect of getting citizens in Poland and other strict communist states to think for themselves and begin asserting their rights. In the late 1980s, changes began to occur throughout the entire Eastern Bloc as Soviet President Mikhail Gorbachev initiated his policies of glasnost (openness) and perestroika (restructuring), which aimed to create an air of openness in public discussions about past and present problems facing the USSR. Perestroika was meant to encourage a new way of thinking about the social, political and economic structure of the communist state and begin establishing a free-market economy with some degree of private ownership and profit-making.

Once the seeds of a market economy had been planted, however, the floodgates opened and people in the east began demanding more freedoms and more accountability from the state. Unintentionally, Gorbachev's policies became the medium for bringing down the totalitarian system that had governed the Eastern Bloc countries for decades. The resultant new economic and social liberties related to religious worship, freedom of speech, freedom to strike and freedom to assemble, destabilized the autocratic governments of Eastern Europe, beginning with the German Democratic Republic (East Germany) in 1989, underscored by the fall of the Berlin Wall, and followed closely by the USSR's Baltic republics (Lithuania, Latvia and Estonia) and other states lying east of the *Iron Curtain* declaring their independency. While these upheavals resulted in newfound freedoms, they also destabilized a long-established system of despotic control and predictability, resulting in increased crime rates, ethnic unrest, economic downturns, increased scarcity of food and supplies and growing poverty levels. Finally, in 1991–1992, the Soviet Union dissolved, forming 15 new independent countries, some of which are discussed below. Likewise, in a ripple effect, Czechoslovakia split into two new countries on January 1, 1993 (the Czech Republic and Slovakia), and Yugoslavia, whose ethnic tensions had been kept in check by the power of communism and the personality of General Tito, dissolved, erupting into a series of bitter civil wars during the early and mid-1990s and into a series of new states (Bosnia and Herzegovina, Croatia, Slovenia, Serbia, Montenegro, the Republic of Macedonia). The Republic of Macedonia, which declared independence in 1991, was the only former republic to gain sovereignty without resistance from the Belgrade-based Yugoslav authorities. The long-term future of the province of Kosovo is still to be decided, although it declared independence from Seribia on with some parties wanting independence, others the creation of a greater Albania, while the Serb minority still wishes to have a political relationship with Serbia 2008.

For tourism these changes were extremely profound for several reasons. First, many of the *post-communist* countries of the east (e.g., Poland, Czech Republic and Hungary) skyrocketed onto the World Tourism Organization's top 20 list of tourist destination countries in the mid-1990s. This is primarily because people of Eastern European descent, who had earlier migrated to the west, were now free to return to their homelands to visit relatives and places they had not see for nearly half a century. However, Hungary has always been the most westernized country and has a potentially large tourism market because of its cultural ties with other central European countries and its accessibility to the markets of Austria, Germany and Italy.

Second, the citizenry of the east became free to travel to the west to explore the lands they had heard of but had never before had opportunities to visit. Third, traveling to the east from the west became easier with fewer visa and currency regulations. The countries of Eastern Europe opened up to floods of tourists from the west and became especially popular owing to the status as *former* communist states, as well as their relatively inexpensive prices in terms of transportation, food and lodging. Today, most countries of the former communist bloc have embraced tourism and have begun to thrive as important destinations. Others, however, such as Belarus and Moldova, have resisted (either intentionally or not) the urge to focus on tourism as a major economic growth catalyst, while others struggle to develop tourism, but in light of negative ongoing associations with civil unrest (e.g., Serbia, Albania, Georgia, Armenia and Azerbaijan), are unable to develop a thriving tourism industry.

The EU Enlargement

In 2004 a number of the former state communist countries of Eastern Europe joined the EU in a process known as accession. In addition to Malta and Cyprus, the Czech Republic, Estonia, Hungary, Latvia, Lithuania, Poland, Slovakia and Slovenia joined the EU. This was the largest number of countries admitted into the EU at one time. On 1 January 2007 the former communist countries of Bulgaria and Romania joined. To join the EU, countries must fulfill the *Copenhagen criteria* – a set of rules that define eligibility to join the Union, first laid out at the June 1993 European Council in Copenhagen, from which they take their name. The criteria include having institutions to preserve democratic governance and human rights, respect and protection for minorities, a functioning market economy and accepting the obligations and political, economic and monetary aims of the EU. Other candidate countries in Eastern Europe include Croatia, which applied for membership in 2003 and the Republic of Macedonia, which applied in 2004. The other successor states of the Socialist Federal Republic of Yugoslavia (Bosnia and Herzegovina, Montenegro and Serbia) have all adopted EU integration as an aim of foreign policy. Albania, Moldova and Ukraine have done likewise. However, given that the EU has had difficulties with its own constitution, there are concerns from existing members that the accession and enlargement process has already been overstretched, particularly as the admission of Albania and the rest of the Western Balkans into the EU has already been set as a priority by the alliance. This situation may make it extremely difficult, or at least delay for many years, the potential future accession of the former Soviet Republics and the South Caucasus: Armenia, Belarus, Georgia, Moldova and Ukraine, although such an enlargement is likely to receive opposition from Russia.

Hungary and Health Tourism

Traveling for health reasons is an important motivation for tourism throughout many parts of Europe. The supply of health tourism products depends on the availability of health-care facilities and natural resources, including appropriate landscapes, climates, mineral springs and the development and promotion of resorts. Hungary has a long history of spa and health tourism due to its large number of thermal springs. For more than 2000 years, people traveled to Hungary for its healing waters. Today, almost 300 out of 1,300 thermal springs are used as public baths. The thermal and medicinal waters are known to have a healing effect on rheumatic problems, cardiovascular disorders, arthritis, skin problems and asthma. Famous spa towns include Hajdúszoboszló, Bükfürdö, Balf, Debrecen, Gyula, Zalakaros, Hévíz, Harkány, Margitsziget and Város1ig.

Germans and Austrians have been traveling to Hungary for dental treatment combined with visits to traditional spas since the fall of the iron curtain. Because of lower wages and utility costs, dental treatment in Hungary is far less expensive for German patients and *tooth tourism* has become a major contributor to the Hungarian economy. Currently, Hungary draws large numbers of patients from Western Europe and the United States for high-quality cosmetic and dental procedures that cost half of what they would in the tourists' home countries.

Spas and wellness have been identified by the Hungary Tourism Organization, the national tourism agency, as one of the country's four most important international tourism products, alongside convention and incentive tourism (MICE), and recreation in the Budapest and Lake Balaton regions. To promote the segment, 2003 was designated and promoted as the Year of Tourism of Health. From an international perspective, the HTO focused its efforts on large-scale press campaigns in Germany, France, Italy, Sweden, Denmark and Finland. According to Tourism Hungary, 5 percent of people used commercial accommodation facilities for health tourism in 2003, and the number of guests in spa hotels increased by 6.7 percent and the number of guest nights by 2 percent compared to 2002. One-third of the 2.3 million German guest nights in 2004 were spent in spa and wellness hotels, and overall thermal hotels experienced an increase of 22.2 percent in guest nights compared to 2003 numbers.

In 2002 the Hungarian government developed a 10-year tourism development program consisting of six sub-sections, one of which specifically deals with the development of the health tourism sector. The so-called *Szécheni Plan* supports health tourism-related projects with an investment of one-third of the total portfolio estimated at approximately €353 million by 2004. The aim of the plan is to increase Hungary's tourism-related revenues. In terms of health tourism, the objectives are the development of competitive products on an international scale, complex service packages, the attraction of new three-generation target groups, encouragement of further investment and extending the tourist season. The following strategies of the Szécheni Plan aim to achieve these objectives for health tourism:

- Modernize existing health resorts and hot springs, and improve their services.
- Promote the use of thermal water resources which are known but not yet used for tourism purposes.

- Develop the infrastructure of health resorts and hot springs through a coordinated and tourism oriented development of health and thermal water-related services and tourism-related infrastructure.
- Develop an institutional and regulatory framework, for example un order to provide an enhanced level of health facilities throughout the country, the Hungarian Government has introduced a rating system which assesses facilities and services such as baths, saunas and steam baths, fitness equipment, skin care services, therapy services and vegetarian food services.
- Ensure appropriate marketing for health and hot spring tourism.
- Develop human resources.

Budapest, Hungary's capital city is one of Europe's gem cities and a very popular tourist destination for western Europeans. Its historic architecture and location on the Danube River provides considerable appeal.

The Former Czechoslovakia

As noted above, on January 1 1993, Czechoslovakia split into Slovakia and the Czech Republic, creating overnight a new international border, complete with customs and immigration stations and border-crossing formalities. With the collapse of communism in the early 1990s, the Czech Republic took off as a tourist destination, partially because of the desire of people of the Czech diaspora to visit the homeland that had been essentially inaccessible for several decades. National parks and wood lands provide much of the tourist appeal of these two new countries, although their capital cities, Prague (Czech Republic) and Bratislava (Slovakia) are well known for their unique urban architecture, picturesque city squares, castles and fortresses.

The Baltic States: Estonia, Latvia and Lithuania

Prior to their forced absorption into the Soviet Union, Estonia, Latvia and Lithuania were independent states in the early 1900s. The United States and other countries never recognized their Soviet integration and kept their embassies open in Washington, DC, anticipating the time when they would once again become self-governing and return ambassadors to their rightful places. These three republics were among the first to declare independence from the USSR, which led to violent forceful tactics by the Soviet military. Soon after, all three were recognized by the world community as independent states, and the USSR had little choice but to let them go.

Today, tourism is a high priority for all three countries. Estonia particularly has close cultural and historical ties to Finland, and therefore is a significant destination for Finns who often travel by ferry boat across the Gulf of Finland for day trips to Tallinn or weekend getaways. The old city of Tallinn has been listed a UNESCO site and is a popular tourist destination and major gateway to the Baltic region. Estonia's coastal islands are popular destinations and are growing in popularity as holiday second-home locations.

Latvia and Lithuania are also burgeoning tourist destinations. Both countries' capitals, Riga and Vilnius, are now vibrant cities with interesting architectural and historic appeal. Castles, music festivals, and scenic rural areas contribute to their international tourist appeal.

Poland

Poland is one of Europe's larger countries and home to many cities with global appeal, as well as scenic rural areas that keep many traditions alive. Kraków's old city possesses architectural treasures from a variety of eras and churches (Poland was one of the few eastern countries where religion (i.e., Catholicism) was able to flourish under communism). Warsaw, the capital, which was nearly destroyed in the World War II, was re-built as a drab communist capital, but today it is a cosmopolitan city with shops, hotels and a variety of tourist attractions. The historic centers of Kraków and Warsaw have been designated UNESCO World Heritage Sites. Gdansk, one of Poland's largest cities, and a major seaport, is very historic with unique architecture and religious edifices. A German-ethnic city before World War II, Gdansk was a city-state or an independent country between 1919 and 1939, when it was annexed by Germany. The city's German heritage is still part of its appeal for German tourists and others.

Auschwitz and other Holocaust concentration camps from World War II are places of *thanatourism* or dark tourism, where sites of human suffering are commemorated. Auschwitz-Birkenau is one of Poland's most important heritage destinations, for it was the largest concentration camp in Hitler's German Reich, where some 1.5 million Jews and other minorities were tortured and killed.

National parks near the borders with the Czech Republic and Slovakia have been designated International Parks, owing to their status as cross-border nature preserves. This has led to a great deal of bi-national cooperation between Poland and its neighbors in the areas of environmental improvements, conservation and nature-based tourism development.

In common with many other countries of Europe, the eastern bloc countries, including Poland, have begun to promote themselves as significant diasporic destinations. This means that they are attempting to cater to people of Polish descent who live in Australia, Canada, United States, the United Kingdom and other diverse places to return to the land of their ancestors to discover their own roots or personal heritage, by meeting distant relatives, studying Polish, conducting family history research and visiting villages and churches where their ancestors might have lived.

Slovenia

Unlike its former Yugoslavian partner republics (e.g., Croatia and Bosnia-Herzegovina), Slovenia was spared much of the violence and bloodshed that were meted out by the Yugoslavian military when the republics began to break away in the early 1990s. Today Slovenia is known for beautiful mountain scenery, lakes and its colorful capital city, Ljubljana.

The EU's Youngest: Romania and Bulgaria

Romania and Bulgaria are the EU's newest members (January 2007). Romania's image was terribly tainted under the dictatorship of Ceausescu, but it has in the nearly two decades since the fall of communism, recovered and become an important tourist destination. Romania is a popular destination on Danube River cruises, which are able to reach the Black Sea. The Transylvania region is home to the Vampire myth of Count Dracula (an actual person but not a vampire). Tourists arrive by the busload to see the famed castle and region made increasingly popular by dozens of movies and novels set in the beautiful, yet feared, forests of Transylvania. Romania's rural lifestyle and peasant traditions are important for tourism, as are its cities as major gateways.

Since its communist rule collapsed, tourism has become an important priority for Bulgaria as well. Like Romania and other neighbors, Bulgaria is a favored stop on Black Sea Danube cruises, and its rural appeal evokes a similar mental landscape of horse-drawn carriages, farmers and small villages.

Eastern Europe – Non-EU Countries

Albania

Before the 1990s, Albania was often counted as the strictest communist country in Europe. United States citizens were forbidden entry, although Europeans could visit if they managed to get a visa, and all visitors were required to *look a certain way*. By way of example, in addition to special permission and difficulty to obtain visas, men were required to have short hair and clean-cut appearances. Likewise, all visitors were required to be accompanied continually by a guide and were virtually prohibited from speaking to Albanian citizens. This built Albania's reputation as the most isolated country in Europe and, in the company of North Korea, in the world. Following the 1992 free elections, a new, more democratic government was put into power and the nation opened up a capitalist market economy. Although Albania suffered some political and economic instability in the 1990s, and some regions were marked as dangerous to visit, tourism is growing and has become a priority for the present government. Most of Albania's tourism resource base is founded on ancient Greek and Roman sites, intriguing village life, and sun and sea along the Ionian Coast.

The Former Yugoslavia

The dissolution of Yugoslavia in the early 1990s was a major turning point for the Balkan region of southeastern Europe in geo-political and tourism terms. While, as noted above, Slovenia was spared significant devastation, Croatia and Bosnia-Herzegovina were not. The Croatian War of Independence (1991–1995) was a brutal conflict wherein Croatia fought with the Yugoslav army for separation from Yugoslavia. During the latter part of this period, the battle was between Croatia's nascent military and the new country's Serb minority, who desired to remain connected to Serbia and greater Yugoslavia. Croatia won the war and is now a thriving, cosmopolitan nation populated primarily by ethnic Croatians. The Bosnian War (1992–1995) involved many players in Bosnia and Herzegovina and was known for its brutality and neighbor-against-neighbor fighting tactics. In this conflict, Croatian, Serbian and Bosnian Muslims fought against each other and destroyed each other's villages and religious buildings and icons. In 1996, a peace treaty (Dayton Accord) was signed, ending the Bosnian War, and forming a federal state that includes large populations of Serbs, Croatians and Muslims. Why conditions have much improved, there are still some underlying ethnic tensions in Bosnia and Herzegovina, and keeping peace is a delicate balancing act.

Tourism is important for Croatia and Bosnia-Herzegovina. Croatia's coastal areas, particularly its famed cities Dubrovnik and Split, are important urban heritage destinations, some replete with notable remains of the Roman Empire. Dubrovnik was targeted and much of it destroyed by the Yugoslav military during the Croatian War because of its nationalistic importance in Croatian identity. The city has healed, however, and many of the damaged buildings have been repaired. The old town is a UNESCO World Heritage Site and one of Croatia's best-known destinations. The dramatic scenery associated with the Dalmatian Alps is a particularly significant tourist draw, and the country's Adriatic coastal and island resorts are booming, particularly popularized by German and other west European tourists.

Bosnia and Herzegovina is a country of significant contrasts. Its beautiful mountain and rural scenery is often a backdrop to the dramatic ruins of the Bosnian War, many of which are still visible in the landscape. Cities such as Mostar and Sarajevo (the capital) were devastated by the war, with many ancient structures and historical sites being targeted and destroyed by warring ethno-religious groups and military factions. Sarajevo was popularized by its hosting the 1984 Winter Olympics, but later was plastered of the world's news headlines as a site of aggressive wartime fighting. The country is quickly recovering economically and socially from the war and focusing more on tourism as a tool for development. The war provides much of the backdrop for tourism, as Mostar and Sarajevo both use it as a tourist commodity, including destroyed buildings and souvenirs made from artillery shells and other wartime devices.

Following its 1991 independence from Yugoslavia, the Republic of Macedonia was called the Former Yugoslav Republic of Macedonia (FYROM) in an effort to appease the Greeks, who objected to the name Macedonia, because of their widely held contention that Macedonia was a historically Hellenic (Greek) region and name. While the official name of the country now is the Republic of Macedonia, Greece still officially recognizes it as FYROM, and many Greeks informally refer to it as *so-called Macedonia*. Macedonia did not experience the conflicts of the Yugoslavian wars in the 1990s, although it did experience some minor skirmished with ethnic Albanian rebels in 2001 and was shaken slightly by the 1999 NATO fighting with the Yugoslav military in Kosovo, which led thousands of Kosovo Albanians to flee to Macedonia. The country today is waiting to become a member of the EU. Macedonia is gaining importance as a European tourist destination and is especially notable for its Roman and Byzantine ruins, churches, natural environment and excellent cuisine and wine.

Russia and the CIS

Russia, the world's largest country, has a vast diversity of natural and cultural landscapes that create widespread appeal for tourists. The expanse of Siberia (see below), mountains and volcanoes, deserts, forests, coastlines and navigable rivers are important natural elements. Numerous cultural regions, languages, ethnicities and religions contribute to a wide array of folk practices (e.g., music, art, cuisine, dress, village layout, agricultural landscapes) that provide considerable charm for tourists. Its cities are perhaps its most visited districts, the most important being Moscow (the capital) and St. Petersburg (known as Leningrad during the communist period). St. Petersburg possesses some of Russia's most valuable architectural and artistic gems, many associated with the ruling Czars and national heritage. Moscow is the lifeline of Russia and houses the government and most central organizations for the arts and sports in the country.

Photo 2.20

The Kremlin in Moscow, on the Moskva river. The Kremlin is fortified complex that has been a center for religion and politics in Russia Since the 14th century

Photo 2.21

The Taiga forest in Siberia. Meandering stream and remnant water bodes in the Taiga, the World's continuous forest, in Russia's Siberia

PHOTO 2.22
Lake Baikal, Siberia. Lake Baikal is the deepest lake in the world and contains about 20 percent of all the fresh water on the planet. The mountains of Olhon Island can be seen in the distance. In winter, large parts of the lake are covered with thick Ice.

For potential visitors, Russia still holds on to many of its old communist-era policies and practices. For example, strict rules are still in place in applying for a visa, and accommodations reservations must often be made and paid in advance, as well as letters of invitation often must accompany visa applications. This old-style approach to tourism differs significantly from several of the former USSR states that have opened their arms to international arrivals and eliminated most visa requirements. In spite of these tight regulations, political instability in several regions (e.g., Chechnya), accusations of corruption at all levels of government, economic crises, and a globally recognized organized crime establishment, there is considerable world demand for travel to Russia.

CIS stands for Commonwealth of Independent States. The CIS was formed in December 1991 after the break-up of the USSR, and includes most of the countries that were formerly Soviet Socialist Republics, the largest of which, by far, is the Russian Federation (Russia). The only former Soviet Republics not part of the CIS are the Baltic countries of Latvia, Lithuania and Estonia – all now members of

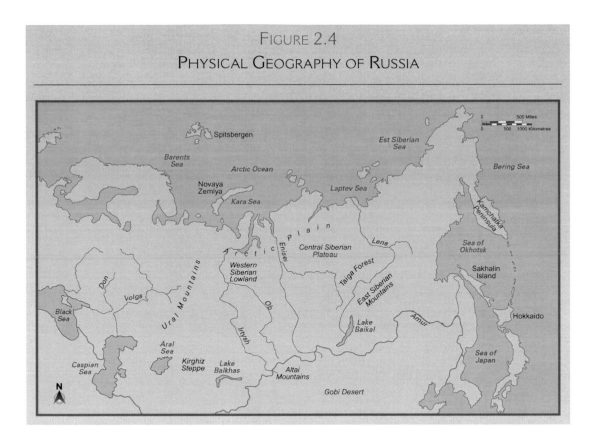

FIGURE 2.4

PHYSICAL GEOGRAPHY OF RUSSIA

the EU. Although Georgia and Ukraine have expressed ambitions to become closer to the EU in the long-term, they presently remain members of the CIS– primarily an economic union (similar to the North American Free Trade Agreement and the EU), which fosters tariff-free trade among member states and facilitates the movement of goods, services, capital and labor. The CIS can basically be divided into two major sub-regions: the Slavic language region, which lies west of the Ural Mountains, and is therefore part of the European continent, and the Turkic languages region that lies mostly to the east of the Urals.

This easternmost region is sometimes referred to as Eurasia, partly because in October 2000, the heads of Belarus, Kazakhstan, Kyrgyzstan, Russia and Tajikistan signed an agreement on the creation of a Eurasian Economic Community. Uzbekistan stated its intent to join in the future, while Armenia, Moldova and Ukraine presently have observer status. Although recognized in Europe, the term CIS has not gained popularity worldwide, and it is still too early to know whether this geographic term will become widespread.

The western portion of the CIS is closely related historically to Europe, although it also has had a history of closer relations with the countries and peoples of Central Asia than have other European countries. The countries that today comprise the European CIS include Belarus, Ukraine and Russia, the Romanian-speaking country of Moldova and the Transcaucasian countries of Georgia, Azerbaijan and Armenia, which have their own distinct ancient languages.

There are many Central Asian minority enclaves throughout the CIS region. The people in these ethnic enclaves settled many hundreds of years ago as part of migrations and invasions that have crossed the Russian lowlands from Central Asia, including Mongolia and Southwest Asia, including Iran (Persia) and Turkey. Further to the west, the European culture and history was closely tied to the seas and oceans through its many peninsulas, bays and rivers because of the opportunities this provided for trade. European influences here included Ancient Roman communities and, more significantly, substantial numbers of Viking communities from the Baltic through to the Black Sea. The CIS part of Europe, on the other hand, is far from large bodies of water, and is instead closely tied to the large Eurasian landmass, and the unique opportunities and challenges that this environment presents.

The European portion of the CIS covers half the land area of the continent of Europe, and a quarter of the land area of the former USSR. The country of Russia spans both this European section and extends far to the east beyond the Ural Mountains and all the way to the Pacific Ocean. Russia is the largest country in the world, covering 11 times zones, which is almost half of the 24 time zones that extend around the globe.

To the east are the Asian countries of the CIS. These include the Central Asian republics (or countries) of Kazakhstan, whose population is half Russian and half Kazakh, Uzbekistan, Turkmenistan, Kyrgyzstan and Tajikistan. (Mongolia and far western China's Xinjiang Province are sometimes considered part of Central Asia but will be discussed in the East Asia reading.) The culture, history and physical geography of Central Asia has much in common with that of the Middle East, with the major exceptions being a much colder winter climate and a long period of domination by Russia and the USSR.

Because the land area of the CIS is so massive, it is well endowed with a great diversity of natural resources. Its size, however, made integration difficult for the Soviet Union because transportation and communication networks were very expensive to build across such a vast territory. Another challenge for this region is that 80 percent of it lies further north than the Great Lakes of North America. St. Petersburg, formerly known as Leningrad, is about the same latitude as Anchorage, Alaska. Moscow is at the same latitude as Ketchikan, Alaska. Ukraine is at the same latitude as the United States-Canada border, while the Caucasus Mountains are about the same latitude as Chicago and New York. Russia also has a longer coastline than any other country in the world, and much of it is frozen and inaccessible in the winter months.

Landforms

The dominant landform in the CIS region is the Great Russian Lowland, which is an extension of the North European Plain. It extends across the eastern half of the former USSR and into the Western Siberian Lowland, which is a vast marsh and taiga forest area situated on the east of the Ural Mountains. The lowlands end at the Siberian Plateau, which is an area of rolling hills and permafrost soils. The northern half of the Russian lowland was covered by continental glaciers 10,000 years ago, as was most of Northern Europe and North America. These glaciers have left behind marsh lands and irregular river networks, along with a variety of moraines and other glacial deposition features across the northern lowlands of Russia.

Like Central Europe, the older mountains of the Urals and other smaller hills often are rich in mineral deposits. Just north of Ukraine is the world's largest mass of iron ore. Coal and peat are found throughout the Russian lowlands, which together with the iron ore formed the basis of the region's industrial core, centered on Ukraine and the Black Sea. Moscow is connected to this region through the Moscow Canal, which connects the Baltic Sea at St. Petersburg to Moscow and the Volga River, flowing south to the Caspian Sea. Other canals connect the Volga River to the Black Sea, which leads to the Mediterranean Sea. This region, extending from St. Petersburg, through Moscow, to Ukraine and the Volga River Valley, to the Caspian and Black Seas, is also the former USSR's breadbasket. It is a rich agricultural land, with mixed dairy, vegetables, grains and livestock.

The Ural Mountains are the only significant mountain range across the Great Russian Lowland. Although there are some smaller hill areas, such as the Ukrainian Uplands, the Central Russian Uplands, and the Volga Uplands, none of them is over 600 ft (180 m) in elevation. The highest peak in the Urals, by comparison, reaches 6184 ft (2080 m), though most far below 3000 ft (915 m). The Urals are similar in the age to the mountain ranges of central Europe (north of the Alps), as well as those of northern Scandinavia and the Appalachian Mountains in the United States. The Urals are also rich in iron ore, bauxite, which is used to make aluminum, asbestos, nickel, platinum, gold and a variety of other minerals. Large oil and coal fields lie to the east and west of the Urals, making this mountain system the most important industrial region in Russia.

Russia's Siberia

Siberia starts on the eastern side of the Ural Mountains with the West Siberian Plain. This plain is an extension of the Great Russian Lowland/North European Plain. It is flat, vast and covered with taiga forest. Russia's taiga forest is the largest continuous forest in the world, containing 20 percent of the world's timber. Much of the West Siberian Plain is completely uninhabited, and large parts are unexplored. North of the taiga forest, Siberia's landscape turns to one of desolate and barren tundra and permafrost.

About 1000 miles (1600 km) or more to the east of the Ural Mountains, the West Siberian Plain gives way to the Central Siberian Plateau. The Central Siberian Plateau extends another 1000–1500 miles (1600 to 2400 km) to the east where it gives way to Russia's Eastern Highlands, an area of Alpine orogeny. Both the Central Siberian Plateau and Eastern Highlands are predominantly permafrost regions, where much of the ground is frozen all year round underneath its surface. The permafrost is more extensive and continuous in the tundra areas in the northernmost areas of Siberia. Permafrost in many parts of Siberia (as well as Canada and Alaska) is starting to melt because of climate change, which makes travel increasingly more difficult as the hard permafrost is easier to travel on for vehicles or for the nomadic herders of the region.

Population centers and human activity in Siberia are concentrated along the Trans-Siberian Railway, which is one of the greatest railway adventures in the world, connecting Moscow to the city of Vladivostok on the Sea of Japan. The railway crosses Siberia's southernmost territories, which, east of the West Siberian Plain are quite mountainous along the borders with Mongolia and China. The Kamchatka Peninsula to the far east of Siberia is a spectacular highly volcanic and glaciated landscape.

There are 29 active volcanoes on the peninsula, including the Klychevskoy Volcano which is the highest volcano in Eurasia.

The climate of Siberia is continental in the extreme. Winters are long and cold. Summers are short and cool to hot. In the city of Verkhoyansk in eastern Siberia, the average winter temperature is −58°F (−50°C), while the average summer temperature is 60°F (−15.5°C). This difference of almost 120°F (65.5°C) from the winter average to the summer average is the greatest in the world. The coldest city temperature ever recorded in the world was also in Siberia, in the town of Bherkliask, which once reached −84°F (−64°C).

Siberia holds considerable opportunity for ecotourism development, although the costs of these experiences tend to be high owing to the region's remoteness and limited infrastructure. Wilderness (hiking and wildlife viewing), sporting activities (fishing and hunting) and arctic activities (dog and reindeer sledding and skiing) are the mainstay of the fledgling tourism industry in interior Siberia. Whale and other sea mammals, birds and volcanoes are attractions along coastal and island areas, especially on the Kamchatka Peninsula. Inuit and other nomadic peoples of the north comprise the cultural attraction of the area. Unfortunately, it is estimated that 10 percent of the wildlife in northern Eurasia (including Central Asia) is seriously in danger of extinction. The region is in need of more concerted conservation efforts, which ecotourism has some potential to facilitate.

Lake Baikal, Eurasia's largest freshwater lake and the world's deepest, is located in southern Siberia just north of Mongolia, and serves as a focus for the region's ecotourism because of its wildlife and accessible location on the Trans-Siberia railroad. Lake Baikal is 3.15 million hectares in size and is the oldest (25 million years) and deepest (5,580 ft; 1,700 m) freshwater lake in the world, containing 20 percent of the world's unfrozen fresh water. Although there is increasing concern over lake pollution from timber and paper mills, it still has very high scenic value and is home to many endemic species.

Economic Development

Although Siberia is very isolated and is sparsely populated it is currently undergoing substantial economic development as it holds major resources of oil, gas and other minerals as well as timber. The Sea of Okhotsk is also one of the richest fisheries in the world owing to its cold currents and extremely large tidal ranges, and produces over 10 percent of the world's annual fish catch, although fishing has actually declined since the collapse of the Soviet Union as has much of the manufacturing base that was moved there during the Soviet period to encourage regional development. Nevertheless, the development of the region's oil and gas fields has given parts of the region a major economic boost.

The physical landscape is also very important in providing the resources for developing tourism. Nowhere is this clearer than the Kamchatka Peninsula. Although the Peninsula has some mineral deposits as well as timber resources the landscape is increasingly being recognized as an important economic resource. The Peninsula is similar to Alaska in terms of its abundance of wildlife and nature, however only limited numbers of tourists currently visit there.

Much of the Peninsula is national park or reserve with a number of reserves being part of the Volcanoes of Kamchatka World Heritage Site, which is regarded as one of the most outstanding volcanic regions of the world. Because of the spectacular landscape the Peninsula is attractive for photography as well as ecotourism. Several of the national parks and reserves are also occupied by some of the local indigenous people who are developing commercial handicrafts as part of cultural tourism. The area also has many geysers and hot springs that feature strongly in the promotion of the area to travelers. As in Alaska the area is also becoming attractive for hunting and fishing tourism.

The Transcaucasus

In the southern part of the European portion of the CIS there are three mountain ranges: the eastern edge of the Carpathian Mountains (a small portion of which is in Ukraine), the Crimean Peninsula (a small mountain range extending out from the north shore of the Black Sea), and the Caucasus Mountains (situated between the Black Sea to the west and the Caspian Sea, which is one of the world's largest inland bodies of water, to the east). The Caucasus Mountains are a high Alpine system of recent geological origin that is rich in mineral resources and lush with semitropical vegetation (due to the neighboring seas) on its lower slopes. Over the past 400 years, this area has served as a shifting boundary between the Ottoman Empire, the Russian Empire/Soviet Union and the Persian Empire.

Because of the many different peoples who have passed through this area, some as conquerors and others as traders, the Transcaucasus (which refers to the mountains and the lowlands to their immediate north and south) is known as the *land of languages* because over 50 different languages and dialects are spoken in this small territory. The major languages are Azerbaijani (a Turkic language); Ossetian and Tatic (Persian-Iranian languages); Armenian (an ancient Indo-European language); the Caucasian languages of Georgian, Chechen, Dagestani, Abkhasian; pockets of Greek; and the Slavic languages of Russian and Ukrainian. On the northern side of the Caucasus are various regions belonging to Russia, including Dagestan, which has some 40 different ethnic groups, many with distinctive dialects.

The Russian territory of Chechnya has been the site of a bloody independence effort by the Muslim Chechens against the Russians for several years. On the southern slopes of the Caucasus range are the independent countries of Georgia, Armenia and Azerbaijan. Azerbaijan has assumed great economic importance in recent years because of its oil reserves, which it has been seeking to expand through an active drilling and exploration program in the Caspian Sea. However, some concerns deal with the potential pollution effects of oil exploitation as the Caspian Sea is already suffering from increased levels of industrial and agricultural pollutants and declines in fresh water entering the sea as a result of water diversion for irrigation schemes. Georgia has been developing strong ties with Western countries and is strategically important because it carries a major oil pipeline from the CIS countries.

The Western Caucasus of the Russian Federation is one of the few large mountain areas of Europe that has not been significantly impacted by humans with its alpine pastures only being grazed by wild animals. The park is also important as it has substantial areas of relatively undisturbed forest and is the home of the European bison (buffalo), which like the American buffalo once roamed over the plains and woodlands of Eastern Europe but is since limited to a small number of protected areas. This World Heritage wilderness area is increasingly attracting ecotourists located as it is only 30 miles (50 km) from the Black Sea. However, an important issue facing tourism development in the region is that many international tourists associate the political instability in the southern Caucasus with the Russian regions that are far more stable.

As already noted, Armenia, Georgia and Azerbaijan share the Caucasus region with Russia. During Soviet times, the region was an extremely favored domestic destination for Russians from the north, who could return home with boxes and suitcases stuffed with fresh fruits and vegetables that were difficult to acquire in other parts of the Soviet Union; the Caucasian republics were known as the fruit basket of the USSR. Today, the three countries boast some of Eurasia's most impressive mountain scenery, and all three are heavily dependent upon religious heritage in their tourist offerings. Armenia and Georgia are overwhelmingly Christian nations with most of their heritage focusing on ancient churches and cathedrals. Azerbaijan is a largely Muslim country, with its religious landscape comprised more of picturesque mosques and other Islamic features. Cuisine, wine, mountain scenery and village life are salient parts of the tourist product, although all three capital cities are important gateways into the region and centers for business tourism. Georgia boasts an affiliation with the ancient saga Jason and the Argonauts, and Azerbaijan boasts its position on the ancient Silk Route, which has become an important UNESCO-endorsed, multinational heritage corridor through Asia and the Middle East.

Other European Former Soviet Republics

As already noted, Moldova is a Romanian-speaking nation, located just east of Romania. Following its departure from the USSR, a referendum was held in Romania to determine if it should absorb Moldova into its territory, given their common heritage and linguistic roots. The result was no, owing partly to the financial and social burden on Romania to upgrade Moldova's infrastructure, economy, social system, education system and health care scheme to meet national standards. Similar problems were encountered by West Germany regarding East Germany when the two states were reunited in 1990. Tourism in Moldova is limited but growing and focuses mainly on rural landscapes, including scenic villages and inexpensive wines.

Moldova is struggling economically but surviving in its new capitalist environment. However, even this relatively small country is experiencing some political conflict. The thin wedge of territory between the Dniester River and the border of Ukraine declared independence from Moldova with support from Russia when the USSR dissolved. The territory, known as Transdniestria or Transnistria (although its self-appointed name is Pridnestrovie), has close relations with Russia and a largely Russian and Ukrainian population. It has established its own government offices, customs and immigration, money, and trade relations with Ukraine and Russia. While it is not recognized by the international community as a sovereign nation, it has become a tourist curiosity, even though visas are sometimes difficult to acquire.

At the time of USSR disintegration, Belarus (White Russia) achieved independence as one of 15 equal Soviet republics. However, it is unique in the sense that this was not the country's desire. Following economic and political turmoil in the earliest days of independence, Belarus desired to be united with Russia, which never came to fruition. Today, Belarus is functioning now independently and has some interest in tourism, although there are influential factions in the country that are trying dissuade tourism development.

Ukraine has become a fashionable tourist destination for personal heritage tourists, because of the widespread Ukrainian diaspora throughout the world, with one of the largest communities being in Canada. Ukraine's tourism promotional efforts spotlight this form of *roots tourism*, wherein people of Ukrainian descent travel to their homeland to do genealogy, meet relatives and see native villages. Like Russia, Ukraine is a large country with an array of natural and cultural environments that exude tourist appeal. Wildlife viewing, mountain trekking and visiting national parks are important elements of tourism, as are golf courses, health spas, Black Sea resorts, religious sites and historic castles. Ukraine also has a thriving *mail-order* bride business, where men from Western Europe, the Americas, Asia, Australia and New Zealand travel to find (i.e., purchase) wives.

TOURISM ISSUES AND INSIGHTS
SIBERIA AND ASIA'S MONSOON CLIMATE

There are no moderating marine air influences in Siberia, which makes it, along with Central Asia, much drier than areas closer to Europe. Because land masses heat much more quickly than water, Siberia is dominated in winter by a high air pressure system and in summer by a low air pressure system. The summer low is caused by the rapid heating of the ground and the rising of air into the upper atmosphere. The winter high is created by the cooling of the ground, and the subsequent descending of air from the upper atmosphere.

High pressure systems are always caused by air that is descending from the upper atmosphere to the ground. Usually this air is very dry, which is why high pressure systems are associated with clear skies. Conversely, low pressure occurs when air near the ground rises up into the upper atmosphere. If a large source of water is available, this will bring moisture into the upper atmosphere, causing clouds to form, which can then bring precipitation (rain or snow). Another feature of low air pressure and high air pressure is that their winds move in opposite directions. The low pressure winds circulate around the center of low pressure in a counterclockwise direction. High pressure winds circulate in a clockwise direction. Because the *Siberian High* in winter and the *Siberian Low* in summer are so intense, they affect the direction of wind patterns for the entire continent of Asia. In the summer the Siberian Low circulates in a counterclockwise direction pushing air off the Asian landmass, across the Indian Ocean toward India and Southeast Asia, across the South China Sea, and up toward Japan. In the winter months, the Siberian high circulates in a clockwise direction, pushing extremely cold air from Siberia down across northern China and into Japan, and circulating winds from the South China Sea across Southeast Asia and across the Indian Ocean toward India and Southwest Asia. This change in wind direction is known as a *monsoon* wind pattern: with a *summer monsoon* coming from one direction, and a *winter monsoon* coming from an opposite direction. Because the summer monsoon is so pronounced when it arrives in India and Southeast Asia, most people refer to the summer monsoon simply as *the monsoon*.

	Population 2006 (1,000)	World population share 2006 (%)	International tourist arrivals (1,000)		Change since 1990 (%)	World market share 2004 (%)
			1990*	2004		
WORLD	**6,525,170**	**100.0**	**436,757**	**776,837**	**77.9**	**100.0**
Europe and Eurasia	**737,666**	**11.3**	**257,964**	**410,718**	**59.2**	**52.9**
Nordic Europe	24,891	0.4	9,945	14,934	50.2	1.9
Northern Europe	190,189	2.9	77,563	98,379	26.8	12.7
Southern Europe	152,098	2.3	132,907	204,901	54.2	26.4
*Eastern Europe-Eurasia**	370,487	5.7	37,549	92,504	146.4	11.9
Top10 Destination Countries						
1 France	60,876	0.9	52,497	75,121	43.1	9.7
2 Spain	40,398	0.6	34,085	52,430	53.8	6.7
3 Italy	58,134	0.9	26,679	37,071	39.0	4.8
4 United Kingdom	60,609	0.9	18,013	27,754	54.1	3.6
5 Germany	82,422	1.3	17,045	20,137	18.1	2.6
6 Russian Federation*	142,894	2.2	2,000	19,892	894.6	2.6
7 Austria	8,193	0.1	19,011	19,373	1.9	2.5
8 Poland	38,537	0.6	19,215	14,290	−25.6	1.8
9 Greece	10,688	0.2	8,873	13,313	50.0	1.7
10 Hungary*	9,981	0.2	2,000	12,212	510.6	1.6

*International Tourist Arrivals: Eastern Europe-Eurasia 1995 instead of 1990; Russian Federation estimated from Soviet Union for 1990; Hungary estimated for 1990

Sources: World Tourism Organization (UNWTO), 2007, Facts and Figures; GeoHive. 2007, The population of continents, regions and
countries (2006–07–01), http://www.xist.org/earth/pop_regions.aspx

Note: All Photos without a Source listed are from iStockphoto.com

3

THE OLD WORLD: CENTRAL ASIA THROUGH AFRICA

3.1. Central Asia

3.2. Southwest Asia and North Africa

3.3. Sub-Saharan Africa

This section covers a vast territory that we call the *Old World*. It extends from Central Asia, through Southwest Asia (also known as the Middle East), across North Africa, and across the Sahara Desert to Sub-Saharan Africa. We call this the Old World because it includes the political and culture hearth of some of the greatest empires of Eurasia (the Mongol Empire, Arab Empire and Ottoman Empire, among others), as well as the probable source of modern humans (in Africa). Africa, overall, is geologically the oldest continent and over 200 million years ago was at the center of the Pangaea supercontinent. The area north of the Sahara Desert (from North Africa to Central Asia), in particular, share many characteristics, including history, the Islamic religion, and largely arid environments. As noted in Section 1, the term *Old World* as used in this book differs from standard usage which refers to the Eastern Hemisphere and includes all of Europe and Asia, in addition to Africa.

PHOTO 3.1
Africa and Southwest Asia from space

Today, the Old World is rich in physical, cultural and historical landscapes, though much of the region's recent emergence from dominance by European powers has resulted in political turmoil and limited tourism development. Ecotourism and heritage tourism, based on archeological areas, have great potential in almost every corner of the Old World. International tourist arrivals are relatively low throughout the Old World, though year-on-year growth rates have been higher than the global average in recent years. This is despite wars and political turmoil that stand in the way of tourism development in many corners of this vast region. There also remains a great need to increase environmental awareness and to address major environmental problems, which is especially challenging in more impoverished countries. As these issues are addressed, the Old World of Central Asia, Southwest Asia, North Africa and Sub-Saharan Africa could blossom as major international tourism destinations.

3.1 CENTRAL ASIA

Central Asia includes the countries of Afghanistan, Kazakhstan, Kyrgyzstan, Tajikistan, Turkmenistan, and Uzbekistan. The suffix -*stan* means *land*, so these are

FIGURE 3.1
REGIONS AND SUBREGIONS OF THE OLD WORLD

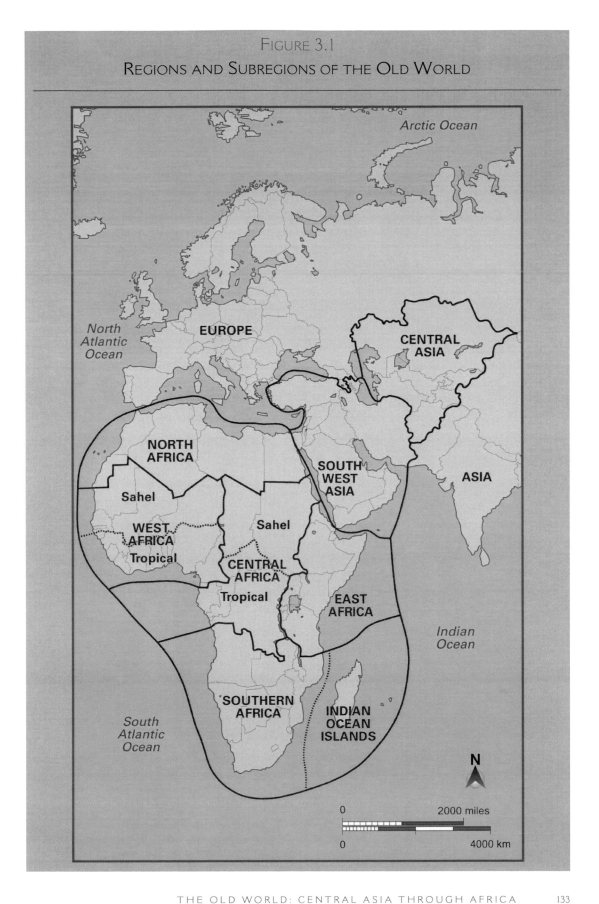

the land of the Afghans, the land of the Kazaks, the land of the Kyrgyz, and so on. Central Asia was formerly known as Soviet Central Asia. It is a predominantly Turkic-speaking Muslim cultural region, with large minority Russian populations in some locations. Its population is the fastest growing among the territories that were once part of the Soviet Union and today is sometimes referred to as the Commonwealth of Independent States (CIS). Central Asia has a mostly arid climate, though rivers from its high mountain areas allow for irrigated agriculture. Ethnic tensions have also been significant in Central Asia, mostly in the form of anti-Russian sentiments following many years of Soviet efforts to *Russify* the region (to make it *Russian*).

Physical Geography

Central Asia's physical landscape can basically be divided into two subregions: (1) the high mountain areas in its southeast, where Central Asia meets the Tibetan Plateau and (2) the flat plains surrounding the Aral and Caspian Seas in the south and west of the region. The two mountain countries of Central Asia are Tajikistan and Kyrgyzstan. Tajikistan is the home of the Pamir Mountains (bordering India and Pakistan) and has Central Asia's highest mountain peaks, reaching over 23,000 ft/7,000 m in elevation in the *Pamir Knot* (also known as the *Roof of Asia*). These mountains are a major tourist attraction, though political instability and intense winter blizzards, which can last for days, make travel to them extremely challenging.

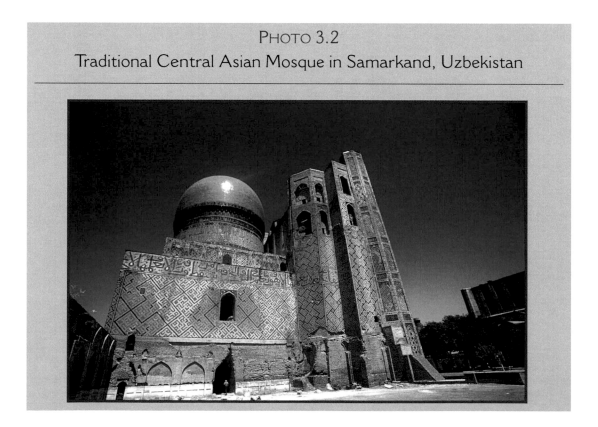

PHOTO 3.2
Traditional Central Asian Mosque in Samarkand, Uzbekistan

Photo 3.3
Trekking in the Pamir range in Tajikistan

Photo 3.4

Playing "Buzkashi" in Kyrgyzstan. Buzkashi is played on horseback throughout the steppes of Central Asia. The general objective is to successfully carry a goat or calf carcass across a goal line

Kyrgyzstan is north of Tajikistan and includes the somewhat lower Tian Shan mountain range, which borders China. The Tian Shan range is a major potential tourism area for both Kyrgyzstan and China and is easier to access for tourists owing to the relatively greater degree of political stability in Kyrgyzstan. The Ala–Archa Canyon is a national nature park not far from the Kyrgyz capital of Bishkek, where numerous trekking trails lead visitors to glaciers on the country's highest peaks. Kyrgyzstan's Issyk Kul Lake is the second largest mountain lake in the world (after Lake Titicaca in the Andes Mountains of South America). Surrounded by snow-capped peaks, it was a major resort destination during the Soviet era and is a growing tourism spot today. Both Tajikistan and Kyrgyzstan have rolling hills and some lower lying plains in their western portions that border the other countries of Central Asia.

Kazakstan, Uzbekistan and Turkmenistan encompass the lower plains that comprise most of the Central Asia region. Kazakhstan is the ninth largest country in the world in land area. The country slopes from its higher mountains in the east, through rolling hills, to vast sand deserts and marshes in its western and southern portions. Uzbekistan and Turkmenistan similarly slope toward lower lying areas in their western reaches as they approach the Caspian Sea. The Caspian Sea and the Aral Sea are both *internal drainage systems*, meaning that while rivers flows into them, they do not flow to an ocean. They were once much larger than they are today but have shrunk considerably over time because of the arid climate and diversion of water for agricultural irrigation. In the case of the Aral Sea, the water has become so salty that the former freshwater fish varieties have now been replaced by saltwater fish.

The northern portions of Central Asia reach toward Siberia and the very center of the Asian continent, and therefore experience the extremes of summer heat and winter cold, though not as extreme as Siberia to the north. Arid conditions are most prominent in the southern lowland areas, with higher precipitation in the mountains in northern Kazakstan, which borders Siberia. Even with the high eastern mountains, virtually the entire region of Central Asia receives less than 20 inches 51 cm of rainfall each year, creating grassland, desert and drought conditions. The arid climate creates highly sensitive aquatic ecosystems in all of the seas and lakes of Central Asia, the largest of which are the Black Sea, the Caspian Sea, and the Ural Sea. These water bodies concentrate drainage from their surrounding watershed and serve as sensitive measures of regional environmental degradation. Most all of them are severely polluted, though concerted international efforts in the 1990s to address these problems have helped to some degree. Ecotourism offers an alternative to the large-scale and heavy industries that have caused this widespread damage.

The intersection of desert, grasslands and mountains also creates a rich diversity of ecosystems that attract hunters and fishers, though some argue that they are starting to threaten some of the region's endangered large game. Migratory bird watching on wetland areas between the sand dunes and drier plains are a major niche tourist attraction in the lowland areas of Central Asia. However, the greater difference between summer and winter temperatures in lowland Central Asia results in large numbers of summer insects, which can be a major distraction for visitors. Because of their location on the former edge of a vast Jurassic sea, the southeastern mountains of Turkmenistan and Uzbekistan have some outstanding dinosaur sites, including the Kugitang Reserve, located on the Turkmen side of their shared border.

FIGURE 3.2

CENTRAL AND SOUTHWEST ASIA PHYSICAL GEOGRAPHY

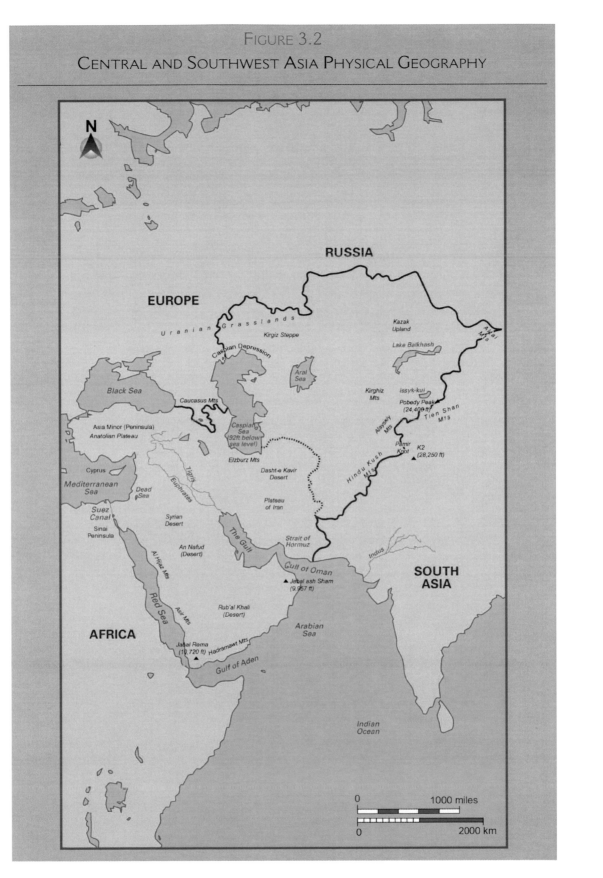

Human Geography

Central Asia shares many characteristics in common with Southwest Asia (also known as the Middle East) and North Africa. All three have low overall population densities, although higher density centers do exist. All three have mostly arid grassland and desert climates. Most of the people of all three regions share Islamic religious beliefs, and historical ties that involve the Arab and Ottoman Empires. The major difference of Central Asia is that it has much colder winter temperatures and a recent history of being part of the USSR.

Central Asian Empires

What we see today in the former Soviet Socialist Republics of Central Asia is the result of the disintegration of one of the world's last great empires. An *empire* is a group of countries and nations ruled by a single supreme authority. This is very different from the nation-state concept, which was a formative historical feature of Europe (Chapter 1). Some of the world's major empires originated in Central Asia, including that of the Huns from the northern portion of the region, whose empire was concurrent with that of the Romans. The Huns attacked China in the 4th century BCE, and conquered the Volga region, including Moscow, in the 4th century CE. Under their leader, Attila, the Huns ransacked Roman Italy in the 5th century CE, marking the final end of the Roman Empire. Genghis Kahn, from Mongolia, unified the Central Asian lands around 1200 CE. The Mongol Empire expanded to control most of Asia and Eastern Europe by 1260 CE. (This was the same time that the European Renaissance was beginning in Southern Europe.) In Europe the Mongols were known as the Tartars; they ruled the European portions of their empire from the Moscow area. In the late 14th century, they were removed from power in China; in 1401, they were removed from the Moscow area, and by the mid-15th century they were completely removed from Russia.

The Silk Road

The Silk Road actually is comprised of many different routes that connected the Chinese city of Chang'an (modern day Xi'an) to cultures of Asia Minor and the Mediterranean Sea. Although there is evidence of ancient Egyptian trade with Southwest Asia, and probably Central Asia as early as 4000 BCE, the earliest Mediterranean connections to China are found in jade dating back to about 1500 BCE. Evidence of Chinese silk in Egypt dates back to approximately 1000 BCE. Some silk trade may have existed earlier than that, but its evidence has completely decomposed over time. The Greek conqueror Alexander the Great is credited with opening the silk route as the major historical trading route that it came to be, starting in the 4th century BCE. China's Han Dynasty greatly expanded trade along the route in the 2nd century BCE, after which the Romans came to develop a near-insatiable desire for Asian goods, especially silk, which resulted in a considerable flow of gold to China and the establishment of a Roman Embassy in Chang'an in 166 CE. Although disrupted by the rise of the Turkish Empire in Southwest Asia, the Silk Road trade routes were re-established under the Mongol Empire (13th to 14th c. CE) and finally declined at the end of the 14th century when sea routes came to dominate trade between the East and West. Today, the Silk Road is promoted as a major tourist attraction, though its isolation and limited infrastructure make traveling there a challenge without a well organized tour group.

Ancient cities of Central Asia still maintain a strong sense of cultural continuity with the past. Herat, Afghanistan, whose citadel was built by Alexander the Great, and the Silk Road city of Merv in Turkmenistan (reputed to have been the largest city in the world in the 12th century) are two examples. Magnificent buildings are found in the Central Asian countries from the pre-European era, many of which were built by Timur (known as *Tamerlane* in Europe), who conquered much of Central Asia (including the Mongols) in the 14th century, establishing the Timurid Empire (1370–1405). His empire was centered in Uzbekistan and covered all of Central Asia, plus large parts of Southwest Asia (southeast Turkey, Syria, Iraq, Kuwait, Iran, Azerbaijan, Georgia) and South Asia (Pakistan and India). His dynasty lasted in some form until 1859. Among the well preserved buildings that date back to Timur's influence are the magnificent Hodja Akmed Yassavi Mausoleum in Jabagly, Kazakhstan, and Registan Square, which was the center of old Samarkand in Uzbekistan.

European Empires

The mid-15 century was the beginning of the age of European exploration, discovery and colonization. This era started with the Portuguese sailing to Africa and Asia, and the Spanish, who focused on the Americas following the explorations of Christopher Columbus in 1492. The Dutch soon followed, settling in South Africa and colonizing Indonesia, along with the British, who moved into Africa, India and North America, and the French, who colonized areas of Africa and Indochina (in Southeast Asia). At the same time the Russian Empire began expanding eastward and westward. The Russian push was led by Muscovite armies after Russian independence from the Mongols in 1401. By 1815 the Muscovite Russian armies had controlled all of the territory in Eastern Europe and Central Asia that would later become the republics of the USSR, and other areas that did not become part of the Soviet Union, including Poland, Finland and Alaska.

In the late 1800s, the Russian Empire was a largely rural, agrarian society. The lands east of the Urals, including Central Asia, had very low population densities, and few Europeans considered the Russian Empire to be a major threat. In 1917, however, a revolution occurred in Russia that overthrew the Czar (Russian emperor). In the confusion that followed, several territories of the old Russian Empire broke away, including the Transcaucasus countries of Georgia, Armenia, and Azerbaijan; the Baltic states Estonia, Latvia, and Lithuania; and Belarus, Ukraine, Moldova, Poland and Finland. The United States had already purchased Alaska from Russia in 1867.

World War II marked the last great push for imperial expansion by the European powers, who now were joined by Germany in Africa, the United States in Asia and the Caribbean, and Japan, which sought control over most of East Asia. By the end of World War II, all of the old Russian Empire, except for Poland, Finland and Alaska, was retaken by the new Russian/Soviet leadership and integrated into the USSR. In addition, the countries of Eastern Europe, from Poland to Yugoslavia, fell within the sphere of Russian/Soviet political domination.

FIGURE 3.3

COUNTRIES, CAPITALS AND MAJOR CITIES OF CENTRAL AND SOUTHWEST ASIA

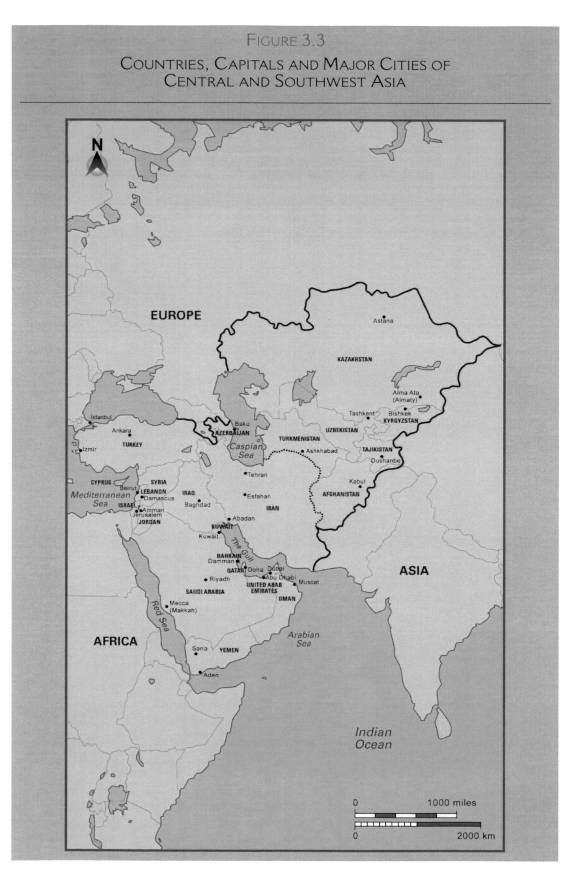

The End of the Empires

Most of the European empires dissolved in the decades following World War II. India and Pakistan gained independence in 1949; in the 1950s, the Philippines, Indonesia and Indochina (Vietnam, Laos and Cambodia) gained independence, along with some African countries. In the 1960s and 1970s most of the remaining African colonies gained their independence. However, it was not until the end of the 1980s and the beginning of the 1990s that the Russian Empire/USSR finally dissolved (being replaced by the decentralized and somewhat smaller CIS organization).

The Central Asian republics have had significant growing pains in establishing legitimate political rule and economic stability following their independence from the Soviet Union in the early 1990s, though their remote locations and poor transportation infrastructure may be even greater barriers for international visitors. Every country in the region has politically sensitive areas, and these issues need to be kept in mind in any discussion of tourism resources in Central and Southwest Asia. The two mountain countries represent two extremes of post-Soviet Central Asia. Despite similar physical geography features, Tajikistan has suffered through civil war for most of the 1990s, resulting in tens of thousands of deaths and hundreds of thousands of refugees. On the other hand, Kyrgyzstan is the most democratic and stable of the Central Asian countries (Figure 3.3).

Afghanistan

In the past, Afghanistan has been included in the South Asia region, mostly because it was not part of the former Soviet Union. Today, however, it is usually included in Central Asia because of its common cultural and environmental characteristics. Like its two northern neighbors, Tajikistan and Kyrgyzstan, Afghanistan is a largely mountains country in its eastern portions, with lower lands in its western and southern portions. The major mountain range in Afghanistan is the Hindu Kush, which is a southern extension of the Pamir Knot, and a western extension of the Himalaya Range. The Hindu Kush region is easily accessible from nearby Pakistan, from which adventure travel into the region often originated prior to the Soviet Union's disastrous invasion of Afghanistan in the 1980s. The famed Panjshir Valley was known for its lush vegetation and hospitable population (the Panjshiris), but has also been a major military battlefield in the war against the Soviet Armies.

In 1978, the communist party of Afghanistan (People's Democratic Party of Afghanistan) took control of the government in Kabul, but there were two or three major factions within the party, each with its own goals for the future of the country. The Soviet Union staunchly supported the new communist country, but concerns about how matters were being handled by the faction in power led to the invasion of Afghanistan by the Soviet military in December 1979. While the Soviet forces never controlled most of the country, they did control the puppet government in Kabul. For 10 years, until its withdrawal in 1989, the Soviet Union fought against various rebel forces that resided in the mountainous north and other isolated parts of the country that did not support the communist government. After the USSR withdrew from Afghanistan in 1989, the country fell into civil war leading to the collapse of the communist government in 1992. The Taliban was one of these factions opposing the government in Kabul. The Taliban were a fundamentalist Muslim group that severely forced religious piety and the inferior role of women in society. In 1996, they seized power in Kabul and effectively controlled most of Afghanistan until the United States invasion of 2001 when the regime was overthrown for supporting the Al-Qaida terrorist network within its borders.

Given its history of war and otherwise political instability, many observers have questioned whether or not tourism could ever be established in Afghanistan. This is particularly the case today. As of early 2008, foreign military troops were still stationed there in search of Osama Bin-Laden and other terrorists who were reportedly living in the rugged mountains along the border with Pakistan. As of early 2008, military conflicts were still occurring in parts of Afghanistan, and most governments had issued warnings against their citizens traveling to the country.

During the 1970s, Afghanistan received approximately 90,000 foreign visitors each year, and tourism was considered one of the most important foreign exchange earners. Tourists visited primarily because of the country's wealth of natural and cultural attractions, including rugged mountains, valleys, ancient cities, and ancient Buddhist cultural sites. Early in the 21st century (2005–2007), Kabul's international airport was receiving international flights from Europe and other parts of Asia, and there was a revival in tourist demand among the more adventurous and intrepid travelers. Several tour companies have recently begun to offer adventure tours to Afghanistan. New hotels are being built and foreign investment, particularly by expatriate Afghanis, is being routed into (re)developing the country's utility and tourism infrastructure. Afghanistan's domestic tourism is growing as well, as middle and upper-class Afghanis and foreign aid workers from the cities spend their weekends in places such as the lakes of Band-e Amir and the cultural sites of Bamyam. In 2005, the government appointed its first tourism minister since the United States invasion to promote Afghanistan as an emerging tourist destination, emphasizing the country's mountains and opportunities for skiing and trekking, as well as heritage sites. There are even plans to establish a tourist destination at Tora Bora, near Osama Bin-Laden's

TOURISM ISSUES AND INSIGHTS
LONELY PLANET AFGHANISTAN

Lonely Planet is one of the most influential guidebooks in the world. In 2007, the Lonely Planet Library added Afghanistan to its list for the first time. Does this signal a renaissance of tourism in the country and acceptability of travel to and within Afghanistan or does it constitute a form of extreme adventure tourism? Arguably tourists are now returning to several parts of Afghanistan anyway, while the country is also host to a number of foreign aid workers, contractors and military personnel on the ground already who would probably appreciate guidance on things to do and see when they are off-duty. Such activities may also help bring income to some business people and communities while the information may also help cultural sensitivities.

Nevertheless, the guidebook does urge caution and discretion. There is a whole section on safety, and risk assessments on each region at the start of the relevant chapter. For example, the message regarding the south is basically you should not go there, although the guide is more positive about traveling to Pakistan on the historic route through Jalalabad and the Khyber Pass. A point of debate therefore is whether the publication of a guide will encourage people to travel there or will it be used more for armchair travel?

TOURISM ISSUES AND INSIGHTS
IS ANY PUBLICITY GOOD PUBLICITY – THE CASE OF KAZAKHSTAN?

The Republic of Kazakhstan covers an area of central Asia the same size as Western Europe, making it the ninth largest country in the world. Its population of 15.3 million is 60% Kazakh, 25% Russian, with smaller proportions of Ukrainians, Uzbekis and Germans. The name of the capital, Astana, literally means *capital!*, although the largest city is Almaty which is the commercial center and is regarded as one of the most cosmopolitan cities in Central Asia. Kazakhstan declared independence from the Soviet Union on December 16, 1991, and was the last of the Soviet republics to declare independence. The president and head of state, Nursultan Nazarbayev, has been in power since independence. The elections in 1999, 2004 and 2005 fell short of international standards according to the Organisation for Security and Co-operation in Europe and intimidation and suppression of political opponents is common. The country also has substantial environmental problems ranging from Soviet nuclear testing, industrial dereliction, and the ecological disaster of the Aral Sea, sometimes regarded as the greatest man-made disaster in the world, where water diverted for irrigation for cotton has shrunk the lake and poisoned the land and people with salt.

However, Kazakhstan is undergoing substantial economic development because of its enormous oil and gas reserves. The government is also hoping to promote tourism to the region primarily focussed on cultural and natural heritage attractions as well as coastal resorts on the Caspian Sea. Unfortunately, although the country has become better known in the west in terms of name as a result of Sacha Baron Cohens' film *Borat* (sub-title: *Cultural Learnings of America for Make Benefit Glorious Nation of Kazakhstan*), a mockumentary about a fictional Kazakh television journalist character who visits the United States of America in a cheap suit and a bad mustache. The film was designed as much as a satirical perspective of American life, particularly with respect to anti-semitism (Cohen is a Jew who is a grandchild of a holocaust survivor), as it was of Kazakhstan. Unfortunately, members of both countries failed to see the comic value of such satire.

The Kazakhstan Government were unhappy about the image it portrayed of their country and culture and first tried to sue Cohen and then hired a public relations firm to launch a debunking marketing offensive, including a four-page advertisement in the *New York Times*, both of which failed and instead gave even more publicity to the film and the character. The satirical Barat character had actually been on British television since the mid-1990s but it was the success of the film that led to expressions of concern from the Kazakhstan Foreign Ministry and other members of the government. The film has been banned in Russia and Kazakhstan and the domain name www.borat.kz was suspended in December 2005. The 2006 United States State Department annual human rights report cited the loss of the .kz website as evidence of the Kazakh government's efforts to curb free speech. Although actually filmed in Romania the film has nevertheless increased awareness of Kazakhstan in the travel marketplace. For example, since the release of the movie the respected British newspaper *The Guardian* has provided several stories on the country (which are generally positive) and not on any of the other central Asian republics.

The Kazakhstan government reportedly invested $40 million in the production of the film Nomad, a historical epic set in 18th century Kazakhstan, where a young boy is destined to unite the country's three warring tribes and free them from the Dzungars a confederation of West Mongolian tribes. The Kazakh language film premiered in 2005 and the English language version was released in the United States of America in 2007. Unfortunately, the film was not a box-office success.

old headquarters. There are still legitimate concerns about landmines, rival mountain rebels, and roadside banditry, but the new Ministry of Tourism is attempting to alleviate people's fears by providing armed escorts for tours.

3.2   SOUTHWEST ASIA AND NORTH AFRICA

The cultural and geological diversity of Southwest Asia and North Africa (and to a lesser degree colonialism) has created more countries in this region than any other part of Asia. Geographically (based on culture and landforms), Southwest Asia can be divided into two major subregions. To the south is the Arabian Peninsula, home of the world's largest true desert and includes the countries of Kuwait, Saudi Arabia, Bahrain, Qatar, United Arab Emirates, Oman and Yemen. Syria, Lebanon, Israel, Jordan, and Iraq are in a geographical transition zone between the Arabian Peninsula to the south, the mediterranean sea to the west, and mountains to the north. The northern part of Southwest Asia (from Asia Minor to Central Asia) is a highland region and includes the countries of Turkey, Azerbaijan and Iran. Cyprus, Armenia and Georgia are sometimes included in the highland Southwest Asia region, though they are also sometimes included in Europe owing to cultural similarities; this book discusses them in the European context.

Algeria, Egypt, Libya, Morocco and Tunisia constitute North Africa. Western Sahara is a stateless territory administered by Morocco, while Sudan shares the Nile River with Egypt. Both of these countries are sometimes included in North Africa, though in this section only Western Sahara is included in North Africa, while Sudan is placed in the Central Africa region of Sub-Saharan Africa. Egypt is sometimes included in Southwest Asia because of its close physical and historical ties to the Arabian Peninsula, though we place it in North Africa in this book based on its geographical location.

The Middle East

Southwest Asia and North Africa are often referred to as the *Middle East*. The term Middle East was first used to define Southwest Asia by the British India Office in the 1850s, and basically referred to the region east the Ottman Empire (today's country of Turkey, was the *Near East*) and centered on the Persian Gulf. This definition, however, was widely criticized for its geographical innacuracy, and later for its Eurocentrism. Until World War II, there continued to be confusion over the use of Near East and Middle East to refer to Southwest Asia, though it was well established that China and Southeast Asia were the *Far East*. In the decades after World War II, however, the term Near East has been largely dropped from popular use (it is still used by historians and archeologists), and Middle East has come into common acceptance. (The United States government, for example, first used the term in an official document in 1957.)

Despite its wide acceptance by news media organizations, the term Middle East is still not clearly defined. Most of the time it refers to the countries of the Arabian Peninsula, plus Turkey and Iran to the north, and Egypt across the Red Sea. However, it can include Afghanistan and Pakistan (which are placed in Central Asia and South

PHOTO 3.5

The Sphinx and Pyramid of Khafre, Giza, Egypt

Photo 3.6

Cairo, Egypt, from the Ibn Tulun Mosque Minaret. With a population of close to 16 million people, Cairo is the largest city on the African Continent

Asia, respectively, in this book), and the remaining countries of North Africa, west of Egypt. The Muslim countries in the Horn of Africa (Ethiopia, Eritrea, Djibouti and Somalia) and the country of Sudan are sometimes included as part of the Middle East, but more frequently are considered to be Sub-Saharan Africa. In other definitions

PHOTO 3.7

Inside the Grand Bazaar in Istanbul, Turkey. Dating back to the mid-15th century, the Grand Bazaar contains some 4000 shops and 58 covered walkways, making it one of the world's largest and oldest shopping centers

the Maghreb Region, comprising the northwest part of the African continent (i.e., Morocco, Algeria, Tunisia, and sometimes Libya and Mauritania), is not included in the definition of Middle East. Because of this confusion, this book refers to the more accurate geographic concepts of Southwest Asia and North Africa.

PHOTO 3.8

Istanbul, Turkey, strides both Europe and Asia. The Hagia Sophia (left) and the Blue Mosque (right) are in the European part of the city. The Bosporus Strait and Asia are in the distance

PHOTO 3.9

Petra in Jordan, one of the New Seven Wonders of the world, is famous for its 2000 year old cave facades

PHOTO 3.10

Expansive sand seas are common throughout the
Arabian Peninsula and Northern Africa

Source: Jarkko Saarninen

Physical Geography of Southwest Asia and North Africa

Geologically, Southwest Asia is a region of considerable tectonic (earthquake) activity. This is where the African and Eurasian continents collide, creating Alpine orogeny mountain systems. These include the Atlas Mountains in Northwest Africa, Asia Minor and the Caucasus Mountains, the Zagros Mountains of Iran, and the Hindu Kush Range, which branches out from the Pamirs and into Afghanistan. (The Himalaya, the Rocky Mountains, the Andes, and the Alps are also part of the Alpine Orogeny, or period of mountain building.) These high mountain ranges provide sources of water in an otherwise very dry region. The active continental movement in this zone results in frequent earthquakes that occasionally cause major damage to human settlements. In 2003, a very large earthquake occurred in the ancient city of Bam, Iran, killing 27,000 people and destroying some 75% of the city's buildings, including its ancient and imposing mud-citadel (said to be the largest adobe building in the world). The damage caused by the 2003 earthquake in Bam meant that the internationally culturally significant parts of the city were placed onto the World Heritage in Danger List. However, there has been an international effort to try and repair as much as possible the damage that was caused to Bam by the earthquake. Bam, the site of an oasis in the desert of the Iranian high plateau, dates to the 6th century BCE; however, between the 7th and 11th centuries Bam's fortified settlement and citadel (Arg) were developed as the city was at the crossroads of silk and cotton trade routes. The citadel contains 38 watchtowers, government quarters, and an historic town with one of the oldest mosques in Iran dating from the 8th to 9th century CE. The modern city of Bam surrounds the old town and citadel.

South of the mountain regions of Southwest Asia are large areas of land that were formerly under water. The Persian (or Arabian) Gulf is a remnant of one of these large seas. The North Africa plain, east of the Atlas Mountains, was similarly once submerged. As old shallow seas, these areas were rich in sea life and vegetation, which over time have been transformed into oil and natural gas. The sand covered flat lands of Southwest Asia and North Africa are estimated to contain two-thirds of the world's oil reserves, and are of strategic global geopolitical importance. The modern economies of some areas, especially on the Arabian Peninsula, have been transformed by the region's oil and gas wealth. Although some oil fields were initially drilled by British and American oil companies in the first half of the 20th century, it was the development of oil by companies owned by the countries in the region in the 1960s and 1970s that provided both the basis for rapid economic expansion in the region, as well as changes in the world's geopolitical balance. These were both caused by the dependence of western developed countries on the region's oil. While the oil economy has provided the basis for the development of petrochemical industries, the countries of the region have been diversifying their economic base, with tourism being a major target industry. In addition, a number of Gulf countries such as the United Arab Emirates (UAE) and Qatar, have developed substantial airlines and airline infrastructure in an attempt to position themselves as global transport, business, tourism and leisure hubs.

The land area in this southern part of the Middle East and North Africa is comprised of massive platforms (known as massifs) of extremely ancient rock. The rock underlying these areas is amongst the oldest in the world, and was part of the core of Pangaea, the ancient supercontinent that comprised all the continents we know today. The Arabian Peninsula is one large massif tilted upward on its western side, where its higher mountains are located, and downward on its eastern side, sloping into the Persian Gulf. (The country of India has a similar geologic structure that is tilted in the same way.) The continent of Africa and the Arabian Peninsula massif are separated by the Red Sea but were once a single geologic structure. However, the movement of molten magma deep inside the earth caused the surface to crack along the Red Sea, the Gulf of Aden, and the Great Rift Valley in eastern Africa, all of which today are slowly widening and pushing their adjacent land areas apart from one another.

These flat land areas are covered by the large *sand seas* of the Sahara Desert and Arabian Peninsula. Together this sea of sand extends 5000 miles (8050 km) from east to west. It was formed by the erosion of the underlying rock by wind, water and time. The area has very little cloud cover, causing extremes of daytime heat and nighttime cold. The Rub' al Khali (*Empty Quarter*) covers much of the Arabian Peninsula and is the largest true desert in the world. A true desert is a solid expanse of sand seas with no vegetation. The entire region, extending across North Africa and into Central Asia, has a hot and dry climate, although the more mountainous northern portions are colder in the winter months.

Arid Climate Zones

From the Atlantic Ocean to the Indian Ocean, and extending into Central Asia, is the largest expanse of dry, arid and desert lands on the planet. The reason for this vast arid climate zone is the location of the African continent on the surface of the earth. *Climate* refers to the average weather conditions in a place over the course of a year. The main variables in climate are seasonal changes in climate and precipitation; arid climates have little or no rain throughout the year. A climate map of the earth shows a belt of tropical, humid climate (high rainfall and high temperature) along the equator. Drier climates are found just north and south of the tropical equator and are either arid (little rainfall), generally found on the western sides of continents, or subtropical (summer hot/winter cool) on the eastern sides of continents. Further north of these regions is another belt of humid climates, including the Mediterranean and Marine West Coast climates on the west coasts of continents, and increasingly colder humid climates on the east coast of the continents. Finally, the North and South Polar regions are vast arid regions that receive very little precipitation, though their soils can be quite water logged and frozen with moisture.

Environmental Adaptation

In the hot and dry desert areas buildings in towns and cities are traditionally built very close together to protect against heat and wind. Although winds from the upper atmosphere are generally not strong, the daytime heat rising from the desert landscape can create very strong convection winds. Making a building very compact is like raising the ground level, with the heat affecting the roof of the houses while the interior space below remains cooler, like a cave in a mountainside. Courtyards provide shade and an opportunity for the circulation of air as winds pass overhead and pull cooler air from below. Round roofs, which are common features of the region's traditional architecture, also contribute to this circulation of air. Some traditional buildings use wind towers, which are about 150 ft (15 m) high and collect air at their top on their windward side (facing into the wind), directing it into the house, and then exhausting the wind out through the windows on the leeward (back) side of the building. Water channels, wells, and water fountains are also used in traditional architecture to keep the indoors cool as the air passes through.

Bedouins

The traditional (pre-modern) economy of North Africa and Southwest Asia consisted of two non-urban lifestyles. The first is nomadic herding and the second is sedentary agriculture. Nomadic herding in Southwest Asia and North Africa is mostly practiced by the Bedouins (*desert dwellers*), who are Arab pastoralists and comprise about 10% of the population in Southwest Asia and North Africa. They live in a delicate balance with the desert ecosystem because overgrazing can permanently destroy a pasture area, turning it into a desert. Most are not truly nomadic, but practice transhumance, which is movement in a prescribed route among pasture areas. They move from one pasture to another to prevent overgrazing, often spending the dry season in higher areas and the wet season in lowland areas. Some only travel short distances within a small area, while others may move up to 600 miles (966 km) a year, which requires almost constant travel. The distance traveled depends on the quality of the pasture land in a region and the seasonal availability of food and water. The area and route traveled is clearly defined and respected by others. Individuals have use and access rights to certain places, even though they may only be there a few days out of the year.

Bedouins travel in family groups, with the sheik, or head man of the tribe or clan, as its leader. They own very little (pots and utensils, jewelry, radios), so they can more easily travel. Their animals are prized possessions and a measure of social and individual value. Sheep are the dominant livestock, producing milk, wool and meat. Goats are often better for drier climates, as they are able to survive on the sparsest vegetation. Camels are kept more for meat and milk, and occasionally for transportation, though that is not their dominant use. Bedouins have a strong attachment to their traditional lifestyle, and often feel discriminated against by urban-based governments in the region. Governments throughout Southwest Asia and North Africa have tried to settle the nomads, which has often led to disease and overgrazing, as well as much resistance. Many Bedouin groups in countries such as Egypt and Jordan have become involved in tourism, offering camel guiding services and overnight experiences (including food and culture) in Bedouin tents.

Ecotourism

Throughout the region, nature-based tourism is poorly developed, with most tours focusing on archeology, ancient cities, churches and monasteries, traditional markets, and village and urban life. On the Arabian Peninsula, the UAE and Oman have been developing tourism based on their desert resources, including safari tourism and Bedouin ethnic tourism. Educational tourism has also emerged in the more developed areas of the region, such as Israel, based on modern and technological adaptations in these arid lands. The arid conditions throughout the region from Central Asia to North Africa create highly sensitive and endangered aquatic ecosystems, the largest of which are the Red Sea and the Persian Gulf, and the Black Sea, Caspian Sea, and Ural Sea in Central Asia. These water bodies concentrate drainage from their surrounding watersheds and serve as sensitive measures of regional environmental degradation. Most of them are severely polluted, though concerted international efforts in the 1990s to address this problem have helped to some degree. In Central Asia, ecotourism offers an alternative to the large-scale and heavy industries that caused some of this widespread damage. However, there remains a great need throughout to increase environmental awareness and to address major environmental problems.

Ecotourism opportunities are actually quite plentiful along the coastal seas and oceans that surround much of the Arabian Peninsula. These include diving in coral areas and sea turtle communities, which are usually away from major cities where pollution has caused considerable coral damage, and coastal wetlands that attract large numbers of birds. The Farasan Islands, for example, support the largest wild gazelle population in Saudi Arabia, in addition to a great variety of birds, dolphins, turtles and whales in marine habitats, which range from coral reefs to mangroves.

Israel has many nature reserves that protect a diversity of wetland ecosystems. A geologic depression in western Jordan includes the Jordan Valley, the Wadi (*oasis*) Araba, Lake Tiberias (aka the Sea of Galilee) and the Dead Sea, the lowest point on any continent. In eastern Jordan wetland parks are managed by the World Wildlife Fund (WWF) in the oases of the Shaumari and Azraq. The famous archeological site of the old trade caravan city of Petra, with its many large buildings and tombs carved into rock walls, is located close to the Wadi Araba in Jordan.

The Maghreb

Maghreb means *the land where the sun sets* in Arabic (al-maghrib) and is the name given to the northwest corner of the African continent. By contrast, Southwest Asia and Egypt are known collectively as Mashriq or place where the sun rises. Traditionally the core of the Maghreb has been Morocco, Algeria and Tunisia, through which the Atlas Mountains run. Today it often includes these three countries, plus Libya and Mauritania, all of which have a large Berber population. In 1989, these five countries formed the l'Union du Maghreb Arabe (UMA), a relatively weak economic trade union. Between Morocco and Mauritania is the territory of the former Spanish Province of Western Sahara, one of the most arid and least populated regions on earth. Today, Moroccan forces control most of Western Sahara, with a small part controlled by the Prolisario Front, which backed by Mauritania, fought for the territory's independence after Spain withdrew in 1975. The Arab League of countries supports Morocco's claims to Western Sahara, while the African Union countries support the Prolisario.

The rugged Atlas Mountains (peaks over 13,000 ft/4000 m) form a geologic spine through much of the Maghreb region. These mountains are part of the Alpine system that extends through Southern Europe and provide great biological diversity to the northwest corner of Africa. Just off the Atlantic coast of the Maghreb region are Spain's Canary Islands and Portugal's Madeira and Azores Islands.

TOURISM ISSUES AND INSIGHTS
VOLUNTEER TOURISM

Volunteer tourism combines travel with voluntary work often of a social or environmental nature, and usually in a location where government or private sector assistance would not otherwise be forthcoming. Volunteer tourism is therefore seen to provide a more reciprocally beneficial form of travel in which both the volunteer and the host communities are able to gain from the experience. The concept of volunteer tourism has therefore come to be strongly related to concepts of sustainable tourism and sustainable development, especially with respect to pro-poor tourism (PPT).

While the concept of international volunteering is by no means a new phenomenon, in recent years there has been a rapid increase in the number of individuals taking part in short term, organized volunteer tourism programs (VTP). The increasing demand for VTPs has been paralleled by an increase in sending organizations that promote, sell, and organize

Continued

programs for volunteer tourists. Sending organizations now offer a large variety of options depending on volunteer tourists' preferred activity, location and duration.

It has been suggested that the interactions encouraged by this form of tourism between volunteers and their hosts lead to improved cross-cultural understanding, with volunteer tourists gaining a sophisticated understanding of the local culture in which they participate, as well as the issues facing their host communities. In addition, some group VTPs attract volunteers from all over the world and the friendships developed between volunteer tourists themselves may also reduce racial, cultural and social boundaries. However, with the growing number of short-term VTPs, recent studies have begun to question whether volunteer tourism does indeed always result in increased cross-cultural understanding. In particular, research relating to the United Kingdom *gap year* (a year taken out between high school and university, or post-university, which often includes an element of voluntary work) suggests that international volunteering may in fact reinforce existing stereotypes and deepen dichotomies of *them and us*. It has also been suggested that certain types of VTPs may represent a form of neocolonialism or imperialism, in which volunteer tourists inadvertently reinforce the power inequalities between developed and developing countries. For example, when volunteer tourists inappropriately take on the roles of *expert* or *teacher* regardless of their experience or qualifications, this may seen to represent the neocolonial construction of the westerner as racially and culturally superior. Therefore, it is essential for programs to be carefully developed and managed in order to ensure the development goals are achieved. Where individuals volunteer through sending organizations, these organizations must play an important role in ensuring that stereotypes are broken, rather than reinforced.

Three key recommendations for sending organizations seeking to achieve cross-cultural understanding have been identified. First, they should develop programmes which will be of genuine value for the local communities. Second, the importance of approaching VTPs as a learning process rather than simply an *experience* should be recognized through the use of experiential learning techniques. Third, opportunities for interaction with other cultures should be deliberately facilitated.

Source

Raymond, E.M. and Hall, C.M. (2008) The development of cross-cultural (mis)understanding through volunteer tourism, *Journal of Sustainable Tourism* (available online)

Human Geography

Civilizations and Empires

Southwest Asia has long been a crossroads of travel between Asia, Europe and Africa. It was the center of the earliest known civilizations of humankind, including the Sumerians (3500 to 199 BCE), ancient Egyptians (3000 to about 30 BCE), and the Babylonians and Assyrians (900 to 500 BCE). As in other parts of the world, sedentary agricultural areas have the largest number of people and are mostly found along the rivers, in more humid highland areas, and in scattered desert oases.

The Nile River Valley and the Tigris-Euphrates Valley were home to two of the oldest civilizations on the planet.

The ancient Egyptian civilization existed along the middle to lower reaches of the Nile River thousands of years, with the dynastic period lasting from about 3150 BCE to 31 BCE. The Egyptian dynasties reached their largest territorial extent about 2000 BCE, and ended when it was conquered by the early Roman Empire. The Egyptian civilization was based on a social structure designed to manage the waters of the Nile River to support agriculture. This included the collective development and management of an irrigation system and a semi-divine ruler to influence the unpredictability of nature. From this grew a writing system and literature, trade relations and military domination over neighboring territories, and an elaborate system of religious beliefs. The pyramids and the sphinx of Giza are one of the great wonders of the ancient world, and continue to be among the most remarkable architectural accomplishments of human history.

Contemporary with the Egyptian Dynasties was the ancient Mesopotamian civilization along the Tigris and Euphrates Rivers (in modern-day Iraq). Ancient Mesopotamia is usually dated from the Bronze Age about 3500 BCE to the arrival of Alexander the Great in the 4th century BCE, at which time Greek culture came to dominate the region. The Tigris and Euphrates Rivers provided similar opportunities to the Nile River for the emergence of highly organized societies. Among the major kingdoms and empires of Mesopotamia were Sumer, Babylon, and Assyria. The Sumerians arose about 3500 BCE, before the Egyptian Dynasties, and lasted to approximately 2800 BCE. The ruins of the ancient city of Ur (birthplace of the Old Testament's Abraham) in southern Iraq date back to Sumerian times. From about 2000 BCE until the dominance of the Greeks, southern Mesopotamia was largely (not always) dominated by Babylonia (capital city of Babylon), while the northern portions of the Tigris and Euphrates Rivers were the home of the Assyrian Empire, which at one time extended their control to the Nile River. The city of Babylonia was famed for the legendary Hanging Gardens of Babylon and the Tower of Babel, though no signs of the city exist today.

Turkey has been the center of two major empires in Southwest Asia. In its early history it was closely tied to Greece and at times was ruled by its Mediterranean neighbor. Along with much of the Mediterranean Sea, which was part of the Roman Empire (31 BCE to 475 CE), and then became the center of the Eastern Roman Empire (also known as the Byzantine Empire, ca. 5th c. CE 1299) after Rome fell to invading groups from other parts of Europe and Central Asia. The Byzantine Empire was based in Constantinople, which was made the Christian capital of the Roman Empire by Constantine the Great in 324. This Greek-speaking empire spread Orthodox Christianity throughout large parts of Eastern Europe, where it is still the dominant religion today. (The empire was named after the Greek city Byzantium, which was named New Rome by Constantine, but soon became Constantinople; it was named Istanbul in 1930, which is a traditional Turkish name for the city.) The Byzantine Empire reached its peak in 550 CE when its empire encompassed much of the Mediterranean Sea. This did not last, however, as within less than a century the Arab Empire would begin to expand outside the Arabian Peninsula. Little of the Byzantine period remains in the cultural traditions of Southwest Asia, or even Turkey, with the exception of its architecture. The Hagia Sophia (St. Sophia) in Istanbul was built as a Christian Church in 532 to 537 CE and is considered by many to be one of the most beautiful buildings in the world. It later became a mosque and today is a museum that continues to dominate the skyline of old Istanbul.

The most influential empire for most of Southwest Asia and North Africa was the Arab Empire (632–1258 in various forms and sizes). One cultural characteristic that all of Southwest Asia and North Africa (except for Turkey) share is their history of being part of the Arab Empire, resulting in shared cultural traditions that reach back to that time, including religion, language and architecture. Arabic today is the dominant language of the region from the Arabian Peninsula to Morocco. It was spoken by the Prophet Mohammed, a trader born in Mecca in the year 570 CE and founder of Islam. Within some 50 years of his death in 632, Arabs from the Arabian Peninsula had conquered the Persian Empire (Iran) to the east, much of the Byzantine Empire (Turkey) to the north, all of North Africa to the west, and most of the Iberian Peninsula (Spain and Portugal). Further to the east, Pakistan in South Asia, and southern portions of Central Asia also came under Arab Empire control. The Arabs built Baghdad as a new capital city for their empire.

The Arab Empire reached its peak in the late 8th century. It was a cosmopolitan empire, blending the wisdom of three continents. Scientific innovation included Arabic numerals (which are still used today), mathematics based on the number zero (which was a relatively new concept), algebra and trigonometry, and medical colleges that produced the first government-certified physicians in the world; free public hospitals were also established in the Arab Empire. Aristotle, Plato and Hippocrates were translated from Greek into Arabic, thereby preserving their writings through Europe's Dark Ages. Baghdad became the richest and one of the largest cities in the world. The dominance of the Arab Empire on the Arabian Peninsula continued until the year 1258 when the Mongols conquered and destroyed Baghdad. The Mongols ruled the city for 200 years, and the Arabs never again were able to establish the unity of former times. The vision of a return to a unified Arab world has, however, continued into recent times; Libya, Syria, Iraq and Egypt have all tried to establish themselves as heirs to the Arab Empire, though none have succeeded.

The most salient legacy of the Arab Empire is Islam. The countries of Central Asia, Southwest Asia and North Africa share the religion and culture of Islam, and over 90% of the people in this region are Muslims. Within Islam there are two major sects: Shia (or Shiite) Islam and Sunni Islam. The Sunnis believe that Mohammed was the last prophet of God, while the Shias believe there were other prophets after Mohammed. Sunni Muslims predominate throughout the region, with the exception of Iran, where Shiites are the most numerous, and Iraq where they comprise the majority population but are not as pervasive. Iraq was ruled by a minority Sunni government for many decades, which brutally suppressed the majority Shiite population, resulting in the Shiites tending to be more impoverished and more fundamentalist in their religious beliefs. Differences between Sunnis and Shias are a major source of tension in some parts of Southwest Asia today. (There are other major centers of Islam and Islamic culture that are not part of the North Africa, Southwest Asia and Central Asia. These include Pakistan and Bangladesh in South Asia, and Malaysia and Indonesia in Southeast Asia. Indonesia has the largest Muslim population of any country in the world.)

After the fall of the Arab Empire, a second Islamic empire arose in Turkey. Asia Minor (the peninsula where Turkey is located) was never part of the Arab Empire, though Islamic religious influences gave rise to the Ottomans, whose empire eventually replaced the Byzantine rulers in Constantinople. The Ottoman Empire (1299–1922) reached its peak in 1526 when it controlled the area from Hungary to the Caucasuses, the entire Arabian Peninsula, and most of North Africa. The empire lasted until World War I, when it was defeated by Great Britain and Russia. Although they saw themselves as heirs to the Arab Empire, the Ottoman leaders exhibited a great distrust of science, commerce, and industry. They isolated non-Islamic peoples, such as Armenians, Jews and Greeks, and political corruption was a major problem throughout the Empire. These characteristics formed the basis of European and other Western stereotypes of much of Southwest Asia and North Africa today. These perceptions are not helped by the political turmoil and unrest that continue to plague many parts of the region making this region among the most dangerous in the world visit. At the same time, strong cultures and traditions, opportunities to see distinctive landscapes, and lifestyles and historic relics give tourism enormous potential.

Non-Islamic Peoples

Most of the region's population today speak Arabic, consider themselves Arabs, and practice Islam. The major non-Arab, yet Islamic, areas are located in the high plateau and mountain regions of Turkey, Central Asia (mostly Turkic speaking), Iran, northern Iraq, and portions of Afghanistan. Besides Islam, Southwest Asia is also a hub of Judaism and Christianity, two other major world religions. The Jewish state of Israel was created after World War II, in a region that historically had a large Jewish population, but also a large Arabic-speaking Palestinian population. Jerusalem, the capital and largest city of Israel, has long been a pilgrimage destination for Jews, Christians and Muslims. It is one of the three most important religious cities in Islam, as Muslims believe that the site atop the Temple Mount is where the Prophet Mohammed ascended to heaven accompanied by the Archangel Gabriel. Unfortunately, competing religious interests in such a small territory have more often served as a source of conflict and division rather than religious tolerance and unity.

The southern portions of Algeria, Tunisia, and Morocco have large Amazigh (Berber) populations, who have lived in this region for over 2000 years. The country of Sudan is Arabic speaking and Islamic in the north with Sub-Saharan African (and Christian) cultures in the south. Similarly, the southern edge of the Sahara Desert is a transition zone where semi-Arab peoples transition to Sub-Saharan Africa populations. Countries there include Mauritania, Mali, Niger and Chad (which are included in the Sub-Saharan Africa region of this book). Although on the edge of the Middle East region, the highlands of Ethiopia are the center of a civilization that dates back over 2000 years, and has evidence of Greek and Egyptian influences, including the adoption of the Coptic Christian tradition, which is related to the eastern Orthodox form of Christianity. Smaller early Christian church populations are scattered throughout Southwest Asia and North Africa, including a large Christian population in Lebanon, Syria and Israel.

Israel

Israel's primary tourist appeal is its religious heritage sites. Christians, Jews and Muslims around the world travel to Israel and the adjoining Palestinian territories to view and experience places significant to their religious traditions. Christmas and Easter are especially popular seasons for Christians to visit the Holy Land. Bethlehem and Jerusalem, sites of important events in the life of Jesus Christ, are the main destinations in Israel for this group. Muslims (who can get permission from their home governments to visit Israel) gravitate to the Haram al-Sharif (Temple Mount to Jews) to see the Dome of the Rock (*Masjid Qubbat As-Sakhrah* in Arabic) and to worship at the al-Aqsa Mosque adjacent to the Dome, located in the Muslim Quarter of Jerusalem. The rock is believed to be the place where the Prophet Mohammed ascended into Heaven to consult with Moses. The existence of the Dome of the Rock renders Jerusalem the third most sacred location for Muslims, following Makkah (Mecca) and Medina in Saudi Arabia. The rock is also venerated by Orthodox Jews as being the location where Abraham was willing to sacrifice his son in the Old Testament.

For Jews, Jerusalem represents the center of their religious and cultural heritage. It was one of the capitals of ancient Israel, and many events took place there, including temple building, which have made the city a holy place. Of particular importance is the Western Wall – the last remaining vestige of ancient Solomon's Temple. Jews travel from all parts of the world to pray and worship at this site, and many young Israelis and other Jews of the diaspora celebrate their bar mitzvahs (boys), bat mitzvahs (girls), and marriages at this location, adding special significance to these events. Unfortunately, the ongoing conflicts between Israel and its neighbors, and the bitter relations between Palestinians and Jews in Israel, have led to many important sacred sites for Jews and Christians being inaccessible and off-limits for security reasons.

Turkey

Turkey today probably has the best developed tourism industry in the entire region from Central Asia to North Africa. Similar to other areas in the region, archeological and historic sites are a cornerstone of tourism in Turkey, which has historically served as the bridge between Asia and Europe. The higher elevations of Turkey and other parts of highland Southwest Asia are considerably cooler than the Arabian Peninsula, and many distinct forested regions are protected in Turkey's nature reserves and 21 national parks. Some of these parks, first established in 1958, were initially designed for archeological and historical purposes, but have since become important ecological habitats protecting biological diversity. Wetlands are also more plentiful on Asia Minor and around the Caucasus Mountains. Trekking in the mountains (including ski-mountaineering in Georgia), bicycle touring, and sun and sand resorts along the Mediterranean coast have become popular travel experiences in these areas.

Iran

After a period of turmoil following the overthrow of the Shah of Iran in 1979, tourism returned by the late 1990s, though visas for independent travel were very difficult to obtain. Rampant urban and industrial development, combined with devastation from the Iran–Iraq War in the 1980s, have caused widespread environmental damage, especially along coastal areas of the Persian Gulf and Caspian Sea. The country has established a few national parks, mostly in forested areas of the Alborz mountain range where the rare black bearded and spiral horned Alborz sheep reside, however these parks are almost entirely unmanaged and unprotected. Iran is a significant Shia Muslim pilgrimage destination, with many sacred mosques and graves of Imams (religious leaders) being significant draws. Iran has several amazing ancient cities, some of which have been listed by UNESCO as World Heritage Sites, although strained relations with the west have prevented tourism from growing at a significant scale.

Saudi Arabia and the Hajj Pilgrimage

As already noted, the dominant religion in the region is Islam; the center of Islam is Saudi Arabia. It is mandatory for Muslims to make the Hajj pilgrimage to the city of Makkah in Saudi Arabia at least once in their lifetime, if financially and physically possible, making this one of the greatest international tourist movements in the world. (There is some debate as to whether or not religious pilgrimage is a form of tourism. Most pilgrims say it is not. However, from an economic viewpoint, there is little difference between religious travel and leisure travel.)

The Hajj is the fifth of the five pillars (or practices) of Islam. The other four are Shahadah (the declaration of faith), Salat (prayer), Sawm (fasting) and Zakat (charitable giving). The Hajj is the pilgrimage to the Holy City of Makkah (Mecca is its anglicized form) during the Islamic month of Dhu'l-Hijjah. Hajj literally means *to set out for a place*. The greater Hajj (al-hajj al-akbar) is performed over 5 or 6 days starting on the eighth day of Dhu'l-Hijjah. Together with the lesser Hajj (Umrah), the Hajj comprises a series of religious activities and ritual acts that must be carried out in a particular order at specific religious locations in and around Makkah that are symbolic of the lives of Ibrahim (Abraham) and Hajarah (Hagar), and which are cornerstones of Muslim faith. Prior to the greater Hajj many pilgrims will visit the city of Medina and the Mosque of the Prophet, where the Prophet Mohammed's tomb is located.

The Hajj attracts over 2 million international and domestic visitors to Makkah and Medina each year (see Table 3.1). It is the second largest religious gathering in

TABLE 3.1
NUMBERS OF HAJJ PILGRIMS 1996–2006

Year	Saudis	Non-Saudis	Total
1416*/1996	784,769	1,080,465	1,865,234
1417/1997	774,260	1,168,591	1,942,851
1418/1998	699,770	1,132,344	1,832,114
1419/1999	775,268	1,056,730	1,831,998
1420/2000	571,599	1,267,555	1,839,154
1421/2001	549,271	1,363,992	1,913,263
1422/2002	590,576	1,354,184	1,944,760
1423/2003	610,117	1,431,012	2,041,129
1424/2004	592,368	1,419,706	2,012,074
1425/2006	629,710	1,534,769	2,164,469
1426/2006	573,147	1,557,447	2,130,594

*Arab calendar year
Source: Ministry of the Hajj, Kingdom of Saudi Arabia

Many westerners have heard of kosher food and have a rough idea that it refers to Jewish dietary laws but few know of halal food. Given the increasing numbers of non-Islamic visitors to Islamic countries and communities and the growing number of Muslim tourists to non-Islamic countries an understanding of halal is therefore extremely important for the tourism and hospitality industry as well as in appreciating Muslim culture.

Halal is one of the most important aspects of Islamic life. Although it is a standard that Muslims around the world live by, many non-Muslims are still unaware about halal food and its significance for the Muslim community. Halal food and drinks must conform to Islamic dietary laws as specified in the Qur'an, the hadeeth (sayings) and sunnah (tradition) of the Prophet Muhammad, as well as in the fiqh (teachings) of the four Islamic Jurists: Hanafi, Shafi'ie, Maliki and Hambali. Other sources of laws are the Ijma (collective approval) and Qiyas (syllogy) of Islamic scholars.

Halal and haram are the two major terms used in Islamic dietary laws. While halal means permitted and legitimate, haram, on the other hand, means unapproved, illegitimate or illicit. Several criteria must be met before food products can be certified as halal. First, the product must be free from any substance or ingredient taken or extracted from a haram animal or ingredient. Halal products are made from naturally halal animals, such as cattle, goat, sheep and chicken that are slaughtered according to the manner prescribed in Islam. Second, halal products should also be processed, produced, and/or stored by using utensils and/or equipment that have been cleansed according to Islamic law. The main idea behind this is that products should be free of contamination and must not come into contact with haram substances during preparation, production and/or storage. In addition, halal ingredients should also not be mixed with objectionable or haram ingredients like enzymes and emulsifiers of porcine origin or other non-halal animals. Any other groups of food, like cheese and meat, may be combined together, as long as no haram or prohibited foods are included in the mixture.

Islam places a very strong emphasis on cleanliness in everything, especially in the context of food and drink. In Islam, eating is regarded as a matter of worship, like prayer and other religious activities. So, just as Muslims perform the ablution as a means of cleansing themselves before their daily prayers, they must also ensure that the food they consume is clean and prepared in the correct manner, starting with the avoidance of items that are prohibited in Islamic dietary laws. The Qur'an clearly prohibits Muslims from consuming the following categories of food: carrion, flowing blood, pork, animals that have been slaughtered with the invocation of a name other than the name of God (this type of food is associated with the practice of idolatry that Islam strictly opposes; this prohibition also addresses the issue of halal slaughtering, in which pronouncing the name of God is a required condition while slaughtering an animal), and alcohol. Islam prescribes that an (halal) animal should first be slaughtered before its consumption, in order to get rid of the blood. The Islamic method of slaughtering an animal is to cut its throat to enable as much blood to run out and not congeal in the veins.

There are also other prohibitions that have arisen either according to the (fiqh) teachings of Islamic jurists or based on the (hadeeth) sayings and (sunnah) tradition of the Prophet Muhammad. These prohibitions include the consumption of all beasts of prey and birds of prey, amphibians; undesirable insects; and vermin or poisonous animals. In addition, Muslims are strictly prohibited from eating meat that has been cut from a live animal.

Continued

According to Islamic law, fish and other sea creatures are exempted from the category of *dead animals*. All marine animals are therefore halal and can be eaten without the requirement of slaughtering and bleeding, although there is some debate among jurists of different schools of Islamic thought with respect to the status of crustacea and molluscs. Human beings are permitted to catch seafood in any manner they like, using methods that are as humane as possible. It also matters not whether seafood comes out of the water dead or alive, as a whole or in pieces, and if caught by a Muslim or a non-Muslim.

Source

Wan Hassan, M. and Hall, C.M. (2003) The demand for halal food among Muslim travellers in New Zealand, In Hall, C.M. et al. (eds) *Food Tourism Around the World*, Butterworth-Heinemann, Oxford.

the world (after the Kumbha Mela pilgrimage in India, which occurs every 12 years and attracted some 70 million people in 2003). In poorer Islamic nations, governments and international organizations offer grants for the needy to assist in paying for the trip to Mecca, and some TV shows offer Hajj trips as competitive door prizes. Because of the large numbers of people that participate in the Hajj over a short period of time, Saudi authorities have developed an extensive infrastructure to manage the pilgrimage. The Saudi government issues special visas to non-Saudi nationals for the purpose of the pilgrimage, and only a set number of visas are allocated to each country that pilgrims come from.

Guides are often hired to help travelers perform the rites of Hajj, organize lodging, and provide meals, drinks, transportation and interpreter services. Women are encouraged to undertake the Hajj in conjunction with a close male relative, although the Saudi government will allow women to travel accompanied by a group of other women if they have written permission from a male relative. Entrance to Makkah is forbidden to non-Muslims as the entire city is regarded as a holy site to Islam.

Makkah and Medina are two of the three most important Islamic religious sites. Their location in Saudi Arabia gives the Saudi government and the Saudi royal family an enormous role and responsibility with respect to Islamic affairs. Together with its significant oil wealth, the Saudi rulers are a major influence in the political affairs in Southwest Asia and North Africa. Nevertheless, the same combination of natural resources monopoly and religious significance have been a source of instability in the region that has often served to harm tourism. Radical Islamists, such as Osama Bin-Laden, are often driven more by their dislike of Saudi government policies than by their hatred of the west.

Saudi Arabia has among the most restrictive international travel policies in the world. The country receives over 9 million visitors a year, about half of whom are guest workers, followed by religious-related travel. Until 2004, Saudi Arabia did not issue tourist visas. The only way a person could enter the country was to attend the

Hajj (on a Hajj visa), or as an invited guest visiting relatives, a company, a university or attending a conference. Tourism is now starting to emerge, though tourist visas are only issued to organized group tours, and visitors are expected to respect the culture and traditions of Saudi Arabia. Homosexuality, drug smuggling, adultery and trying to convert a Muslim from Islam are all punishable by death, as are the religious practices of the Jehovah's Witness and Bahai faiths. Non-Muslims are not allowed to visit the holy cities of Makkah and Medina.

Growth of Leisure Tourism

As noted in the Israel and Saudi Arabia examples above, religious pilgrimage is a primary form of tourism in Southwest Asia, followed by heritage tourism based on the archeology of ancient empires. Compared to other parts of the world, tourism has not been a major economic growth engine in Southwest Asia and North Africa. Part of the reason for this has been the idealistic contentions of religious conservatives who view tourism as promoting hedonism, immoral behavior, and cultural degradation. In the view of many clerics and government officials, the negative religious and social impacts of tourism (e.g., prostitution, nudity, open affection between genders, immodest attire, alcohol use, irreverence for sacred places and ceremonies, gambling, etc.) outweigh the economic and social benefits that the industry might offer. Even though countries such as Turkey, Morocco, Tunisia and Egypt have become important leisure travel destinations, especially for Europeans, most of the Muslim-dominated states of the region have been cautious to accept tourism.

Religious beliefs in primarily Muslim nations profoundly affect the growth, operation and management of tourism. Forms of tourism that emphasize culture over recreation tend to be emphasized, and tourist resorts are more likely to be located inland rather than near beaches on the coast. Beach and coast-based tourism, in particular, is generally seen as a major promoter of vices by openly promoting recreation and bodily pleasures. This worldview has led to the encouragement of domestic and intra-regional travel rather than catering to non-Muslim outsiders, which serves as a protective measure to reduce the influences of Western tourists on destination populations. Of this, Aziz (2001: 154) notes, "... no Islamic country has yet managed to accommodate the needs of Western tourists without compromising the religious and cultural expectations of most of its own people."

Although total numbers are relatively low compared to more developed regions of the world, in recent years Southwest Asia and North Africa have been among the fastest growing regions for international tourism in the world. This may seem surprising given the wars and civil unrest that many parts of the region have experienced in recent decades (including Iraq, Iran, Azerbaijan, Egypt, Tunisia, Lebanon and Israel/Palestine). Nevertheless, the gulf states of UAE, Qatar, Kuwait and Oman have been reinvesting large amounts of oil money into tourism and related leisure and sports developments as part of a strategy of economic diversification. Dubai, one of the seven emirates that comprise the UAE, has become a leader in this area, building a post-modern landscape of man-made islands (in the shape of giant palm trees), indoor ski runs (the world's largest), and the world's tallest building (160 floors, to be completed in 2009). Even Saudi Arabia, among the most religiously conservative countries in the region, is gradually encouraging more international tourists.

Investment has been focused in hotel, leisure, sports and shopping developments as well as airlines. In fact, in the same way that in Southeast Asia there has been intense competition between Kuala Lumpur and Singapore for hub status, so the Gulf States have also been competing for the growing international tourism and travel market to the gulf region, as well as the development of stopover tourism between Southern Asia and Europe. From the Persian Gulf, where much of this competition is concentrated, London is 7 hours away by air, Frankfurt is 6 hours, Cairo is 4 hours, and Hong Kong is 8 hours by air.

Egypt, with over 8 million visitors in 2005, is the dominant non-religious international tourist destination for the Old World region (Central Asia, Southwest Asia and all of Africa). Egypt has long been an important group tour destination in the Middle East, particularly in conjunction with visits to Israel. In the late 1970s, a peace treaty was signed between Egypt and Israel, paving the way for the development of tourism between them and opening doors through which Israelis now vacation in Egypt, and Egyptians spend their holidays in Israel. Elsewhere in North Africa, Tunisia has become an important resort destination for Europeans, while Morocco is a well established adventure and youth travel destination. Libya has been largely closed to the world following military clashes with its neighbors and accusations of supporting terrorist attacks against the United States and Europeans in the 1970s and 1980s. That changed in 2006 when the country agreed to settle its international disputes and began to allow its first Western tourists in decades.

United Arab Emirates

Dubai (one of the UAE's emirates) is one of the best examples of a place expanding tourism and seeking to develop a transportation, business and leisure hub. In 2006, Dubai was serviced by 91 airlines connected to over 130 destinations and had over 280 hotels. In addition to airport development Dubai also developed a cruise ship terminal that opened in 2001. The importance attached to tourism development in Dubai is illustrated by the fact that the tourism organization, the Dubai Tourism and Commerce Marketing's (DTCM), is chaired by the UAE Vice President and Prime Minister and Ruler of Dubai, His Highness Sheikh Mohammed bin Rashid Al Maktoum. As well as its head office in Dubai, the DTCM has 14 overseas offices, located in New York (USA and Canada), London (the United Kingdom and Ireland), Paris (France), Frankfurt (Germany), Stockholm (Scandinavia), Milan (Italy), Moscow (the Russian Federation, CIS and the Baltic States), Sydney (Australia), Johannesburg (South Africa), Mumbai (India), Hong Kong (East Asia), Tokyo (Japan), Saudi Arabia and Zurich (Switzerland and Austria).

The growth of tourism in Dubai has gone hand-in-hand with an aggressive aviation development policy which combines an *open skies* policy with the development of the national airline, Emirates, the international airline of the UAE, which is wholly owned by the government. Growth of Emirates Airlines has been substantial, doubling in size every 5.5 years in its first 11 years since its establishment in 1985, and every 4 years since 1996. As of mid-2006 Emirates flew to 93 destinations in 57 countries with almost 550 flights per week flying out of Dubai. Dubai has built this economy on loans from its more oil rich Emerate neighbors, creative business acumen, and an open and global economy. To attract international tourists Dubai has expanded beyond the traditional tourist attractions of Southwest Asia and North Africa. Those tend to include cultural attractions (Arab culture, historical cities and archeological sites) and natural attractions (desert caravans, marine tourism and birdwatching). Instead, Dubai has focused on developing sporting facilities, such as golf courses, and a meetings and conventions industry. It is also relatively liberal with respect to alcohol, dress and the mixing of sexes, which allows Dubai to promote itself as an international pleasure tourist resort that can cater to a wide range of tastes and markets. Likewise, Dubai is one of the most desired shopping destinations in the world.

Other emirates (e.g., Sharjah, Abu Dhabi and Rash al Khaimah) in the UAE have followed Dubai's lead and have started testing the tourism waters. Aside from Dubai's shopping, amusement parks, and other commercial attractions, UAE tourism is based largely on business travel (oil) and desert safaris.

Qatar, Bahrain and Kuwait

The three Gulf states of Qatar, Bahrain and Kuwait are interested in tourism as an economic growth mechanism to supplement their large oil supplies. Like other petroleum-producing countries of the region, business travel comprises a large part of their international market. Qatar and Bahrain are especially interested in developing tourism based on beaches, historic sites and cities. Kuwait became known to the outside world as the center of the Gulf War in the early 1990s and has some tourism based on that legacy. All three countries are well connected throughout the region, and Qatar Airways, like the UAE's Emirates Airline, is working to become a major air transport hub between Europe, Asia and Africa. Bahrain is physically connected to Saudi Arabia by a large bridge, or causeway, providing another vital form of transportation linking large Saudi Arabia with tiny Bahrain.

Extreme Tourism

Extreme tourism is defined as travel to dangerous places or participating in dangerous activities. Sometimes called *shock tourism*, it is related to extreme sports and dark tourism, but may place the tourists in even more life threatening, but adrenaline pumping, danger than either of those. One form of extreme tourism is travel to the most dangerous places of the world – places that most leisure travelers would avoid. War torn areas of the Old World (from Central Asia through Africa), where civil disorder is the norm, are the types of destinations that draw the small, niche extreme tourism market.

Central Asia, Southwest Asia and North Africa have suffered more than their share of global conflict in recent decades. Some of these have included the Iran–Iraq War (1980–1988), the hostilities between Israel and the Palestinians (since World War II) and between Morocco and the Prolisario Front in Western Sahara (1975–1991), the two United States-led invasions of Iraq (1991 and 2003), Soviet (1979–1989) and American (2001) invasions of Afghanistan, Turkey's invasion and splitting of the island of Cyprus (1974), civil war in Lebanon (1975–1990) and Tajikistan (1992–1997), ongoing civil war in southern Sudan (since 1955) and recent genocides in western Sudan (since 2003), and political uprisings in Algeria (1992–2002). In addition, the entire region has a long history of powerful rulers for life and insurgent terrorism related to ethnic divisions and the rise of extreme versions of Islamic fundamentalism. Many of these are examples of both the internal struggle for scarce resources in this hostile yet fragile environment, as well as the result of external influence and interference by European, Russian, and American interests after centuries of colonialism. It is amazing that despite these challenges, some form of tourism still persists in every country in this region.

Iraq

Iraq is an example of a nation attempting to develop its tourism economy while experiencing internal war. In March 2003, based on suspicions that Iraq's leader, Sadam Hussein, was manufacturing weapons of mass destruction (WMDs, e.g., nuclear and biological weapons), which he might use against the United States and Israel, the United States invaded Iraq and overthrew its autocratic leader. As of mid-2007, WMDs had not been found; however, the United States maintained its presence in Iraq with the goals of bringing democracy and human rights to a nation that had been ruled for decades by a despotic dictator, as well as to break any possible links between Iraq and al-Qaida terrorists based in Afghanistan. As of early 2008, United States troops and some allies were still stationed in Iraq fighting against warring insurgents, attempting to redevelop the country's infrastructure, and seeking to restore political control to the Iraqis. On nearly a daily basis, the media has reported roadside explosions, murders, kidnappings, and general lawlessness.

Despite the problems in Iraq, there have been nascent efforts to begin promoting and developing tourism in the midst of the conflict. In the face of social chaos and obvious dangers, the first organized tour of the country since the United States-led invasion took place in September 2003, arranged and operated by Hinterland Travel in the United Kingdom. Since then, there have been many media reports of tourists visiting Iraq on small, organized tours or individually. Not all of Iraq is subject to the frequent violence of Baghdad, and domestic tourism is beginning to thrive in some areas. In addition, Iraqi tour operators have organized trips for Iraqis to neighboring countries – something they were not permitted to do under Sadam Hussein's regime.

Several courses in hotel and tourism management are now being offered at colleges and universities in the far northern part of the country, which has been a protected region since the first United States-led invasion of the country in the 1991 Gulf War. Although it understands the difficulties of developing the industry in the face of war and insurgent attacks, the Iraqi Tourist Board is making preparations now for tourism development in the future when peace is achieved. In the midst of the insurgency, the tourist board continues to employ over 2,000 staff who are busy in 14 centers throughout the country checking on hotels and restaurants and issuing business licenses.

Lebanon, Syria and Jordan

Lebanon endured a bloody civil war between 1975 and 1990, spurred by religious conflict between the country's Muslims and Christians. Lebanon's internal strife was exacerbated by the country's small size and proximity to Syria and Israel. Prior to the civil war, tourism was a major sector of Lebanon's economy. Beirut, the capital, was often referred to as the Paris of the Middle East due to its extensive French colonial influence. However, much of Beirut was destroyed during the civil war, and visitation ceased almost entirely. Warnings were issued by the governments of the United States, Canada and various European countries against travel to Lebanon. Between 1990 and July 2006, however, with only a few minor skirmishes, including those associated with the September 2005 withdrawal of Syrian troops from the country, Lebanon had a more stable political, social and economic environment.

At the close of the 1970s and 1980s civil war, adventurous Europeans, particularly Belgians, Germans, Dutch, Italians, French and expatriate Lebanese quickly returned to visit the country, and the tourism industry once again began to flourish, albeit at a smaller scale than before the war. However, in July 2006 Israel invaded Lebanon once again, at first to find two Israeli solders who had been captured by Islamic Hezbollah fighters. However, as the invasion and attacks on Lebanon's infrastructure continued, the Israeli government's justification was to prevent Hezbollah from attacking Israel with rockets launched from Lebanese territory. Unfortunately, the destruction wrought by the Israeli invasion meant that much of the social, economic and tourism infrastructure that had been rebuilt following the civil war was again destroyed, but perhaps more seriously for the longer-term development of tourism in the region had served to reinforce the negative image of war and political instability that existed among many potential Western tourists.

Syria has many desirable attributes: Roman heritage, religious sites (Christian and Muslim), interesting cultures, and a well-known cuisine. Suspected support of Hezbollah and other militant factions bent on destroying Israel and the United States has led to souring relations between Syria and the United States, as well as other western nations. The United States government claims Syria to be a hotbed of terrorist support and strongly warns Americans from visiting Syria, which has many spillover effects on other United States allies. Likewise, recent tensions between Syria and Lebanon have given way to reduced cross-border travel between these two countries since the early 2000s.

Like Egypt, Jordan signed a peace treaty with Israel in 1994, which opened the border to cross-border to and from its Jewish state neighbor. Israelis regularly visit Jordan today, and many more progressive-minded Jordanians visit Israel on day trips or longer as business tourists, pilgrims or on pleasure holidays. Jordan is a well-known heritage destination, particularly associated with Petra on the old spice trading routes, and Roman ruins scattered throughout the country. As already noted, Bedouin culture is also becoming a new attraction for people willing to spend time in the harsh desert environments (badia) of Jordan.

3.3   SUB-SAHARAN AFRICA

This section covers the region of Africa located south of the Sahara Desert. Sub-Saharan Africa has historically been among the most impoverished region of the world, and poverty and short life expectancies are continuing challenges for much of the region. It was completely controlled by different European powers during the colonial era, and today it remains among the more remote and exotic destinations for tourists from the developed countries of North America, Europe and Japan. Sub-Saharan Africa is believed to be the place of origin for humankind, and is the most

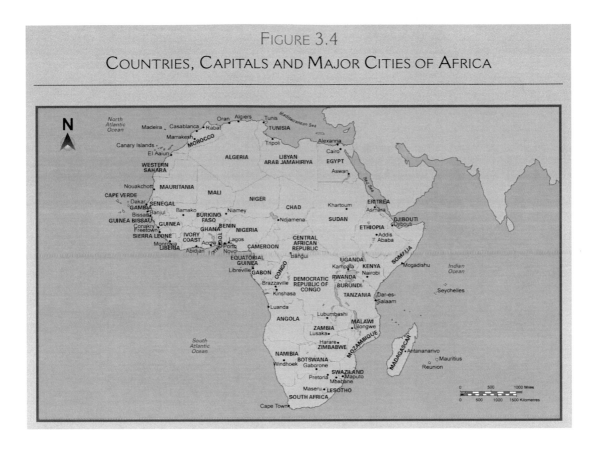

FIGURE 3.4
COUNTRIES, CAPITALS AND MAJOR CITIES OF AFRICA

culturally and ethnically diverse region in the world today. At the same time, it has a significantly lower population density than many other areas of the world. The physical geography, however, is not all that complicated for an area that is three times the size of the United States.

Physical Geography of Sub-Saharan Africa

Unlike Europe, and indeed much of the Eurasian landmass, Africa (the entire continent) is a very compact continent. It has no large, penetrating bays or seas. It is a relatively flat continent, with a generally uniform elevation and only a few high mountain regions. Most of Africa is a plateau surrounded by a narrow coastal plain. Over 90 percent of the continent is more than 500 ft (150 m) in elevation. The exceptions to this plateau character of most of Africa are the Atlas Mountains in the northwest extreme of the continent, which are an extension of the Alps in Europe; Mount Kilimanjaro, which is an extinct volcano and Africa's highest peak at 19,340 ft (5895 m); the Cape Range in South Africa, which is a major source of gold and diamonds; and the Great Rift Valley, which is the largest Rift Valley region in the world, averaging 30 miles (48 km) wide and up to 3000 ft (915 m) deep. (A *rift valley* is formed by a continent splitting apart, with each side of he valley moving in an opposite direction.)

Africa's larger landforms are relatively easy to comprehend. Africa has several large river basins, in addition to the major mountainous regions that rise above the

PHOTO 3.11

A sign marking the Tropic of Capricorn in the
Namib Desert of Namibia

Source: Jarkko Saarninen

continent's plateau-like topography. Starting in Southern Africa, the Kalahari Basin is an arid internal drainage basin. The rivers in this basin flow from higher elevations that receive more precipitation down toward the center of the basin (home to the Kalahari Desert) where they dissipate into the soil. (They do not flow out to the ocean.) North of the Kalahari is the Congo Basin, which is the drainage for the Congo River. The Congo Basin is in the most humid portion of Africa with dense tropical jungles. The Congo River flows over a large number of waterfalls as it makes its way down from the higher fringes of the basin toward its center and out to the Atlantic Ocean. These waterfalls prevent navigation into the interior of the Congo, and along with similar ones in other basins, kept much of interior Africa a mystery until only about 200 years ago.

Northeast of the Congo Basin, the Nile River flows through the Sudan Basin and out to the Mediterranean Sea. To the east of the Sudan Basin is the Chad Basin, another internal drainage system in a very arid landscape (the Sahara Desert). West Africa is the home of the Niger River, which flows through the arid Djouf Basin before it enters the Atlantic Ocean (Figure 3.5).

Climate

Most people in the more developed countries of the world imagine the landscapes of Southwest Asia and North Africa as little more than deserts. For Sub-Saharan Africa the image is mostly that of a jungle (tropical rainforest). While these images

FIGURE 3.5

PHYSICAL GEOGRAPHY OF AFRICA

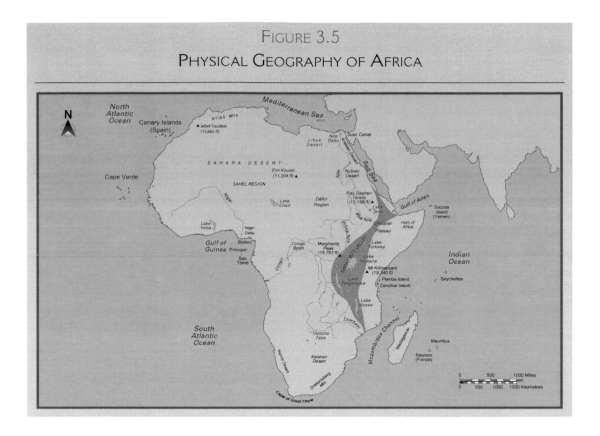

are accurate for large portions of these regions, each also has a much greater diversity of climatic conditions. Africa is the only continent that sits astride the equator. Africa extends almost the same distance north and south of the equator. The northwest African coast and the eastern portions of the Mediterranean Sea, have a Mediterranean climate with rainfall in the winter and drought in the summer. These areas have among the highest population densities in Africa, because their rainfall helps make their soils more productive.

Moving south, the climate of Africa quickly changes to steppe grasslands and then desert. Some desert areas here only receive recorded rainfall once in 10 or more years, with recorded temperatures reaching 150°F (65°C). This area has the lowest population density in Africa, mostly because of the lack of water. Where water is available, settlements can be very dense, such as along coastlines and along the Nile River. Elsewhere, nomadic lifestyles predominate.

South of the Sahara Desert is the Sahel region, which is a transition zone to more humid grasslands further to the south. Here Arab and Berber cultures from the north and Black African cultures from the south meet and interact with one another, sometimes in violent ways. This region also extends through Ethiopia. Rainfall in the Sahel region is very unpredictable, with some years receiving adequate precipitation for agriculture and grazing, while other years experience severe droughts. Desertification (the southward expansion of the Sahara Desert), has become a serious problem due to overgrazing and not allowing vegetation to regenerate. These problems have grown due to increasing population pressures in the region, and all of the countries along the Sahel have experienced famines over the last several decades.

The unpredictability of rainfall in the Sahel is due to the pattern of wet and dry climatic zones that surround the globe. Along the equator around the entire globe is a zone of tropical climate with year-round high temperatures and high rainfall. This area is known as the intertropical convergence zone, or ITCZ. Air from north and south of the equator meets along this zone and rises up (low pressure), creating clouds and rain throughout the year. The fact that most of the equator is ocean contributes to the high rainfall in the ITCZ.

The air that moves into the upper atmosphere along the equator eventually must descend back to the earth. This happens to the north and south of the equator in regions known as the *horse latitudes* (also known as the Calms of Cancer north of the equator, and Calms of Capricorn to the south, and more formally as the Subtropical High). In these areas, the air that descends from the upper atmosphere (high pressure) is generally dry with calm winds. The Sahara Desert in the northern part of Africa and the Kalahari Desert in the southern part of Africa are both situated in the horse latitudes, as are the Australian Outback and North America's Sonora Desert. The reason these areas are called the horse latitudes is because early sailing ships would sometimes be stuck in these regions of the oceans for many days at a time and sailors are said to have thrown their horses overboard in hopes that a lighter boat would more easily move in the calm winds.

The ITCZ and the Subtropical High follow the sun, moving northward in the northern hemisphere summer, and southward in the northern hemisphere winter. Thus, in the summer months of the northern hemisphere the ITCZ brings precipitation to the Sahel region and the edges of the Sahara Desert. The problem is just how far north ITCZ will travel in any year. In good years the ITCZ travels well north and stays there for a long time bringing plenty of moisture to the Sahel. If this extends over several years, people will migrate to the region. However, it is just as possible for the ITCZ to stay south of the Sahel, causing extended years of drought, famine and out migration.

Humidity increases further southward. In the southern part of West Africa (on the Atlantic Coast) and in the Congo Basin the ITCZ is present most of the year, creating tropical rainforests of the Congo Basin. In between the tropical climate and the transition region of the Sahel are grassland and savanna (sparsely forested grasslands) climates and vegetation. These subtropical grasslands exist both north and south of the Congo Basin and are the homes of Africa's large game animals, including giraffes, elephants, lions and zebras. The very southern part of Africa has a Mediterranean climate, which is the same climate as that found in the very northern tips of the continent.

Human Geography of Sub-Saharan Africa

Poverty

Sub-Saharan Africa has a population of about 733 million (2004), which is 11.5% of the world's population (6.396 billion in 2004). This is a relatively low population given the large land area that Sub-Saharan Africa encompasses. It is also one of the poorest regions in the world, accounting for only 1% of the world's gross domestic product (GDP). In urban areas, over 60% of the people live in slum and squatter areas. High infant mortality rates exist in most countries of this region and Sub-Saharan Africa is the only major region in the world where poverty has increased since 1980. The region contains 70% of the world's 50 poorest nations.

Photo 3.12

The Okavango Delta (or Okavango Swamp) in Botswana is the world's largest inland delta. The Okavango River drains into this interior basis, which was a lake 10,000 years ago, instead of the sea. The diversity of big game wildlife is a major tourist attraction

Source: Jarkko Saarninen

The biggest challenge today for Sub-Saharan Africa is AIDS. Of the estimated 34.3 million people in the world who have had AIDS by the year 2000, 24.5 million of them live or lived in Sub-Saharan Africa, and 19 million of them have already died from the disease. A quarter of those deaths have been children under the age of 15. AIDS has reduced the life expectancy in Sub-Saharan Africa from 59 years to 49 years, or less (the global average of 62 years). In Zimbabwe alone it has been reduced from 61 to 33 years, and in Chad it is only 32 years. The overall impact of AIDS by 2010, is projected to have reduced the population of Sub-Saharan Africa by 71 million people – this includes people who would have been born if it were not for the deaths of women of childbearing age. This number is more than twice the 30 million Europeans (1/3 of the population at the time) who died of the bubonic plague (1347–1352 CE), which was previously considered the worst outbreak of disease in world history.

Despite these difficulties, several countries in Sub-Saharan Africa have thriving economies. Good governance and sound fiscal policies, have created bustling and robust economies in Botswana, Ghana, Uganda, Senegal, Gabon, Mauritius and the Seychelles. Ghana, for example, has had one of the strongest stock markets in the world over the past decade.

Traditional Economy

Much of Sub-Saharan Africa has been relatively isolated from the rest of the world throughout history, and even in modern times. North Africa and East Africa have been important trading routes and have been closely connected to world trade for a long time. However, West Africa and areas further to the south were cut off from the major European, Asian and North American trade routes due to deserts, seas and jungles.

Vasco de Gama, from Portugal, was the first European explorer to sail around the Cape of Good Hope (southern tip of Africa), which he accomplished in 1497. This route became the major transportation corridor between Europe and Asia for the next 300 years. During that time, Europeans became very familiar with coastal settlements, but knew nothing of the interior regions of Africa, which they perceived to consist of only deserts and jungles. The plateau character and river navigation challenges made explorations of the interior difficult.

The traditional economy of Sub-Saharan Africa (also known culturally as Black Africa) was primarily subsistence agriculture. Diets consisted mostly of starches, with small amounts of protein. This was true on the savanna and grassland areas, where maize (corn), sorghum and millet were the staples, as well as in the forests and jungles, where sweet potato, cassava and fruit were major foods. These traditional diets were supplemented by the hunting of wild game, which led to the extinction of many large animals.

Shifting cultivation was a common practice, especially in the savannas and jungles of central and eastern Africa. On the savanna, entire families would move as farmers shifted from one field to another. In the jungles, villages usually remained in one place while farmers shifted from one field to another. In both cases, the fields that were left behind were allowed to lie fallow for several years to regain their nutrients. Also in both areas, land holdings were communal, based on the tribal society, and each family received a sufficient amount of land to provide for a subsistence livelihood. In the colonial period, land came under private ownership. This resulted in the migration of landless farmers to the cities, and increased incentives to produce surplus cash crops for sale and export. This directly led to overuse of the soil, shorter fallow periods, and less productive farm lands.

Pastoral herding lifestyles were found on the savanna and on the steppe or grassland areas. Sheep and cattle were the dominant grazing animals and outnumbered people in most of these herding areas. Nomadic and transhumance herding were common in the

PHOTO 3.13

Source: Lauren A. Hall-Lew

past but very rare today. Most of the sedentary herding populations today supplement their cattle and sheep raising with crop production. Cattle, especially, are highly prized symbols of social status in these areas, and are important in marriage ceremonies and religious sacrifices. African cattle breeds are very hearty and resistant to diseases, but tend to be poor milk producers.

Africa today has what is known as a *dual economy*. Traditional agricultural economies (lower circuit) exist outside of the cities, while urban centers have more modern market economies (upper circuit); and there is very little trade between these two groups. In the dual economy model, the upper circuit economy is a money-based system that is tied to international trade. This exists in the coastal urban areas of Sub-Saharan Africa, which have been more influenced by European trade. The lower circuit is a non-monetary barter system that is mostly local. This characterizes many of the non-urban areas of Sub-Saharan Africa.

Empires and Kingdoms

Several empires have arisen in Sub-Saharan Africa over the centuries. The Ethiopian empire, which we discussed briefly in relation to the Middle East, is the earliest major civilization of Sub-Saharan Africa, dating back to pre-Christian times. Ethiopia is the dominant country of East Africa. Legends indicate that the Ethiopian Empire was founded by Menelik I, the son of King Solomon of Israel (960–922 BCE) and the Queen of Sheba (an early name for Abyssinia, located near Ethiopia on the Red Sea). The royal line of Menelik I ended in 1974 with the death of King Haile Selasie.

Poverty reduction has become an important item on the tourism agenda. In 2007, the United Nations World Tourism Organization (UNWTO) identified poverty reduction, along with climate change, as a global challenge to the tourism industry. One particularly important aspect of the interest in equity and human well being as a tourism development goal has been the growth of academic and development agency interest in the relationship between tourism development and poverty-reduction strategies – what is often referred to as pro-poor tourism (PPT). As with the relationship between tourism and sustainable development, the PPT field has developed in great part as a result of interchange between researchers and public and non-government organizations with interests in the less-developed countries. However, also as with sustainable development, the PPT field has become increasingly open to contestation and critical debate.

The focus on providing tourism employment to the unemployed or under-employed is not far removed from the goals of many regional economic development programs. Although PPT advocates tend to suggest that there are qualitative differences with respect to its approach with respect to the poor. However, critics suggest that it fails to address the structural reasons for the north–south divide as well as internal divides within the developing countries, particularly with respect to international trade. For example, in the area of agriculture the European Union (EU) and the United States of America have been strongly against free trade which developing countries have been seeking. Nevertheless, despite such concerns, the UNWTO has resolved that the liberalization of the conditions governing trade in services is compatible with sustainable tourism development and the protection of social and cultural values and identities, and advocate the concept of *tourism liberalization with a human face*.

The idea that openness is good for growth and human development has become deeply ingrained in many development institutions such as the World Bank. However, other agencies, such as the United Nations Development Program (UNDP), have commented that in practice, the relationship between trade and growth is determined by a complex array of domestic and external factors and cross-country evidence provides little foundation for the use of loan conditions or world trade rules to promote rapid liberalization. The UNDP as with many other commentators do argue that liberalization of trade in services, such as tourism, offers potential benefits to developing countries, yet according to the UNDP the industrial countries have focussed on areas that threaten to undermine human development prospects, while failing to liberalize areas that could generate gains for poor countries. However, at a local scale there are a number of PPT initiatives being carried out in Africa with South Africa in particular being a laboratory for the testing and evolution of new approaches towards the planning of local economic development.

Sources

Hall, C.M. (ed.) (2007) *Pro-poor Tourism: Who Benefits? Perspectives on Tourism and Poverty Reduction*, Channel View Publications, Clevedon.

Rogerson, C.M. (2006) Pro-poor local economic development in South Africa: The role of pro-poor tourism, *Local Environment*, 11(1): 37–60.

In 324 CE, the King of Ethiopia converted to Christianity, and ancient Coptic Christian churches are still found in the highlands of Ethiopia. Black Jews from Ethiopia, who practiced a very old form of Judaism, have immigrated to Israel, based on an Israeli law that permits Jews in from around the world to live in Israel.

The Ethiopian empire prospered through its trade with Arabs, supplying gold, ivory and spices from inner Sub-Saharan Africa. In the 19th century the Ethiopians were defeated by invading Italian forces, who in 1936 colonized the country. It was freed by a British invasion in 1941 in the early years of World War II. Today, the highlands of Ethiopia are considered the Switzerland of Africa and a Christian enclave surrounded by Islamic peoples, and lowland areas that have been troubled by famine, war and civil unrest.

West Africa is a major cultural hearth for much of Black Africa. Early civilizations arose along the Niger River. The Ghana Empire existed from the 8th to 12th century, at the same time that the Arab Empire and Chinese Empires were at their peaks. They controlled all trans-Saharan African trade during that time. The Mali Empire replaced the Ghana Empire from the 13th to 15th century. In 1324 its emperor, Mansa Musa, made a pilgrimage to Mecca and visited Arab leaders. Upon his return, he made Mali one of the major Muslim countries in the region.

In Southern Africa, Zimbabwe was the center of the Karanga Empire in the 11th century. Through trade with Arabs to the north, they became very advanced in mining industries, agriculture and trade with South Asia. The word *Zimbabwe* was the name of a religious shrine that was built in the 12th century by the Karanga people, which demonstrated their high level of architectural skill. When the white dominated government of Rhodesia was voted out of office in 1979, the new leaders of Rhodesia renamed their country Zimbabwe after this religious shrine.

In the 15th century, Bantu-speaking peoples from the tropical savannas and rainforests of West Africa spread into the Congo Basin, pushing the indigenous pygmy tribes into the Kalahari Desert to the south. The Bantus established the Congo Kingdom, which covered a wide area and prospered through trade with its neighbors. In the 16th century its king adopted Christianity and began a process to modernize the Congo Kingdom, using Portugal as a model. However, in the 17th century the kingdom declined following wars with its neighbors and the demoralizing impacts of the slave trade. In 1665, it was invaded and colonized by Portugal.

Slavery

All of Sub-Saharan Africa's empires and kingdoms were in decline when the Europeans arrived in the 16th century. The major product that the Europeans wanted from Africa was slaves. Slavery has existed in Sub-Saharan Africa since Egyptian times. Arab traders sold Black slaves to the Greeks and the Romans. (Early Greece had more slaves than free men.) Slavery was also common in Sub-Saharan Africa itself, and existed there long after it was abolished elsewhere in the world. Some say that slavery still exists in pockets of Sub-Saharan Africa to this day.

In the late 16th century, the Portuguese brought African slaves to work on the first plantations in the New World that they established in Brazil. Brazil was an area with a very low native population density, so the Portuguese relied on imported labor to work their agricultural lands. In 1602, the Dutch brought the first African slaves to North America, putting them to work on their colonies in the Caribbean. The first

PHOTO 3.14

The cape coast castle and dungeon in Ghana was a major center for the Trans-Atlantic Slave Trade in the late 1600s and early 1700s, and later became the administrative center for the British gold coast colonies

Source: Lauren A. Hall-Lew

black Africans came to the British colonies as indentured servants in 1619, a year before the Mayflower brought the Pilgrims to New England. By the late 1600s most Black Africans were brought to the colonies as slaves. Large numbers of West African Blacks came as slaves to the Americas in the early 1700s to work on the plantations of the British colonial South, the Caribbean and Brazil.

The British were the main source of African slaves to their colonies. They brought fabrics, costume jewelry and other manufactured goods to West Africa where they traded these for slaves. They also brought to Africa corn, peanuts, sweet potatoes, coconuts, bananas and citrus fruit (from other tropical lands), all of which greatly improved the traditional diet of Sub-Saharan Africa. From West Africa they brought slaves to the West Indies (the Caribbean), and the colonial southern USA. Only about 85% survived the trans-Atlantic journey. (Although this number was much higher than in East Africa where only about 10% survived to the Arab slave trade.) The peak of the African slave trade to North and South America was in 1791 when about 75,000 slaves were brought by the British, Portuguese, Dutch, French and Danish. In total an estimated 11 million slaves were brought to the Americas.

In 1807, Great Britain banned slavery within the British Isles. In 1834, the British banned slavery throughout to the British Empire. The United States banned the slave trade in 1808, though it was not enforced on a regular basis. The reasons the

PHOTO 3.15
Colorful festival in Swaziland

Source: Jarkko Saarninen

trans-Atlantic slave trade lasted more than 200 years were several. First was the need for inexpensive labor in the plantations of the New World, especially in areas that had low native populations or where natives were uninterested in working for Europeans. Second was the competitive nature of African tribes. Tribal groups that relied on hunting required vast areas of land to meet their resource needs, and they often fought violently with intruders. Herding tribes needed access to grasslands and savannas, and resented being enclosed by other groups which prevented them from practicing transhumance. Sedentary tribes needed access to the best agricultural lands, and along with shifting agriculturalists, struggled to keep cattle and game animals out of their crops. Competition for scarce resources among these lifestyles has long been an issue in Sub-Saharan Africa. Rather than killing one's enemies, the tradition arose to enslave them, and sometimes sell them as slaves to others.

Tribalism

The word *tribe* is often used to describe the social organization in Sub-Saharan Africa. The definition of *tribe* is any group of people who share the same customs and languages, and who believe they descended from a common ancestor. There are an estimated 600 to 1000 tribes in Sub-Saharan Africa, many of which speak their own separate language. (There are an estimated 900 to 1500 different languages spoken in

Sub-Saharan Africa and most Africans speak more than one language.) Tribes range in size from a few thousand to several million members. Tribes are a form of communal association. They support individuals in times of need, and they expect conformity to customs, traditions and other basic laws governing behavior. Most tribes also include some form of shared work among their members. In Sub-Saharan Africa there are often tribal marks that people carry, such as a cut on the face of some kind, that were used in the past to identify one's tribal affiliation.

In Anglo North America, the rights of the individual are often considered more important than the groups or social organizations that they belong to. Examples include the right to free speech and a general belief that an individual has the right to do as one wishes. For much of the rest of the world, however, the group is considered more important than the individual. To many Africans, the family, the clan and the tribe are more important than either the individual or the country in which they live. In part, this is because the African countries that exist today were created by Europeans – they did not exist prior to colonialization and they have little relation to traditional tribal boundaries. Most are not nation-states and their citizens have not had a long history of identification with today's African countries.

Political Boundaries

The political boundaries of most of the countries of Africa today were created at the 1884 *Berlin Conference* where the European colonial powers divided up the African continent among themselves. This was before most of the interior of Africa was colonized or even explored. Because the older empires and kingdoms of Africa were almost non-existent by this time, the European powers had little difficulty in dividing them up indiscriminately. (They had done the same in the Middle East, but were unable to do this in the rest of Asia.) The result was that the former empires of Africa, along with all of the major tribes, were split or joined in a manner that made little sense based on ethnic territories. This was the complete opposite of the nation-state form of countries that had evolved in Europe. Traditional political systems that were based on tribes were shattered, and to this day separatist movements and inter-tribal warfare exist in many Sub-Saharan African countries.

The worst recent outbreak of tribal tensions occurred in Burundi and Rwanda, two former Belgian colonies. In 1994, militias from the majority population Hutu tribe in Rwanda slaughtered 937,000 members of the ruling Tutsi tribe and moderate Hutus. This event is known as the Rwanda Genocide. The genocide was sparked by events in neighboring Burundi, where Hutus and Tutsis had been in a state of civil war since 1993. These tensions have a long history. In 1972, for example, the Rwanda Tutsis killed between some 200,000 Hutus, including all educated Hutus, in an effort to suppress any attempt to overthrow the Tutsi rulers. Other countries that have experienced large-scale tribal conflicts in recent decades include Nigeria (between Muslims in the north and Christians in the south), Somalia, and more recently Sudan (both in it its southern region and western region), Zimbabwe, Eritrea (which fought a successful civil war against Ethiopia), Liberia (which is a country created by the United States as a place for former Black slaves to return to Africa), and elsewhere.

While a logical approach to this problem may be to redraw the map of Africa, this is no longer a viable option. Although tribal allegiances remain strong across political boundaries, new political and economic interest groups have been formed based on the countries as they exist today. Contemporary politics in Africa requires the appeasement of various ethnic groups within a country's boundaries by giving them some form of limited autonomy and providing funding for economic development.

Most of the major conflicts in Sub-Saharan Africa are largely ignored in the developed Western countries. This is so for several reasons: (1) there is often limited television coverage of events there by the news media in the West, (2) there are seldom any political or economic consequences of these conflicts for Western countries, (3) the cultural and social ties of Sub-Saharan Africa to the West are limited and (4) the West expects things like this to happen in Sub-Saharan Africa. This last explanation is probably tinged with a degree of racism.

Coups d'etat and Political Discord

Largely owing to the role of colonialism, autocratic power brokers, and poverty, Sub-Saharan Africa has experienced considerable political unrest since the mid-1900s. Nearly all countries of Africa have since independence been directly affected by warfare or other forms of political instability. A common phenomenon to have plagued several African countries is coups d'etat, or a military overthrow of the government. In many cases, coups occur repeatedly in various countries, such as Ghana throughout the 1960 to 1990s. These events have major implications for tourism. The immediate effects include closing of international borders and airports, which impedes the flow of people into and out of the country. Coups also result in questionable safety and security for tourists, a lack of investment in tourism infrastructure and relations with other countries often being strained. Africa has also experienced wars and acts

PHOTO 3.16

View from Capetown and Table Mountain, South Africa, from Robben Island. Nelson Mandela was imprisoned on Robben Island for 27 years during the country's apartheid era

Source: Lauren A. Hall-Lew

of genocide, which clearly create negative images and thwart tourism development plans. The ethnic tensions in Rwanda and Burundi during the 1990s, for example, essentially ceased all tourism operations in those countries as international media reports scared off would-be visitors by stories of mass murders and widespread kidnappings and other crimes. Likewise, the present civil war in Sudan, the political chaos and lack of functional government in Somalia, and the current wars in Guinea, Sierra Leone, Eritrea and Ethiopia present an image of Africa that is not conducive to the development and growth of tourism.

Regions of Sub-Saharan Africa

There are about 45 different countries and territories in Sub-Saharan Africa, which is about 20% of all the countries in the world. The major regions of Sub-Saharan Africa include: West Africa, East Africa, Central Africa, Southern Africa and the island of Madagascar.

West Africa

West Africa is the region lying south of the Sahara Desert and bordering the Atlantic Ocean. It is geographically divided into two distinct subregions, each of which has distinct environmental and cultural characteristics. The first region consists of countries in the Sahel region that border the semi-arid environment along the southern Sahara Desert. These countries include:

Burkina Faso	Cape Verde	Chad
The Gambia	Mali	Mauritania
Niger	Senegal	

The second region consists of countries that line the Atlantic Ocean on the humid and tropical Guinean Coast. These countries include:

Benin	Cameroon	Cote d'Ivoire (Ivory Coast)
Equatorial Guinea	Ghana	Guinea
Guinea-Bissau	Liberia	Nigeria
Sierra Leone	Togo	

The Niger River flows through much of the region, although numerous smaller rivers flow from the interior highlands to the ocean. The Guinean Coast, in the southern portions of this region, is a humid tropical rainforest that receives year-round precipitation. Mangrove swamps are common along the coast near the mouths of rivers. Rainfall decreases considerably as one moves northward toward the Sahara Desert. Some countries span both the humid and arid regions of West Africa. Nigeria, for example, is both the wealthiest country in West Africa (due to its large coastal oil reserves) and the most populated country on the African continent. Political tensions between Nigeria's more Muslim north and more Christian south, however, have been a contributing factor in the country's political instability and continuing individual poverty. (West Africa is sometimes referred to as *Western Africa* to avoid confusion with the Economic Community of West African States (ECOWAS), which is sometimes shortened to *West Africa*. ECOWAS is a political and economic association that does not include all of the countries listed above. We use the term *West Africa* in here because its more general definition is widely used outside of the region.

West Africa is among the less visited international destination regions of the world. Nigeria receives the most international visitors, due to its large population and economic importance. Senegal (769,000 international visitors in 2005) is the second most visited country in West Africa. This designation, however, may reflect the fact that The Gambia is surrounded on three sides by Senegal, and cross-border travel between the two countries constitutes international travel. The Gambia has also seen rapid tourism growth in recent years. Ghana is the third most visited country in West Africa (584,000 in 2004), especially for English-speaking tourists, followed by Cote d'Ivoire (Ivory Coast). Nigeria and Ghana are English-speaking countries, while in Senegal and Code d'Ivoire French is the official language. Despite the region's tropical climate and diversity of cultural groups (from interior nomads to coastal agriculturalists and urban settlers), it is the colonial history that forms the basis of Western Africa's international tourism today.

Western Africa was the principal source of slaves brought to the Americas between the 16th and early 19th centuries. The slave trade from Africa resulted in the widespread (forced) migration of people from their African homelands to many other parts of the world. Today this African diaspora has significant implications for tourism, primary of which is a large and growing worldwide desire among people of African descent to visit the land of their ancestors. This form of tourism is sometimes referred to as existential tourism, defined as travel to a place that holds special meaning for the tourist's personal identity. Existential tourism by diasporic populations is widespread today as international transportation has become easier and both voluntary and forced migrations have become commonplace.

Because of its historical role, as dark as that may be, international tourists of African descent have become an extremely important tourist market for Western Africa. This is especially so for tourists who come from regions with higher standards of living, levels of education, and better paying jobs, such as in North America, Europe, and the Caribbean. Many travel agencies and tour operators in the United States, for example, have started to specialize in ancestral travel to Africa, particularly in cities with large African-American populations, such as New York, Chicago, Los Angeles, Philadelphia, Washington DC, San Francisco, Atlanta and Miami. These agencies arrange international trips for African-Americans, typically selling them as *going home* or *motherland* tours.

Ghana has a high concentration of slave-related visitor attractions and is the second most important international tourist destination in Western Africa, receiving 584,000 visitors in 2005. Because of its British colonial history, it is the primary destination of choice in Western Africa for African-American and African-British tourists because it has a higher likelihood of being the origin of many slaves from Western Africa who were brought to the English-speaking countries of the Americas. In addition, the widespread use of English as the country's lingua franca, makes Ghana an easy place to visit for American and British tourists. With this realization, Ghana has focused considerable attention on diaspora tourism, and its current 15-year National Tourism

Development Plan (1996–2010) places slave heritage at the center of the country's tourism development efforts.

Also related to the historical slave trade of Western Africa, UNESCO has put considerable effort into developing and designating a Slave Route through the region. The purpose of the Slave Route is to conserve, commemorate and educate the world about the atrocities associated with the slave trade. However, the UNESCO designation, which is similar to the designation of a World Heritage Site, also adds to the tourist appeal of the region and is a good example of multi-national cooperation in developing a large-scale tourist route.

East Africa

East Africa includes the area known as the Horn of Africa, which contains the countries of Djibouti, Ethiopia, Eritrea and Somalia. East Africa also includes the coastal countries of Kenya and Tanzania, and the East African Rift countries of Uganda, Rwanda and Burundi. The Horn of Africa, along with Rwanda and Burundi, have been the site of some of the most troubling political instability on the African continent in recent years. The lack of a central governing authority in Somalia occasionally spills over into the tourist regions of neighboring countries, while Uganda has the longest running civil war on the African continent. Despite these challenges, East Africa is the second most visited region in Sub-Saharan Africa, after Southern Africa.

The East African Rift System winds its way from north to south through East Africa, forming its western boundary in the south. It is here that the famous lakes of Victoria, Albert, Tanganyika and Nyasa (Malawi) are found, along with some of the most fertile lands on the African continent. The area has a very complex ethnic makeup, with many different languages and language groups, along with a large number of Europeans who were attracted to the agricultural potential during the colonial period, and the remnants of the Arab Empire that once ruled a large part of East Africa.

Kenya is the most visited country in East Africa (1.2 million international visitors in 2004), and one of the third most visited countries in all of Sub-Saharan Africa. Tanzania and Uganda each receive about a half million international visitors a year. Safari tourism, to see big game animals in the wild, forms the basis of tourism in East Africa. In Kenya there are 60 designated wildlife protection areas, which are divided into *parks* that are administered and financed by the country's central government, and *reserves* that are set aside by local authorities, though they are partially financed and administered by the central government. In total, between 6% and 12% of Kenya's land area is protected in these ways. (The land area varies as the boundaries of the protected areas fluctuate from year to year according to management needs.)

A goal of many safari tourists is to see the *Big Five* animals. The term was originally coined by big-game hunters to designate the five most difficult animals to hunt, but now is used by big-game tourists with their cameras. The Big Five include the lion, the African elephant, the African buffalo (or Cape buffalo in South Africa), the leopard and the black rhinoceros. While these animals are also among the most dangerous in Africa, the list does not include the hippopotamus, which is possibly the most dangerous animal when it is in water. Wildebeests, gazelles and zebras are among the other big game animals that are distinctive to the safari lands of East Africa and Southern Africa.

Photo 3.17

Mount Kilimanjaro in Tanzania from Amboseli National Park in Kenya. This extinct Volcanic mountain is the highest peak in Africa at 19,340 ft/5,895 m, and is considered the tallest free-standing mountain in the world, rising 15,100 ft/4,600 m from its base

Tanzania is home to Mount Kilimanjaro (although part of it lies in Kenya), the Ngorongoro, and the Serengeti and had, prior to the 1970s, been in direct competition with Kenya for leadership in safari tourism in East Africa. However, the country fell behind during two decades of ineffective government policies. Mount Kilimanjaro is the highest peak in Africa (19,340 ft; 5,895 m). It is an inactive stratovolcano that is geologically related to the Great Rift Valley, and although it is famous for its snow-capped peak, the current trend in global warming is making that a scene from the past. The Nogorongoro Conservation Area is in the Great Rift Valley, and Serengeti National Park is located on the plains adjacent to this in the northern part of Tanzania. The Serengeti is also home to the Maasai people and is famous for being home to an estimate 1.5 million large game herbivores and predators.

The Great Rift Valley in East Africa has created a series of large lakes that are known collectively as the Great Lakes of Africa. The most famous of these are Lake Victoria and Lake Tanganyika. Lake Victoria (or Victoria Nyanza) is the world's second largest freshwater lake, and the largest lake located in a tropical region of the world. Its oval shape lies prominently within a large plateau on the east side of the Great Rift Valley. It is bordered by the three major tourism countries of East Africa: Tanzania, Uganda and Kenya. Uganda's Ssese Islands, a large collection of islands in the northwest of the lake, have become a popular tourist destination in recent years. Lake Tanganyika is the world's second deepest lake and the world's second largest in total water volume. It fills the Great Rift Valley towards its southern end, forming a long (418 miles; 673 km), relatively narrow (about 60 km; 40 miles), and very deep (4820 ft; 1,470 m) body of water. While Lake Victoria is the source of the White Nile River, which flows north to the Mediterranean Sea, Lake Tanganyika's waters flow into the Congo Basin and out to the Atlantic Ocean.

TOURISM ISSUES AND INSIGHTS
MANAGING THE SAVANNA LANDSCAPE

The special appeal of the African savanna landscape for western tourists is well recognized. The African savanna is widely viewed as the archetypal wild environment, a place of unspoilt nature. The appeal of this *safari* landscape – scattered thorn bushes, wide vistas, yellow grass, herds of animals – is reinforced by countless wildlife documentaries, tourist brochures, films and web advertising. Yet such images tend to obscure the fact that these are environments over which bitter struggles have been fought for. Whether or not visitors and tour operators recognize their presence, people that inhabit these environments are often clinging to a precarious livelihood in marginal economic and environmental conditions. In east and southern Africa, for example, the colonial and post-colonial state has had a major role in reshaping the landscape, creating huge national parks in conflict with the interests of both settled local communities and nomadic pastoralists who find themselves in competition with wildlife for the use of savanna plains. As a result, local people in extreme environments often have contested relationships with agencies of the national government. They have often been moved around at its behest and are unlikely to trust power emanating from a distant capital city. Commercial tourism agencies, also often closely linked to the very states that created this crisis of marginalization, may fail to grasp the highly political nature of questions of environmental sustainability in dry environments.

The devastating social effects of forced removals and reduction of grazing lands through the creation of national parks and other protected areas is now widely recognized. It is increasingly acknowledged that in the process of expanding conservation areas and tourist operations, local property rights need to be protected as far as possible, particularly given that the appropriation of all resource rights by governments and centrally managing them has not worked to the benefit of either conservation or local economic development. In the last two decades, various experiments in community-based tourism and attempts to give communities greater local rights over wildlife and land, have been pioneered in dry environments. In fact, such an approach is now widely viewed as the only hope for sustainable wildlife tourism.

Source

Preston-Whyte, R., Brooks, S. and Ellery, W. (2006) Deserts and savanna regions, In S. Gössling and C.M. Hall (eds) *Tourism and Global Environmental Change*, Routledge, London.

Central Africa

Central Africa is a large region that straddles the equator and is largely drained by the Congo River system flowing out of the Congo Basin. In the north, Central Africa includes the southern Saharan Desert countries of Chad and Sudan. The humid, tropical climate zone begins in Cameroon and the Central African Republic, which form the northern part of the Congo Basin. Further to the south are the countries of Gabon, Republic of the Congo (Brazzaville), and the Democratic Republic of the Congo (Kinshasa), formerly known as Zaire. The island country of Sao Tome and Principe is also included in this region. Most of these countries were once part of French Equatorial Africa and have had long administrative ties to the former Belgian Congo.

Central Africa is characterized by a hot and wet climate. The ITCZ hovers over this region 12 months out of the year and there is no significant dry season. Although rainforests predominate in the lowlands of the Congo Basin, these are surrounded by flat savannas and open forests on the higher plateau lands (up to 3000 ft; 900 m) to the north and south and around the higher elevations that surround the Congo Basin. Unlike the Great Rift Valley region to the east, the population density is very low throughout central Africa. Large areas of tropical rainforests are completely devoid of people and the first cities in this region were not established until the Europeans arrived in the 15th century. Most of the people today still live in rural communities that are very traditional.

The countries of Central Africa have among the least-developed economies in Africa and the region overall is the least visited in Sub-Saharan Africa. Gabon is the big exception to this. Due to it coastal oil reserves (similar to Nigeria), Gabon's capital city, Libreville, has very modern buildings, roads, and casinos. It is also one of the most expensive cities in the world, and one of the safer capital cities of Sub-Saharan Africa.

By contrast, Kinshasa, the capital of the Democratic Republic of the Congo, is a sprawling and dusty city of colorful, yet impoverished people. *The Congo (Kinshasa),* as the country is also known has long been acknowledged to have among the richest natural resources on the African continent, not the least of which are diamonds and coltan (which is used in all mobile phones). Corrupt and ruthless governments and civil wars have, however, devastated the country and caused widespread malnutrition. They have also threatened the great biodiversity of the country's tropical rainforests, which include many rare animal species, including common and pygmy chimpanzees, mountain gorillas, okapis and white rhinos. The country has five national parks that are listed as World Heritage Sites, all of which have been listed as *In Danger* in recent years as the poor economic conditions of the over 63 million people in Congo (Kinshasa) have pushed many of them to turn to bushmeat (wild animal meat) as a food source. Because of these problems, the Congo Basin has come to symbolize the *dark* side of the African continent.

Southern Africa

Southern Africa includes the countries of Angola, Botswana, Lesotho, Malawi, Mozambique, Namibia, South Africa, Swaziland, Zambia and Zimbabwe. Southern Africa transitions from the more humid Congo Basin in the north to the dry Kalahari Desert in its central region. Milder Mediterranean type climates are found further toward the Cape of Good Hope (at the southern tip of the African continent).

In August 2007 the WWF-UK (World Wildlife Fund-United Kingdom) released its annual league table of the plants and animals most commonly brought illegally into the United Kingdom. Many of the seized items derived from species protected under the Convention on International Trade in Endangered Species of Wild Fauna and Flora (Cites), the worldwide agreement that bans trade in 827 species and strictly controls the movement of more than 32,000 others. The items confiscated included snakeskin goods, elephant ivory carvings and, top of the list with the highest number of seizures, 605 kg (more than half a ton) of traditional Chinese medicines that contains endangered species such as tiger, rhinoceros, seahorse and deer musk. In total there were 429 seizures in 2006–2007, up from the previous year's total of 302.

Traditional Chinese medicines, the subject of 97 seizures, can contain material from threatened species such as tigers, rhinos, leopards, bears and seahorses. There were also 221 seizures of elephant ivory and skin products, 44 seizures of snake and lizard products such as handbags and shoes, and 39 seizures of similar crocodile and alligator products. The United Kingdom authorities also seized almost 1,000 live reptiles such as snakes, chameleons, tortoises and terrapins. In total United Kingdom Customs confiscated more than 163,000 illegal wildlife trade items, many made from highly endangered species, and more than 158,000 plants, including orchids and cycads. More than 1,270 kg of coral was also stopped in a total of 23 seizures. According to Heather Sohl, wildlife trade officer at WWF, many tourists could be unwittingly helping to push some of the world's most endangered species to the brink of extinction for the sake of exotic souvenirs, with the majority of seizures not being bought in by criminals but by holidaymakers as souvenirs. The message of the WWF is therefore *if in doubt don't buy*.

Source

WWF, Endangered Species (also see Wildlife trade link on same page): http://www.wwf.org. uk/researcher/issues/rarespecies/

Southern Africa attracted many European colonialists, and as a result has experienced a long history of political and economic struggles between the white elite and emerging Black nationalism. South Africa is the dominant industrial power of Southern Africa, and the wealthiest country on the African continent. Mozambique, on the other hand, is by some measures considered the poorest country in the world.

Southern Africa as a whole received the most international tourists of any of the regions in Sub-Saharan Africa. With 7.5 million tourists in 2005, the country of South Africa was second only to Egypt (8.2 million) in visitor arrivals for the entire African continent. Zimbabwe was second in visitor arrivals (1.8 million in 2005) in Sub-Saharan Africa. Botswana, Namibia (a former German colony), and Zambia each receives between half a million and one million visitors a year. Zambia and Zimbabwe share one of the most famous attractions in Southern Africa; Victoria Falls. At Victoria Falls, the expansive Zambezi River (Africa's fourth longest river) flows into a series of deep chasms. Zambia and Zimbabwe also both share large areas

PHOTO 3.18
The Namib Desert in Namibia

Source: Jarkko Saarninen

of pristine nature preserves that have considerable tourism potential. Zambia, however, suffers from poor transportation and accommodation infrastructure to support international tourism.

In contrast to Zambia, Zimbabwe has a well-developed transportation network and tourist resorts, much of which was built when by the White minority that ruled the country under the former name of *Rhodesia*. In addition to Victoria Falls, Zimbabwe has four other World Heritage Sites, and all of them are threatened by the social unrest and instability brought on by the country's dictocratic leadership. Rhodesia was once the breadbasket of Africa, but Zimbabwe today is a country of malnutrition, low education rates, high crime rates, and an average life expectancy of only 36 years in 2006.

South Africa

South Africa is probably the most diverse country in Sub-Saharan Africa, both culturally and environmentally. It has snow-capped winter peaks, the Atlantic, Antarctic and Indian Oceans, subtropical forests and grasslands, and high plateaus. Its wildlife preserves are the most diverse in Africa, including the Greater St. Lucia Wetland Park, which is the only estuary in the world where both ocean sharks and the freshwater hippopotamus share the same habitat. Just as diverse is the human population, which consists of several African tribes and Dutch Boer, British, and South Asian immigrants.

Photo 3.19
Beachfront hotels and condominiums in Durban, South Africa

Source: Alan A. Lew

Between 1948 and 1994 the country of South Africa practiced a form of political and social racial segregation under a policy known as apartheid. Apartheid affected all aspects of life in South Africa. It dictated what types of transportation people could use, what educational institutions they could attend, where they could live and work, and where they could eat and sleep. Black South Africans were essentially relegated to the marginal areas of the country and had few legal rights. As a result of its racial policies, South Africa was constantly criticized by the global community, and sanctions limited international trade and tourism.

Apartheid policies resulted in the formation of four black *independent homelands*, which were set aside as places for African natives who were not a part of South Africa. Like American Indian reservations, Ciskei, Transkei, Venda and Bophuthatswana were established in poor resource areas for the sole abode of Black Africans. These lands were treated by the South African government as independent countries, although no other countries in the world recognized them as such. Owing to their unique sovereign status and limited natural resources, all of these homelands pursued tourism as a form of economic activity. They especially developed forms of tourism that were not permitted in the religiously conservative South Africa. This included large-scale resort development with an emphasis on gambling, prostitution, and other illicit activities that appealed to the white and colored (mixed race) peoples of South Africa. Like the state of Nevada in the United States, South African tourists frequently traveled to the homelands to indulge in these activities, which were strictly forbidden in the white controlled areas. With the dissolution of apartheid policies and the election of a primarily Black government in 1994, the homelands were dissolved and reintegrated back into the Republic of South Africa, though their resorts continued to thrive.

The almost half a century of apartheid policies in South Africa had a significant impact on the country's heritage tourism. The Black African past had essentially been written out of the country's official history, and tourism development (museums and monuments) focused primarily on the history of the White minority. In 1994, however, this also changed, and the country is beginning to experience a rebirth of its indigenous heritage, focusing on their struggle for political and social recognition. Black African museums and heritage sites have opened up and now surpass the number of *white* establishments, and tour itineraries are now more balanced and objective in their treatment of both Black and White heritages in the country.

Madagascar and the Indian Ocean Islands

The islands off the southern Indian Ocean coast of Africa are considered part of the African continent, though culturally they share much in common with the larger Indian Ocean region, extending to South Asia and Southeast Asia. Madagascar is the fourth largest island in the world, and the largest, by far, of the Indian Ocean island countries. It has a very distinct language (Malagasy) and culture that are more related to Indonesia and the South Pacific than to Africa. Geologically, it was part of India until 70 million years ago when it wandered off on its own. Because it has been isolated for so long, Madagascar has a unique biology, including being the home of lemurs, an early cat-like monkey, and many other plants and animals found only on the island. This unique biology has significant potential as an ecotourism resource for the country, if it can survive threats of extinction caused by the destruction of natural habitats.

The eastern side of the island of Madagascar is the windward side and the natural vegetation is one of dense tropical rainforests. However, this is also where most of the population lives and much of the natural vegetation has been cut for fuel wood and agricultural purposes. Traditionally, shifting cultivation was a sustainable form of agriculture in which farmers would work a plot of land until the nutrients were depleted, then leave it to regenerate while working on a different plot of land. The growing populations of eastern Madagascar do not give the land sufficient time to regenerate, however, resulting in the massive loss of topsoil and downstream flooding.

International tourist arrivals to Madagascar are only a fraction of those to the small island of Mauritius, which received 761,000 international tourists in 2005. The Republic of Mauritius consists of several small, formerly volcanic islands, where South Asians comprise just over 50% of the population. It has over a million people and in addition to traditional agriculture, its economy is based on beach tourism, off-shore banking and small-scale manufacturing. Reunion island is similar in these characteristics, except that it is still governed directly by France. The Comoros islands are an Islamic republic and one of the poorest countries in the world. The nearby Seychelles are a popular beach tourism destination and is both the smallest independent country in Africa, and the continent's wealthiest on a per capita basis.

TOURISM ISSUES AND INSIGHTS
THE ENVIRONMENTAL IMPACT OF TOURISM –
THE CASE OF THE SEYCHELLES

The Seychelles is a republic of just over one hundred islands in the southwest Indian Ocean. Tourism is the second most important source of foreign exchange for the islands. Because the environment is an extremely significant component of its attractiveness, especially for water-based tourism such as scuba diving and snorkeling, the country has made extensive conservation efforts. However, one of the biggest issues in the study of the environmental impact of tourism is the area of study. Do we just focus on what happens at the destination or do we try and incorporate the environmental effects of traveling to and from the destination? In a study of the 118,000 international leisure tourists who visited the country in 2000 it was found that 97% of the environmental impact (in terms of energy consumption and production of greenhouse gases) was a result of tourists traveling to and from the Seychelles from their homes in Europe, South Africa and elsewhere. The environmental impacts of a typical holiday journey to the Seychelles (10.4 days) were the equivalent of the environmental impacts of the average human being in a year. Such a finding therefore presents a significant challenge to our understanding of how to evaluate the environmental impacts of tourism as well as how to manage such impacts. For long-distance destinations such as the Seychelles it also present multiple problems. Are the conservation efforts at the local level that are often funded through tourism being overwhelmed in the longer term by the environmental impacts of *getting there*? In addition, a second issue is that for island microstates that are often distant from their major markets what other economic alternative is there?

Sources

Gössling, S., Hansson, C.B., Hörstmeier, O. and Saggel, S. (2002) Ecological footprint analysis as a tool to assess tourism sustainability, *Ecological Economics*, 43: 199–211.
Gössling, S. and Hall, C.M. (2006) *Tourism and Global Environmental Change*, Routledge, London.

	Population 2006 (1,000)	World population share 2006 (%)	International tourist arrivals (1,000)		Change since 1990 (%)	World market share 2004 (%)
			1990*	2004		
WORLD	**6525170**	**100.0**	**436757**	**776837**	**77.9**	**100.0**
Old World	**1272166**	**19.5**	**32698**	**94281**	**188.3**	**12.1**
Central Asia	91175	1.4	1821	3955	117.2	0.5
Southwest Asia and North Africa	432342	6.6	24006	72683	202.8	9.4
Sub-Saharan Africa	748649	11.5	6871	17643	156.8	2.3
Top 10 Destination Countries						
1 Turkey	70413.96	1.1	4799	16826	250.6	2.2
2 Saudi Arabia	27019.73	0.4	2209	8579	288.4	1.1
3 Egypt	78887.01	1.2	2411	7795	223.3	1.0
4 South Africa	44187.64	0.7	1029	6815	562.3	0.9
5 Tunisia	10175.01	0.2	3204	5998	87.2	0.8
6 Morocco	33241.26	0.5	4024	5477	36.1	0.7
7 Bahrain	698.585	0.0	1376	3514	155.4	0.5
8 Syria	18881.36	0.3	562	3033	439.7	0.4
9 Jordan	5906.76	0.1	572	2853	398.8	0.4
10 Zimbabwe	12236.81	0.2	636	1854	191.5	0.2

*Central Asia International Tourist Arrivals 1995 instead of 1990.
Sources: World Tourism Organization (UNWTO), 2007, Facts and Figures.

ASIA AND OCEANIA

THE ASIA AND OCEANIA REALM

This section covers about half of the world, both in total area and in total population. It includes the countries of East Asia, Southeast Asia and South Asia (from Japan to Pakistan), the continents of Australia and Antarctica, and most of the island nations and territories of the Indian and Pacific Oceans. Asia, Antarctica and Australia comprise about 35 percent of the Earth's land area, and over half of the planet's total surface when the Pacific and Indian Oceans are included. Asia and Oceania realm has about 60 percent of the world's population, with India and China having populations of over one billion, and Indonesia, Pakistan, Japan and Bangladesh all with over 100 million.

Given the vast territory covered, it is not surprising that each of the major regions of the Asia and Oceania realm has distinct cultural and environmental characteristics. East Asia has relatively homogeneous cultures that share sinitic (Chinese) influences. South Asia and Southeast Asia are culturally more diverse, though the giants of India and Indonesia still manage to keep their many ethnic groups united under one

PHOTO 4.1
Asia and Oceania from space

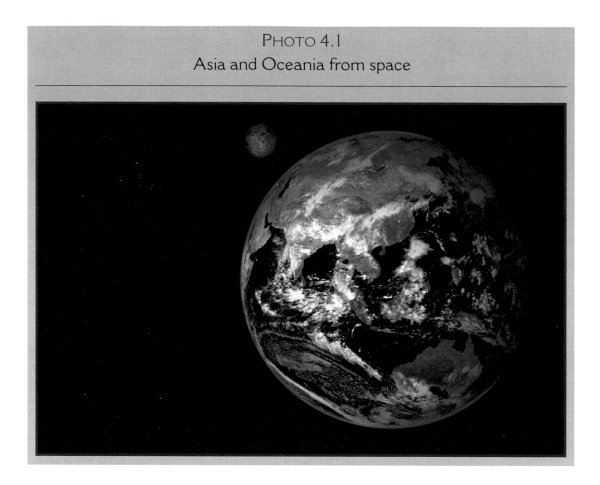

government. Southeast Asia sits as a culture and economic crossroads between East Asia, South Asia and Oceania. Oceania is divided between the European influenced Australia and New Zealand, and the widely dispersed islands of the Indian Ocean and the South Pacific, with Antarctica possibly being the most distant and isolated land of all. With the equator running through its middle, most of the Asia and Oceania realm is tropical and subtropical, though cold extremes are found in the far north and in the Antarctic (Figure 4.1).

4.1   SOUTH ASIA

Physical Geography

South Asia includes the countries of India, Pakistan, Bangladesh, the island nations of Sri Lanka and the Maldives, and the Himalayan countries of Nepal and Bhutan. South Asia is sometimes referred to as the Indian Subcontinent because it is dominated by the country and peninsula of India. It is a very diverse region, but like Africa, its physical geography is fairly straightforward and easy to comprehend. The Indian peninsula is a large tilted block of land that is actually connected to Australia and has moved north-ward and collided into the larger Asian continent. On the western side of this peninsula

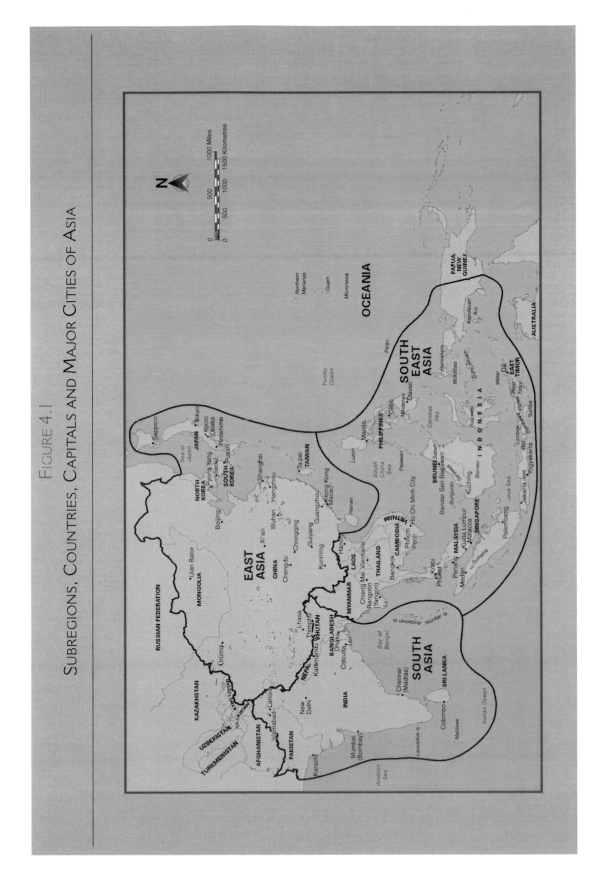

FIGURE 4.1

SUBREGIONS, COUNTRIES, CAPITALS AND MAJOR CITIES OF ASIA

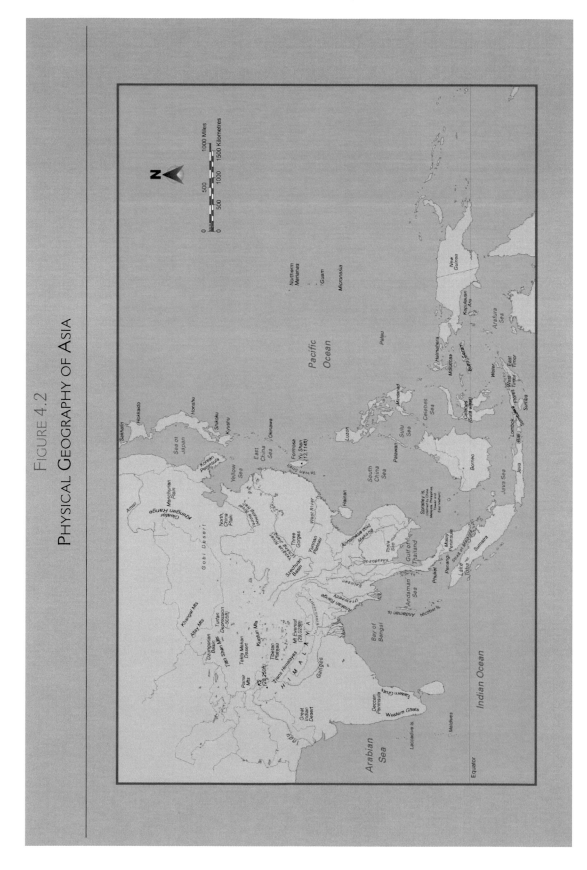

FIGURE 4.2

PHYSICAL GEOGRAPHY OF ASIA

A Buddhist stupa a Mong La Pass (13,117 ft/3978 m) in the Khumbu region of Nepal, on the trail to Mt. Everest, which is in far distance in the left of this scene.

Source: Alan A. Lew

are the Western Ghats mountains, and on the eastern side are the lower Eastern Ghats mountains. In between these two mountain systems is the Deccan Plateau.

The north of the South Asian subcontinent is surrounded by high mountains. In the west the dominant range is the Sulaiman Mountains, found in Pakistan and along its border with Afghanistan. This comparatively low mountain range extends northward to the Pamir Knot, which is where the Himalayan Mountain Range starts. The Sulaimans were the gateway to South Asia for invading groups from Central Asia and the Middle East.

The Himalayas extend across most of the width of South Asia from west to east, and include most of the highest mountain peaks in the world, including Mount Everest (29,028 ft; 8,864 m) and K2 (28,250 ft; 8,611 m). North of the Himalayas is the Tibetan Plateau, with a base elevation of 15,000 ft (4,570) above sea level. At the eastern end of the Himalayan Range the Indian Subcontinent is bounded by the Chin Hills and the Arakan Range which form India's border with Myanmar in Southeast Asia.

South Asia has three major rivers: the Indus, the Ganges, and the Brahmaputra. All three flow out of the Himalayan Mountains and the Tibetan Plateau. The Indus River flows through Pakistan to the Arabian Sea. The Ganges River begins near the origin of the Indus but flows eastward across northern India and out to the Bay of

Bengal. The vast flat area these two rivers traverse is known as the Indo-Gangetic Plain. The Brahmaputra River also begins near the origin of the Indus and Ganges but flows eastward across the Tibetan Plateau side of the Himalayas and down through Bangladesh, where it joins the Ganges River flowing into the Bay of Bengal.

The term *monsoon* refers to a climate where winds shift direction between the summer and winter seasons. Properly used, there is a *winter monsoon wind* and a *summer monsoon wind*, although most people around the world use the term *monsoon* simply to refer to summer rain storms, which are often more intense than winter rains. South Asia has the most distinct monsoonal climate in the world caused by the large mass of the Asian continent. In the summer season, the Asian continent heats up, causing air to rise and forming a low pressure air system over Siberia. The opposite occurs in the winter when a very cold Siberia forms a high pressure air system.

The summer Siberian low pressure system circulates in a counterclockwise direction, while the winter high pressure circulates in a clockwise direction. The change in direction of these winds in Siberia changes the monsoonal wind patterns in South Asia. The counterclockwise summer wind directions over the continent of Asia pulls air across the Arabian Sea and Indian Ocean, where the air picks up moisture. The air then moves to the Indian Peninsula, bringing the heaviest rainfall to the Western Ghats and Bangladesh, and the mountains that form India's border with Myanmar. When the air system is working well, these winds bring rain throughout much of the Indian subcontinent. When the summer monsoon fails to arrive, as it occasionally does, the result is drought, crop failures and possibly famine. When they are too strong or too concentrated, they can result in widespread flooding and crop and property damage.

The Winter Monsoon moves in the opposite direction, bringing moist air from the Bay of Bengal to the Eastern Ghats of the Indian Peninsula. However, it tends to be drier than the summer monsoon, and while it brings rain, it has less of an impact on the entire South Asian region. (The winter monsoon tends to have a greater impact on East and Southeast Asia.)

Because of the summer and winter monsoons, the natural vegetation of large parts of South Asia is either tropical rainforest or semitropical rainforest. This vegetation is particularly pronounced on the island of Sri Lanka, on the western coast of India, in the Western Ghats, in Bangladesh and on the southern slopes of the Himalayas. The year-round rainfall in most of these areas, along with high temperatures, also make them major rice growing regions. Deciduous trees and shrublands are the most common vegetation in the rest of India. These are found on the central Deccan Plateau, which lies in the rain shadow of the Western Ghats, and on the Indo-Gangetic Plain. Drier grasslands and deserts are also found in South Asia, especially in the lower reaches of the Indus River Valley, where the Thar Desert is located, and in the Sulaiman Range of Pakistan. The Tibetan Plateau is also mostly grassland.

Human Geography

Boundaries within India are mostly based on ethno-linguistic lines. South Asia contains one of the greatest diversities of ethnicity in the world. The region is dominated by India, which has a population of just over a billion people (about 1/6 of the world's population) and is incredibly diverse. The national language of India is Hindi, which is only spoken by about 35 percent of the population; in addition, English is widely used as a lingua franca, which allows all educated people in the country to communicate in a common language. In addition to Hindi there are 14 other official languages in India, each of which is associated with a different ethnic group and several of which have their own writing systems. Altogether there are at least 1650 languages and dialects spoken in India. Political borders in India are often based on ethno-linguistic lines. The major racial groups include the Indo-Aryan peoples who live predominantly in the north, and the Dravidian peoples, who are mostly in the east and south. Australoid-Negrito people reside in smaller numbers in the central hills of the Deccan Plateau, and Mongoloid peoples (related to Tibetans and Chinese) predominate in the northern mountains and in Assam in the northeastern portion of the country.

The other countries of South Asia are less diverse than India but still face the challenge of ethnic diversity within their borders. Pakistan, for example, has four major ethnic groups, each of which is associated with a different province. Its capital, Islamabad, was built as a new city in a central and neutral location. The island country of Sri Lanka is 72 percent Sinhalese (which is related to the Indo-Aryan race), 20 percent Tamil (who are a Dravidian racial group mostly found in southern India), and 6 percent Moors (who came to the island as traders from North Africa). Over the past couple of decades a civil war has been fought by the Tamils of Sri Lanka against the dominant Sinhalese rulers of the island. Nepal is mostly Hindu in its southern portions bordering India, and mostly Buddhist in its mountains bordering Tibet. The smallest countries of South Asia are the Himalayan Kingdom of Bhutan and the Islamic country of the Maldives in the Indian Ocean. Afghanistan was considered part of South Asia during colonial times, but is more often grouped with the Middle East today.

Indo-Aryan Invasions

One of the distinct characteristics of South Asia is the influence of the Hindu caste system. The caste system is believed to have originated with the Indo-Aryan invasions of the ancient Indus River Valley civilization – one of the oldest on earth. It dated to about 3000 BCE, which made it concurrent with the early Egyptians and Mesopotamians. Much of the Indus River civilization of that time has been buried underground by the waters of the Indus and Ganges Rivers. Archaeologists believe that the Indus River civilization was a matriarchal society, based on evidence that they worshiped a female fertility goddess. They were dark skinned and short in stature, and were probably vegetarians.

The Indo-Aryans probably originated somewhere in Central Asia. They invaded Europe, Southwest Asia and South Asia between 2000 and 1500 BCE (although some argue that this was more of a migration than a military invasion). Common linguistic features can be found in the languages of all three regions dating back to this time period. The Indo-Aryans were cattle herders with highly developed military capabilities. They were probably light-skinned and taller in stature than were the people of the Indus River, and they were meat eaters. They never united the entire Indian subcontinent, nor even the entire Indo-Gangetic Plain, mostly due to constant warfare among themselves. These battles formed the basis of the Mahabarata Epic, which is a classical and semi-religious set of stories of early India. The Indo-Aryan peoples arrived by sea in Sri Lanka in the 6th and 5th centuries BCE, skipping over much of central India.

The Caste System

The Indo-Aryan social structure consisted of three major groups: priests and teachers, warriors and rulers, and herders and manual laborers. In Europe these became the three social groups of the Middle Ages: priests, nobles and peasants. (Some claim that in the United States this later became the basis for common references to upper, middle and lower socioeconomic classes.) In India the three groups became the Brahman caste, the Kshatriya caste and the Vaisya caste, respectively. In addition to these three principal castes, two other caste groups were developed: the Shudras, who were Dravidians living in the Indus Valley, and the Dalits, who included everyone else. Thus, the five basic caste groups of Hinduism were formed in India. Some scholars argue that these casts were not a clearly fixed hierarchy in India until the late 1800s when the British shaped it to more resemble the class system they were accustomed to:

- Brahmans are the priests, scholars and educated caste; they eat no meat, a trait that they picked up from the Dravidians. They live in temples and in the town centers where the temples are located. They can be very poor, having given up attachments to the material world. Sometimes they work as cooks in restaurants because everyone else can eat the food they cook, including other Brahmans.
- Kshatriyas are warriors, landowners and rulers. They are also the merchants in northern India, and live in the center of the commercial districts. They eat chicken, but no pork or beef. In southern India they often form the highest caste group, because very few Indo-Aryans migrated to south, with the exception of Sri Lanka.
- Vaisyas are herders, peasants and farmers. In southern India they are often the merchant caste. They eat chicken, and they can eat pork on special occasions, but no beef.
- Shudras are the laborers, crafters and peasants. They eat chicken and pork, but no beef. The original Sudras were Dravidians, who were vegetarians, whereas the original Indo-Aryan were meat eaters. Over time these roles have completely reverse themselves. The Sudras traditionally lived outside of the city and were responsible for slaughtering animals. Sometimes they carry out animal sacrifices in the temples of the Goddess Durga (the demon killer).
- Dalits are also known as the Harijans and Untouchables. They are not considered part of Hindu religious society and social structure, and were therefore not considered human. For many years they were not counted in the local population census in some parts of India. All non-Hindus are automatically Dalit, which is technically not a caste. Because they are outside of the caste system, they can eat any kind of meat, including beef. Their traditional roles are butchers, tanners and fishers, all of whom must kill animals as part of their livelihood. They also slaughter cows for certain sacred festivals, but they cannot cook for anyone in a higher caste group. In Japanese society, the Eta social group serves a similar role, and also is considered at the bottom of social classes.

The caste system was officially abolished in the 1950 Indian constitution, and many Indians today pay little heed to it. They eat what they want and socialize with anyone, without regard to traditional caste rules. The caste system, however, continues to be a very important and influential force within the more traditional rural areas of India.

PHOTO 4.3

Pashupatinath temple complex on the Bagmati river near Kathmandu, Nepal. This is a major pilgrimage destination for hindus from throughout South Asia. Note the body at the bottom of the steps that is being prepared for cremation

Source: Alan A. Lew

Although the caste system is frequently criticized, it has had the influence of uniting the great ethnic diversity of India. Caste designation transcends ethnic and language differences. For example, in traditional India a Kshatriya in Tamil Nadu Province in southernmost India could more easily marry a Kshatriya from northern India than someone of another cast in her/his hometown.

Religion

Buddhism

Buddhism is another major world religion that originated in South Asia. It is sometimes called Hinduism without the caste system. However, there are some other significant differences between Hinduism and Buddhism. Unlike Hinduism, Buddhism teaches that people can change their individual situation if they take the initiative. Buddhism also considers itself superior to other religions, and it seeks converts, which Hinduism generally does not. This makes Buddhism a proselytizing religion, like Christianity and Islam. Hinduism and Judaism are not proselytizing religions.

Buddhism was founded by Siddhartha Gautama (563–483 BCE). He was a prince in the foothills of the Himalayas and gave up his royal life to seek the reasons for so much suffering in the world. His answer was that attachment to worldly goods was the cause of suffering, and renunciation and detachment from the world would lead to freedom from suffering and ultimately to Buddhahood. Buddhism became the dominant religion in the Mauryan Empire which was founded in 325 BCE. Asoka, its second Emperor, united all of the Indo-Gangetic Plain for the first time, including today's Afghanistan and a good part of the Deccan Plateau. In 275 BCE, Asoka adopted Buddhism and sent Buddhist missionaries as far as Greece and Egypt. This was the height of Buddhism in South Asia, and the arts and sciences both flourished under Asoka's rule.

Hindus saw Buddha as the 10th incarnation of the Hindu god Vishnu, one of the Hindu trilogy of supreme gods, Brahma and Shiva being the other two. Buddhism, therefore, was absorbed back into Hinduism, and almost completely disappeared in South Asia after Asoka's rule. It continued to be followed in Tibet and Nepal in the Himalayas, and on the island of Sri Lanka, where it is the dominant religion today.

Islam in South Asia

Islam is the third major religion of South Asia. It was founded in the 6th century CE in Saudi Arabia by the Prophet Mohammed, who viewed it as an extension of Jewish and Christian traditions. It rapidly spread across North Africa and into Central Asia after Mohammed's death. Islam did not enter into South Asia until the 10th century CE, when it was introduced by Arab traders. Dalits were more open to this new religion because of their exclusion from Hinduism and because Islam had no caste system. Islam was especially popular in the Bengal region of India and today's country of Bangladesh. Some of the remaining Buddhists in India were also attracted to Islam.

The Moghal Empire was the peak of Islamic rule in the region, and the empire covered much of the same area as the Buddhist Mauryan Empire. The Moghals ruled from 1526 to 1857 when the British took control of a highly disorganized India. The Moghal Empire's leaders were Muslims, although most of the land they ruled remained Hindu. The Taj Mahal was built during this time (1632–1648) and is considered the masterpiece of Mogul art and architecture. The Taj Mahal is actually a mausoleum located in Agra, south of India's capital city, New Delhi. It was built by the Mughal Emperor Shah Jahan after the death of his favorite wife, Mumtaz Mahal. The mausoleum building combines elements of Persian, Turkish, Indian and Islamic architecture, and includes a large garden and a variety of out buildings.

PHOTO 4.4

The Taj Mahal in Agra, India. This Mausoleum was completed in 1648 by the Muslim Mughal Emporer Shah Jahan for his favorite wife

Hinduism was always able to absorb other religions but was unable to absorb Islam because of major differences between the Hindu-Buddhist tradition and the Judeo-Christian-Islamic tradition. The following comparisons apply to these major religious traditions in their broadest sense. The actual religious teachings and practices of any individual church, temple, teacher or minister may vary considerably.

- The Jewish-Christian-Islamic tradition believes in human equality before God; whereas the Hindu tradition (but not Buddhism) is based on the caste hierarchy, in which a higher caste person is closer to God than a lower caste person.
- The Jewish-Christian-Islamic tradition believes that humans have a free will and can change their lives; Hinduism (but not Buddhism) believes that there is no free will and that all is based on fate (karma). In fact, trying to change one's position in society is wrong because it increases one's karma (resulting in more reincarnations) and is against the will of the gods.
- Hinduism believes that one can only improve one's next life by fulfiling the duties of this life. Buddhism, on the other hand, teaches that the only way out is a total rejection of all material things, which is the Brahman caste role in Hinduism. Buddhists basically believe that everyone can become a Brahman.

- The Jewish-Christian-Islamic tradition believes that the world is real and can be changed; the Hinduism-Buddhism tradition believes that the world is an illusion and that the spiritual world is the only reality.
- The Jewish-Christian-Islamic tradition believes that the world and life can be enjoyed; the Hindu-Buddhist tradition believes that the world and life only bring pain and suffering – enjoyment is only possible in the spiritual world.
- The Christian and Islamic traditions (but not Judaism) believe that their religion (and their God) is the only true religion. Hinduism (but not Buddhism) believes in millions of gods that are constantly changing, and that all religions are equally valid. Traditional Buddhism believes that there are no gods at all; salvation is entirely up to the individual. Later forms of Buddhism introduced the concept of Bodhisattvas, which are somewhat similar to saints in the Catholic tradition.
- Islam (but not Judaism and Christianity) teaches that the use of pictures and statues is idolatry and therefore forbidden; Hinduism (but not traditional Buddhism) profusely uses pictures and statues.
- Judaism-Christianity-Islam teaches that there is only one life per person in which one can prove oneself; Hinduism and Buddhism believe in reincarnations that can last forever.
- Judaism-Christianity-Islam teaches that the world will end, and that this is very important; Hinduism-Buddhism believes that the world and spiritual reality are both infinite and eternal, and therefore time has no real meaning. Hinduism measures time in 64 million year cycles; the current cycle, the Kali Yuga, is considered an evil time in which to be reincarnated.

These differences between Islam and Hinduism were simply too great to be reconciled and became the basis of the partition of British India into Hindu-dominated India and Muslim-dominated Pakistan, which included East and West Pakistan, at India's 1947 independence.

Sikhs

The Sikhs are a major religious and ethnic group in the Punjab Province of India. The Punjab regions of both India and Pakistan are at the top of the Indo-Gangetic Plain, between the drainage of the Indus and Ganges Rivers. Sikhism was founded by Guru Nanak (1469–1539 CE), who sought to combine the best of Islam and Hinduism. Sikhism is a monotheistic religion that opposes idolatry (like Islam), yet it teaches that all religions are equally valid. Like Hinduism, it also incorporates meditation.

The Sikhs were militarized under Govind Singh (1666–1708), who was the 10th and last guru (master teacher) of the Sikh religion. He created a warrior fraternity within Sikhism, introducing the wearing of turbans, the non-cutting of hair and the tradition of always carrying a knife. The Sikhs were famous for their military skills as mercenary soldiers for the British Empire. In 1947, 2.5 million Sikhs left Pakistan's Punjab region and migrated to Indian Punjab as part of the partition of South Asia, because they were promised complete autonomy under the Indian government. Sikh separatists have been fighting a war of independence to create a separate country (which they call *Kalistan*), although they only comprise about half of the population of Indian's Punjab Province.

British Legacy and Colonialism

The British have long been blamed for many of the problems of India in the 20th century, especially the conflicts between Hindus and Muslims. The major impact of British rule, however, has been the modernization of the Indian subcontinent. The British built the most expansive and heavily used railway network in the world in India, which extends to many of the smaller and more isolated districts of the country. The British also built a comprehensive road network. The British built industries, introduced a European-style education system, a legal system based on English Common Law (similar to the United States, Canada and Australia), and a parliamentary political system. In addition, the British united and integrated all of South Asia for the first and only time in its history. India's transportation system has helped enhance the movement of people from one region to another for employment and tourism purposes.

Modernization has also had negative impacts. It has increased ethnic tensions and forces that push to divide the Indian subcontinent. Greater education has resulted in greater demand for the use of local languages instead of the national language, which has reinforced local identity over the national identity. Knowledge of other places within South Asia made people realize the great differences in levels of economic development and standards of living, resulting in accusations of favoritism, rather than a shared sense of similarity and goals. Muslims in India increasingly identified with Muslims in the Middle East where they see more similarities to their values and traditions, rather than with the Hindus who are their neighbors.

Partition

The one thing that brought the Hindus and Muslims of South Asia together was their desire to rid themselves of British colonial rule. This shared goal, however, did not bring about a lasting unity between the two groups, as trust was never fully achieved. In 1947 India was granted independence, following almost 50 years of anti-British protests and the weakening of the United Kingdom in World War II. The British sought to keep India as a single country, which was also the goal of the Hindu leaders (including Mahatma Gandhi). Muslims, however, wanted an independent Pakistan. The partition of South Asia resulted in about 5 million deaths from ethnic violence, and the migration of 13 million people between India and Pakistan. Even after partition, there were as many Muslims in India as there were in the new country of Pakistan – about 100 million.

Partition created the new country of Pakistan, which originally comprised West Pakistan and East Pakistan (Bangladesh). The only similarities between these two territories were that they were both predominantly Muslim. Almost everything else about them was different. West Pakistan had a dry climate where drought was a constant threat, whereas East Pakistan had a humid tropical climate, with an overabundance of water. Agriculture in West Pakistan was primarily grain production (mainly wheat), while in East Pakistan's agriculture was primarily wet rice production. West Pakistan, at partition, had an average annual per capita income of US$350 (£175); in East Pakistan it was less than half that at US$150 (£75).

The West Pakistanis were light-skinned and more of the Indo-Aryan racial stock; the East Pakistanis were darker skinned and of the Dravidian racial stock. Each of these territories had more than 100 million people, but East Pakistan was only one fourth the size of West Pakistan, resulting in a much higher population density. West Pakistan was much closer to the Middle East, and much more closely integrated with

Middle Eastern economies; West Pakistan was economically and culturally closer to India. The Indian state of Bengal was adjacent to East Pakistan, and its major city Calcutta was the central industrial center for the region. The conflicts that these differences engendred results in East Pakistan declaring its independence from West Pakistan in March 1971. A civil war was fought in which one million East Pakistan Bangladeshis died. India intervened with its army on the side of the Bangladeshis and independence was finally achieved in December 1971, followed by the adoption of the new country's name of Bangladesh.

Irredentism

When people in one country desire to separate and join with people in an adjacent country to form a new country, this is known as *Irredentism.* irredentism is a major problem for Pakistan with its neighbors to the west, and is also a major issue for India in the Jammu and Kashmir region in the far north, where 75 percent of the population is Muslim, but the rulers have traditionally been Hindu. At partition, the Hindu rulers of Jammu and Kashmir sided with India. However, Pakistan has long supported the desires of the Muslim population in Jamu and Kashmir to separate from India and join Pakistan. Because of this, India and Pakistan have been in an almost continuous state of war since 1947. This situation is especially tense with both countries having nuclear weapons (Indian since 1974 and Pakistan since 1998) and the rise of militant Islam in the border areas of Pakistan and Afghanistan.

Tourism Issues in South Asia

In common with all other areas of the world, physical and human geography are fundamental elements in tourism in South Asia. The vast physical and cultural geographies of the region form the foundations for tourism development but also erect many barriers to its success.

Supranationalism, Conflict and Poverty

Supranational organization exists in South Asia in the form of the South Asian Association for Regional Cooperation (SAARC). Member countries include Bangladesh, Bhutan, India, the Maldives, Nepal, Pakistan and Sri Lanka. While the goals of SAARC are to promote the socio-economic interests of the region and the cultural development of the people, in part through tourism, there are several obstacles that prevent its successful implementation. The ethnic conflict in Sri Lanka and the dispute over Kashmir between India and Pakistan are two of the most challenging problems facing the region in terms of tourism and economic cooperation. These and other conflicts have tainted the region's image and impacted the growth of intra-regional tourism.

SAARC has also had a limited effect in improving the impoverished conditions that many of the people of South Asia live in. South Asia has the second lowest average incomes of any major region of the world, after Sub-Saharan Africa. Poor populations are widely seen in the densely populated larger cities of South Asia, and Western visitors often respond to this life-on-the-street with culture shock. It is common for Western-oriented hotels to emphasize how modern they are, providing a sheltered enclave in which to recover from the culture shock of some parts of South Asia. Rural areas are also very impoverished with many remote areas still lacking electricity and running water. By Western standards, however, the cost of living in South Asia is extremely inexpensive and there is a vast network of alternative accommodations that cater to backpack tourists from through the world. Many younger backpack travelers from Europe and North America will spend months and years traveling on very little money through South Asia.

Mountain Adventures

The Himalayas are one of the major tourist attractions of South Asia. In Nepal, Mount Everest (also known as Sagarmatha and Chomolungma) and the Kumbhu Valley that leads to it are one of the most trekked regions in South Asia. This is the home of the Sherpas, who originally migrated to Nepal from Tibet and continue to practice Tibetan Buddhism. Edmund Hillary and Tezing Norgay first climbed Everest in 1953. Today some 500 people a year typically attempt the peak, though harsh climate prevents many from achieving their goal, and several die each year in the attempt. Annapurna, which has five peaks over 24,000 ft (7,400 m), is another major trekking region in Nepal.

Although it only reaches some 3,510 ft in elevation, a trip over the Khyber Pass in northern Pakistan is one of the top adventures of South Asia. Historically, the pass has been one of the most important trade and transportation routes between Central Asia and South Asia. The pass cuts through an extension of the Hindu Kush range that was used by the Indo-Aryans who invaded South Asia some 3000 years ago, Alexander the Great from Greece who conquered the Indus River region in 326 BCE, and the Muslim Mughul Empire, which controlled northern South Asia from 1526. The British also used the Khyber Pass to invade Afghanistan in the 1800s and 1900s. Today the Khyber Pass has significant tourism potential, but it is known as a haven for bandits and an epicenter for conflict between Afghanistan and Pakistan, and most tourists are encouraged to avoid it.

Between Nepal and Pakistan is the Kashmir region of India. Kashmir has been a popular tourist destination for Europeans since the late 1800s, and a pilgrimage site for Hindus and Buddhists long before that. Its mountainous landscape with many trekking and winter skiing opportunities, its mild summer climate, distinctive gardens and houseboat rentals available on Dal Lake, located next to the city of Srinagar, are the main attractions of the Kashmir region. Unregulated residential and tourism development on the banks of Dal Lake have caused it to shrink to a fraction of its original size. This in addition to tensions between Pakistan and India over the Kashmir region, causing periodic terrorist and military actions, have affected visitation in recent years.

Pilgrimage or Religious Tourism

Religious pilgrimage is a unique form of tourism and shares many characteristics in common with recreational and leisure travel. Infrastructure needs, including transportation, accommodations and meals, are almost identical. The sites visited are often the same for both religious pilgrims and secular tourists, and pilgrims typically include visits to non-religious sites, as well. Managers of both religious and secular destinations must develop policies that protect the site while ensuring consistent experiences for large numbers of visitors over time. Some argue that religious and leisure travel have similar motivations and experiences, as well. These includes motivations to experience social shared values, places of authenticity and a search for meaning beyond that found in the home place.

Throughout South Asia are major religious sites for Buddhists, Hindus, Sikhs and Muslims. Many of these are in the form of temples that commemorate sacred sites and attract large numbers of devotees from within the region and from abroad. The Kumbha Mela, the largest pilgrimage/religious tourism gathering in the world, is held four times every 12 years rotating among four cities in India. In 2001, the Great Khumbha Mela event (once every 12 years) attracted close to 30 million pilgrims who bathed in the Ganges River at its confluence with the Yamuna River. Similarly, hundreds of thousands of pilgrims travel each year to Lumbini, Nepal, the birthplace of Buddha. Many of these pilgrims come from Sri Lanka, Southeast Asia and East Asia where Buddhism is more widely practiced than in India. Japanese and Southeast Asian Buddhist organizations have specially built accommodations facilities that cater to their different cultural needs.

In India, among the most important pilgrimage destinations that are also major tourist sites are The Golden Temple of the Sikhs and the Hindu holy city of Varanasi. The Golden Temple is located in the Indian Punjab city of Amritsar and is the most sacred site for Sikhs, who come from throughout the world to pray there. The gold-colored temple, officially named *Harmandir Sahib*, sits in the middle of a small lake and symbolizes the spiritual and political independence of Sikhism.

India

As noted above, India is a significant religious tourism destination, both for domestic and international pilgrims of Hindu, Sikh and Buddhist faiths. What the Golden Temple is to Sikhs, the entire city of Varanasi is the Hindus. Varanasi (also known as Benaras and Kashi) sits on the sacred Ganges (Ganga) River in the Indian state of Uttar Pradesh, one of India's poorest regions. It is considered one of the oldest places of continuous habitation on the planet, dating back to over 3000 BCE, and is the single most important pilgrimage destination for all sects of Hinduism. More than one million Hindu pilgrims come to the city each year to bath in the Ganges to cleanse their sins, and to burn their dead on funeral pires. It is believed that dying in Varanasi will end the continual suffering of reincarnation. Varanasi is also where Gautama Buddha is believed to have given his first sermon on the principles of Buddhism, making it one of the four pilgrimage sites that all Buddhists should visit. The others are Lumbini, Nepal (where Guatam Buddha was born), Bodh Gaya, India (where he gained enlightenment), and Kushinagar, India (where he died).

Another significant form of tourism in India is visiting friends and relatives or VFR tourism. This may be the most significant form of tourism in India in actual numbers, although there are no data to substantiate such a claim. The Indian diaspora (spread of an ethnic group abroad from the homeland) is scattered throughout the entire world, with places such as Fiji, South Africa, Guyana, the United States, Canada and Australia having substantial populations of Indian origin. These people are known for traveling back to their homeland to visit relatives and friends, to experience the land of their ancestors, and to participate in religious and other festivals.

India's 28 states and seven territories have unique tourism products, and most tourism centers on large cities and other urban areas. Jungle tours involving tigers and elephants are popular, while adventure travel and ecotourism are being actively promoted by the Ministry of Tourism in the country's many national parks and protected areas. Desert safaris and the cooler hill stations of the northern mountains are popular destinations and activities. The hill stations were popular holiday spots during colonial times for the British, who needed a respite from the hot interior lowlands; now they are again popular among wealthy Indians and foreign visitors alike.

In addition to the British, India's soil was also occupied at some point in history by the French, Portuguese, Dutch and Danish. However, only the British, French and Portuguese had colonies into the 20th century. The French transferred sovereignty of its four small territories in eastern India (Puducherry, formerly Pondicherry) in 1954, in response to India's 1947 independence from the United Kingdom. Portugal was the last to leave India. It gave up its territories of Goa, Daman, Diu, Dadra and Nagar Haveli in 1961 under military pressure from India. Puducherry and the former Portuguese colonies have become important tourist destinations and centers of Christianity in South Asia. Goa and Diu are important beach resorts, and the European architecture of all the territories appeals to people interested in cultural heritage. Many of the older people in these areas still speack French or Portuguese.

Bangladesh

Since the partition of the subcontinent, more than 200 million Hindus have migrated out of Bangladesh, while a similar number of Muslims have migrated into the country. Bangladesh is 95 percent rural. Its major industry is the growing of jute, which is used to make burlap bags and rope. It is grown in Bangladesh and sent to factories in Calcutta for processing. The warm climate and ready availability of water allow three rice crops a year to be grown. Almost half of the country is flooded every year by the Ganges and Brahmaputra rivers, as well as by tidal floods caused by typhoons from the Bay of Bengal. Because much of the country is low lying, it is regarded as being extremely susceptible to climate change and sea-level rise. Transportation is a problem because water is everywhere, and it can take up to 20 hours to get from Dhaka, the capital of Bangladesh, to the mouth of the Ganges River. Although Bangladesh has some tourism based on beaches, jungles and architectural heritage, severe climatological disturbances have prevented the development of large-scale tourism in the country. In addition, because the country's population is over 80 percent Muslim, it has suffered much as other largely Islamic populated nations from sometimes perceived security concerns.

Pakistan

Pakistan was the first Islamic Republic in the world. When it was founded, the Muslims there shared a high level of religious intensity because of their finally gaining independence after many decades of living under Hindu rule. Islam was a unifying force for the people of Pakistan (which means *land of the pure*), who named their new capital city Islamabad (City of Islam).

Pakistan is made up of four major ethnic groups; Balochistan is where the Balochis reside. There are also large numbers of Balochis in southern Afghanistan and eastern

Iran, who have long desired their own country – a cause supported in the Cold War era by the former Soviet Union. The Sindh Province is dominated by the Sindhis, who mostly migrated from northern India and the Ganges Plain. This is where Karachi, the largest city in Pakistan and the country's main seaport, is located. The Sindhis speak Urdu – the national language of Pakistan, which is closely related to Hindi, the national language of India. Punjabis live in the Punjab Province of Pakistan, which adjoins the Punjab Province of India, homeland of the Sikhs. The Punjab province is the wealthiest and most populated in Pakistan. It shares many similar climatic and economic conditions to India's Punjab, which is also a relatively wealthy region. The fourth major ethnic group in Pakistan are the Pashtuns, who live in the Northwest Frontier Province, although most ethnic Pashtuns are located in neighboring Afghanistan. Like the Balochis, they were divided into two different countries by the European colonial powers so they could be more easily controlled. The Pashtuns also have long desired their own country. The former Taliban rulers of Afghanistan were Pushtuns who went into hiding in the Pushtun area of Pakistan after the United States government overthrew their leadership in the Afghanistan War of 2001.

VFR tourism is a very important part of the tourism economy of Pakistan. This is critical in a country that has suffered considerably from the conflict in neighboring Afghanistan. Little other tourism presently exists, not for a lack of natural and cultural resources, but because of the broader conflict in the region and the resultant fact that most developed countries have placed Pakistan on their travel warning lists. There is promise of growing cross-border travel between India and Pakistan, but presently, heavy restrictions have been placed on Indians crossing into Pakistan and vice versa, owing to the conflict between the two nations, which many world observers fear has escalated to nuclear capabilities in recent years. Indian visas for Pakistanis and Pakistani visas for Indians are difficult to acquire, but citizens of other countries can pass over the border relatively easily. One interesting tourism phenomenon popular among both nationalities is to visit the border itself, where every evening at the Wagah crossing just east of Lahore, the changing of the border guards, a fancy ceremonial affair, takes place. Bleachers and souvenir shops have been set up on both sides, and it is one of the most popular attractions in the region.

The Himalayan Kingdoms

The two other major regions of South Asia are the Himalayan kingdoms of Nepal and Bhutan and the Indian Ocean island countries of Sri Lanka and the Maldives. Nepal and Bhutan are buffer countries between the larger countries of China (and Tibet) to the north and India to the south. Like India, they formerly were under British colonial influence. Both were ruled by hereditary monarchs and have very traditional agricultural societies. Nepal is a mostly Hindu country (although Buddhism dominates in its northern mountain regions), while Bhutan is a Buddhist country. Buddhist practices in both countries are closely associated with Tibetan cultural influences. Bhutan and Nepal are among the poorest countries in the world, with tourism as their main export industry. Both are also dependent on India for political and economic support, as well as their major source of tourists.

Nepal has existed as a kingdom centered in the Katmandu Valley for more than 1,500 years. It has nine of the fourteen highest peaks in the world, including Mount

Everest and Annapurna I. In recent decades, Nepal has suffered from a Maoist-based (a form of Chinese communism) insurgency that had come to control most of the rural countryside, with the central government controlling the cities. Many thousands of Nepalese have died in the struggle between the two groups, though most tourists have not been directly affected by this conflict. Peace agreements in 2006 brought Maoists into the government and significantly reduced the influence of the monarchy.

Nepal's world-famous mountain trekking on and near Mount Everest has received a great deal of tourism industry and academic attention. The region is viewed as an ultimate goal for mountain climbing enthusiasts, who typically employ members of an ethnic group known as Sherpas, to guide them and carry their camping and hiking equipment. This trekking tourism phenomenon has come under heavy scrutiny in recent years by researchers for its culturally and environmentally questionable practices. The utilization of Sherpas as *pack animals* has been criticized as a neo-colonialist and Euro-centric practice of ethno-economic oppression. Likewise, it is common practice for supplies to be carried into the mountains, but little of it is carried out. The resultant litter is left to accumulate along trails, streams and scenic valleys, creating an unappealing site for tourists and ecologically unsustainable conditions for the environment.

The Kathmandu Valley is on UNESCO's World Heritage List due to seven major sites, monuments and buildings that demonstrate the historical continuity of the kingdom of Nepal. These sites include Durbar Squares of Hanuman Dhoka (Kathmandu), Patan and Bhaktapur from the days when each was a separate city-state trying to outdo the other in architectural splendor. In addition, the Buddhist stupas of Swayambhu and Bauddhanath, and the Hindu temples of Pashupati and Changu Narayan all continue to be important South Asian pilgrim destinations. As noted above, Lumbini, the birthplace of Lord Buddha, is a very important tourist site and a vital pilgrimage goal from Buddhists from around the world.

Bhutan is about one-third the size of Nepal, and has a population of approximately 2 million. The precursor of Bhutan was the country of Lhomon or Monyul, which existed from 500 BCE to 600 CE, when Buddhism was introduced to the region. Various Buddhist sects fought for political control for many centuries thereafter (with additional influences from Tibet) until the 17th century when a theocratic government united the country. From that time until 1907, the Kingdom of Bhutan (or Drukyul – *Land of the Thunder Dragon*) had a system of shared civil and spiritual (Buddhist) rule under an absolute monarchy (the Dragon King). The monarchy is absolute, but the king is admired and respected, unlike the King of Nepal, who was largely despised by the people.

Bhutan has four major ethnic groups: Ngalop (Tibetan origin); Sharchop (Indo-Mongoloid origin); aboriginal or indigenous tribal peoples; and Nepalese. Fear of the increasing number of Nepalese in the population has prompted the government to adopt policies in the 1980s to support and enhance a Bhutanese cultural identity that is different from that of Nepal, which has caused an increase in ethnic tensions and large numbers of Nepalese leaving Bhutan for refugee camps in Nepal in the 1990s. Bhutan has more Buddhist monks than soldiers, has no traffic lights, and the King only allowed television into the country in 1999. In December 2004, Bhutan became the first country in the world to ban the smoking of cigarettes in public and the sale of cigarettes within its borders. Individuals can import them if they pay a 100 percent tax, however.

Bhutan's primary tourism resources are its well-preserved culture (lifestyles, dress, village life, festivals and celebrations, unique architecture, religion) and its natural

TOURISM ISSUES AND INSIGHTS
THE DANGERS OF CLIMBING EVEREST

Since the growth of commercial guided expeditions in the early 1990s, Mount Everest has become a playground for those with time and money seeking high-altitude adventure experience. In the northern spring of 2007 more than 600 people reached the summit and there were six deaths. Most climbers were been part of commercial operations that charge between $10,000 and $65,000 (£5,000 to £32,500) for a guide, Sherpas, equipment and backup.

There has been a significant change in the profile of climbers on the mountain since the first successful climb. In the early decades, less than 20 percent were 40 or over but between 2000 and 2005 almost half the climbers were in this age bracket. In the same period over-60s have increased from 0.3 percent to 3.6 percent. Since 2000 an average of 13 sexagenarians have attempted the climb each year. Edmund Hillary and Tenzing Norgay were 33 and 39 when they became the first men to climb Everest in 1953. Around a third of those under 40 make it to the summit, but by age 60 only around 13 percent succeed. This lowered success rate does not seem to be due to older climbers using their experience to back off from difficult situations. One in 20 are killed on the mountain, around three times the overall average. If they do make it to the summit they have an even higher chance of death – a quarter do not make it back down, more than 10 times the average. Gender made no difference to success or death rates.

Sources

Huey, R.B. and Salisbury, R. (2003) Success and death on Everest: How the main routes and seasons compare. *American Alpine Journal*, 2–9.

Huey, R.B., Salisbury, R., Wang, J.-L. and Mao, M. (2007) Effects of age and gender on success and death of mountaineers on Mount Everest. *Biology Letters*, Vol. 3 (No. 5, October 22) 498–500.

bounties in its Himalayan setting. Bhutan has long been closed to mass tourism; even today only small numbers of high-paying tourists are allowed into the country, and only some of the country's regions are open to foreign visitors. A visa quota is in place. In 2006, for instance, less than 18,000 tourists were permitted to enter. Tourists must pay a certain amount of money per day, and the entire trip, including transportation to Bhutan and internal travel, as well as food and accommodations, must be pre-paid. Independent travel is not permitted, as even individual tours must be organized and pre-planned by the Bhutan Tourism Corporation. The theory goes that if small numbers of tourists are allowed in, but a high fee is charged for each person per day, enough money will be earned by fewer tourists that mass tourism is not required. This unique policy among the world's nations has much to do with avoiding the negative socio-cultural and environmental changes that typically accompany tourism development.

The Indian Ocean Insular Countries

Both the Maldives and Sri Lanka have long been major sun, sand and sea tourist destinations for Europeans. They are also island countries. Beyond that, however, they are very different from one another in size, ethnicity and contemporary issues.

Sri Lanka lies off the southern tip of India, almost in the center of the Indian Ocean. Its summer monsoon rains bring lush vegetation on the southern half of the island's mountain slopes, the highest peak of which is Pidurutalagala at 8,281 ft (2,524 m). However, the northern half lies in the summer monsoon's rainshadow and is a relatively dry zone. The island is dominated by the Buddhist Sinhalese, who originally arrived from north India in about 500 BCE. They created a high civilization from the 3rd century BCE to the 12th century CE that was known for its engineering prowess. Sri Lanka came under Portuguese and Dutch control until finally becoming a crown colony of Britain in 1802. Sri Lanka has had a democratic tradition dating back to the 1930s, and in 1960 the Sri Lankans elected the world's first female prime minister. Today the Sinhalese comprise about 74 percent of the country's population, while 13 percent are Hindu Tamils, who are related to the Hindus in India's nearby province of Tamil Nadu. Ethnic tensions between these two groups date back to the 1950s, and the conflict was only somewhat calmed in the aftermath of the December 26, 2004, Indian Ocean tsunami disaster that killed more than 30,000 Sri Lankans.

Sri Lanka receives many accolades as an enjoyable tourist destination, largely because of its remarkable beaches and cultural heritage. Its forests team with leopards and exotic birds, and its human past affords many opportunities for interactions with ancient temples, villages and colonial buildings. Sri Lanka was one of the hardest hit countries by the Asian tsunami of December 2004, which virtually devastated the beach resorts on the island. Many of them have since been rebuilt and recovery has been quick, although there are many areas still struggling to recuperate from the disaster. In addition, the longstanding civil war conflict between the nation's two main ethnic groups has curtailed tourism development and concentrated it in the southern end of the island.

The Maldives consists of some 1,200 coral islands, grouped in a chain of 27 atolls. These coral atolls comprise live coral and sand bars that sit atop an undersea mountain range, which runs north to south for 600 miles (960 km) southeast of the Indian Peninsula. The rising ocean level is threatening the future of the Maldives, as it threatens other low-lying islands throughout the world, which is particularly poignant in this small country because the highest elevation is only 2.4 m above sea level. About 200 of the islands are inhabited, though many have very small numbers of people on them. The Maldives has a population of about 300,000 and is a primarily Muslim country and another former British colony.

Like Bhutan, the Maldives has a unique tourism system designed to minimize the negative social impacts of tourism. Maldivian tourism caters to affluent Europeans and is the most important sector of the economy, so the government and population want tourism, but they do not want the behavior of the tourists to clash with their own conservative Islamic values. Therefore, many of the islands are used exclusively as self-contained resorts, with Maldivians working, but not living permanently on them. When tourists travel to the Maldives, they essentially book into a single-island resort, where they have only limited interaction with locals–resort employees. Tourists are not encouraged to visit Male, the capital and most populated island, although they may if they dress and behave appropriately. This spatial segregation between tourists and Maldivians is a unique model that appears to be working for this country. The international airport is on a small island, and inter-island transportation is done via boat. The Maldives is known as a *paradise* with white sandy beaches and clear blue water. In addition to beaches, the islands have become popular for scuba diving in recent years.

PHOTO 4.5
Buddha Statue in Kandy, Sri Lanka. Kandy is in the mountains in the Center of Sri Lanka and is an important center for Theravadin Buddhism, which is practiced in Sri Lanka and Southeast Asia.

4.2   SOUTHEAST ASIA

Southeast Asia is the large area of land and water situated between India to the west and China to the north. Older terms for this region include *Indochina* and *Further India*, both of which referred mostly to the peninsular part of Southeast Asia (from Myanmar to Vietnam, and excluding Indonesia and the Philippines). The island realm of Southeast Asia was historically known as the *East Indies* and the *Spice Islands*, though the latter term also referred to the Moluccas, a group of islands that are part of Indonesia. Compared to its neighboring regions, Southeast Asia has a relatively low population density. Its estimated population in 2004 was about 560 million, which is half the population of India and of China. About 20 percent of the population of Southeast Asia (110 million) lives on the Indonesian island of Java.

Situated between South Asia (dominated by India) and East Asia (dominated by China), Southeast Asia is a cultural shatterbelt where many different cultural influences have merged through history. (This is similar to the Balkan Peninsula and the Transcaucasus between Europe and Asia.) Today, the dominant cultures in the region include Burmese (Myanmar), Thai, Vietnamese, Cambodian (Khmer), Malay, Chinese, Indian and European. Large numbers of people are followers of Buddhism, Islam and Catholicism, all of which may be combined with older animist traditions. Ruling governments adhere to political ideologies that include communism, capitalism, democracy, dictatorships, monarchies and military rule. Large areas were formerly under the colonial control of the Netherlands, Great Britain, Spain, France and the United States. The diversity of economies in Southeast Asia today include some of the wealthiest countries in the world (Singapore and Brunei) and some of the poorest (East Timor, Laos, Myanmar and Cambodia).

Physical Geography

The major physical geography distinction in Southeast Asia is between Peninsular Southeast Asia and Insular Southeast Asia. Peninsular Southeast Asia consists of most of the countries directly attached to the Asian continent: Myanmar, Thailand, Laos, Vietnam and Cambodia. Insular Southeast Asia consists of the mostly island countries of Malaysia, Singapore, Brunei, Indonesia, East Timor and the Philippines.

Peninsular Southeast Asia is very mountainous in its northern areas bordering China, though these areas are also sparsely settled. The mountain ranges extend southward from southern China and the Tibetan Plateau, and are rich in minerals, including tin, iron, bauxite (aluminum) and oil. The highest peak in Southeast Asia is Hkakabo Razi (19,240 ft; 5,881 m), which is actually on the edge of the Himalayas in northern Myanmar. Between these north–south mountain ranges run the major rivers of Southeast Asia, which have their origin on the Tibetan Plateau and in Southwest China. Most of the population of Peninsular Southeast Asia resides along these rivers, especially on the coast where they enter the sea. The major rivers include:

- *Mekong River* – touching all of the countries in Peninsular Southeast Asia and entering the South China Sea near Ho Chi Mihn City, Vietnam;
- *Irrawaddy River* – in Myanmar and entering the Andaman Sea near Yangon (Rangoon);
- *Salween River* – in Myanmar, touching on the border with Thailand and entering the Andaman Sea in eastern Myanmar;
- *Chao Phraya River* – in Thailand and entering the Gulf of Thailand near Bangkok (Krung Thep);
- *Red River* – in Vietnam and entering the Gulf of Tonkin near Hanoi.

The Mekong River is the most significant of these because it connects to all of the countries of Peninsular Southeast Asia and the ethnically diverse province of Yunnan in Southwest China. Regional development programs have focused on the Mekong River Basin to encourage a more integrated transportation system among the countries of Peninsular Southeast Asia (and China), and to promote international tourism.

A popular point along the Mekong River is where the countries of Myanmar, Thailand and Laos meet. Known as the *Golden Triangle*, this region was once infamous for growing poppies for heroin production. Today, however, former heroin traders run tea and souvenir shops for tourists who flock to the Golden Triangle, where Myanmar has built a large casino, and tour boats take visitors over the border to Laos (without a visa) where they can send postcards with relatively rare Laotian stamps. Trekking to visit the minority hill tribes in the mountains of northern Thailand, out of the cities of Chiang Mai and Chiang Rai, is a long popular activity that has spread to Laos and northern Vietnam since the mid-1990s.

Insular Southeast Asia consists of a large arc of volcanic islands formed by the collision of the Eurasian continental plate with the Pacific Ocean floor (Pacific plate and Philippine plate) and the Indo-Australia continental plate. In the middle of this arc is the island of Borneo, which is politically divided between three countries: Malaysia, Indonesia and Brunei. Borneo, which is not geologically volcanic, is instead part of the Asian land mass. It is the second-largest island in the world (after Greenland), and its highest peak is Mount Kinabalu (4,095 m, 13,435 ft), which is a popular hiking trip out of the town of Kota Kinabalu in the state of Sabah, Malaysia. Sabah also has one of the world's top scuba diving destination on the island of Pulau Sipadan, which is the tip of an ancient volcano covered with coral, and a popular breeding ground for sea turtles. Similar spectacular diving is found throughout Insular Southeast Asia. In 2006, biologists exploring the Indonesian waters off New Guinea found 50 new species of fish, shrimp and coral in an area that contains more than 1,200 types, 600 species of coral, whales, sea turtles, crocodiles, giant clams, manta rays and dugongs (related to the manatee).

While few of the internal islands of insular Southeast Asia are volcanic, almost all of the outer islands are, from Indonesia's Sumatra to Java, to Timor on the west and west of the region, to the Philippines in the northeast. All of these islands have active seismic systems that produce rich agricultural lands and lush green landscapes, punctuated by steep volcanic peaks that occasionally wreak havoc on the surrounding countryside.

Climate and Ecology

Insular Southeast Asia sits directly astride the equator and receives year-round rainfall from the Intertropical Convergence Zone (ITCZ). As discussed in Chapter 3 the ITCZ is an area where air from the north and south collide and rise into the upper atmosphere, forming clouds and rain. This occurs throughout the year, though the ITCZ does move northward in Summer (June–August) and southward in Winter (December–February), following the sun. Along the equator, winds and ocean waters mostly move from the east toward the west. To the east of Southeast Asia is the vast Pacific Ocean, which gets quite warm in the summer months, causing a lot of moisture to evaporate into the atmosphere. The rising air forms tropical storms that occasional become typhoons (in Asia) or hurricanes (in North America). In the northern hemisphere summer, the typhoons tend to hit the Philippines more than any other place, causing widespread flooding and landslides. (In the southern hemisphere summer the hurricanes tend to hit northeastern Australia.)

Peninsular Southeast Asia and the southernmost portions of insular Southeast Asia experience a hot summer dry season because they are further away from the ITCZ and its cooling rains. Like South Asia, all of Southeast Asia has a monsoonal climate pattern. In the winter, the Siberian High Pressure system circulates air over the Asian continent in a clockwise direction, bringing moisture to Southeast Asia from the South China Sea, which is located northeast of Southeast Asia. In the summer, the Siberian Low Pressure system circulates air over Asia in a counterclockwise direction, pulling moisture into Southeast Asia from the Indian Ocean. For Peninsular Southeast Asia, the winter monsoon tends to bring more moisture than the summer monsoon. The Korat Plateau in northeast Thailand is the driest area in Peninsular Southeast Asia, and the poorest region in Thailand. Because it is in the interior of peninsular Southeast Asia, it is in the rainshadow of mountains that keep out both the summer and winter monsoon rains.

The tropical rainforests of Indonesia are home to the second greatest biodiversity in the world, after Brazil's Amazon rainforest. Its flora and fauna are a mix of Asian and Australian species. The line between these species, known as the Wallace Line after British naturalist Alfred Wallace, roughly runs between the islands of Borneo and Sulawesi, and between Bali and Lombok. The line marks a deep water trench between the Asian and Australian continental land masses that many animals could not cross when sea levels were lower during the ice ages. The area to the west of this line is clearly part of the Asian continent and much of it was exposed land in the past, allowing it to be populated by tigers, rhinoceros, orangutans, elephants and leopards. While once common, these large animals are rare today, especially with the annual practice of burning rainforests in the spring dry season to expand land for agriculture. These mostly illegal burnings reduce the habitat for large and small animals and cause widespread air pollution throughout Southeast Asia, and threaten the survival of 140 species of mammals, as identified by the World Conservation Union (IUCN).

East of the Wallace Line the flora and fauna are more closely related to that of Australasia with the island of New Guinea having been part of the Australian continent several times during the ice ages. This southeast corner of Southeast Asia is less populated and less visited than most of the rest of the region. War and civil unrest in East Timor and on the Indonesian side of New Guinea (formerly known as Irian Jaya, but changed to West Papua in 2006) have kept outsiders out of this part of the world until recent years. In 2005, an international group of scientists visiting the Foja Mountains (also known as the Pegunungan Van Rees) on the north coast of West Papua discovered a virgin tropical rainforest that is one of the few places on the planet not directly impacted by humans. Although the situation has improved in recent years, a separatist movement continues to struggle against Indonesian control of West Papua. Travel to this emergent ecotourism destination is growing slowly, making it one of the more challenging, and potentially rewarding, destinations in Southeast Asia.

Orangutan

One of the most critically endangered mammals it the orangutan (or orang hutan, meaning *human of the forest*). Orangutans once roamed throughout Southeast Asia but today are only found in the rainforests of Borneo and Sumatra – and in the homes of people throughout Asia who adopt infant orangutans as pets. They are known for their reddish-brown hair and incredibly high level of intelligence, and are becoming increasingly rare in the wild. While cute and cuddly as infants, when they become

Source: Alan A. Lew

adults they can easily toss a human across a room. Several centers have been established on Borneo and Sumatra to rescue orangutans who have been displaced by fires or abandoned as pets and reintroduce them into the rainforests. These centers have also become popular ecotourism destinations, which supports their operations, although their biodiversity goals usually take precedence.

Human Geography of Southeast Asia

Humans have lived in Southeast Asia almost as long as they have resided in Africa. The Negrito people include the Orang Asli, or original/aboriginal people, in Peninsular

Malaysia; the Aeta, Ati and at least 25 other tribes in the Philippines; the Mani of Thailand, and 12 Andamanese tribes of the Andaman Islands in the Indian ocean. They probably migrated to Southeast Asia from Africa as long as 70,000 years ago, though they are not closely related to any modern day African ethnic group. They were recently found to have one of the purest DNA of any contemporary genetic group. They comprise a very small percentage of the population of Southeast Asia today, though they were once the dominant group. They are short in stature (about 4 to 5 ft), black skinned, and practice hunting, gathering, and slash and burn agriculture in the mountains of Southeast Asia. They were widespread during the European colonial period, but the remaining 50,000 or so are today mostly found in the interior mountains of Borneo and the Philippines, and on the Andaman Islands in the Indian Ocean (part of India). Negritos are generally considered to belong to the Australoid race, which includes the aborigines of Australia, the Papuans on the island of New Guinea, the Melanesians in the South Pacific, the Veddahs of Ceylon and possibly the Ainus of northern Japan.

Malays

Insular Southeast Asia is dominated by the Malay race (which is distinct from the Malay-speaking ethnic group found in Malaysia, Borneo and Sumatra). The Proto-Malay (early Malay) probably originated in Southwest China (Yunnan Province) and migrated into Southeast Asia about 5000 BCE. There are only a few pockets of Proto-Malay groups remaining in Southeast Asia, mostly in South Vietnam, southern Thailand and on some of the islands of Indonesia. The rest of the Malay population (including most of the people of the Philippines, Indonesia and Malaysia) are a mix of Proto-Malay with other migrants from South Asia, China and the Tibetan highlands. The Malay language is the national language of Malaysia (Bahasa Malaysia) and Indonesia (Bahasa Indonesia).

Early Malay society was matriarchal. Women were responsible for household chores and agriculture, and held the rights to property. This gave women considerable economic influence, and in traditional Malay culture the man moved to the woman's household after marriage. Even today, Malay wedding rituals are based on a ceremony in which the man is welcomed into the woman's household. Most of the Malay race today practices Islam, although there are some major exceptions, including Filipinos and East Timorese, who adopted Catholicism under Spanish and Portuguese rule, respectively, and the Balinese who still practice a form of Hinduism that was common in Southeast Asia prior to the arrival of Islam.

The Khmer

The Mon-Khmer people migrated into Peninsular Southeast Asia about 3500 years ago, after the Malays. They were possibly pushed into the region by Tibetans. They became a dominant civilization in Peninsular Southeast Asia, displacing the early Negrito and Malay populations. Today, the Mon are situated in Myanmar on the Thailand border, while the Khmers comprise about 90 percent of the population of Cambodia. One of the peak periods of Khmer political power was during the Angkorean Empire in the 9th to 13th century CE. At this time the Khmer controlled most of present-day Cambodia, Laos and Thailand, and built the capital city of Angkor and its famous Angkor Wat (temple). With over one million people at it peak, Angkor was once the largest pre-industrial city in the world. The rise of Tai kingdoms in the 13th and 14th centuries, along with over-exploitations of Cambodia's natural resources to support the city, eventually resulted in the almost total destruction of Angkor in 1431 by Tai armies, and the enslavement of some 90,000 Khmers. Today, large populations of Khmer-speaking people reside in areas of Thailand and Vietnam that are adjacent to Cambodia.

Hill Tribes

The mountains of peninsular Southeast Asia also contain many smaller ethnic groups, most of whom reside in more than one country. These groups are often referred to as *Hill Tribes* and visits and stays in their villages are a major part of the trekking experience in their mountain homelands. Some of these (and their approximate populations) include:

- Akha (120,000 people) Myanmar-Laos-Thailand-Vietnam.
- Cham (20,000) Cambodia (where they are Muslims) – Vietnam (where they are Hindus).
- Chinese (400,000), Kachin (600,000) and Shan (6 million) Myanmar.
- Hmong or Meo (1.6 million) Myanmar-Laos-Thailand-Vietnam-China.
- Jarai (220,000) southern Vietnam.
- Karen (2 million) Myanmar-Thailand.
- Lisu (500,000) China-Myanmar-Tibet.
- Montagnards (800,000) Vietnam highlands.
- Wa (400,000) Myanmar-China.
- Yao (1 million) China-Vietnam-Laos.

Indochina

Over 2000 years ago, during the Han Dynasty in China, the Empire of China made a major expansion out of North China and into South China. This initiated a major migration of non-Chinese people of South China and into Southeast Asia. The Vietnamese, also known as Annamese, migrated from Southeast China down the east coast of Southeast Asia at that time. Vietnam has historically had the closest cultural ties to China of any country in Southeast Asia. It was administratively part of China until the 10th century CE, and the Vietnamese practice the same form of Mahayana Buddhism mixed with Confucianism that is common in China. They also practice a very labor intensive form of rice cultivation, similar to that of southern China. Because of these similarities, older geography textbooks often included Vietnam in East Asia instead of Southeast Asia.

Vietnam, Cambodia and Laos comprise the former French colony of Indochina, although *Indo-China* was sometimes also used to describe all of Peninsular Southeast Asia, as well. France controlled this region since the 1880s, taking some of it in a short war with Thailand in 1893. Japan took control of Indochina in World War II, and France tried to take it back after the Japanese surrender in 1945. However, the Vietminh under Ho Chi Minh (whom the United States supported against the Japanese), fought to keep the French out in the first Vietnam War (1945–1954), after which Vietnam was divided into North Vietnam (which was communist ruled and supported by China) and South Vietnam (which was capitalist and supported by the United States). With China's support, North Vietnam sought to reunite the country under its rule, resulting in the Second Vietnam War, which lasted from 1959 until the last United States troops pulled out in 1975. The Communist Party of Vietnam still rules the country, though today it is open to tourism and Western investment.

Early Indianization of Southeast Asia

About 2000 years ago traders from China to the north and India to the west entered Southeast Asia. For most of Southeast Asia it was the Indian influence that was most significant. The Indians referred to Southeast Asia has Suvardvira (or Suvard Bumi), the *Golden Land*. Most of the Indian traders were Sudras, from the bottom of the caste system. They were generally uneducated adventurers. Around the 1st century CE, the higher Kshatriya cast entered Southeast Asia as merchants. This was the second-highest caste group in India, and they were primarily looking for goods to trade with the Roman Empire. They were a more educated caste and they introduced Indian political structures into Southeast Asia.

At about the same time the village chiefs in Southeast Asia were gradually expanding their areas of rule beyond the village to larger territories. Some of these local rulers traveled to India where they were impressed by the large Indian armies, cities and priestly elites. The Kshatriya merchants brought Brahmin priests to Southeast Asia to perform ceremonies that helped legitimize the emerging rulers. As late as the 1930s, Hindu priests from India still had the role of inaugurating the kings of Southeast Asia.

The Brahmin priests and Buddhist monks from India brought new ideas to Southeast Asia, including the idea of a *god king*, which views the king as a reincarnation of the Buddha or of a Hindu god. This was the basis of Angkor Wat, which was originally built for the Hindu god Vishnu. The Indian priests and monks also brought new architecture, a bureaucratic and court system, and a military framework. Mahayana Buddhism was flourishing in India, especially in the 4th to 6th centuries CE, and was brought by Bhuddhist monks to Southeast Asia. By 800 CE, when construction of the Mahayana Buddhist monument of Borobudur is believed to have started, Hindu- and Buddhist-based kingdoms were common throughout Southeast Asia; and Southeast Asia's first major empires had emerged on the island of Java, on the island of Sumatra, and in Cambodia, Thailand and Myanmar. The largest of these was the Majapahit Empire centered in Java in the 13th century.

Hinduism, Buddhism, Borobudur and Angkor Wat

Hinduism and Mahayana Buddhism in Southeast Asia were largely restricted to the ruling elites and are often referred to as court cuts. Their ceremonies were used to grant legitimacy to the rulers and conquerors. The religions did not filter down to the common peasants, who continued to practice animist traditions. It was not until Theravadin Buddhism was introduced to Peninsular Southeast Asia and Islam and Catholicism to Insular Southeast Asia that the common people moved somewhat away from their traditional beliefs.

In the 12th century CE, refugees from internal wars in Myanmar fled to Sri Lanka where they learned Theravadin Buddhist teachings, which they brought back to Myanmar. From there it spread rather quickly throughout Peninsular Southeast Asia. Theravadin Buddhism is closer to the original teachings of the Buddha, which focuses more on self development and eschews praying to saints and idols. In practice, however, it is mixed with older Hinduism, and Mahayana Buddhist and animist beliefs.

Source: Alan A. Lew

Borobudur is the largest Buddhist monument ever built, and is believed to have been a precursor to Angkor Wat in Cambodia. It is located in Central Java, Indonesia, and comprises six square levels topped by three circular levels that are adorned with 2,672 relief panels and 504 Buddha statues. Pilgrims follow a path from the base to the top of the stupa that takes them through the three levels of Buddhist cosmology: Kamadhatu (the world of desire); Rupadhatu (the world of forms); and Arupadhatu (the world of formless). Borobudur was abandoned in the 14th century after Islam came to be the dominant religion in Insular Southeast Asia. Today the restored Borobudur is the single most visited site in Indonesia and is a pilgrimage destination for Mahayana Buddhists, mostly from East Asia.

Construction of Angkor Wat first began in the 1100s as a Hindu temple at the center of the capital city. The original temple, however, was largely destroyed by the Cham Kingdom in Vietnam in 1177. It was later rebuilt and changed to a Theravadin Buddhist temple around 1400, which it continues to be today. The temple, which includes the *temple mountain* (highest point, representing Mount Meru, the home of the Hindu gods) is surrounded by temple galleries with bas relief carvings and a moat. It is the epitome of classical Khmer architecture style. It has also become a symbol of modern-day Cambodia, appearing on its national flag, and it is one of the leading tourist attractions in Southeast Asia. Angkor Wat underwent major renovation in the 20th century, mostly by foreign aid organizations. Renovations were interrupted by Khmer Rouge control of Cambodia in the 1970s and 1980s, but began again in the 1990s. A rapid growth in tourism to Cambodia in recent years (reaching one million international visitors in 2004) has seen a correspondingly large increase in visitors to Angkor

Wat. The temple complex has been modified only slightly to accommodate the increase in visitors, with ropes and wooden steps being used to protect the bas-reliefs and floors.

Islam and Christianity

In the 14th century, Muslims were in power in South Asia and large numbers of Arab traders were visiting Southeast Asia. It was at this time that Marco Polo visited China and returned to Europe through Southeast Asia. The Arabs introduced Islam to the trading ports where many had settled. Local leaders adopted Islam to strengthen their trading ties with the Muslim merchants. Through this process, Islam became the dominant religion in Insular Southeast Asia by the 16th century.

The result of this history is that Peninsular Southeast Asia has a mix of Hindu and Buddhist cultural practices, while Insular Southeast Asia has a mix of Hindu and Muslim traditions. The major exceptions to this include Vietnam, which has a strong Chinese influence, including Mahayana Buddhism (from Tibet), Confucianism and Taoism, and the Philippines and East Timor, which are mostly Roman Catholic due to European colonial influences. Some of the minority hill tribe populations, especially in Myanmar, have also adopted Christianity. While most of the country of the Philippines is Catholic, its southern island of Mindanao has a large Muslim minority that has been fighting a separatist movement since Spanish colonial times. Although dangerous to visit in the past, peace talks in recent years have opened Mindanoa to tourism, with the old sea gypsy port of Zamboanga being the island's top tourist destination.

Early European Colonies

The Portuguese were the first of the European powers to establish a colony in Southeast Asia. They conquered the port city of Melaka (also spelled Malacca) in modern-day West Malaysia in 1511, which was a year after they had established their colony of Goa in India. In 1556 they established control of the eastern half of the island of Timor. By controlling Melaka, the Portuguese controlled the Strait of Malacca, the most heavily used trading route between China and India. They could easily stop every ship traveling through the narrow passage between Malaysia and the island of Sumatra and force them to pay a tax to continue.

Magellan arrived in the Philippines in 1521, during his voyage around the world. Starting in the 1560s, Spain sought to conquer the sparsely settled and remote islands of the Philippines, and in 1571 they captured Manila, the largest town in the Philippines (which at that time had a population of 15,000). Under Spanish rule, large numbers of people, especially from China, migrated to the Philippines. By the late 17th century over half of the population of the Philippines was Chinese. The Spanish language and Spanish culture formed the basis of the Filipino elite. Following the Spanish American War in 1898, the Philippines became a colony of the United States, which lasted until 1946 – much longer than Filipinos had expected. During that time, much of the Spanish influence was eroded and replaced by American cultural influences, although many place names and family surnames still reflect a strong Spanish influence.

In 1596 Dutch ships entered Indonesia for the first time after they had been banned from Portuguese ports. In 1610 they signed a treaty with the King of Jakarta allowing them to sail to the Spice Islands (the Moluccas). The most valuable product from Insular Southeast Asia for Europeans were the spices that were used to preserve and enhance meat. From their initial base in Java, the Dutch were able to dominate almost the entire

PHOTO 4.8

Children playing in Balikpapan in West Kalimantan on the Island of Borneo in Indonesia

Source: Alan A. Lew

territory that is today the country of Indonesia. In 1641 in the Dutch completely leveled the Portuguese colony of Melaka, which then became a Dutch colony. They were helped by local Malay sultans who had come to hate the ruthlessness of the Portuguese.

The British were latecomers to European colonization in Southeast Asia. In 1685 they established themselves in Bencoolen, on the south side of the island of Sumatra. In 1796 they signed a treaty with local Malay rulers to establish a colony on the island of Penang, located at the north end of the Strait of Malacca. In an effort to break the Dutch monopoly over trade in Southeast Asia. In 1819 they signed a treaty that allowed them to establish the city of Singapore, which would eventually become the dominant economic center for all of Southeast Asia.

The British were much more diplomatic than were the Portuguese, and even the Dutch. To establish Singapore they learned of a conflict between two brothers over which of them would become the Sultan of the territory in which the island of Singapore was located. Sir Stamford Raffles, who spoke fluent Malay and was a scholar of the history of the region, signed the treaty for Singapore with the older brother who had fled into hiding on the island of Sumatra. The younger brother could not stop the power of the British Navy and the British claims that it had signed a treaty with the rightful ruler of the territory (the descendants of whom still reside in the Sultan's compound in Singapore). The British came to control Myanmar as a further extension of their colonization of India, and eventually expanded their control from Singapore to all of present-day Malaysia.

The former British colonies of Penang, Melaka and Singapore together are know as the Straits Settlements. All three of them have predominantly Chinese populations.

Some of these Chinese are descents of early Chinese merchants who married Malay women and settled in the Strait of Malacca 700 years before the arrival of the Europeans. In Malay they are known as Peranakan Chinese, and exhibit a distinct culture that is a fusion of Chinese and Malay. Peranakan culture is seen in the architecture, cuisine and traditional clothing of the three Straits Settlements cities. The old central town of Melaka probably demonstrates Peranakan culture best, as well as ruins of the Portuguese era and administrative buildings dating back to the Dutch period. The colonial heritage is increasingly being promoted by the Malaysian government as a tourist attraction.

Tourism in Southeast Asia Today

The political boundaries of the countries of Southeast Asia today directly reflect the European colonial boundaries of the 19th century.

Thailand and the Tai

The Tai people migrated from Southwest China and formed the basis of a language group that today is spoken in Thailand (Thai), Laos (Laotian), Myanmar (Shan minority group) and the southern China provinces of Guangxi (Zhuang minority group) and Yunnan (Dai minority group). Across this region, some 35 million people speak versions of the Tai language and its dialects. This does not mean that all of the different Tai speakers can speak to one another. Laotian, for example, is part of the Tai language group; however, Laotian itself has four major dialects, each of which is further subdivided, and most of which are mutually unintelligible. Thailand's population is about 75 percent Thai, 15 percent Chinese and 3 percent Malay. The Chinese are mostly in the larger urban areas. Thailand is a constitutional monarchy and democracy, and the King commands great respect in the country. Many of Thailand's northern Hill Tribes have become the backdrop for extensive trekking routes that have become very popular among adventure tourists.

In the 19th century, Siam was able to play off rivalries between the British and French colonizers of Southeast Asia, which enabled it to be the only territory in Southeast Asia that was never made a colony. Concessions to the British, however, resulted in three mostly Malay provinces being made part of British Malaya. However, one other Malay-dominated province remained in Thailand, and Muslim separatists in that province (which borders Malaysia) have caused civil unrest and terrorist attacks on police and Buddhist Thais in recent years.

The Thai are the predominant people in the country of Thailand (Thai here means *freedom* in the Thai language). Thailand was formerly known as Siam, and the Buddhist kingdom of Sukhothai (1238–1368) is considered the first of Siamese kingdom. It was eventually conquered by the second Siamese kingdom of Ayutthaya (1350–1767). Following the destruction of Angkor in 1431, most of the Hindu Khmer court were brought to Ayuthaya, and Khmer customs and rituals were adopted by the Siam court. Ayuthaya was sacked by Bhuddhist Burmese in 1767, and in 1782 the capital of Siam was moved further south to Bangkok. The ruins of Ayuthaya are today a major cultural heritage site and tourist attraction in Thailand.

Thailand today is one of the most visited countries in Asia, and its capital, Bangkok, is a major hub for air travel into and out of Southeast Asia. Tourism to Thailand rose

Source: Alan A. Lew

rapidly in the 1970s after the Vietnam War, when Thailand offered a popular break for United States servicemen. Much of Thailand's tourist reputation has been influenced by the sex industry, which grew to serve visiting soldiers. That still exists today, though it is a much smaller part of the formal tourism economy, which now includes temples and cultural sites in the Bangkok area. Sex tourism in Thailand is supported overwhelmingly by male visitors from Australia, Japan, North America and Europe who travel, sometimes exclusively, for sexual encounters. This form of tourism has received a great deal of negative press in the past decade, and efforts are being made by the Tourism Authority of Thailand to downplay its pervasiveness and replace it with new forms of tourism, such as shopping.

Today, about 65 percent of the visitors to Thailand come from the Asia-Pacific region, with Malaysia and Japan being the main sources, and China a growing source of visitors. Western tourists to Thailand also favor the country's beach resorts on the Gulf of Thailand and on many of Thailand's scenic islands (including Phuket and Koh Samui). Asian tourists tend to focus on Bangkok and historic sites such as Ayuthaya. Medical tourism is a growing segment of Thailand's economy (also popular in Singapore and India). Medical tourists tend either to come from highly developed

PHOTO 4.10

Source: Alan A. Lew

countries (where medical care is very expensive), or from developing countries where the more wealthy have difficulty finding high quality medical care.

Vietnam

Vietnam, with over 85 million people, has the largest population in Peninsular Southeast Asia. It is 87 percent Vietnamese, with the remainder being ethnic Chinese and various hill tribe populations. One of Vietnam's most popular tourist attractions is the World Heritage Site of Ha Long Bay, located on the coast near the border between China and Vietnam. It consists of a large cluster of 1,969 limestone islands that rise steeply from the sea. Many of the islands have limestone caves with stalactites and stalagmites, and some have floating villages attached to them. Both the French and American legacies provide foundations for tourism to the country today. Hanoi, the capital of colonial Indochina, is the most French city in Asia and is renowned for its European influenced cuisine and architecture. American soldiers who fought in Vietnam have been taking tours to the country since the late 1990s to revisit sites that they knew in the war and to reacquaint themselves with the people of Vietnam under more favorable circumstances.

Cambodia and Laos

Cambodia is one of the smallest and poorest countries of Southeast Asia. At the end of the Vietnam War (1975) the Khmer Rouge (Red Khmer) communist government came to power and adopted policies that resulted in the death of 1.7 million of its population of 8 million at that time. This event is popularly known as *the Killing Fields* after the movie made about the event in 1984. In 1978, Vietnam invaded and removed the Khmer Rouge from power. While Cambodia is still under communist rule, tourism has begun to flourish there. Although Angkor Wat is the country's premier attraction, the dark tourism Killing Fields also attracts curious visitors, and the country has had the unfortunate designation of being one of the most popular child prostitution destinations in Asia.

Laos is the only landlocked country in Southeast Asia, and is also among the poorest. It is located between the Mekong River, separating it from Thailand to the west, and the Annamite Mountain Range, which separates it from Vietnam to the east. About half of its population is ethnic Lao, who live in the lower valleys, while the other half are a mix of hill tribes who live in isolated and remote mountainous areas. Vientienne is the capital, although Luang Prabang is the more popular tourist destination. Luang Prabang was the pre-communist capital of the kingdom of Laos and has been designated a World Heritage Site by UNESCO for its many temples.

Myanmar

Myanmar (also known as Burma) has a population of 42.5 million people, about 75 percent of whom are Burmese and 25 percent of whom are either South Asian or hill tribe groups. The South Asians, mostly from India, reside in the lowland cities, such as the capital Yangon (Rangoon), where most of them are merchants. Myanmar is also among the poorest countries in the world and is ruled by a military junta, which took power during a coup in 1988 in which the country's name was changed from Burma to Myanmar. In protest over the dictatorial and oppressive policies of the military regime, some countries (including the United States, the United Kingdom and Canada) have rejected this name change. Politically and socially Myanmar is the most isolated and least westernized of all the countries in Southeast Asia. Calls for tourism boycotts of the country are common because money spent there supports the military government, which is deemed by most observers and foreign governments to be brutal and lacking in human rights. At the same time, the untouched nature of the country makes it a very special and memorable place to visit for those who have visited, and the country's cultures and built heritage are among the most spectacular in the region.

British Insular Southeast Asia: Malaysia, Singapore and Brunei

Malaysia's population is comprised of 45 percent Malay, 33 percent Chinese, 9 percent South Asian and 5 percent tribal people. Large numbers of Chinese and South Asians are in Malaysia because of its importance along the trade route between India and China. They were also brought to Malaysia by the British to work on rubber and palm oil plantations. Malaysia is the world's largest producer of natural rubber and palm oil, as well as tin. Malaysia is divided into West Malaysia, which is predominantly Malay, and East Malaysia, where non-Malays are the majority population. The two parts are separated by the South China Sea; West Malaysia forms

PHOTO 4.11

The Merlion is the symbol of the city-state of Singapore.
Singapore is a major financial center for Southeast Asia

Source: Alan A. Lew

part of Peninsular Southeast Asia, whereas East Malaysia is comprised of two states, Sarawak and Sabah, on the island of Borneo. Malaysia gained its independence from the United Kingdom in 1963, bringing together the British colonies on the Malay Peninsula (Malaya and Singapore) and the British colonies on Borneo. Ethnic tensions between Malays and Chinese were a major source of friction within Malaysia, and resulted in the island of Singapore becoming a separate country from Malaysia in 1965.

Malaysian tourism is based largely on urban heritage (e.g., Melaka and Kuala Lumpur), beach resorts along the country's coastlines, and rainforest-based ecotourism on Borneo. There is a steady flow of cross-border travel between Malaysia and its southern neighbor Singapore, particularly for shopping by Singaporeans in the border town of Johor Baru.

Singapore is an island city-state at the southern tip of the Malay Peninsula. It is 237 sq miles (697) sq km in size, and Chinese are predominant at 77 percent of the population, although they come from several different areas of China and speak a variety of Chinese dialects. Malays comprise 15 percent of Singapore's population, and Indians make up 6.5 percent. Singapore is one of the wealthiest countries in the world and enjoys a very high standard of living. The country consistently ranks as having one of the least corrupt governments in the world, although it is often criticized as having a lack of press freedom. (Myanmar and Cambodia, by contrast, are among those countries with the highest levels of government corruption).

Singapore is a very important gateway and air hub for all of Southeast Asia. In fact, its Changi Airport is considered one of the best *shopping malls* in the world. Shopping otherwise tends to dominate tourist activities in the dowtown area. Because Singapore is a small country with a large and urbanized population, Singaporeans often seek quick opportunities to travel abroad. Given its small size and close proximity to neighbors, this is quite easy to achieve. Day and weekend trips across the border into Malaysia and Indonesia are common among Singaporeans. In Malaysia, they can shop, visit historic Melaka, or spend time on a beach. Quick ferry services to Indonesia's nearby Bintan and Batam islands allows easy access for Singaporeans to golf courses and beach resorts.

Although some tensions continue to underlie politics and race relations in Malaysia and Singapore, the different ethnic groups live harmonously together and provide these countries with a colorful display of festivals, food, and ethnic shopping districts, such as Chinatowns and Little Indias. Most of the street food hawkers are now in government regulated food centers where they serve Malay, Chinese and Indian specialties, as well as fusion cuisine unique to the Malay archipelago.

Brunei Darussalam (Brunei) is one of three countries sharing the island of Borneo. It is an oil exporting Islamic sultanate that achieved independence from the United Kingdom in 1984. When Malaysia gained its independence from Britain in 1963, Brunei decided not to join with Malaysia but rather remain a protectorate under British control. Brunei is about the size of the US state of Delaware, making it one of the smallest of the world's countries, though it is also one of the largest oil producers east of the Middle East. Because of its vast oil deposits, Brunei's ruling sultan is one of the wealthiest men in the world. Although tourism is not a high priority for Brunei, there is some tourism, particularly sport tourism and business-related travel.

Indonesia and East Timor

Indonesia, with a population of almost 225 million, is demographically the fourth largest country in the world, after China, India and the United States. It has more than 18,000 islands (6,000 of which are inhabited), more than 300 distinct ethnic groups, and more than 250 different languages. As a *lingua franca* that could be understood by inhabitants of the Indonesian archipelago, the Indonesian language was invented early in the 1900s to bridge the gap between the country's hundreds of languages. The Javanese people comprise 45 percent of the total population, followed by the Sundanese at 14 percent, and ethnic Chinese at 2 percent. Islam is the religion of 90 percent of the population in Indonesia, making it the world's largest Muslim-populated country. However, the vast majority mixes their Islamic faith with pre-Islamic animist and Hindu influences. Indonesia's economy is based primarily on tropical agriculture, including coffee, tea, tobacco and tapioca. It claimed independence from Dutch colonial rule in 1945, although the Dutch did not relinquish control until 1949. Over 110 million people live on the island of Java, where the country's capital of Jakarta is located. The Hindu island of Bali is also part of Indonesia and is a major beach resort destination, especially for Australians.

Despite the threats to Indonesia's rainforests, trekking and touring the jungles and islands of Indonesia is very popular, making the country the leading ecotourism destination in Asia, and possibly in the world. In the 1990s, most tourists who traveled to Indonesia for trekking, bird and animal watching, diving and visiting the diverse ethnic communities scattered throughout the islands were from the more developed countries of the world. This has changed in recent years, as Asians, and especially Indonesians, have become wealthier and more interested in the natural wonders the country has to offer. The rise in intra-regional travel within Southeast Asia has also been prompted by the growth of low-cost airline carriers, making travel to nearby destinations more attractive than long-haul trips to Europe or North America.

As noted earlier in the chapter, Borobudur is one of Indonesia's most notable attractions. Nearby is the spectacular Prambanan Hindu temple complex, which, like Borobudur, has been designated a UNESCO World Heritage Site. Java is replete with ancient religious temples, many of which are still in ruin and many that have been reconstructed, attracting large numbers of tourists. Gamalan music, religiously based dances, living folkways and cultural performances provide most of the backdrop for Indonesia's cultural tourism. While tourism has historically been centered on Java and Bali, many other countries have begun to appear on the tourist circuit in the past quarter century. Lombok, just east of Bali, is growing as a beach resort destination. The Komodo Islands are home to the famous and endemic Komodo Dragons. Sulawesi, Sumatra, Sarawak (on Borneo) and many of the other outlying islands have grown into important tourist destinations, primarily visited for their cultural traditions, village life and natural environments. The orangutans noted earlier and Sumatra tigers are examples of famous fauna species found in Indonesia that add to its tourist appeal.

Several events have affected the growth of tourism in Indonesia in recent years. For instance, the epicenter of the December 2004 tsunami that affected most of Southeast and South Asia was located off the coast of Indonesia's Sumatra island. The Aceh province was hit particularly hard with hundreds of villagers losing their lives, and tourism to Indonesia nearly collapsed altogether. Terrorist bombings in 2002 and 2005 in popular Bali tourist spots killed many Indonesians and foreign tourists. These events, together with the outbreak of SARS and the Bird Flue early in the 2000s severely curtailed tourism, and there are continuing terror threats in Indonesia that have foreign governments, tour companies and tourists on alert.

East Timor (officially Timor Leste) comprises the eastern half of the island of Timor, the western half of which is part of Indonesia. When Portugal withdrew from East Timor in 1975, the Indonesian government forcibly took control of the former Portuguese colony, an illegal action not recognized by the United Nations or international community. Following a bloody civil war, East Timor gained its independence from Indonesia in 2002 with the military support of Australia and the global community. In 2004, East Timor had the lowest per capita GDP (roughly equates to per capita income) in the world, at about US$500. Living conditions for its approximately one million citizens are very difficult as it attempts to recover (with considerable Australian aid) from the ravages of war. In 2002, the new government was anxious to begin developing tourism, which in fact did begin. However, in recent years, political instability has plagued the new nation, and today there are widespread worries of government corruption, violence and other criminal activity – all of which have prevented the industry from developing in this fragile country.

The Philippines

The Philippines has more than 7,000 islands and is also a very diverse country. The largest ethnic group is Cebuano (around the island of Cebu), comprising 24 percent of the population. Tagalog is the national language, although the Tagalog ethnic group makes up only 14 percent of the country's population. More than 90 different Malay languages are spoken in the Philippines, though at least 50 percent of the population uses English as their *lingua franca* – a legacy of a half century of American rule (1898–1946). The Philippines is 85 percent Roman Catholic, 8 percent Protestant and 5 percent Muslim. Under Spanish rule, land was used to reward those who supported the Spanish. The result was an elite class who controlled the best land in the country, while the impoverished peasants had the worst or no land. Land reform today is still the number one issue in the Philippines. Muslim separatists on the southern island of Mindanao have been attempting to break off from the Catholic Philippines since the country's independence and have resorted to terror tactics and kidnappings (including tourists) in recent years, with the effect of declining arrivals in the entire country.

The Philippines has had a long history of close relations with the United States military, and like Thailand, it has a reputation for sex tourism that was at least partially related to the foreign military presence. This has declined considerably, though not completely, since the withdrawal of the last United States troops in 1992. Filipinos comprise one of the largest and fastest growing immigrant populations in the United States and the Middle East. The mailing of remittances (money) back to relatives in the Philippines is important to the survival of many Filipinos. Large numbers of Filipinos can regularly be seen at major international gateway cities in the United States with large packages to take back to their friends and relatives in the Philippines. The United States military personnel who were formerly based in the Philippines also comprise a sizeable portion of the country's international visitors. In addition to prostitution, the country is best know for tropical resorts and rainforests where people undertake wildlife watching, hiking and mountain trekking.

4.3 EAST ASIA

East Asia is racially one of the most homogeneous regions of the world. China is 90.5 percent ethnic Han Chinese, Japan is 98.4 percent Japanese and Korea is about 99 percent Korean. By comparison the United States is about 60 percent non-Hispanic Caucasian. Even though it covers an area larger than most of the other regions covered so far, there are only five countries in East Asia: China, Japan, North Korea, South Korea and Mongolia. In addition, there are the Chinese territories of Taiwan, Hong Kong and Macau, which are largely autonomous from mainland China. Culturally, East Asia has been dominated by China, and all of its countries look to classical China as part of their early influences. For example, both Mahayana Buddhism (which came to China from Tibet) and Confucian values predominate throughout East Asia.

Source: Alan A. Lew

Physical Geography

The western reaches of East Asia extend into the center of the Eurasian continent. Western China and Mongolia share many similar characteristics with the countries of Central Asia. It is a land of high mountains and vast basins, most of which are very arid. From the Pamir Knot in Tajikistan, the Tian Shan Mountains extend northwest to form China's western border with Kyrgyzstan. The Altun Shan and Kunlun Shan mountain ranges form the northern boundary of the Tibetan Plateau, while the Himalayas comprise its southern boundary. The Tibetan plateau (known as the Qinghai-Xizang Plateau in China) has a base elevation of about 15,000 ft, from which higher mountains rise.

North of the Tibetan Plateau are the deserts and grasslands leading to Central Asia and the border between China and Mongolia. These include the Tarim Basin (home of the Taklamakan Desert) and Gobi (or Shamo) Desert. Southeast of the Tibetan Plateau is a rugged mountain region with steep valleys through which many of the great rivers of East and Southeast Asia flow. In one area, the Salween (Myanmar), Mekong (Indochina) and Yangtze (China) rivers flow parallel to one another within a 50 mile (80 km) distance. These mountains become lower further away from the Tibetan Plateau, though most of southern China is still mountainous all the way to the South China Sea.

North of the Yangtze River lies the North China Plain, and north of that, across the Bo Hai Sea is the Manchurian (or Heilongjiang) Plain. The North China Plain was once covered with water, but was gradually filled in by sediment carried from the west by China's two major rivers. In the north, the Yellow River (or Huang He) flows from

PHOTO 4.13

Popular view of Hong Kong harbor from The Peak on Hong Kong Island. Hong Kong is a special administrative region of China

Source: Alan A. Lew

the Tibetan Plateau through the Gobi Desert and on to the North China Plain. The Yellow River is known as *China's Sorrow* because it is *undrinkable, unnavigable and unforgiving* in its flooding of the North China Plain. It is *Yellow* because of the large amounts of mud that it carries from the loess areas of the Gobi Desert. *Loess* is a type of loosely compacted soil made up of wind-blown dirt. Further to the south is the Yangtze River (Changjiang or Long River, in Chinese), which is the most important river in China. It flows from the Tibetan Plateau, through Chongqing (Chungking) and the Red Basin of Sichuan Province (the most densely populated region in China), through the Three Gorges of the Yangtze, through the Twin Lakes area near Wuhan, and out to the East China Sea at Shanghai.

Ring of Fire

Coastal East Asia is part of the *Pacific Ring of Fire*, which refers to a ring of volcanic and earthquake areas that encircles much of the Pacific Ocean. In Asia, this ring of active seismic activity extends from Alaska's Aleutian Islands, down the Kamchatka Peninsula of Russia, to Japan, Taiwan and the Philippines, then to New Guinea and New Zealand. Between these islands and on the East Asian mainland are major seas, including the Sea of Japan (between Japan and the Asia mainland), the Yellow Sea (between the Korean peninsula and China), the East China Sea and the South China Sea (between China and the Philippines). Japan's Mount Fuji is part of the Ring of

Photo 4.14

Halong bay on the coast of Vietnam near China is a dramatic landscape of almost 2000 Limestone Islands. This world heritage site is one of the more popular nature-based tourist destinations in Vietnam

Source: Alan A. Lew

Fire; it is a large volcano cone and the highest peak in Japan (12,389 ft; 3,776 m), which last erupted in 1707 CE. It is a popular hiking destination, with many overnight huts and panoramic views of Tokyo and Honshu Island.

Climate and Agriculture

East Asia lies in the northern latitudes. It extends from the tropics in the southernmost areas of China to cold northern latitudes in Mongolia, Manchuria (China) and Japan's island of Hokkaido. Mongolia and Western China experience a harsh continental climate that is very cold in the winter and hot in summer. The eastern coastline of China and the islands of Japan, Korea and Taiwan have some maritime (ocean) influences. However, because they are on the east coast of the Eurasian continent, they are downwind from the cold winter winds and the hot summer air masses that originate in Siberia and Central Asia. This makes the difference between summer and winter weather conditions much more extreme than one would find in coastal areas on the opposite side of the continent, such as in Europe. This is especially true for the more northerly latitudes of China, Korea and Japan.

Along the east coast of East Asia the climate varies with changes in latitude (from south to north). The southernmost areas are tropical and subtropical, meaning they are located below the Tropic of Cancer and have the sun directly overhead at the peak of their summer months. The southernmost island of Hainan in China has a tropical rainforest climate. Further north from Hainan the summers are equally hot and humid, but cooler winter temperatures create a subtropical climate. The warm and humid climate of southernmost China allows for two and sometimes three crops of rice to be grown in a single year. In the mountainous areas of southern China, tea and upland dry rice are often grown.

East Asia is also subject to typhoons that form in the Pacific Ocean east of the Philippines in the summer months. From the Philippines the typhoons turn northward, following the wind flow of the summer Siberian High Pressure system. They usually make land fall along the coast of southern China (from Hainan to Taiwan). Occasionally they will even make their way northward to southern Japan. In the winter, the Siberian Low turns a clockwise direction, bringing occasional blasts of frigid cold out of the interior of Asia to much of East Asia. While this sounds like a monsoonal climate, with wind directions changing from summer to winter, it is not usually described as monsoonal due to the relatively dry winters.

Most of southern Japan, South Korea and eastern China south of the Yellow River, has a humid subtropical climate. However, because they are further to the north, the winter months are longer and colder. This is similar to the climate in the southeastern United States, and is characterized by relatively warm temperatures and rainfall throughout the year though especially in the summer months. The growing season for rice, however, is shorter and only one crop in a year is more common. Even further north, wheat is grown instead of rice.

The densely populated North China plain near Beijing experiences more intense winter conditions. In this area wheat and soybeans are the dominant agricultural crops. The more sparsely settled area of Manchuria is a major breadbasket for East Asia. The Korean Peninsula and the islands of Japan have a similar transition from rice growing in the South to soybeans and other crops in their northern areas.

East Asia consists of more than just these coastal areas, though this is where most of the region's population resides. There is also a major east to west climate transition. The further west, the drier the climate becomes. This is true of all continents that are not situated on the equator. Along the coast humid and warm conditions allow for intensive agricultural activity. Further to the west, agriculture becomes extensive with a focus on the production of wheat and other grains, and the grazing of animals. In the far western reaches of China, oasis agriculture is common due to the harsh arid conditions. This is true in both the Gobi Desert and on the Tibetan Plateau.

Human Geography

Since the end of World War II, East Asia has undergone a remarkable transformation in social and economic development. Japan led the way, quickly recovering from the ravages of war to become one of the wealthiest countries in the world with one of the most successful economies. The Japanese enjoy one of the longest life expectancies in the world, and their approach to export-based economic development has served as a model for South Korea, Taiwan, Hong Kong and Singapore, who were among the first newly industrializing countries (NICs) in the developing world. These countries were known as Asia's *little dragons*, with Japan being the big dragon. All of these countries, including Japan, have a strong Chinese cultural influence. The most remarkable economic transition in world history has occurred in China, which has moved from being one of the poorest countries in the world to a leading world economic power in only two decades. In East Asia, only the countries of North Korea and Mongolia have been struggling in their economic development efforts.

China's Dominance

With a population of about 1.3 billion people, China is the most populated country on earth. It is also the world's oldest, continuous nation and civilization. Although at times it was fragmented into opposing feudal kingdoms, it has had an identity as a single cultural realm since at least 2000 BCE, and probably earlier. Versions of Chinese writing date back to 3000 BCE and the earliest Chinese historical records make reference to the Xia (or Hsia) Dynasty 1994 BCE. The Xia Dynasty in was located on the Yellow River, just west of the North China Plain near the city of Xi'an, which was the cultural hearth of Chinese civilization. The earliest dynasty that has significant historical records is the Shang (or Yin) Dynasty, which existed from 1523 to 1027 BCE. This dynasty had a complex agricultural society and government bureaucracy, along with a well-established social class system. It was during this time that contemporary Chinese writing and the Chinese lunar calendar were established.

The Chou Dynasty, 1027 to 256 BCE, was concurrent with the Greeks and is considered the classical period of Chinese civilization. This was the time that Confucius and Lao Tze, the founder of Taoism, lived. Early Chinese laws were codified at this time and the world's first paper money was introduced. It was also a time of feudal divisions and warfare on the North China Plain (known as the Warring States Period).

During the Chin Dynasty (247–221 BCE) all of the smaller kingdoms of China were unified for the first time by Chin Shih Huang Di (the Yellow Emperor of the Chin Dynasty). He was an extremely ruthless emperor, known for the massive burning of books and the murder of scholars, resulting in the loss of much of the earlier historical records of China. He was also responsible for creating the first Great Wall of China by connecting a series of smaller defensive walls that were built in earlier times and located farther north than the Great Wall of today. His tomb in Xi'an, with its over 8000 life-size terracotta soldiers, is one of China's most significant archeological finds. However, the Yellow Emporer's dynasty did not last beyond his death. The Han Dynasty followed in 202 BCE, and lasted up to 220 CE. It was concurrent with the height of the Roman Empire, with whom the Chinese traded along the Silk Route. The Han Dynasty continued the unification and expansion of China into modern-day southeast and southwest China.

The Great Wall of China is not only the country's most recognized icon, but also has much symbolic significance for how China relates to the outside world. On the one hand it was built to protect China from nomadic northern tribes that periodically invaded the country. The Huns, for example, invaded China in the 4th century BCE.

PHOTO 4.15

View of the Tokyo Bay area of Tokyo, Japan

(These were the same Huns that invaded Europe and sacked Rome in the 4th century CE.) The Great Wall also played a role in keeping China Chinese, by maintaining cultural uniformity to the south of the wall. In some periods of Chinese history, Chinese were not allowed to leave China, and were considered no longer Chinese if they did.

Chinese civilization has historically been based on settled agriculture. This made China very different from the nomadic cultures that existed in the grasslands and deserts to the north and west of the North China Plain. The Great Wall marks the change in vegetation between the drier region to the north that is better suited to animal grazing and the more humid region to the south of the wall. Throughout the world a cultural division exists between settled agriculturalists and nomadic people. This was seen previously in Section 3.3, and to a lesser degree in North Africa. Nomadic people see themselves as free and self-reliant. They view settled agriculturalists as weak and dependent. Settled agriculturalists, on the other hand, see themselves as civilized and educated, and view nomadic peoples as vulgar and ruthless. Historically, nomadic peoples have demonstrated military prowess and have often invaded settled agriculturalist societies. This was seen in the Indo-Aryan invasions of South Asia (2000 BCE).

Nomadic peoples also tend to be easily absorbed into the cultures of the settled populations that they conquer. This has happened in China, though only two nomadic groups ever completely controlled all of China. The Mongols under Genghis Khan did so from 1260 to 1368 CE (Yuan Dynasty), when China was part of the largest empire that the world has ever known. This was also when Marco Polo visited China. After the fall of the Mongolian Yuan Dynasty, the Chinese Ming Dynasty (1368–1644) revived the idea of the Great Wall and built the current structure that millions of tourists visit today. It marked the northern border of China, separating it from Mongolia.

There is a famous claim that is often repeated of the early American astronauts claiming that the Great Wall was the only manmade object that they could see from space. Actually, the Great Wall cannot be seen from space because it is much more narrow than any American freeway or German autobahn. What the astronauts probably saw was the change in vegetation that occurs along the approximate location of the Great Wall.

The Ming Dynasty also built the Imperial Palace (also known as the Forbidden City) in Beijing. The Ming Dynasty fell to non-Chinese nomads from Manchuria who established the Qing (Ching) Dynasty from 1644 to 1911 CE, which was the last dynasty of China before the establishment of the Republic of China. Under the Qing Dynasty, China became the wealthiest empire in the world up through the 18th century. However, China was in considerable decline by the time European traders started arriving by sea in the 19th century.

Post-Dynastic China

For most of the 19th and 20th centuries, China has been in a state of political disarray and internal turmoil. In the final years of the Ching Dynasty, China had lost large amounts of territory to neighboring countries and China's 21 provinces and five autonomous regions were battling amongst each other over who should rule the country. When the Republic of China was established in 1911 by Dr. Sun Yat-sen, this period of internal turmoil had not yet been settled. The situation was further complicated by the rise of the Chinese Communist Party, first in the major cities, and later in the more rural parts of the country. After World War II, the Chinese Communist soldiers, under Mao Zedong, pushed the Republic of China government out of the mainland and to the island of Taiwan.

In 1949 the People's Republic of China was established and for the following three decades China was essentially closed off to the rest of the world. For China, this was a period of intense political infighting centered on the ideology of communism. With some exceptions, mass starvation was mostly eliminated under the Communists, though standards of living stagnated. In 1976, China's revolutionary leader, Mao Zedong died and Deng Xiaoping came to power. His reforms gradually, but successfully, brought free market economic principles to China, although the Chinese Communist Party still maintains strict political control. The result has been a rapidly rising standard of living for most of the people of China, although those in the coastal provinces have benefited more than those in the interior of the country, and the gap between the rich and poor has increased dramatically from Mao Zedong's China.

Chinese Tourism

One indicator of how China has changed since the death of Mao Zedong is seen in its tourism economy. In 1978, China received about 230,000 international foreign tourists, mostly because of the severe limitations that the government placed on who was allowed to visit the country and who was not. In 2006, China received over 22 million foreign visitors. These numbers are calculated by China's National Tourism Organization

(CNTO) and include day visitors who do not stay overnight in China, but excludes visitors from the *compatriot territories* of Hong Kong, Macao and Taiwan. The latter would add another 100 million visitors to China's total. Using the data from the World Tourism Organization (UNWTO), which only includes overnight visitors and does include the Chinese compatriots, China received 41.8 million visitors in 2006, making it the fourth most visited country in the world. If its current growth rates continue, China will be the most visited country in the world in 2017. In addition to the large numbers of international tourists to China, the country recorded over 1.2 billion domestic trips taken by Chinese in 2005.

As an export industry (one that brings money into a country or destination), those numbers are good for China. However, the most significant impact for the rest of Asia and the world is the rapidly growing numbers of Chinese tourists who are traveling to other countries. In 2006 some 34.5 million mainland Chinese trips were taken outside of China. China has more outbound tourists than any other country in Asia, though they are mostly concentrated in Hong Kong and Macao (71 percent). The impact of Chinese outbound tourism is starting to be felt in Asia (17 percent), with far fewer going to Europe (5 percent) and elsewhere, although arrivals to Australia have grown tremendously in the past few years since it was placed on China's approved destination list. In addition, members of the rapidly growing middle class in China are among the biggest spenders when they travel overseas, making them a highly desired market.

Mainland Chinese are currently able to take leisure trips to many countries in the world – those that have been approved destinations by the Chinese government. The United States has not yet been placed on the approved list, so Chinese are still restricted from visiting the United States as pleasure tourists, although they can visit relatives and visit as students and business people. Canada has been negotiating its position on the list and expects to be an approved destination in the near future. By 2020 China is projected to produce 100 million outbound trips going to every corner of the globe, making it the largest producer of tourists in the world, by far. Destinations should begin to prepare for the onslaught of Chinese tourists, as the population of that country is increasing in affluence, ability to travel and freedom to travel, and will become a coveted market segment in the future.

Chinese Landscape

How people experience and interact with the natural environment is influenced by the culture they grew up in. Even more than other Asian countries, the people of China have a distinct perspective on the relationship between humans and the environment, and how that relationship is expressed. Mountain peaks have been seen as places of respite and contemplation, with monasteries being one of the few proper forms of development allowed. This is best seen in the traditional landscape paintings made with simple black ink on an off-white paper. The classical painting would show a series of steep mountains, similar to the limestone (karst) mountains of Guilin, with one or more very small representations of people and buildings scattered in the valleys and on mountain trails. The scenery represents the Taoist philosophy of harmony and balance, values that are actually common in many traditional societies.

The close cultural relationship to mountain areas means that most mountains show some signs of human impact, typically in the form of a pagoda, a rock carving, or a monastic building situated in particularly attractive locations. Pristine wilderness is rare, though they do exist. Many foreign visitors are surprised when they visit a popular mountain and see a large Chinese character carved into a rock face; and they are even more surprised by the Chinese interpretive material, which typically makes reference to ancient Chinese history and legends that all Chinese know, but which are unknown to foreign visitors. (These stories are taught through the textbooks used for learning Chinese reading and writing.) The more fundamental difference is that for the Chinese, virtually every mountain and rock feature is associated with an element of Chinese history and legend, and has a cultural significance. The scientific significance is also there, but for the masses the cultural meanings are more accessible and immediate. For many foreign visitors from the West, the opposite is true.

China's Minority Areas

Most of the ethnic Han Chinese in China live in the eastern, coastal parts of the country. The more remote northern, western and southwestern regions have large non-Chinese populations who together number over 120 million (about 9.5 percent of China's population). China's one-child policy does not apply to its minority groups, who are growing at rates many times faster than Han Chinese. The 11 largest non-Chinese ethnic groups, among the 55 that are officially recognized by China, are:

Southwest China (bordering Southeast Asia)

- *Zhuang (16 million)* – Tai-speaking people mostly in the Guangxi Zhuang Autonomus Region.
- *Miao (8 million)* – several different hill tribe ethnic groups, including the Hmong, who live along China's border with Southeast Asia.
- *Yi (7 million)* – Tibeto-Burmese speaking minority who live along China's border with Southeast Asia.
- *Tujia (7 million)* – Tibeto-Burmese speaking minority who mostly live near the borders of Guizhou, Hunan and Hubei Provinces.
- *Buyei (3 million)* – Tai-speaking people who live along China's border with Vietnam.

Northern China
- *Manchu (10 million)* – in Northeast China, which was formerly known as Manchuria;
- *Mongols (5 million)* – in the Inner Mongolia Autonomous Region of northern China;
- *Koreans (2 million)* – along the border with North Korea.

Western China
- *Hui (9 million)* – a Muslim population in Xianjiang and other western provinces.
- *Uyghur (7 million)* – a Central Asian Muslim people mostly in the Xinjiang Uyghur Autonomous Region.
- *Tibetans (5 million)* – a Buddhist people in the Tibet Autonomous Region.

Each of these ethnic groups, and the many others that are officially and in officially recognized, has a distinct material cultural and traditions around which they have built tourism economies. Southwest China is known for its many different ethnic groups, most of which are also found in neighboring countries in Southeast Asia.

The old town of Lijiang in Yunnan Province has been identified as the closest to the legendary *Shangri La*, and is also in a popular mountain trekking region. Western China is best known for the ancient Silk Road trading route, which includes oasis cities and high mountains in China and neighboring Central Asia. Tibet is a very special place where traditional Mahayana Buddhist practices are seen in their purist forms, but the region is also changing rapidly since the Qinghai-Tibet Railroad (the highest in the world) was opened in 2006.

Taiwan, Macau and Hong Kong

Taiwan, Hong Kong and Macau are all considered territories of China. However, they were not under the control of the Chinese Communist Party when the People's Republic of China was established in 1949. The government of the Republic of China fled to Taiwan and re-established itself after the communist takeover of the mainland. Hong Kong had been a British colony since 1842, while Macau had been a Portuguese colony since 1557. In 1997, Hong Kong was returned to mainland Chinese control, while Macau reverted back to mainland control in 1999.

Although China considers Taiwan part of its sovereign territory, Taiwan (the Republic of China) considers itself to be the original China and an independent state. Taiwan has a long history of not effectively being part of China. The indigenous people of Taiwan are Malayo-Polynesians, who probably migrated to the island from the Philippines some 12,000 years ago. Genetically, the 12 official aboriginal nations (tribal groups) on the island are among the most homogeneous people on earth, indicating a very long period of isolation. The first Chinese to settle on the island arrived in the 1400s, although this is disputed by historians. Chinese settlers also arrived after the Dutch colonized Taiwan in 1624. The Dutch were ousted by the Chinese pirate, Koxinga, in 1662, who established the Kingdom of Tungning. His kingdom lasted until 1683 when mainland China took over the island as part of its efforts to stop piracy in the South China Sea. In 1895, following China's defeat in the Sino-Japanese War, Japan took control of Taiwan, which it ruled until 1945 when Japan returned the island at the close of World War II.

Some two million refugees fled from mainland China to Taiwan in the period between 1945 and 1949. Today, the population of Taiwan is almost 30 million, of which about 84 percent are native Taiwan Chinese (not related to the post-World War II refugee migration). The original Malayo-Polynesians number less than 400,000 and live as minorities in the island's high mountains. Taiwan has one of the highest per capita incomes in Asia, and its capital, Taipei, had the world's tallest building until 2007. An important attraction in Taipei is the National Palace Museum, which is one of the finest museums of Chinese art in the world. Most of the items on the rotating display were brought from mainland China by refugees fleeing the Communists. Although Taiwan does not have large volcanoes, it is part of the Ring of Fire and has dramatic mountains that reach over 13,000 ft (3960 m), most of which are protected with national park status. The Taroko Gorge is a deep and narrow canyon that cuts through the center of the mountains with a dramatic road carved into the granite walls. One of the most recent tourism-related debates in Taiwan is the establishment of casinos in the Penghu Islands, just off Taiwan's west coast. Many Taiwanese observers see gaming as an economic opportunity, while others consider it evil and against Chinese tradition.

Macau was given to Portugal in 1557 by the Emperor of China as a reward for Portuguese assistance in defeating a notorious pirate in the South China Sea. It is a very small area, consisting of a peninsula and two small islands. In 1974, following a leftist revolution in Portugal, the Portuguese offered to give Macau back to China. China was not ready to accept the return of Macau at that time, but officially designated it as *Chinese territory under Portuguese administration*. Historically, Macau has been a backwater to nearby Hong Kong, and has been much more politically dependent on mainland China than has its British counterpart. The small population of Macanese culture is a mix of Chinese and Portuguese, and is related to similar places where Portuguese have intermixed with local populations, such as in Melaka (Malaysia) and Goa (India).

Macau is mostly known for its gaming industry, and serves both nearby Hong Kong and mainland China as a gambling center. In 2004, the first international casino companies were permitted to open in Macau, bringing new life (and Las Vegas-style casinos) to the city's former monopoly gaming industry. The rise in mainland Chinese tourists to Macau has transformed it into the largest gaming city in the world, in terms of gaming profits. The Macau Grand Prix has also been a major event for several decades. Besides gaming and tourism, textiles, garments, fireworks, toys and electronics are major areas of employment in Macau. Many people visit Macau on side-trips from Hong Kong, as the two territories are well connected by fast boats and hydrofoils.

In the early 1800s European trade with China was basically a one-way arrangement. The Europeans purchased silk, tea and fine Chinese pottery from China. There was little, however, that the rather sophisticated Chinese economy was interested in purchasing from the Europeans in exchange. Therefore, the European traders used silver to purchase Chinese goods, which put a strain on the central banks of European countries. The Portuguese were the first to introduce opium into China as an alternative product for trade. The opium was grown in South and Southeast Asia. Opium was illegal in China but was traded openly in the southern port city of Guangzhou.

Because of the opium trade, silver began leaving China and the Chinese government decided to confiscate the opium from the foreign settlements to stop its trade. They also forced most of the foreigners out of the ports in southern China. Most went to Macau, but the British were not allowed to go there by the Portuguese, so instead they anchored at a nearby fishing village called Hong Kong. The British traders called on the British Navy to retaliate against China and the British Navy subsequently bombed cities along the Chinese coast all the way to Beijing. In 1842 they forced the Qing Emperor in Beijing to grant the island and nearby peninsula of Hong Kong to the British.

Other Europeans also fought opium wars with China to force China to allow them to establish trading communities in the major port cities. But only the British actually established a permanent colony. Under British law, Hong Kong flourished as a trading center. It offered a much better port facility than Macau, and the British had a reputation for treating most people fairly in a largely free-market economy. Hong Kong today, even under mainland Chinese rule, is consistently rated as having one of the most free and open economic systems in the world. Less can be said for democratic rule, which even the British suppressed until their last days in Hong Kong.

As much as 75 percent of the land in Hong Kong is mountainous and covered with lush subtropical vegetation. This steep terrain makes the harbor and city view from

Victoria Peak on Hong Kong Island one of the most scenic urban landscape views in the world. The steep terrain also exasperates the density of crowding in the city. Hong Kong could not survive without considerable support from China in providing basic water, food, petroleum and electricity needs.

Hong Kong today is a major global financial center, having lost much of its manufacturing base to the less expensive areas in neighboring China. It is the most visited tourist destination in Asia, receiving well over 20 million visitors a year, the majority coming from mainland China to shop for high-end goods. It has also been a major gateway to China, especially in the period before the 1990s when direct international flights into China were very limited. Taiwanese still mostly entered China through Hong Kong, though that is slowly changing with more direct flights between Taiwan and mainland China to be introduced, probably sometime in the coming decade.

Japan

Japan has a population of more than 127 million people, making it the tenth largest country in the world. The land area of Japan is slightly smaller than the US State of California. It is an insular country made up of four large islands and about 3000 smaller islands that extend almost to Taiwan. The Japanese have a cultural tendency only to occupy lowland areas, leaving the interior mountains uninhabited, except for temples and resorts. As a result, most Japanese live in very high-density urban areas on the southern coast of the island of Honshu, which is the largest island in Japan. This includes the Tokyo-Yokohama metropolitan area – the world's largest urban agglomeration at 35 million people. Kyushu and Shikoku are the two southernmost islands and are warmer and more subtropical than the rest of Japan. Hokkaido is the northern frontier island and is famous for its winter Snow Festival and large ice sculptures in Sapporo. Hokkaido is relatively sparsely settled and connected to Honshu by the Seikan Tunnel (53.9 km; 33.4 miles), an underwater railway that is slightly longer than the *Chunnel* between England and Belgium.

Japan is ethnically the most homogeneous country on earth. As mentioned above, 98.4 percent of the population is Japanese. Koreans and Chinese each make up 0.4 percent of the population, and the Ainu of Hokkaido comprise some 0.1 percent. The Japanese take great pride in their racial purity; a former prime minister, Yasuhiro Nakasone, commented in 1986 that the United States education system was falling behind Japan because of its ethnic impurities. (The United States view is that the multiplicity of ideas and perspectives are what has made the United States the success that it is today.) The homogeneous culture of Japan is due, in part, to its geographic isolation. The islands of Japan are physically separated from the main areas of the Asian continent, with the Korean Strait and the Sea of Japan providing protection from invasions. The Mongols, for example, were not able to incorporate Japan into their massive empire despite several attempts. In addition to geographic isolation, Japanese have been very isolated culturally, taking considerable measures to protect themselves from outside influences.

Japan has some of the largest and most crowded cities in the world, yet it is also one of the safest countries in the world. This is a benefit of the strong influence of Japanese culture throughout the society. The Japanese have a strong adherence to cultural and social norms of behavior. Deviants are treated harshly. Improper behavior results in a loss of face and social ostracism, not just for the individual, but also for the groups that the individual belongs to, including family, community, school and workgroup. All these groups lose face and share in the blame of an individual's improper behavior.

This strict adherence to social norms has its cost. The Japanese education and work system tends to wear people out by their early 30s because of its strenuous social demands. In addition, Japan has one of the highest child suicide rates in the world, and has the highest suicide rate among elderly women, who find that they have only a limited role to play in society after their children leave home. The result is a disciplined society that is adaptable to large-scale organization and mass production assembly manufacturing, and produces highly skilled labor. This has placed Japan at the cutting edge of industrial and high technology development, and contributed to the country's economic recovery after World War II. Related to this, two of the most popular tourist destinations in Tokyo are Ginza, famous for its department stores and luxury brands, and Akihabara, considered by many to be the electronics capital of the world, as well as for Otaku culture. Otaku culture refers to the *obsessive hobbyist*, which in Japan typically means those who follow anime (Japanese graphic novels), computer nerds and game players, military geeks, pop culture fans and other kitsch fads and fetishes.

Japan has a history of openness to incorporating and adapting foreign ideas. During China's Sui Dynasty (581–619 CE), Tang Dynasty (618–907), and early Song Dynasty (960–1279) Japan sent scholars and government officials to China to learn everything they could about Chinese arts, culture and government. (This was roughly concurrent with the Arab Empire and the Dark Ages of Europe.) Most went for a two to three year period and upon their return were placed in positions of authority to implement what they had learned. Buddhist teachings and Chinese art, architecture and city planning were adopted from China at this time. One example is Japan's former capital city, Kyoto, which was designed after the Tang Chinese capital city of Chang'an (modern day Xi'an), and using Chinese geomancy (feng-shui) principles. Kyoto was the imperial capital of Japan for 11 centuries, although Japan was not fully united for all that time. Having been spared from the fire-bombings of World War II, Kyoto is one of the best preserved cities in Japan. Today it has some 2000 Buddhist temples and Shinto (Japanese traditional religion) shrines, plus many palaces and gardens. It provides a welcome difference from the ultramodern Tokyo landscape, and tourism is a major part of Kyoto's economy.

The tradition of sending Japanese to China lasted some 600 years, after which Japan entered a feudal Dark Ages in the 12th century. During this time Japan was fragmented by powerful clans and regional families (daimyo), and the military rule of warlords (shogun). During the European colonial period (starting in the 15th and 16th centuries), Japan benefited from its great distance from Europe. It was essentially closed to the rest of the world, until 1850 when the United States Navy, under Admiral Perry, forced Japan to open its doors to trade with the West. Concern over encroaching Western powers, the Japanese came together in 1868 and overthrew the Shogun of Japan, the most powerful feudal lord, and restored the Emperor Meiji to power. This is known as the Meiji Restoration.

Japanese students and entrepreneurs roamed the world to learn all they could about why and how the West had become so successful economically and militarily. They quickly learned and adopted Western technology and management practices, and in the 1890s fought successful wars against Russia and China. As Japan's economy grew, it sought to expand its colonial control over most of East Asia to secure access to raw materials for its growing industries. This was similar to the colonial motivations of the

PHOTO 4.16

South Korean tourists at Mount Kumgang in North Korea.
This is one of only a few destinations in the North that
South Korean Tourists can visit

Source: Dallen J. Timothy

European powers in their industrial revolution in the 1800s. These moves ultimately resulted in World War II, and although Japan lost that war, today it is a major global economic power, with considerable influence throughout the East and Southeast Asia realm.

Three major tourist attractions reflect this history of Japan. The Nijo Castle in Kyoto was built in 1603 by Tokugawa Ieyasu, one of Japan's most powerful shoguns and founder of the Tokugawa Shogunate. The almost entirely wood castle was a symbol of the power of the Tokugawa and is today filled with fine art. The Meiji Restoration moved the capital from Kyoto to Tokyo, where the Meiji Shrine is among the most visited temples in Japan. It is a Shinto temple and museum and was built after the death of the Emperor Meiji (died 1912) and his wife, the Empress Shoken (died 1914), though the original building was destroyed in World War II. The third major historical attraction is the Hiroshima Peace Memorial Park and the Peace Memorial Museum, which commemorates the destruction of Hiroshima by the world's first atomic bomb on 6 August 1945. The park, which was built in 1949, also includes the Children's Peace Monument and the ruins of the A-Bomb Dome, and is a symbol of international peace. In addition to these historic sites, Mt Fuji is a symbol of Japan that is known throughout the world and has become somewhat of an iconic image for the country.

Korea, North and South

Korea has long served as a buffer between China and Japan. Chinese culture entered Japan mostly through the Korean Peninsula. The Go-Joseon Empire (also called Tan-gun Joseon, which means *land of the morning calm*) rose in 2333 BCE in Korea and at one time controlled Manchuria to the north and coastal areas of the North China Plain. This empire lasted until its defeat by the Han Dynasty of China in 108 BCE. Korea has been considered a tributary state of China for most of the time since then, which meant that it maintained a degree of autonomy, but paid tribute to the Emperor of China. Korea was under Japan's control from 1905 to 1945. Unlike other areas of East Asia that were colonized by Japan, the Japanese fully annexed Korea in 1910 because they saw the Koreans as more like themselves than other Asians. The Japanese then tried to erase Korean culture forcibly and replace it with Japanese culture. This led to great devastation in Korea and resentments that are still strong today.

At the end of World War II, Korea was divided into a Soviet Union sphere of influence in the north and a United States sphere of influence in the south. (Germany and Austria were similarly divided in Europe.) The Korean War was fought from 1950 to 1953 after North Korea attacked South Korea. United Nations troops, which included many American soldiers, pushed the North Korean soldiers to the border with China. China, however, decided to enter the conflict and pushed the UN armies southward to where the present border lies between North and South Korea. The border today is known as the Demilitarized Zone (DMZ), which is an uninhabited area 155 miles/ (248 km) long and about 2.5 miles/(4 km) wide. It is also a significant tourist attraction on both sides of the border. Tours from Pyongyang (North Korea – the Democratic People's Republic of Korea) visit, as do tours from Seoul (South Korea – the Republic of Korea). The abandoned village of Panmunjom is in the center of the DMZ and is where North and South Korean representatives meet to discuss border issues. Other than brief visits to Panmunjom, few humans have entered the DMZ since 1953, making it one of the best preserved temperate wildlife areas in the world, although this is complicated by the large number of land mines that both sides have placed over the years.

Although ethnically one people, North Korea and South Korea are vastly different countries. North Korea is ruled by a dictatorial communist government that controls all aspects of life in the north, including recreation and tourism. It is very mountainous and has an abundance of hydroelectric capacity. The mountains also contain considerable mineral wealth, including coal and iron, which are key for heavy manufacturing. North Korea's climate is much more continental than South Korea's, and it has a much smaller population. North Korea is very dependent on industrial factories because it has limited agricultural land. It must sell manufactured products to pay for food imports to feed its people. Malnutrition and starvation have been major problems in North Korea since the collapse of its primary supporter, the Soviet Union.

South Korea also has mountains, but it has much more lowland area that is suitable for agriculture. It has a more humid temperate and subtropical climate, which even allows double cropping in its southernmost areas. South Korea is a food exporter, despite having a population that is over twice the size of North Korea. It has the largest cities on the Korean peninsula including Seoul, with some 24 million in its metropolitan area, and Pusan, the main industrial city on the peninsula. South Korea is a close ally of the United States, and has had successful democratic elections in recent years. South Korea is a newly developed country with a strong and globalized economy. Tourism in the south centers primarily on cultural festivals and religious historic buildings. The southernmost area of the peninsula, particularly subtropical Jeju Island, is considered a very desirable destination among domestic Korean tourists and is a favorite honeymoon getaway for young Korean couples.

North Korea is one of the most closed countries in the world today, though it has very gradually opened to tourism since about 2000. Until recently, there were no communications (e.g., mail, Internet, transportation, telephone) connections between North and South Korea, and citizens from either country were not allowed to visit the other. Today, however, South Koreans can visit a few selected locations in the North, most notably the Mount Kumgang area, which is considered sacred for all Koreans. Organized tours take southerners to the north by boat around the DMZ, or more recently, across the DMZ in motorcoaches. United States citizens are not typically permitted to visit North Korea, although most other nationalities can get visas and have been able to since the 1990s. Most tourist activities in the north are geared toward extolling the virtues of the Great Leader Kim Il Sung and his son, the current leader, Kim Jong-Il. Visits to schools, monuments to the leaders, circuses and festivals comprise the bulk of tour itineraries in North Korea; independent travel is not permitted, as one must always be with a North Korean guide. Most North Koreans are not permitted to leave their country, the exceptions being government officials, ship workers, airline attendants and a handful of others. Domestic travel is virtually nonexistent, as the government rarely allows people to leave the villages and cities where they are assigned to live. There is a steady stream of defectors who are able to get to China and South Korea, and the Republic of Korea welcomes them with open arms.

Mongolia

The popular view of Mongolia is a broad expanse of monotonous landscape with little differentiation. While true for a large part of the country, the eastern portion does contain the high, snow capped Altai Mountains and the Mongolian Plateau. Some of the major rivers of Central Asia originate in this area, which has many lakes and streams. These rivers have created rich pasture lands which have been central to Mongolia's economy throughout history. Most of Mongolia, however, is arid with steppe grassland vegetation, because it is too far from the ocean to benefit from the prevailing onshore summer monsoon winds. The Gobi Desert area has a hard surface and is known for its strong winds. The climate of the Mongolian steppe has made the development of agriculture challenging. Mining, however, is the country's biggest foreign exchange earner, and industrial activities are centered in the capital, Ulaan Baatar, and are primarily related to mining and agriculture, with some handicraft production.

Historically, Mongolia has had a major impact on its neighbors, China and Russia. The Mongol Empire in the 1300s was the largest empire that the world has ever known, stretching from China to Eastern Europe and the Middle East. Today the Mongolian language (Khalkha Mongol) is spoken by people extending to the north and south beyond the country's borders. Mongolian is an Altaic language, related to the languages of Central Asia, Turkey and Manchuria. Culturally, Mongolia is very homogeneous, with 96 percent of the population practicing the Lamaism form of

Buddhism (closely related to Tibetan Buddhism). Herding and hunting are the bases of traditional life among the nomads of Mongolia. The most popular tourist activity in Mongolia is a stay in a yurt (known locally as a gir) tent village on the Mongolian steppe, including eating traditional food and riding horses and camels. The country has several national parks and is home to some of the earliest paleantological sites in Asia. Because the Mongolians are a nomadic people, who do not live in urban settlements, the Soviets insisted on the establishment of cities and towns and erected many buildings similar to the bland Soviet style in Russia. Ulaan Baatar has little to offer visitors other than its role as the nation's gateway and government center, although the city has a high population of German and other European expatriates, and one of its most important market segments is Koreans, who, it is believed, have racial and genetic connections to the Mongolians.

4.4 OCEANIA: AUSTRALIA, NEW ZEALAND, THE PACIFIC ISLANDS AND ANTARCTICA

This region encompasses a vast area of relatively low population density, a lot of open water, and inhospitable deserts, tropical rainforests and vast fields of ice. It includes the continents of Australia and the adjacent islands of New Zealand, and the islands of the South Pacific this Chapter also includes the continent of Antartica. These lands are the most southerly on the planet, with New Zealand and the southern tip of South America being closest to Antarctica and the South Pole. Both South America and Australia have been isolated from much of the rest of the world in recent geologic history. This has produced a unique flora and fauna in both of these continents. Australia, New Zealand and South America have been major colonial settlement areas for Europeans. The South Pacific islands have also had a long history of European colonization, though actual European settlement has been much more limited.

Australia is regarded as either the smallest continent or the largest island in the world. It is 3/4 the size of Europe, the second smallest continent. It is three times the size of Greenland, the world's largest island. Australia is considered a continent rather than an island, in part, because of its cultural difference from surrounding regions. Culturally, Australia is primarily European with a small population of Asian and aboriginal minorities. If it were settled by Malayo-Polynesian peoples, such as Indonesia to the north and Polynesia to the east, Australia may have been considered an extension of Asia and the world's largest island, instead of a separate continent. However, a significant geological reason for regarding them separately is that the island of New Guinea and the continent of Australia share a distinct continental plate. In fact during the Ice Ages when sea levels were lower, New Guinea and Australia were part of a single land mass. Even now the islands off Cape York in the far north of Queensland in the Torres Strait are so close together they can be traveled by canoe all the way to New Guinea on the northern edge of the strait.

Australia's population has over 21 million people (Australia Bureau of Statistics), which is about the same population as the islands of Sri Lanka and Taiwan, but it has considerably less than the annual increase in population of India or China. A major limitation on Australia's population is the continent's low carrying capacity. Only 8 percent

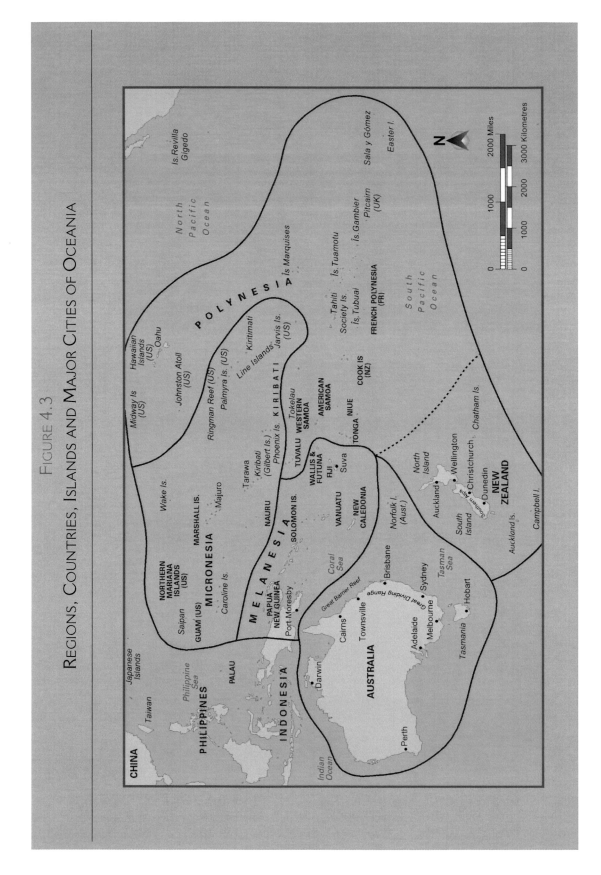

FIGURE 4.3

REGIONS, COUNTRIES, ISLANDS AND MAJOR CITIES OF OCEANIA

of Australia's land is arable (suitable for agriculture), and only 1 percent is suited to intensive agriculture, such as that found in the central United States and in the Ukraine. Climate change is having a profound impact on Australia's agricultural production as the country is getting warmer, and the increased likelihood of low-frequency, high-magnitude weather events, such as floods and droughts, has increased.

To the north of Australia is the island of New Guinea (comprised of Papua New Guinea and Indonesia's West Papua Province), which at 320,000 sq miles (828,796 sq km), is the world's second-largest island (after Greenland). New Guinea is part of the Australian continental plate and was pushed up by Australia's movement to the north and collision with plates that make up the Pacific Ocean floor. To the southeast of Australia is New Zealand, which is about a third the size of New Guinea. New Zealand is about the same size as the British Isles or the Philippines and, like New Guinea, was formed by the collision of the Australian plate with the Pacific plate. New Zealand has a population of just over 4 million people, 75 percent of whom are of European origin. The Maori, the Polynesians who were the first human settlers of New Zealand approximately a 1000 years ago, comprise 15 percent in the country's population, while other South Pacific peoples make up 6.5 percent and Asians 6.6 percent. (The total is more than 100 percent because people are permitted to designate up to three ethnicities in the national census.). Both Australia and New Zealand are experiencing an increase in the proportion of population of the population with an Asian background as a result of migration, while both countries have moved much closer to Asia in political and economic terms.

Physical Geography

The supercontinent Pangaea split over 200 million years ago, forming the continents of Laurasia and Gondwanaland. Some 135 million years ago, Australia, New Zealand and Antarctica broke away from Gondwanaland to form their own separate continent, which has allowed the development of unique plant and animal species. Approximately 80 million years ago Australia and New Zealand detached from Antarctica, and from each other, and moved northward, while Antarctica migrated south to the South Pole. This breakup was relatively late in geologic time and occurred at about the same time the Rocky Mountains, the Alps and the Andes Mountain Range rose, at the time the dinosaurs came to an end.

Australia has the lowest average elevation and relief (change in elevation) of all the continents. Much of Australia is ancient, exposed rock, from the old Gondwanaland shield. The continent's highest mountains, the Great Dividing Range, extend along much of the east coast, with its highest peaks reaching over 7,000 ft (2135 m) in the Snowy Mountains between Sydney and Melbourne. However, much of the Great Dividing Range is below 5,000 ft (1525 m) in elevation in southeastern Australia, and below 2000 ft (610 m) in the northeast of the continent. The northern and northeastern parts of Australia have a rainforest climate with occasional typhoons coming from the ITCZ along the equator. Along the ITCZ, air moves from east to west, so most of the tropical storms that hit Australia come from the Coral Sea and across the Great Barrier Reef. There are a few other highland areas in Australia, all with their highest peaks below 5000 ft (1525) in elevation. These older mountain systems have been heavily eroded, exposing considerable mineral wealth. Coal deposits, for example, are

PHOTO 4.17

Chinatown in Melbourne, Australia. The large numbers of Asian Immigrants to australia over the past several decades has created many colorful ethnic neighborhoods and restaurants

Source: C. Michael Hall

widespread and able to meet most of Australia's energy needs. Australia also has major deposits of iron, lead, zinc, copper and uranium, and is a major supplier of raw materials to Japan and China.

To the east of Australia's Great Dividing Range is a large grassland area, which is home to some of the largest sheep herds in the world, as well as millions of cattle in its more humid areas. Further westward the grasslands turn into tropical savannas in the north and deserts in central Australia. This is the famous Australian *Outback*, which contains the Simpson Desert, the Great Sandy Desert and the Great Victoria

Desert, among others. Nearly in the middle of the continent is Uluru, also known as Ayres Rock, the world's most famous monolith (single rock outcrop), and an Aboriginal sacred site. The Australian Outback is situated in the band of high air pressure that resides north and south of the ITCZ. This means that dry air descending from the upper atmosphere is the dominant climate pattern for much of the interior of Australia, causing desert-like conditions.

Population densities throughout the grasslands, savannas and deserts of Australia are very low, and people are widely dispersed, making transportation and communication a challenge. At the far southwestern tip of Australia is another grassland region where the city of Perth is located. The southernmost regions of Australia are part of the southern upper latitude low pressure storm track. Low air pressure storms (called cyclones) move from west to east, approaching southernmost Australia from the Indian Ocean. Perth has a Mediterranean climate, with a dry summer (in January) and wet winter (in July). Most of the population of Australia lives on the southeast coast of the continent where it is relatively warm and humid throughout the year. The island of Tasmania has a Marine West Coast climate (similar to the British Isles and North America's Pacific Northwest) because it is much closer to the South Pole than the rest of Australia.

New Zealand consists of two major islands: the North Island and the South Island. They both have mountains, with those on the South Island referred to as the *Southern Alps*. The mountains in the north are smaller and less dramatic, with most of the flat

PHOTO 4.18
The Southern Alps on New Zealand's South Island

Source: C. Michael Hall

farmland located on the North Island. Human settlement is primarily in coastal areas due to the mountainous interiors of the islands. New Zealand is further south than most of Australia and has a more humid, Marine West Coast climate with year-round rainfall. The highest mountains of New Zealand reach over 12,000 ft (3660 m) on the South Island and are home to permanent glaciers. New Zealand is an active volcanic and earthquake region, which is especially evident in the volcanoes and thermal areas on the North Island. These geothermal phenomena provide much of the North Island's tourist appeal in the form of geysers, volcanic calderas, mineral springs and hot mud baths.

In Australia, 95 percent of the fauna and 85 percent of the flora diversity are endemic, which means they are found only in Australia. Among Australia's native plants and animals, non-endemic species are mostly found in the northernmost part of the continent, having migrated there from Southeast Asia. The deserts and steps of central Australia kept these migrants to the north of the continent and away from the endemic species further to the south. Among Australia's endemic animal species, 58 percent are placental mammals, and 43 percent are marsupial mammals. The placental animals probably migrated to Australia from Southeast Asia long ago. Nearly a third of the placentals are rats and mice, 25 percent are bats, and the largest is the dingo dog (wild dog) at 0.3 percent.

Marsupials are a very old type of mammal, which originated in North America during the dinosaur era (80 million years ago) and arrived in Australia after traveling through South America and Antarctica. Two-thirds of all marsupial species today are found in Australia and New Guinea, with most of the rest in South America. Marsupials carry their growing fetus in pouches, as opposed to placental mammals, which carry their growing fetus in the mother's womb. This added protection has allowed placental animals to replace marsupials throughout the world, except in Australia, which has a large variety of marsupial species, and South America, which has a few. In North America the only native marsupial is the possum, which was probably reintroduced from South

PHOTO 4.19

The Sydney, Australia Skyline, with the famous Sydney Opera House on the right

Source: C. Michael Hall

PHOTO 4.20
Uluru, or Ayers Rock, in Central Australia. Aborigineal people discourage climbing the rock, but it is still legal to do so, as can be seen in the hikers high on the ridgeline in this photo

Source: Alan A. Lew

America. The giant panda in China is a marsupial that appears to be a cross between a bear and a possum. Marsupials come in many different forms to fill a wide variety of ecological niches. In Australia there are marsupial mice, cats, anteaters, moles, wolves (the extinct Tasmanian tiger), marmots (wombats), dogs (Tasmanian devil), and koalas, in addition to the more distinctive wallabies and kangaroos (of which there are 50 species). Large kangaroos are grazing animals, similar to cows and sheep in other parts of the world. Marsupial cats and wolves are meat-eating predators, whereas koalas are tree-dwelling vegetarians. Australia is also home to the most ancient type of mammal, the monotreme, which nurses its young with milk, which all mammals share in common, but lays eggs like reptiles. The only existing species are the platypus and the echidna (resembles a hedgehog).

New Zealand has been isolated from Antarctica for an even longer period than Australia. There are no marsupials in New Zealand apart from introduced species such as possums and wallabies, with the possums being regarded as a major pest because of the damage they cause to native forests. In fact prior to human settlement there were only three native species of mammals, all bats, one of which is now extinct. Like other Gondwanic island systems, such as Madagascar, New Zealand was

PHOTO 4.21

Source: Alan A. Lew

home to a spectacular array of birds, many of which are now extinct or endangered, including some endemic flightless birds (e.g., kiwis and moas (now extinct)). The first wave of introduced species, such as rats and dogs, probably arrived by island hopping through the South Pacific, along with the Maori Polynesians who settled in New Zealand. Today, numerous placental animals have been introduced to Australia and New Zealand from other continents, and they compete for the ecological niches with native animals. Sheep are the major grazing animal in both Australia and New Zealand, which are leading exporters of wool and mutton. Domestic sheep, wild goats, wild pigs, and placental rats and mice have led to the loss of numerous animal and plant species in both Australia and New Zealand.

Bushfires and Cyclones

A major challenge for environmental interpretation for tourists in Australia is explaining the impacts of natural changes in the environment. These can be such things as bushfires or the effects of cyclones. Bushfires are an essential element of the environmental health of most of Australia's ecological communities, which are highly fire-adapted with many species, such as acacias and banksias, actually being fire dependent for the dispersal of their seeds. In addition, bushfires are excellent in eliminating weeds and other undesirable exotic plant and animal species. Indeed, the biodiversity and high degree of endemism associated with many Australian natural heritage sites, such as national parks or even World Heritage areas like Kakadu, is critically dependent on the maintenance of fire regimes. However, for many people bushfires are perceived as a negative because of the blackened landscapes they produce in the short-term.

Cyclones and storm events also can have a major impact on the environment, but they should also be regarded as part of the natural cycle of environmental change. In the case of Cyclone Larry, which hit the tropical rainforest of northern Queensland in 2006, the immediate impact was the full or part closure of 30 Queensland parks and state forests, as well as physical damage to rainforest habitat and several communities. However, although unsightly, occasional disturbance may actually contribute to biodiversity by helping maintain mosaics of different stages of forest growth and canopy cover in which different species occupy different habitats. Yet, this situation occurs in healthy rainforest. The problem in much of Queensland, as elsewhere in Australia, is that the forest has become fragmented and isolated as a result of human clearance, so that their capacity to regenerate has been substantially reduced. Just as with bushfires in Australia's pyrogenous forests, the impacts of cyclones in rainforests also need to be explained to visitors as being a natural part of the ecosystem.

Human Geography

The Aborigines of Australia were the continent's first people, although they never grew to a very large population. Today they comprise approximately 1 percent

(200,000) of the country's over 20 million people, which is about half their number at their maximum population size (about 250,000 to 500,000 in the late 1700s). Only about a third of them are pure Aboriginal; they are usually regarded as descendants of the Negrito peoples of South and Southeast Asia, although there is evidence suggesting an earlier wave of human settlement. Australia's indigenous people have black skin and wavy to curly hair. Their traditional lifestyles and religious beliefs are closely related to their environment, and prior to European settlement Australia was culturally part of Melanesia. They arrived in Australia at least 60,000 years ago, and 40,000 years later they had settled the entire continent, including Tasmania. Under white European rule, they have been victims of considerable discrimination and poverty.

Arab and Chinese legends told of the presence of Australia, but without any degree of accuracy, and the Portuguese were probably the first Europeans to see the continent, which appeared on their maps as early as 1528. In the early 1600s, the Spanish probably sailed the northern coast of Australia in an expedition that originated in Peru, and the Dutch drew the first navigational chart of Australia's northern coastline. Tasmania was named after a Dutch sea captain (Abel Tasman), who sailed there from Batavia (modern-day Jakarta, Indonesia) in 1642. He was also likely the first European to visit New Zealand. In 1770, Captain James Cook reached Australia and made landfall in several places accompanied by Joseph Banks, a botanist, who later became director of Kew Gardens in London and a leading natural scientist of the day. Cook and Banks also recognized the potential for colonization and settlement, and the French were active in exploring and attempting to colonize Australia in the 1770s.

The American Revolution of 1776 had a major impact on Australian settlement. Prior to the Revolution, British prisoners were sent to the American colonies, but after 1776 they were sent to new penal colonies in Australia, with the first settlers arriving in 1788. It is therefore not surprising that Australian historian Robert Hughes described Australia as the world's first *gulag*. Later these penal colonies became known as free colonies after the prisoners had served their sentences. Other periods of major European population growth in Australia occurred in 1851 when gold was discovered in the southeast, and in 1891 gold was discovered in Western Australia. The sheep industry also grew to importance in the late 1800s in southeastern Australia. For many years Australians with a convict heritage often tried to hide their embarrassing ancestry, although from the 1970s it became a source of pride as Australia increasingly began to express its own cultural identity.

Beginning with New South Wales in 1788, several colonies were established under British rule on the continent. Each was based on a settlement which later became a major city: Sydney (New South Wales), Hobart (Tasmania), Melbourne (Victoria), Brisbane (Queensland), Adelaide (South Australia), and Perth (Western Australia). Later, Darwin became the capital city of the Northern Territory, although the Territory is still denied full statehood with the federal government retaining the right to overrule Territory law. These coastal cities and their colonies often competed with one another for resources and immigrant populations, but in 1901 they joined together to form the Commonwealth of Australia as a federation of states and territories.

The Commonwealth of Australia consists of six states and two territories joined in a single federal state or government. In the federal system, each state retains certain rights, with the other specific rights granted to the central government. The system is similar to that established in the United States but was also greatly influenced by Westminster parliamentary traditions in Great Britain. In Australia the central government retains less power than in the United States, but the areas it has authority over have increased over time. For example, aviation did not exist in 1900 when the Australian Constitution was enacted, but under the Constitution new areas became the responsibility of the Commonwealth (federal) government. Although it should be noted that some areas that exist under the United States Constitution, such as the right to bear arms and freedom of expression do not exist under the Australian constitution.

Australia is therefore somewhat similar to the European Union, although in the case of the EU the central government is much weaker than in Australia or the United States. Also for many years people primarily identified with their state rather than Australia. However, as communication and transport linkages grew, and wars were fought, a sense of nationhood developed, although state rivalry still exists. A single gauge rail linking all the capital cities was not completed until 2004 with the line between Adelaide and Darwin. Competition between Sydney and Melbourne also led to the creation of a new capital, Canberra, and the Australian Capital Territory, which is approximately midway between these two principal cities of Australia. Canberra was designed by the American architect Burley-Griffin, who also designed the planned capital Brasilia, Brazil. Today, Canberra is also known as the bush city because of the extent to which native vegetation has been conserved.

Historically, Australia had a selective immigration policy aimed at making and keeping the country racially white. Some 80 percent of Australia's population descends from the British Isles, with the rest originating in other parts of Europe. Since World War II, Australia received considerable criticism of its white-preferred population policies, which have been a major topic of debate in the country. Australian Aborigines only became citizens of their own country in 1966 following a national referendum. Today the Australian government has established reparation programs for the Aboriginal people, who lost much of their traditional lands, and Australia has become more accepting of its absolute location next to Southeast Asia. Nevertheless, significant issues still remain with the Federal Liberal Government under Prime Minister John Howard during the late 1990s and early part of the twentieth century, often being regarded as racist because of its treatment of Aborigines and policies toward illegal migrants or refugees. Such was the extent of perceived racism that it was even regarded as being at odds with national tourism promotion and the attempt by the country to portray itself as a welcoming destination for visitors. The Australian government is increasingly active in Southeast Asian politics and recognizes common security interest with its neighbors to the north. An increasing number of Southeast Asians have immigrated to Australia both legally and illegally, which is changing the complexion of the country.

As mentioned above, New Zealand has a sizeable minority population made up of Maori and other Polynesian peoples. The Maori are known for their traditionally fierce hunting skills. Maori has cognates in other Polynesian languages such as the Hawaiian *Maori*, the Tahitian *Maori*, and the Cook Islands Maori which all share similar meanings. The word as used in contemporary English means *native, indigenous* or *aboriginal* (with a small a). Maori people themselves often use the term *Tangata whenua* (*people of the land*) to describe their relationship with a particular area of land – a tribe (iwi) or sub-group (hapu) is therefore *tangata whenua* in one area, but not others.

Archaeological and linguistic evidence indicates that there were probably several waves of migration from Eastern Polynesia to New Zealand between AD 800 and 1300. Maori oral history describes the arrival of the ancestors from Hawaiki (a mythical homeland in Polynesia) by large ocean-going canoes (waka), although there is possible evidence of earlier Polynesian settlement although the numbers of people, if any, were likely very small. The settlement patterns of Maori was primarily determined by the climate and the capacity to grow kumara (a type of sweet potato) of which the southern limit is about the area of Christchurch in the South Island, below that latitude Maori were primarily dependent on fishing and marine gathering, hunting and trade. Therefore, the vast majority of Maori were settled in the North Island and the far north of the South Island. As population pressures built up inter-tribal warfare by Maori for access to resources became increasingly common particularly as the Maori killed off native species such as the Moa which was a major food source. In 1769, Captain Cook claimed New Zealand for England, and Christian missionaries from various countries and faiths soon followed. Christianity and the eventual acceptance of British law eventually brought an end to Maori inter-tribal warfare and cannibalism, although different coalitions of Maori tribes fought against each other in cooperation with the British with the New Zealand Maori Wars or Land Wars not completed until the 1870s and passive resistance remaining until 1881. With the outcome being a massive loss of Maori land to the British, with reparations still being sought and decided to the present-day. Today there is considerable interracial harmony between Maori and the European populations of New Zealand. In recent decades there has been a major revival of Maori culture in New Zealand. Auckland is the largest city in New Zealand, and the largest Polynesian city in the world, with over 90,000 Maori, Samoans, Tongans, Cook Islanders and others, and it often uses this feature in its tourism promotion.

The presence of a large indigenous population makes ethnicity a topic of considerable debate in New Zealand. Multiple ethnicity is increasing, and people's ethnicities may change over time. In the 2001 Census, 9 percent of New Zealand's population identified with more than one ethnic group, this had increased to 10.4 percent in 2006. In 2006, 19.7 percent of people aged under 15 years identified with more than one ethnicity. Indigenous Maori people are the largest non-European ethnic group, accounting for 14.6 percent of the population in the 2006 census. Although people could select more than one ethnic group, slightly more than half (53 percent) of all Maori identified solely as Maori. People identifying with Asian ethnic groups account for 9.2 percent of the population, increasing from 6.6 percent in the 2001 census, while 6.9 percent of people are of Pacific Island origin. According to Statistics New Zealand's population projections, in 2021 Maori will comprise 17 percent of the population, 9 percent will identify with a Pacific ethnicity and 15 percent with an Asian ethnicity. Population projections suggest that 70 percent of the population will identify with a European ethnicity in 2021, making European the largest ethnic/racial group.

Although the country is often noted as having a strong British influence in its political and cultural institutions it should be emphasized that there are significant regional differences in settlement patterns that have lingering effects to the present day. For example, the Otago and Southland areas had a substantial Scottish Protestant influence to the extent that the small city of Dunedin has much of its old streetscape laid out as for the city of Edinburgh from which it derives its name. However, as a rule the larger the urban settlement the more diverse the population, therefore cities such as Auckland, Wellington and Christchurch have the most diverse populations, as well as the most diverse economic base.

The Murray River is Australia's second-longest river (1,470 miles; 2,530 km). Together with the Darling (1,700 miles; 2,740 km) and Murrumbidgee (1050 miles;

1,690 km) Rivers, the Murray comprises the Murray-Darling Basin. The Murray-Darling Basin covers 409,835 sq miles (1,061,469 km^2), equivalent to 14 percent of Australia's total area. The basin extends over the states of New South Wales, Victoria, Queensland, South Australia and the Australian Capital Territory. The basin accounts for over 40 percent of Australia's gross value of agricultural production. Approximately 70 percent of all water used for agriculture in Australia is used by irrigation in the basin. The Murray River is of immense cultural, economic and environmental significance. Gravesites at Roonka and Big Bend demonstrate that Aboriginal communities lived there continuously for at least 35,000 years. The river was discovered by Hamilton Hume and William Hovell in 1824. Originally named the Hume River, in 1830 Captain Charles Sturt renamed it the Murray after Sir George Murray, the British Secretary of State for the Colonies. The publication in London in 1833 of Sturt's account of his river explorations indirectly led to the establishment of the state of South Australia.

For many years in the Nineteenth Century the Murray was Australia's main inland transport route. In 1852 the first shallow draft paddle-steamer from South Australia reached Echuca in Victoria. Such was the economic importance of the Murray that in 1863, almost 40 years prior to federation, a conference was held between New South Wales, Victoria and South Australia regarding improving the navigability of the river. Although the river is still used for river boats, including tourist craft, the loss of natural water flow as a result of upstream vegetation clearance, dams, irrigation and silting up, has created some major environmental issues with respect to salination, species loss and water quality, which the state, territory and federal governments are seeking to solve. Since the early 2000s, sand dredging machines have operated at the Murray River mouth to maintain a minimal flow from the sea. Without the dredging, the river mouth would silt up and close, cutting the supply of fresh sea-water into the Coorong lagoon system which is part of the Murray Estuary. Unfortunately, the environmental problems of the Murray are only expected to get worse given the climate change scenarios for Australia.

Comparing Australia and New Zealand

Both Australia and New Zealand have a strong British heritage and are major agricultural countries where sheep are the most common agricultural animal and cattle are second. Both countries are major exporters of agricultural products with Australia being a major cereals exporter and New Zealand dairy products, such as milk and cheese. Both countries also export significant amounts of horticultural produce to Asia and North America. In recent years specialist production has also started to develop such as truffles and boutique cheese and wine in Tasmania, Australia, and saffron and walnuts in the Canterbury region of New Zealand.

Australia and New Zealand share the problem of having small internal markets that are not large enough to support local production of most consumer goods without tariff protection, which are therefore imported from abroad. They are both geographically isolated from their main markets although they have become much more oriented toward Asia in recent years. Despite having strong traditions associated with the *bush* or the countryside and natural areas – images that are often part of national tourism promotion – they are both highly urbanized, with a large proportion of their population living in cities: 85 percent in New Zealand and 86 percent in Australia.

TOURISM ISSUES AND INSIGHTS
TOURISM AND URBANIZATION

Tourism is regarded as a major contributor to urbanization, especially in coastal areas. It does this in two main ways. First, as a very specific form of development in which urban settings are produced to supply demand for tourism, leisure and the temporary resident or mobile visitor. These can be described as urban tourism destinations. Second, as apart of broader processes of urbanization in which, even though urban development is not being undertaken just for tourists, certain locations within the urban area are seen as having a tourism or leisure enabling function. There are a number of features that can be used to distinguish places associated with tourism urbanization, as they are:

- Spatially and functionally different from other urban places. The amenity driven nature of much tourism means that along many coastal areas tourism urbanization is highly linear running along the coastline where permitted. For example, in Cyprus 95 percent of the tourism industry is located within 2 km of the coast;
- Symbolically different, with various brands, images and symbols being used to promote the tourist function;
- Characterized by rapid population and labor force growth in the early stages of development. Even as urban growth slows the population and labor force tends to have a relatively high degree of transience, with considerable underemployment and unemployment as a function of construction cycles and tourism seasonality;
- Distinguished by flexible forms of production, particularly in terms of a highly flexible labor force organized to meet daily, weekly and seasonal change in demand (usually through high-rates of short-term, part-time and casual employment and low-rates of unionization).
- Dominated by government intervention and public–private partnerships, whereby government indirectly invest in facilities infrastructure with a view to encouraging further inward investment;
- Associated with large-scale tourism service production that simplifies the local economy and requires substantial importation of goods, services, water and energy from outside the resort region in order to meet the demands of a highly mobile population;
- Substantial transformation of natural or rural landscapes for tourism production and consumption; and
- Foci of transport networks because of the need to import and export not only goods and services but also the tourists themselves.

They both have social welfare systems similar to Northern Europe, with medical care, housing assistance, education and old-age care supported by relatively high taxes.

Physical geography is a major difference between Australia and New Zealand. Australia is many times larger than New Zealand and is known for its vast desert outback, while New Zealand is known for its green lowlands and Southern Alps. However, the southern state and island of Tasmania (Australia) is much more comparable to New Zealand in terms of its geography. Australia's indigenous heritage is Negrito-Melanesian, whose modern-day Aboriginal descendents have had very poor relations with the European settlers. New Zealand, on the other hand, is part of the Polynesian world, and modern-day Maori have a relatively good relationship with the dominant European (Caucasian) settlers. Both countries have become much more cosmopolitan and economically diversified in recent years, with Australia arguably being more conservative, particularly with respect to politics at the national level. Nevertheless, the two countries are very closely related. Under the Australian Constitution, for example, New Zealand is entitled to become a member of the Australian Commonwealth. There is an economic union between the two countries known as the Closer Economic Relationship (CER) and something approaching a common labor market. The extent of the closeness is also judged by the fact that tentative discussions have also started to develop about having a common currency. The two countries have also fought beside each other in a number of wars, which means they share the same remembrance day (ANZAC Day, 25 April), so perhaps it is a matter of time before economic union starts to approach becoming a political one.

The indiginous people aboriginals of both countries form a considerable part of the tourism product. Tourism in New Zealand focuses overwhelmingly on nature (mountains) and Maori culture, and the Maori people are heavily involved in the production of tourism experiences. Likewise, by law they are active participants in tourism legislation, and all use of their cultural emblems for tourism purposes must be approved by the Maoris themselves. This is not the case in Australia, where the indigenous people have had little say in tourism development and the use of their heritage for tourism purposes. Nonetheless, their sacred places, musical and dance traditions, and bush culture have become popularized aspects of Australian tourism. Film-induced tourism plays a major role in both countries, with Australia-associated movies, such as *Crocodile Dundee* and *Kangaroo Jack* bringing international visibility to the Australian Outback, driving many tourists to the country in search of similar experiences. In New Zealand, the *Lord of the Rings* movies and books have presented new opportunities for people to experience the *Down Under* and movie sets.

Oceania

Australia and New Zealand are part of a much larger human and physical geography realm that is generally known as Oceania. Oceania extends from the islands of Australia, New Guinea and New Zealand, and across the Pacific Ocean as far north as Hawaii and as far east as Easter Island off the coast of Chile. Antarctica is sometimes included in this realm, as well. What this vast region shares in common are its ethnicity and its close relationship with water and ocean travel. With some major exceptions, the biogeography of Oceania is also very similar. Australia and New Zealand are the major international tourist destinations in the region accounting together for about 1.5 percent of global international tourism arrivals.

Most of Oceania is dominated by islands. Australia, at 3,000,000 sq miles (7,769,964 sq km), if it were not a continent, could be considered the world's largest island. New Guinea, at 320,000 sq miles (828,796 sq km), is the world's second-largest island (after Greenland). Other large land masses include the islands of New Zealand, as well as New Caledonia (a French overseas territory). Most of the rest of the islands of this vast realm are much smaller. Many are volcanic in origin, and some are very active, including Hawaii and Fiji, while others are coral atolls that have developed over many millennia.

The term South Pacific is generally applied to the island microstates of the southern Pacific Ocean that lie south of Hawaii, although the political and economic organizations of the region often include Hawaii (USA), Papua New Guinea, Australia

Source: Alan A. Lew

and New Zealand. The island microstates, which are dominated by the Polynesian, Melanesian and Micronesian cultures, have few natural resources except large ocean territories (i.e., fishing) and access to sun, *sea and sand*. The islands' isolation has resulted in substantial species endemism, dependence on the natural environment, diversity of cultures and language and vulnerability to natural disasters. The region's colonial heritage means that states remain economically linked to their former colonial occupiers, while the region's image as an *island paradise* is also a colonial legacy rather than an actual reality, given histories of occasional political unrest and natural disasters (e.g., cyclones).

The South Pacific region accounts for only 0.15 percent of global international tourist arrivals, and most of the travelers come from Australia, Japan, New Zealand and the United States. Nevertheless, tourism is a vital component of the regional economy and a major, though seasonal, employer. Cooperative agreements between South Pacific nations have been established with respect to economic development, fishing, conservation and tourism. The South Pacific Tourism Organization (SPTO) is the lead intergovernment tourism agency for the region. SPTO members include the following Pacific Island nations and territories: the Cook Islands, Fiji, Kiribati, New Caledonia, Niue, Samoa, the Solomon Islands, Tahiti (French Polynesia), Tonga, Tuvalu, Vanuatu and Papua New Guinea, as well as China and over 180 private tourism operators. The SPTO was initially established as a development and marketing organization for tourism in the region with EU support, but the agency has increasingly narrowed its focus to marketing and promotional activities.

High and Low Islands in the South Pacific

Within the area known as the South Pacific (east of Australia, New Zealand and the islands of the Pacific Ocean), and the northern Pacific islands, there are basically two physiographic types of islands: high and low. High islands typically have a tall volcanic mountain in their center. This mountain causes the humid ocean winds to rise, forming clouds and precipitation. High islands tend to have year-round rainfall (an important source of fresh water) and tropical forests. The populations tend to be much larger on high islands because the rainfall and rich volcanic soils are able to support agriculture. Low islands are usually coral atolls. They were once high islands but were eroded away by wind, rain and waves and the original islands are now often well below sea level. On top of the original island, coral has grown and the hard outer shell material has eroded to form sandy stretches of land above the sea. Some of these are quite large, and they sometimes have a freshwater lagoon in their center. Because their elevations are not high, they do not capture much precipitation from the passing winds, and they tend to be much hotter and drier, with some exhibiting almost desert-like conditions. Fishing is the main source of food on low islands, and their populations tend to be smaller than those on high islands. Both high and low islands in the Pacific were formed primarily by collisions of several large oceanic plates, causing earthquake and volcanic activity.

Human Geography of Oceania

The Negrito people (first introduced in the Southeast Asia chapter) were the earliest to settle Oceania. It is uncertain how long they have lived in Southeast Asia and Australia, though they clearly predate the arrival of the Malay people. Today, their closest descendents survive in small numbers on the islands and interior hills of South and Southeast Asia. They are characterized by black skin, short stature and wavy to curly hair. The Aborigines of Australia and the Melanesians of the South Pacific also trace back to the early Negrito people. *Mela* means black, and Melanesia is one of the three major regions of the South Pacific. Included in Melanesia are Papua New Guinea, the Solomon Islands and New Caledonia, all among the largest islands in the South Pacific.

The Malayo-Polynesian people migrated through peninsular Southeast Asia, into insular Southeast Asia, and across the oceans to Madagascar to the west and the South Pacific to the east. They are a brown-skinned people, who probably arrived on the Pacific islands some 25,000 years ago. By 1000 BCE they had settled most of the South Pacific. Approximately 1500 years ago they reached Hawaii and New Zealand, which were among the last of their major settlement areas. The Polynesians used stars and ocean currents to navigate the vast waters of the Pacific Ocean. The Malayo-Polynesians have three major groupings. The first is located in insular Southeast Asia, including Malaysia, Indonesia, the Philippines and aboriginal groups in Taiwan and possibly Japan. The second major group is in a region known as Micronesia, which consists of many small islands located east and northeast of Peninsular Southeast Asia as far as the international dateline. The major racial distinction of Micronesians is their straight hair. The islands of Micronesia are almost all low islands.

The third major settlement area of the Malayo-Polynesian peoples is the area known as Polynesia. This consists of the islands located in a triangle from New Zealand to Hawaii, all the way to Easter Island off the coast of South America. Racially, the people of Polynesia tend to have curly hair and lighter skins than Melanesians. The word *poly* means many, referring to the large number and variety of Islands found in Polynesia. Both low and high Island lifestyles and environments exist in Polynesia. The major high islands are the Hawaiian chain, and the archipelagos of Fiji, Samoa, Tonga and Tahiti. The indigenous people of New Zealand and Madagascar are also Polynesians.

Melanesia includes West Papua (Indonesia), Papua New Guinea, the Solomon Islands, Vanuatu, New Caledonia and Fiji. Micronesia includes Palau, the Federated States of Micronesia (FSM), Nauru, Kiribati, the Marshall Islands, the Northern Marianas (USA), Wake Island (USA) and Guam (USA); Guam is the largest of the Micronesian islands. All of the other island groups on the map, including New Zealand, comprise Polynesia. Norfolk Island and Pitcairn were settled by mutineers from Captain Bligh's ship, the Bounty, who married Polynesian women, creating a mixed blood population.

Migration and mobility are inherent to the peoples of the Pacific Ocean. From Polynesian migration throughout the islands of the South Pacific (including New Zealand) during the pre-European period to the labor migrations in comparatively recent decades from the islands to Australia, New Zealand and the United States, mobility remains a central component of the lives of many Pacific islanders. Yet although island populations are highly mobile in terms of employment and education, substantial bonds of kinship and relationships to village and land remain. The magnitude and importance of migration from the Pacific Islands has strong historical roots. The interface created between expanding colonial powers and indigenous peoples in the nineteenth century helped broaden the base of movement in the region. Between the 1950s and 1970s, the rate of migration from the Pacific Islands, particularly Samoa, to New Zealand was substantial. The size of the Samoan population in New Zealand rose from 6,481 in 1961 to 27,950 in 1976. The primary reasons for migration were employment and family connections. Labor shortages in the New Zealand economy, which existed until the mid-1970s, provided both short- and long-term migration opportunities. In the 1950s the main point of migration was to seek financial returns for the home community, with single females often being selected by communities to migrate, because they were regarded to be more likely to remit their wages. By the 1960s, migration began to have a greater family focus with reunification becoming an important migration impetus.

While post-war economic growth within the countries bordering the Pacific islands has, overall, been strong, many island nations have experienced considerable fluctuations in their own economies. Many Pacific nation-states, for example, struggled under the recession in the early 1980s, which was largely a result of the reliance on relatively few economic activities (i.e., agriculture and fishing). As a consequence, while the region was on the extreme economic periphery, movement to nations that were more developed, such as Australia, New Zealand and the United States, where some family connections also lay (i.e., American Samoans), was facilitated. As more migrants elected to emigrate, family members often joined their kin in their new homelands.

Policies in the receiving countries with respect to migration, particularly the restriction of numbers, have also played an important role in influencing migration patterns. Many restrictions operate within the larger sphere of international economic conditions and thus dictate the rate and flow of migrants. Some of the islands also have direct political connections to more developed countries, such as American Samoa and the United States. Nationals from the Cook Islands, Niue and Tokelau are also New Zealand citizens, so their movement is legally and politically unrestricted. In addition, political unrest has influenced some migration flows in the region, particularly the Fijian Indian community, in the case of military coups that have occurred several times in the island nation. Unfortunately, in the case of Fiji, this has often meant that many of the best educated of the Fijian Indian community (e.g., physicians, teachers, academics) have emigrated.

Tourism in the South Pacific

In tourism and broader development terms, the major handicaps of the South Pacific islands are their small size and isolated/remote location. Because the islands are small, they tend to have high population densities and land use pressures relative to their carrying capacities. Because they are remote, shipping goods and transporting visitors to and between the islands is very expensive. Likewise, several of the islands are so remote that access can be gained only once or twice a week by air or monthly by ship. Although some have had useful mineral resources in the past, for the majority, the advantages are natural and cultural amenities, including their natural landscapes, warm climates, unique cultures and recreational opportunities.

Europeans arrived in the South Pacific in the latter half of the 1700s. Captain Cook made several sailings between 1768 and 1779. Captain Bligh (made famous by the book, *Mutiny on the Bounty*) charted the South Pacific from 1787 to 1789. Cook and Bligh's charts were used by European navigators well into the 20th century. In the early 19th century, whalers and missionaries entered the Pacific, settling on islands that had been claimed by various European powers. In the late 19th century, steamships and the first Western tourists arrived in the Pacific; the steamships reduced the time it took to reach the South Pacific from the coast of North America to only a few weeks.

Air travel has played a major role in overcoming the isolation of the South Pacific, though it is still quite expensive to reach many of the islands. In 1935, Pan Am's China Clipper made the first trans-Pacific flight from the United States west coast to Australia. The trip took six days with 60 hours of flying time. The flight followed the charts drawn by Captain Cook and Captain Bligh and was funded by the United States Post Office, which initially used the China Clipper for postal services. Later, commercial and government/diplomatic travel were the primary users of the China Clipper, although the first tourists to fly across the Pacific did so as early as 1936.

Following World War II, there was a major expansion of air travel across the Pacific. The war made Americans more aware of the Pacific (through the soldiers who fought there and media coverage) and generated more interested in traveling there. In 1947, it still took 6 days to travel by ship from California to Hawaii, 14 days from California to Asia, and 20 days from California to Australia. In contrast, by airplane it only took 13 hours to fly from California to Hawaii. In 1957, Boeing introduced the first successful passenger jet aircraft (the 707), which brought flying times closer to those of today (about 3 hours from California to Hawaii). The development of airline technology after World War II led to airports being built and upgraded throughout the Pacific region, along with new and expanded accommodations and services for tourism development.

Today, many of the islands are heavily dependent upon tourism for their financial well-being. Fiji, the most popular destination in terms of annual arrivals, is especially favored by North Americans, Australians and New Zealanders. The country has been the focus of much resort development in recent decades, with new resorts currently being built. Fijian culture, including visits to cultural centers, and beaches are the main products in Fiji. Many of its smaller, outlying islands, have become resorts in their own right, attracting particularly young, fun-loving spring break and schoolies students from overseas. As alluded to earlier, military coups have plagued Fiji for the past few decades, including a recent non-violent coups in December 2007, which effectively halted tourism to the islands for a few months, although it has since recovered well. Most of the islands (e.g., Cook Islands, Samoa, Tonga) have similar products as famous sun, sea and sand destinations. Political unrest in recent years has all but completed curtailed tourism in the Solomon Islands, and the country has appeared on warning lists throughout the world.

Nauru is a unique case, wherein the island desires to grow tourism, but it has little by way of tourist offerings. It has a few beaches, but most of the island was destroyed in the 20th century by phosphate mining, which has since ceased production. There is little industry on the island, although there is a minor fishing sector. Most citizens rely on monthly remittances from overseas, and the island's budget is based largely on the interest from a lawsuit won against the British and Australians for depletion of the Islands only natural resource (phosphate). Travel to Nauru is expensive and infrequent; the island has its own airline, Air Nauru, but the company continues to operate at a financial loss, being heavily subsidized by the government of Nauru, and provides only periodic flights to a few other islands in the region.

The Micronesian islands, particularly Palau, the FSM, Guam, and the Marshall Islands, are best known for deep sea diving, which focuses on the countries' white sand, blue waters and vast array of coral reefs. Guam is still an integral part of the United States, but FSM, the Marshall Islands and Palau only recently (1980s and 1990s) gained their independence from the United States-administered UN Trusteeship, whose sovereignty over the islands resulted from the defeat of Japan in World War II. As a result, relations with the United States are still very strong, and most of the islands' tourists come from the United States and Japan.

Antarctica

The land mass surrounding the South Pole is the continent of Antarctica. It is larger than Europe, but has no permanent human population and has minimal other forms of biological life. Massive sheets of ice and almost constant stormy seas kept Antarctica isolated from much of the rest of the world until the late 1700s and early 1800s. Antarctica remains a frontier region hostile to human habitation and seldom visited except by scientists and adventure tourists.

Along with South America, Africa, Madagascar, India, Australia and New Zealand, the Antarctic was part of the supercontinent Gondwana and 200 million years ago. At that time Antarctica was a land of lush vegetation and many animals. Fossils and thick coal beds are what remain of that time today. However, a number of Gondwanic species can still be found in the Americas, Australia and New Zealand, including Nothofagus (beech), rattites (flightless birds such as Darwin's Rhea, Emu and Ostrich) and marsupials (in Australia and the Americas).

Ice covers nearly all of Antarctica; its average thickness is 7,000–8,000 ft (2,134 to 2,440 m), although at its deepest it is almost 3 miles (5 km) thick. The ice sheets are as old as 14 million years and contain 90 percent of all the ice and 70 percent of all the fresh water in the world. Should global warming melt the thinnest portions of this ice sheet, which is possible, world sea levels would rise about 20 ft (6 m). Some 2 percent of Antarctica is ice-free; these small areas are known as oases, and are located on the continent's edge. Antarctic ice flows very slowly into the oceans that surround it, and extends over the oceans in ice shelves. The largest of these, the Ross Ice Shelf, is larger than France and is an average of 1,000 ft (300 m) thick. In winter, July in the southern

FIGURE 4.4

ANTARCTICA

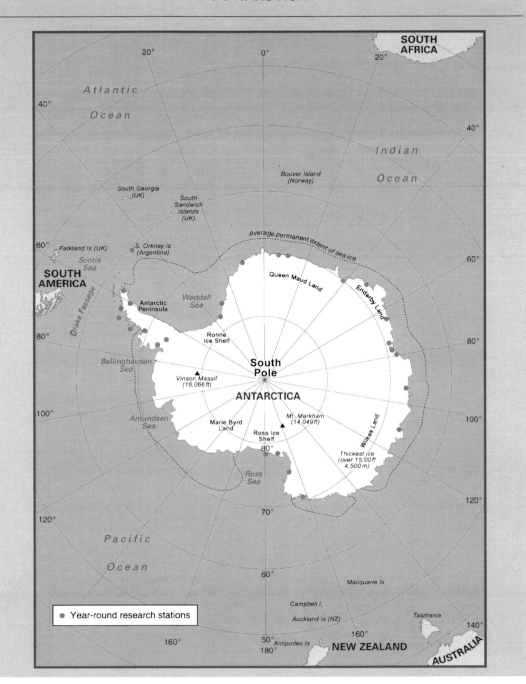

hemisphere, the outer edge of the ice shelves can extend up to 1,000 miles (1,600 km) from the continent. The edges of these shelves periodically break off and float as icebergs northward toward warmer waters.

The *Antarctic Convergence* is a zone located approximately 1,000 miles (1,600 km) off the coast and is the transition area between the icy cold waters that surround

Antarctica and the warmer waters of the oceans further to the north. Also surrounding the continent is the Antarctic Circumpolar Current, which moves clockwise, or eastward, around the continent and is the longest ocean current in the world. Antarctica has the world's lowest recorded temperature, −128.6°F (−89.2°C). The average temperature in the interior is −70°F (−57°C), while the warmest temperatures are on the Antarctic Peninsula and can reach as high as 59°F (15°C) in the Antarctic summer (January). The interior of Antarctica is in fact a desert, owing to the high pressure air system that resides over the South Pole. The average precipitation is only 1 to 2 in. (2.5–5 cm) of rainfall equivalent a year.

The limited plant and animal life in Antarctica includes many species that are only found there (endemic). Some bacteria, lichens and algae grow close to the South Pole. Insects are the most abundant animal life, of which there are 76 species, nearly all of which are only found in Antarctica. Forty-five species of birds live south of the Antarctic Convergence, including several penguin species. Four species of seal live only in the Antarctic region. Fish are quite abundant and have evolved blood that enables them to live in waters as cold as 28°F (−2°C). Krill are a small shrimp that exist in huge numbers in the waters surrounding Antarctica and comprise the basic food for birds, seals and whales.

Human Exploration

James Cook was the first known visitor to Antarctica between the years 1772 and 1775, though he never landed on the continent. In 1820, British and American seal hunters joined a Russian expedition and made the first landfall on the Antarctic Peninsula, but the first recorded landing on the main continent of Antarctica did not occur until 1895. On December 14, 1922, Roald Amundsen of Norway became the first person to reach the geographical South Pole. Antarctica entered the modern age in the International Geophysical Year (IGY) of 1957 to 1958. That year some 50 permanent research stations were established, including one at the geographical South Pole (the center of the earth's, rotational axis), and one at the geomagnetic South Pole (the center of the earth's geomagnetic field and of the southern hemisphere auroras). (In addition, there is the magnetic South Pole, which is the point on which compasses align.)

Seven countries have claimed pie wedge-shaped sectors extending out from the South Pole. Three of these sectors overlap, and one region remains unclaimed. Most other countries of the world do not recognize these claims, and these areas, according to international law, are not considered part of the sovereign territories of the claimants. Twelve countries were part of the IGY agreements to protect Antarctica's resources and preserve them for scientific use, which was codified in the 1959 Antarctic Treaty. These included Argentina, Australia, Belgium, Chile, France, Japan, New Zealand, Norway, South Africa, the United Kingdom, the United States, and Russia (Soviet Union at the time). The Antarctic Treaty does not allow military activities except for scientific and peaceful purposes, and other countries have since joined the Antarctic Treaty.

Tourism to Antarctica occurs in the summer months, between the end of November and early April. According to the International Association of Antarctica Tour Operators (IAATO), the 2003–2004 summer season saw the arrival of 27,537 tourists, along with 16,200 staff and crew. Norway has become a major player in

Antarctic tourism, with nearly 20 percent of Antarctic tourists visiting on Norwegian Cruise ships. Many other cruises depart regularly from the Chilean and Argentinian portions of Tierra del Fuego, and day-long helicopter overflights of the South Pole can be purchased from New Zealand. A typical 15-day cruise, including airfare from North America and 12 nights on the cruise ship, costs approximately US$5,700. Tourism is strictly controlled and its impacts have so far been minimal. The greatest concern is the introduction of exotic plant and animal species that could endanger the unique biogeography of Antarctica.

| | Population 2006 (1,000) | World population share 2006 (%) | International tourist arrivals (1,000) | | Change since 1990 (%) | World market share 2004 (%) |
			1990*	2004		
WORLD	6,525,170	100.0	436,757	776,837	77.9	100.0
Asia and Oceania	3,690,063	56.6	53,292	14,7150	176.1	18.9
South Asia	1,528,357	23.4	3,304	9,272	180.6	1.2
Southeast Asia	581,909	8.9	21,469	48,309	125.0	6.2
East Asia	1,546,659	23.7	23,367	79,412	239.8	10.2
Oceania	33,138	0.5	5,152	10,157	97.1	1.3
Top Destination Countries						
1 China	1,313,974	20.1	10,484	41,761	298.3	5.4
2 Malaysia	24,386	0.4	7,446	15,703	110.9	2.0
3 Hong Kong*	6,940	0.1	6,000	13,655	127.6	1.8
4 Thailand	64,632	1.0	5,299	11,737	121.5	1.5
5 Singapore	4,401	0.1	4,842	8,329	172.0	1.1
6 Macau	453	0.0	2,513	8,324	231.2	1.1
7 Japan	127,464	2.0	3,236	6,138	89.7	0.8
8 South Korea	48,847	0.7	2,959	5,818	96.6	0.7
9 Indonesia	245,453	3.8	2,178	5,321	144.3	0.7
10 Australia	202,664	3.1	2,215	4,774	115.5	0.6
11 India	1,095,352	16.8	1,707	3,457	102.5	0.4

*Hong Kong International Tourist Arrivals estimated for 1990
Sources: World Tourism Organization (UNWTO), 2007, Facts and Figures, GeoHive. 2007, The population of continents, regions and countries (2006–07–01)

THE AMERICAS

5.1. Anglo North America

5.2. Latin North America

5.3. South America

This chapter covers the continents of North America and South America. Culturally, the North American continent is divided into three major regions that share little in common other than geographic proximity and a European colonial heritage. There are actually two uses of the term *North America*. The first is the North American continent, which is everything north of the South American continent. The second is the mostly English-speaking cultural region of the United States, Canada and the island of Greenland (a territory of Denmark). This cultural region is also referred to as Anglo North America, and is covered in the first section of this chapter. The term *Anglo North America* is used primarily to distinguish this region from the mostly Latin speaking areas to the South. It is not entirely accurate given the large Francophone region of Quebec in Canada, as well as Danish Greenland.

From Mexico southward is the mostly Spanish-speaking region of North America, which includes the major subregions of Mexico, Central America, and the islands of the Caribbean Sea. In addition to the language differences, the long border between the United States and Mexico marks one of the few places in the world where a highly industrialized country is directly adjacent to an economically developing country.

PHOTO 5.1

The Americas from space

Source: NASA BlueMarble

The Caribbean is only partially Spanish speaking, with major French-, English- and Dutch-speaking islands, as well. Although geographers have traditionally referred to this region as Middle America, the second section of this chapter is called *Latin North America*, to distinguish it from Anglo North America. Because physical geography does not always follow linguistic boundaries, some of the physical geography of Latin North America is discussed in the Anglo North America section.

The geographic term *Latin America* usually refers to all of the regions covered in section 5.2 of this chapter, plus all of South America. The continent of South America has several significant subregions, including the Andes Mountains, the Amazon Basin, and the Pampas in the south. These are all discussed in the third section of this chapter.

5.1   ANGLO NORTH AMERICA

Physical Geography of North American

Physiography refers to the shape of the surface of the earth. This is also known as topography, although the formal definition of topography also includes vegetation and built structures on the land. The physical landscape of Anglo North America is comprised the following physiographic regions (Figure 5.1):

FIGURE 5.1

PHYSICAL GEOGRAPHY OF ANGLO NORTH AMERICA

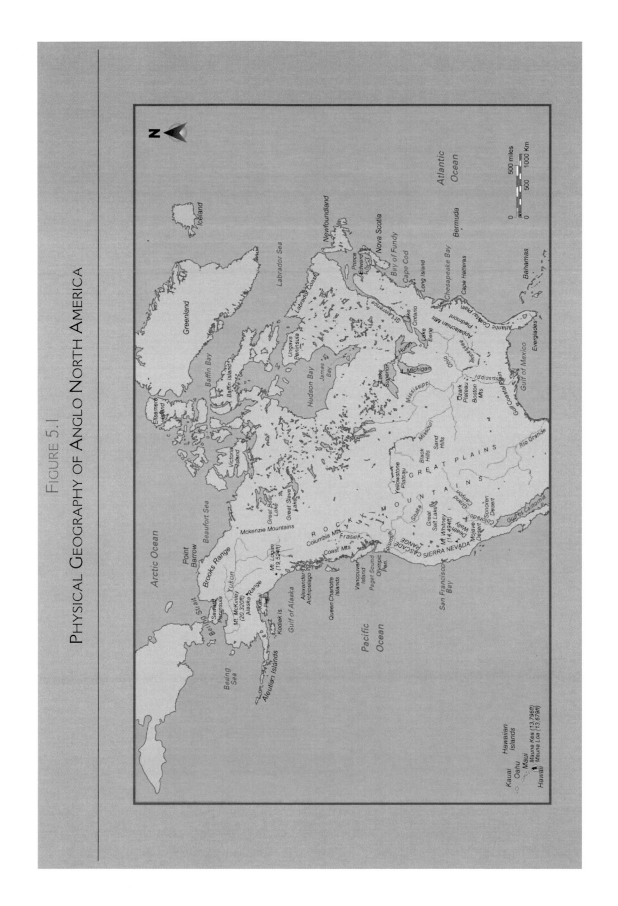

1. *The Interior Lowlands and Coastal Plains*, which, from north to south consists of the Arctic Coastal Plain, the Canadian Shield, the Central Lowlands and the Great Plains, and the Gulf and Atlantic Coastal Plains.
2. *The Appalachian Mountain System*, which includes the Appalachia region, the mountains of New England and the Canadian Maritime Provinces.
3. *The Western Mountains and Basins*, extending along the entire Pacific Ocean length of the continent, and consisting of the Rocky Mountains, the Pacific coastal mountain ranges, and the basins and plateaus that lie between these mountain systems.

The Interior Lowlands and Coastal Plains

Over half of Anglo North America is flatland. The largest expanse of flatland is located between the Appalachian Mountains in the east and Rocky Mountains in the west. This vast Interior Lowland region stretches from the Gulf of Mexico in the south to the northern tip of Canada. Mexico's Yucatan Peninsula is the southern-most outlier of this lowland region. The southern and eastern portions of the Interior Lowlands are made up of the Gulf and Atlantic Coastal Plains, which wrap around the Appalachian Mountains and gradually slope into the sea.

Underlying more than 1 million square miles of the Interior Lowlands of Canada is the Canadian Shield, which is centered on Hudson Bay, the largest bay in Anglo North America. The Canadian Shield contains some of the oldest exposed rock on the surface of the earth, created 4 billion years ago in the Precambrian Period. While the Canadian Shield is almost entirely in Canada, geologically important extensions of it lie in northern Michigan, Minnesota and Wisconsin. In New York, the Adirondack Mountains are part of the Shield. The metamorphic processes that created the Canadian Shield resulted in zones that are rich in metallic mineral deposits. During the great ice ages, vast sheets of snow extended out of the Hudson Bay area, covering much of lowland Canada and the Northeastern United States. Successive periods of glacial cover removed most of the sedimentary material that once covered the Shield, exposing its valuable ores. Canadian Shield iron from northern Minnesota and Canada were one of the main resources allowing for the development of the American and Canadian heavy manufacturing industries (including the car industry) around the Great Lakes.

A string of lakes and other water bodies surrounds the edge of the Shield to the south and west. The Great Lakes, Lake Winnipeg, Great Slave Lake and Great Bear Lake are the largest lakes on the North American continent. They, along with the St. Lawrence River and Lake Champlain Lowland (between New York and Vermont), and the Mackenzie River in the far north demarcate the boundary between the Canadian Shield and surrounding upland areas. Most of the Canadian Shield is vegetated with skinny spruce and aspen forests, with the exception of the far north, which has a treeless tundra vegetation. The tundra line also marks the southern limits of continuous permafrost soils. (South of the tundra line, permafrost exists, but is discontinuous and not in a solid mass.)

The Great Lakes are on the border between the Canadian Shield to the north and the Central Lowlands to the south. The lakes fill in eroded layers of sedimentary rock that encircle a large bulge in the earth's crust, centered on the state of Michigan. Continental glaciers that were over 5000 ft (1500 m) thick carved out the weaker layers of rock that were then filled in with water when the glaciers last receded about

12,000 years ago. Glacial action has also affected the river drainage pattern of the Great Lakes and upper Mississippi, Ohio and Missouri Rivers. The path of the Missouri and Ohio Rivers roughly mark the southern reach of continental glaciers during past ice ages.

The Great Lakes have a significant impact on the regional climate of the upper Midwest. Winds that cross the lakes pick up moisture, which increases precipitation (including snowfall) on the eastern shores of each lake. The lakes also have moderate air temperatures (as the oceans do), creating longer growing seasons on the eastern lakeshores. As a result, the Niagara Peninsula, north of Lake Erie and surrounded by three of the Great Lakes, is the major fruit-growing region in Canada.

The Great Plains rise in elevation from near sea level at the lower Mississippi River to just over a mile high (1 mile = 5,280 ft and 1609 m) in Denver at the foot of the Rocky Mountains. The Great Plains are composed of layer upon layer of sedimentary rock washed out from the Rocky Mountains to the west. Rivers such as the Platte, Missouri, and Red, parallel one another as they flow from west to east down this gentle grade.

While most of the Great Plains is flat and undistinguished, it does contain some distinct physical anomalies. In Nebraska, a belt of sand hills has been formed by wind and the outwash of the last continental glaciers. In South Dakota, however, water erosion has created a vast *badlands* landscape of deeply cut and barren soils. The one major mountain system that interrupts the evenness of the Great Plains is the Black Hills of South Dakota, which rise to over 7000 ft (2134 m). Here, old crystalline igneous rock breaks throughout the surface in a dome-like swelling that is believed to be an outlier of the Rocky Mountain system. The oldest and largest gold mine in the United States, as well as the famous Mount Rushmore, are both located in the Black Hills.

The Great Plains becomes more narrow as it extends into Canada and gradually disappear in northern Alberta. North of Edmonton (the capital of Alberta), where the prairie grasslands give way to a belt of mixed coniferous and deciduous forests. Eventually, these become spruce, fir and aspen forests, also known as *taiga*, which dominate the cold northern latitudes all the way to Alaska, both on the Canadian Shield to the east and the Rockies to the west.

Further to the south, the Gulf Coastal Plain slides into the Gulf of Mexico, while the Atlantic Coastal Plain borders the Atlantic Ocean. This is the lowest and flattest part of the Interior Lowland. These plains are also among the youngest exposed land in Anglo North America. When the Rocky Mountains were first beginning to rise some 70 million years ago, almost all of the Gulf and Atlantic Coastal Plains were under water. The coastal plains were gradually built up by unconsolidated (and easily eroded) sediments washed out from the Appalachian Mountains, the Central Lowlands, and the Great Plains. They are now being threatened by rising sea levels and more frequent hurricanes.

Along much of the coastline are swamps (wet forests), marshes (wet grasslands), and lagoons, along with sand bars and reefs. These characterize a transition zone between land and sea. Florida lies entirely within the Gulf and Atlantic Coastal Plains. Its highest elevation is only 345 ft (105 m), and it is mostly sandy with large swamp and marsh areas. The southern tip is dominated by the 5000 sq mile (12,950 sq km) Everglades marsh. A shallow continental shelf extends up to 250 miles from the coastline to the edge of North America. Coastlines that have a broad coastal zone and wide continental shelf situation are known as *trailing coastlines*, because they are often found on the coast that is trailing behind a migrating continent. The North

American continent has been moving westward, toward the Pacific Ocean (the leading coastline) and away from the Atlantic Ocean (the trailing coastline).

Interior Lowland Climate

The region north of Hudson Bay remains at freezing and below throughout most of the year, with very short summers when high temperatures reach about 45°F (7°C). (Only interior Greenland averages below freezing all year round.) The major air mass influencing this region is the dry and cold continental polar system. This air mass is weaker in the summer, but comes on strong in the winter months. Annual precipitation is under 10 in. (25 cm) for the entire Canadian Shield, except for the areas to the east and south of the Great Lakes. The southern two-thirds of the Canadian Shield experiences mild summers (50°F to 70°F; 10°C to 21°C) and cold (below freezing) winters.

The climate throughout the southern eastern lowlands, below the Great Lakes area, is humid subtropical, with summer rains. Temperatures are moderate in the winter and hot in the summer. Annual rainfall is over 40 in. (102 cm) for the entire coastal plains area, with over 60 in. (152 cm) in the Everglades. This drops to 20 in. (51 cm) further to the west on the Great Plains. Rainfalls below 20 in. typically indicate desert conditions, and the Great Plains was originally known as the *Great American Desert* by early European arrivals.

The major air mass that influences the climate of the Southern Interior Lowlands comes from the Gulf of Mexico. It brings warm and moist tropical air in the summer months, which is when most of the precipitation falls in this region. This air mass is weaker in the winter when occasional strong Arctic air masses reach deep into the Southeastern United States, destroying the region's fruits and vegetables. Vast areas of needle leaf evergreens make the Southeastern US one of the two major timber-producing regions in Anglo North America (the other being in the US Pacific Northwest and Canada's British Columbia). Further to the north, temperatures are cooler and growing seasons are shorter, though summers can still be quite warm due to the continental climatic conditions of the interior of Anglo North America.

The entire Central Lowlands, known as the Midwest in the United States), and most of the Great Plains, are drained by the Mississippi River and its tributaries, including the Missouri and Ohio Rivers. Good soils, flatland, and the navigable rivers made the Midwest an easy region to cross and settle in. Large grain shipments, coal (from the Appalachian Mountains), and iron ore (from the Canadian Shield) could also be transported easily on these waterways. These attributes contributed to making the Midwest and Southern Ontario the agricultural heartland and the heavy industry core of the United States and Canada.

The Appalachian Mountain System

The Appalachian Mountain system comprises a band of mountains that run from Canada's Newfoundland in the northeast to Alabama in the US in its southwest. The system can be divided into four sections:

1. A Northeastern section that covers northern Maine and the Maritime Provinces of Canada, and which has been heavily eroded by continental glaciers.
2. A New England section, which has been somewhat less eroded by glaciers and has some steep sloped mountains and a jagged, glacier carved coastline.

Source: Alan A. Lew

3. The Appalachians proper, which is culturally known as *Appalachia*, and which starts in Pennsylvania and includes the Allegheny and Cumberland Plateaus.
4. The Ozark Plateau and the Ouachita Mountains (pronounced waw'-chee-taw), which were the southernmost part of the Appalachian system, but were cut off from the rest of the range by the Mississippi River.

The Appalachian Mountains were once the principal mountain system in North America, rising as high as the Rocky Mountains today. It was created by the intense uplifting and folding of sedimentary rock as North America shifted and slid against Europe and Africa some 570 million years ago. This was caused by the tectonic force of swirling molten magma inside the earth that causes continental and ocean plates to move about on the earth's surface. Starting about 200 million years ago, North America began to break away from Europe and Africa, forming the Atlantic Ocean. As a result of this process, a portion of the Appalachian system continues across the Atlantic through Northern Ireland, Scotland and Norway.

The Appalachians mostly stopped growing after the continents separated from one another, though it is still the dominant mountain range in the eastern US. Continuous erosion has brought most of the peaks down to under 5000 ft (1524 m) in elevation. Narrow valleys, steep hillsides, and thin soils have resulted in low population densities throughout this mountainous region, and has kept its cities small. This has also been true of the Ozarks and Ouachitas. Metallic minerals (especially copper and iron ore) have been largely mined out of the Appalachians, though coal still remains in abundant supply.

New England and the Maritime Provinces

A portion of New England and most of the maritime provinces of Canada were subjected to mountain-building processes that involved huge intrusions of igneous rock (known as *batholiths*). The hard rock underlying this land, much of which is granite, has experienced considerable scraping and erosion from continental glaciers and resembles the landscapes of the Canadian Shield. The St. Lawrence River and the Gulf of St. Lawrence form a water boundary between the northern Appalachians and the Canadian Shield of Quebec and Labrador. Two north–south trending mountains dominate the Appalachians in New England. The Green Mountains in the west (mostly in Vermont) are lower in elevation. Their peaks have been rounded due to continental glaciers that once covered them. The higher White Mountains (mostly in New Hampshire) include Mount Washington, the tallest peak in the Northeastern United States at 6288 ft (1917 m).

Even though the New England part of the Appalachian Mountains is close to the coast, the climate is continental because of the west-to-east flow of air. Cold polar air masses from the Canadian Shield regularly blow across the northern Appalachians region, bringing winter snow all the way to Boston and New York. The climate is generally one of mild summers and long, cold winters in the Canadian portions, with hot summers and shorter winters in the southern parts of New England.

Because large amounts of the earth's surface water was stored in ice during the glacial advances, sea levels were about 450 ft below their current levels. Much of the North American continental shelf was exposed and a land bridge existed to Asia. Because rivers seek to erode until they reach sea level, the lower sea levels allowed rivers to cut deeper valleys, especially in coastal areas. When sea levels rose, these valleys were filled in, creating Chesapeake Bay (Susquehanna River), Delaware Bay (Delaware River) and New York Harbor (Hudson River). Bays that are created by the filling in of river valleys are called *estuaries*. The result is that the northeastern US coastline has many bays, peninsulas and islands, and contributes to giving North America the second longest coastline among the world's continents, after Asia.

Appalachia

Starting in Pennsylvania, the Appalachians proper are found. Portions of this part of the Appalachians formed the edge of the carboniferous era swamp that covered the interior lowlands of North America some 300 million years ago. These old swamp lands form the basis for the rich coal deposits found throughout this part of the Appalachian system. The transition between the Appalachians and the Central Lowlands of the United States Midwest is sometimes called the *interior low plateaus*. It consists of the Allegheny Plateau in Pennsylvania and the Cumberland Plateau further south. They are, for the most part, sandstone underlain by limestone, which creates a karst topography with limestone caves. The largest cave in North America is Mammoth Cave in Kentucky's Cumberland Plateau. When the sandstone cover is removed by erosion, limestone basins are created, such as the Blue Grass Basin of

Kentucky and the Nashville Basin of Tennessee. Both have rich soils and good farm land.

In the southern part of the Appalachians are the Blue Ridge Mountains. These mountains reach an elevation of over 6000 ft (1829 m) in the Great Smoky Mountains National Park, along the North Carolina and Tennessee border. The Smokies are the highest mountains east of the Rocky Mountains, reaching 6684 ft (2037 m) on Mt. Mitchell. To the west, the mountains are heavily folded ridgelines that are parallel to one another and are known as the *ridge and valley* region. The north-flowing Shenandoah River and the south-flowing Tennessee River run through this area. Most of the Appalachians proper experience a hot and humid summer and cool to cold winter.

The Ozarks

The Ozark Plateau and Ouachita Mountains consist of a group of low mountains sometimes called the *interior highlands*. On the southern edge of the Ozark Plateau are the Boston Mountains, the peaks of which are exposed granite rock. To the south, across the Arkansas River, are the Ouachita Mountains. They are a folded belt that resembles the ridge and valley area of the Appalachians. At its highest points this region is under 2700 ft (823 m). The climate of the Ozarks and Ouachitas is similar to that of the surrounding warm and humid lowlands. This is in part because these interior highlands are an east–west trending system, which benefits little from altitudinal zonation and rain shadow impacts.

Earthquakes in the Eastern United States

Although more commonly associated with the Pacific Coast, the strongest earthquakes ever to occur in the US were in the areas around Memphis, Tennessee and Madrid, Missouri, in 1811 and 1812, respectively. Other devastating quakes have occurred in Charleston, South Carolina, and New York City's Jamaica Bay. Geologists estimate a very high probability of a destructive earthquake occurring in the eastern United States within most of our lifetimes. Because earthquakes are so infrequent in this region, none of the buildings have been constructed to resist tremors, as they have in California, and predictions are very difficult to make.

The Western Mountains and Basins Region

The Western Mountains and Basins comprise about a third of Anglo North America and most of Mexico and Central Aemrica. The major subsections of this diverse region are:

1. The Rocky Mountains in Canada and the United States, which extends to (the Sierra Madre ranges in Mexico).
2. The Intermontane Basins and Plateaus region, wich is located between the Rocky Mountains and the Pacific Coast ranges, and including interior Alaska and central Mexico.
3. The Pacific Coast Mountain and Valley region, including the Alaska Range and the Aleutian Islands in the far north and Baja California in Mexico to the south.

Photo 5.3

The Bellagio hotel and Casino in Las Vegas. The shopping center in the foreground is designed to replicate a Mediterranean town

Source: Alan A. Lew

The Western Mountains were created by the rapid speed with which the North American continent moved westward, colliding into and over the Pacific Ocean Plate. About 80 million years ago, this mountain-building uplifted the western half of the continent where a long series of sedimentary beds lay evenly spread over the ancient continental floor. This disturbance was accompanied by volcanic activity and is known as the Laramide Revolution. It resulted in a great uplift of the sedimentary beds, folding and faulting, and metamorphic changes. In some places, the uplift was followed by the erosion of the sedimentary layers and the exposure of the underlying igneous rock. In other places, the older layers were preserved. The resulted is a great mix of sedimentary, igneous and metamorphic rock across western North America, along with a diversity of landscapes.

The Intermontane Basins and Plateaus region was the first portion to be uplifted, creating a large mountain range through present-day Nevada some 80 million years ago. The Rocky Mountains were formed 60 million years ago. Today, the Front Range of the Rockies still rises a mile above the Great Plains at Denver, Colorado. And mountain building is still taking place today, causing earthquakes along the Pacific Coast, down to the mountains of Central America.

Photo 5.4
Warning sign on the edge of the Grand Canyon in Arizona

Source: Alan A. Lew

The Rocky Mountains and the Sierra Madres

The main part of the Rocky Mountain system lies in Canada (the Canadian Rockies) and in the United States from Montana and Idaho (the Northern Rockies) to Colorado (the Central Rockies) and New Mexico (the Southern Rockies). Disconnected outliers of Rockies include the Brooks Range in northern Alaska and the Sierra Madre Occidental (west) and Oriental (east) in Mexico. Although of different origin, the highlands of Central America, south of Mexico, shares a similar geographic role as the more northern mountain systems.

Climate in the Rocky Mountains is generally cold in the winter and mild in the summer. Highland climates, however, are difficult to classify because of the great variation in micro-conditions between valley floors and mountain peaks. In addition, south-facing slopes often receive much more sunshine and are very different from colder, north-facing slopes in their climate and vegetation. Latitude plays a major role, with the mountains located farther to the north being much colder and having more permanent snow and active alpine glaciers than those to the south.

Intermontane Basins and Plateaus

West of the Rocky Mountains (as well as south of the Brooks Range in Alaska) lies the Intermontane Basins and Plateaus region. This diverse area was created by crustal faulting, volcanic activity, and intense recent erosion and downcutting by rivers. The basic form of this region is that of a series of high-elevation plateaus, older mountains that have eroded into low-lying hills, internal drainage basins with sand dunes and flat playas, as well as the deepest river valleys on the continent.

In Alaska this area forms the vast drainage basin of the Yukon River, with its rolling hills and wide, braided rivers. The Yukon River originates on the Yukon Plateau (a higher-elevation area) in Canada's Yukon Territory. It flows through the *Cold Triangle*, which is an area enclosed by Fairbanks in Alaska, Snag in Canada's Yukon Territory, and Good Hope in the Northwest Territories of Canada. This area regularly has the coldest temperatures in North America, with −60°F to −80°F (−51°C to −62°C) cold periods lasting for weeks at a time. Dawson, on the Yukon River, and the *Klondike Region*, bordering Alaska and Canada, were major gold mining districts in the late 1890s that lie at the center of the Cold Triangle. Summer high temperatures in this area are typically in the 70s F (low 20s C), although temperatures in the 90s F (mid-30s C) are also common. In the summer the melted marshlands of the far north become infested with vast numbers of mosquitoes.

The great extremes of summer and winter temperatures at higher latitudes (closer to the poles) is due to the earth's tilted axis. Because the earth moves around the sun on a tilted axis, the northern hemisphere faces toward the sun in June and looks away from the sun in December. These extremes become most pronounced closer to the poles. North of the Arctic Circle, Alaska and Northern Canada's summer solstice had 24 hours of sun, while the winter solstice has 24 hours of cold darkness. At the other extreme, the length of days in the Caribbean Sea remain about the same all year round, and average winter temperatures are only a couple degrees less than average summer temperatures.

In Canada, a deep fault line separates the Rocky Mountains from the lower mountains of the Interior Basins and Plateaus and the Coast Mountains further to west. This trench is the headwaters for the Columbia, Fraser, Peace and Yukon Rivers. The Fraser Plateau comprises much of central British Columbia, situated between a narrow band of the Rockies and the Coast Mountains. It is made up of large areas of extrusive igneous lava. The entire plateau is drained by the Fraser River, which enters the sea at Vancouver.

The Columbia Plateau is another vast area of lava rock that underlies most of the state of Washington and portions of Oregon and Idaho. It is drained by the Columbia River and the Snake River. Like the Fraser Plateau, the Columbia Plateau was created when giant fissures opened up and poured forth 200 ft (61 m) thick lava flows. Over time they created a 50,000 sq mile (129,500 sq km) area of old lava several thousand feet thick. The Columbia River Basin, also known as the *Inland Empire*, lies in eastern Washington at the center of the Columbia Plateau. Along with the *Great Sandy Desert* in southeastern Oregon, it is the driest area in the Pacific Northwest region of the United States (less than 10 in., 25.4 cm, of rain a year). This is mostly because it lies in the rain shadow of the volcanic Cascade Range. The large rivers that flow through this desert region provide water that make it one of the richest wheat-growing areas in North America. Hells Canyon, on the Snake River between Oregon and Idaho, is also in this area and is the deepest canyon in the

United States. It forms a V-shaped canyon as the river cuts straight down through the old lava rock.

The Great Basin is centered on the state of Nevada, though it also includes areas of neighboring states. It is the largest of the internal drainage basins in the Intermountain West. During the last ice age it was filled with large lakes that have since evaporated, often leaving behind much smaller salty remnants, such as the Great Salt Lake. The landscape of the Great Basin consists of ancient mountains that have been eroded away into widely dispersed smaller ridge lines. Their eroded sediments now form flat expanses and outwash plains. This landscape is known as the *basin and range* and extends well into northern Mexico.

Rainfall is generally under 5 in (13 cm). throughout the basin and range deserts of the American West and northern Mexico. This is due to the high-pressure systems that dominate this area, as well as the rain shadow affect of the Pacific Coast mountain system in California. Irrigated fields rely on water from the plateaus and higher peaks. On the higher mountains there is a well pronounced increase in precipitation and one can often travel from desert to alpine conditions within 100 miles (160 km). Groundwater is another important source of irrigation, although it is becoming more difficult to reach as water tables drop. Most of the rain that does fall in this region comes in the summer months, from summer monsoon moisture originating in the Gulf of California and the Gulf of Mexico.

The most prominent plateau in the Intermontane Basins and Plateaus region is the Colorado Plateau, which is centered on the *four corners* where Colorado, New Mexico, Arizona and Utah meet. It is made up of sedimentary rock that was uplifted at about the same time as the Rocky Mountains. Today, the Colorado Plateau has an average base elevation of 5000 ft (1524 m). As the Colorado Plateau lifted upward from a former shallow sea bed, the Colorado River carved down through it to form the Grand Canyon. Unlike Hells Canyon, the different layers of sedimentary rock that form the Colorado Plateau created a multi-colored, stepped canyon of mesas and rock monuments.

The Pacific Coast Mountains and Valleys

The Pacific Coast of Anglo North America is very diverse. Along it are found the highest peaks and the most active volcanoes on the continent. Like the rest of the mountainous west, the Pacific Coast was shaped by plate tectonic activity. In the south, the Baja California peninsula (including the city of Los Angeles, California) is actually part of the Pacific Ocean Plate that is currently sliding northward against the North America Plate. The granite peaks of the Sierra Nevada Mountains in California are an exposed intrusive igneous (mostly granite) formation, while the Cascade Range further to the north is made up of extrusive igneous (lava) rock. Farther to the north, Canada's Coast Mountains and the Alaska Range in Alaska are intrusive igneous formations, similar to the Sierra Nevada. The Coast Mountains of British Columbia are the world's highest coastal mountain system, while the Alaska Range contains the highest mountains on the continent, including Mt. McKinley (also known as Denali) at 20,320 ft (6194 m).

Both the intrusive and the igneous rock that comprise the higher Pacific Coast mountains come from the melting of the Pacific Ocean sea floor plates that have been pushed under the North American Plate in a process known as *subduction*. The melting of the ocean plates result in molten rock squeezing upward through cracks in the North America plate, creating the Alaska Range, Canada's Coast Mountains, the Cascade Range, and the Sierra Nevada range. (The Rocky Mountains and Sierra Madre Range were also formed this way.) As these mountains were uplifted, the area immediately to their west was sunken to form a depression. The depression originates as the Gulf of California in Mexico and continues as the Central Valley in California, the Willamette Valley in Oregon, the Puget Sound lowland in Washington, the coastal straits and Inland Passage of British Columbia, and the Alexander Archipelago in the Alaska Panhandle (southeast Alaska).

Today, a small ocean plate (the Juan de Fuca Plate) continues to subduct under Oregon and Washington, keeping the Cascade Range volcanically active. Subduction and active volcanism are also still occurring in Alaska from about Anchorage out through the Aleutian Islands. In Mexico, California and British Columbia, however, subduction has mostly stopped, and instead the North American Plate is sliding sideways against the large Pacific Ocean Plate. This causes lateral (or strike-slip) faulting and frequent earthquake activity in most of the Coast Range of California, as the Pacific Plate moves northward at about 2 in. (5 cm) a year.

The low-lying Coast Range of California, Oregon and Washington, (which is different from the Coast Mountains in Canada) were formed by crumpling the edge of the North American continent. The Coast Range continues as Mexico's Baja California peninsula in the south (though its geologic origin is different from that in California, Oregon and Washington) and as Vancouver Island and Queen Charlotte Island in British Columbia to the north. The Alaska Peninsula, which contains more active volcanoes than anywhere else on the continent, and the Aleutian Islands can also be considered an extension of this coastal edge. Unlike the eastern trailing coastline, the western coasts are all *leading* coastlines. They are steep and show signs of emergence, or rising up from the sea, with older coastlines now hundreds of feet up slope in some areas.

West Coast Rain Shadows

The two north–south trending mountain systems in the Pacific Coast (the Coast Range and the Sierra Nevada/Cascade Range) create two rain shadow patterns. The first and smaller rain shadow occurs in the inland valleys of California, Oregon, and Washington and the coastal channels of British Columbia. Thus, Sacramento, Portland, Seattle and Vancouver (British Columbia) all lie in a warmer and less rainy rain shadow area compared to the mountains to their west and east. A more significant rain shadow exists east of the Sierra Nevada, Cascade Range, and Canada's Coast Mountains. This rain shadow extends the naturally occurring deserts of the United States-Mexico border area far north to the Canadian border. In Canada and Alaska, the dry polar desert that exists over the North Pole is extended southward by the same rain shadow process behind the Coast Mountains in Canada. Dry rain shadows are also found in central Alaska, where the north–south mountains shift to an east–west moisture barrier in the Alaska Range.

The Climate of Anglo North America

The rings of high- and low-pressure air masses encircle the globe shape the weather and climate of the North America continent in different ways. The eastern half of the United States and Canada are primarily influenced by interactions between cold

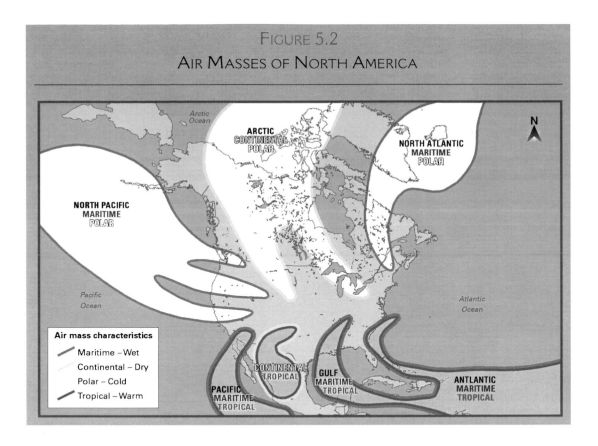

FIGURE 5.2
AIR MASSES OF NORTH AMERICA

Arctic
Ocean

ARCTIC
CONTINENTAL
POLAR

NORTH ATLANTIC
MARITIME
POLAR

N

NORTH PACIFIC
MARITIME
POLAR

Pacific
Ocean

Atlantic
Ocean

Air mass characteristics

Maritime – Wet
Continental – Dry
Polar – Cold
Tropical – Warm

CONTINENTAL
TROPICAL

GULF
MARITIME
TROPICAL

ANTLANTIC
MARITIME
TROPICAL

PACIFIC
MARITIME
TROPICAL

and dry continental air coming down from the high-pressure North Pole, and warm, humid air rising from the equator and the Caribbean Sea. The warm tropical air brings most of eastern North America's rainfall in the summer months. This is true for both Anglo and Latin North America. The humid air spins around the *Bermuda High* pressure system, which circulates in a clockwise direction in the Atlantic Ocean, approximately around the island of Bermuda. The cold polar air keeps the winter months frigid and comparatively drier than in summer in eastern Canada and the United States. Winter precipitation occurs when humid, low-pressure systems move in from the Pacific Coast and intermix with the polar air mass (Figure 5.2).

For most of Anglo North America, the predominant wind pattern is from west (the Pacific Ocean) to east. For Latin North America, the predominant wind pattern is from east (the Atlantic Ocean) to west. Smaller local exceptions to these patterns sometimes occur, and the whole system of air masses moves northward in the summer months and southward in the winter months. As the warmer air masses move northward, it warms up the Atlantic Ocean east of the Caribbean Sea. Starting in June each year, warm and humid air rises from the Atlantic Ocean off the coast of Africa and then moves toward the Caribbean Sea. Occasionally these air masses become tropical storms and hurricanes. The hurricane season lasts through the end of November, when the warm air masses shift further southward. Unfortunately, the hurricane season occurs during the summer holiday season for North Americans, which can cause vacation trip cancellations in the Caribbean and on the coastal plains when inclement weather is forecast.

The Rocky Mountains and the prevailing west-to-east wind pattern (from the Pacific) keep the tropical and polar air masses that affect the eastern United States from entering the western half of the continent most of the time. Occasionally the polar air mass makes its way into the Pacific Northwest in winter, and the tropical Caribbean air mass regularly affects Mexico and the United States Southwest in the summer months.

Western North America is affected by a dry high-pressure air mass in the southern portions (the southwestern United States and northwestern Mexico) that creates desert conditions that extend to the Canadian borders due to the mountain rain shadows, as mentioned above. Further to the north, an upper latitude humid low-pressure system brings year-round humid weather to the Pacific Northwest all the way up to southern Alaska. Central and northern Alaska and Canada are under the influence of the dry polar air mass that affects eastern parts of the continent in the winter months.

California is famous for its Mediterranean climate. This climate exhibits a distinct summer dry and winter wet pattern, which is different from that found anywhere else in North America. This climate transitions into a desert climate on the northwest coast of Mexico, and then to a summer-wet tropical climate in southern Mexico and Central America. North of California, the Mediterranean climate gradually changes to the Marine West Coast climate on the coast from Oregon to southern Alaska. The Marine West Coast climate is wet all year round, although, like the Mediterranean Climate, it also has a winter peak. Because the moisture hitting the west coast comes off the ocean, it has a moderating maritime influence on the coast and coastal snow is very uncommon, except in Northern British Columbia and Alaska.

Human Geography of Anglo North America

Pre-Columbian Settlement

Migrants from Asia are generally believed to have arrived in the New World at least 12,000 years ago, at the end of the last ice age. (though some archeological finds suggest possibly pushing the earliest crossing date back to 45,000 years ago.) At the time Europeans arrived, the area that today constitutes the United States contained perhaps 5 million Native Americans, with an additional 2 million in Canada, including Inuits. The Caribbean Islands had from 500,000 to 1 million people, and Mexico and Central America had 25 to 30 million inhabitants. In Anglo North America, the native peoples were sparsely scattered, with major concentration in the Central Valley of California, the Pacific Northwest, the US Southwest, and portions of the US South. Most of their societies were technologically primitive, though some developed highly organized social systems. However, their population densities were never large enough to allow for sustained high civilizations.

Native Americans is a general term used in the United States that applies to all pre-European contact people in North America, including Hawaiians and Inuits. In Canada the preferred term is *Aboriginal*, and sometimes *First Nations*. *American Indians* is the term used in the United States to refer to pre-European contact people in the North America, excluding Hawaiians, Inuits, and several northern ethnic groups who are more closely related to ethnic groups in Arctic Asia and Europe.

The tribe was the basic unit of social organization for American Indians in North America. A *tribe* is any group of people who share the same distinct customs and language and who believe that they have descended from a common ancestor, whether real or mythological. At the time the Europeans arrived, the tribes of North America spoke several hundred languages and led a variety of lifestyles, from settled agriculturalists (such as the Hopi) to nomadic hunters and herders. Some of these groups got along very well (such as the Iroquois Federation); others did not.

Common European diseases, especially smallpox and measles, killed large numbers of Native Americans because they had no resistance to them. In the early years, Europeans hotly debated whether or not Native Americans were humans or animals. Even when they were finally declared to be human, they were often treated inhumanely. Large numbers were forced to relocate as Europeans came to dominate the continent, and many were killed trying to protect their homelands in the Indian Wars in the United States (1865–1885). Indian place names, however, are common throughout the United States and Canada. The word *Canada* itself may have come from the Iroquois word *Kanata*, meaning town or village.

One of the major differences between the European colonialists and the Native Americans was how each group viewed ownership of land. In Native American societies, land was owned communally by the tribe. An individual had the right to a particular parcel of land only as long as he or she worked that parcel. As soon as the work stopped, it went back to communal ownership. The concept of land as a private commodity that could be bought or sold did not exist in any of the civilizations of the New World, with the possible exception of the feudal land ownership among the Aztecs in Mexico. European settlers brought with them the concepts of private land ownership (freehold tenure), the right to do whatever one wishes with one's land (fee simple ownership), and the ability to buy and sell land (property deeds). These concepts were fundamental to the founding values of the United States and Canada.

For the most part, the northern European settlers in the New World preferred to ignore Native Americans as much as possible. The cultural gap between the two groups was considered too large to bridge, and the preferred means of dealing with the situation was to remove Native Americans to isolated and undesirable lands. Today, many Indian reservations have been found to contain valuable mineral deposits and have demonstrated considerable development potential.

Native Americans constitute less than 1 percent of the population of the United States and a little more than 3 percent of Canada's population. Their absolute numbers are only slightly larger than when Europeans first arrived. In the United States they are mostly settled in the western states, with especially large concentrations in Arizona, Oklahoma, South Dakota and California. Large non-Indian native populations reside in Alaska and Canada's Nunavut province (mostly Inuit people), and in Hawaii (Hawaiians).

European Colonial Settlement

Columbus landed in the Bahamas in 1492. In the 1500s, colonial settlement in the New World was primarily from Spain (to Mexico) and France (to Canada). In the 17th century, increasing numbers of settlers were starting to arrive from the British Isles and Germanic Europe, settling in the British colonies in the United States and Canada. Soon after the American Revolution (1776–1778), 60 percent of the Americans in the 13 colonies were from the British Isles, 20 percent were from German-speaking Europe, including The Netherlands (Germany did not yet exist), and 20 percent were from

PHOTO 5.5

Independence hall in Philadelphia, Home of the declaration of
Independence and the United States constitution

Source: Alan A. Lew

Africa. Today, approximately 40 percent of the population of the United States are
descendants from German immigrants, more than any other national origin.

The French were the first Europeans to settle in Canada, settling in Acadia (modern-day Nova Scotia and New Brunswick) in 1605, and founding the city of Québec
in 1608. The British arrived about a decade later and the Québec area changed hands
between the two several times until 1760 when the British took control of Montreal.
In 1763, the Treaty of Paris gave all of French Canada to the British. At that time
there were an estimated 60,000 French settlers in Canada.

After the British took full control of Canada, some of the French-speaking Acadians
migrated to the New Orleans, Louisiana area, where they are today known as *Cajuns*.
A few years later, British loyalists, fleeing the colonies after the American Revolution,
settled in the new colony of New Brunswick. After the United States gained its independence from Britain large number of British immigrants started to settle in Canada,
eventually coming to predominate over the French-speaking inhabi-tants who are
today centered in province of Québec.

The Confederation of Canada was established on July 1, 1867, which included
today's provinces of Ontario, Québec, Nova Scotia and New Brunswick. Later,
Manitoba (1870), British Columbia (1871), Alberta (1905) and Saskatchewan (1905)
joined Confederation. Britain transferred its jurisdiction over the Yukon Territory and
the Northwest Territories to Canada in the 1880s. In 1999, the Nunavut Territory
was created from a portion of the Northwest Territories as a homeland for the Inuit
people. This large area, however, only has a population of a little more the 24,000.

The Industrial Revolution

The industrial revolution had a major impact on European migration to Anglo North America. The industrial revolution started in England in the late 1700s and entered Northern Europe in the early 1800s. In each area where it took hold, a similar pattern of development occurred. Death rates declined, populations exploded, massive migration from rural areas to industrial cities took place, and poverty increased dramatically. The Irish and British were the first to come to North America to escape the squalor of England's industrial cities. They were followed by the Germans and the Dutch when industrialization occurred in Northern Europe.

Southern and Eastern Europe experienced the industrial revolution at the end of the 19th century, leading to the migration of large numbers of people from these areas to the Anglo North America (and to southern South America). The United States population was 14 times larger in 1900 than in 1800 (growing from 5.3 million to 76.2 million). The impact on Canada was more limited because its potential for large-scale settlement was less. Massive European migration to North America ended with the outbreak of World War I in 1914 and has been very low since then.

Since about the 1950s and 1960s, North America has entered a postindustrial era in which tertiary (service-sector) employment has replaced secondary (manufacturing) employment as the leading source of jobs. This is not the case for many other countries in the world, where manufacturing continues to employ more people than any other sector. Europe and Japan have only recently begun to transform into postindustrial economies. In the postindustrial economy both industries and workers are highly mobile and less place-bound. Because of this many companies and employees have moved from the old industrial core near the Great Lakes to higher amenity *Sun Belt* states in the US South and on the east and west coasts. At the same time, the postindustrial economy is characterized by lower paying service jobs (compared to manufacturing), higher rates of mass-consumerism, very low savings rates by employees, and higher job turnovers. All this makes for less security in employment and in life for the postindustrial North American population.

Population Distribution

Today, the overall North American settlement distribution shows three distinct geographic patterns (Figure 5.3):

1. *The Northeast Manufacturing and Financial Center*, which includes the northeast coast, the Great Lakes region, southern Ontario and Quebec, is the most densely settled region of Anglo North America. It has the largest concentration of major metropolitan areas, even after a couple of decades of migration that has favored the Sun Belt. This is still a highly productive manufacturing region and the center of both United States and Canada financial services. Ethnically, the rural parts of this region are of English and French heritage in the east and in Canada, and of Germanic and Scandinavian heritage west and south of the Great Lakes. Urban populations have larger concentrations of Southern and Eastern Europeans, as well as Blacks who migrated from the South after the US Civil War (1861–1865) and more recent Spanish-speaking arrivals.
2. *The Agricultural Interior Lowlands*, which includes the US Midwest, the Great Plains, and much of the US South is characterized by a very even distribution

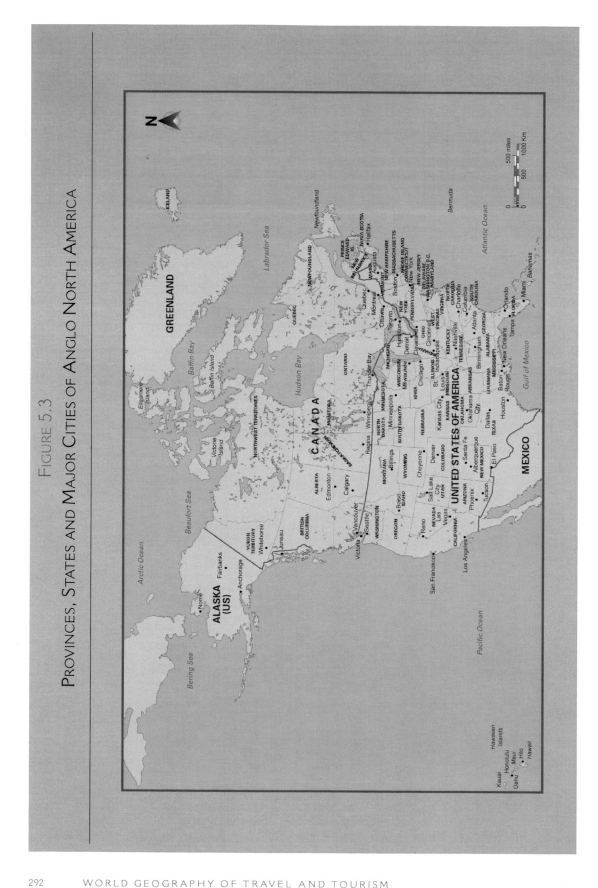

FIGURE 5.3

PROVINCES, STATES AND MAJOR CITIES OF ANGLO NORTH AMERICA

of population and cities over a largely flat terrain. This distribution models a classic spatial pattern in human geography, known as *Central Place Theory*, in which the service area of different size settlements distributes them in an even grid-like pattern across the landscape. The density of this settlement distribution pattern become increasingly spread out as one moves into Canada's northern areas. Ethnically, the European settlers of the Southeastern United States, including the southern Great Plains, were predominantly of Scots-Irish descent (these were Scottish migrants to British Northern Ireland, who then migrated to the American Colonies). On the northern Great Plains and in the American Midwest they were mostly of Germanic and Scandinavians, with some Russian settlement areas, and significant French areas in Canada.

3. *The Dispersed Western Settlements* exhibit a settlement pattern that is highly dependent on the location of natural resources, especially water and minerals. Water enabled agriculture was the basis for most of the largest cities in the interior of western North America. Other cities, mostly smaller in size, were based on mining in the past and recreation today. Port locations were important for Pacific Coastal cities. Vast areas with low populations exist between these larger western settlements. This pattern extends up the western mountains system into Alaska. Ethnically, western North America is a great mix of diverse populations. American Indians are a major population group here, along with immigrants and their descendents from Europe (Utah is mostly of English descent), Central America (especially Mexico), and Asia (China, the Philippines and Japan being the main source countries.) Los Angeles alone is the largest Mexican city outside of Mexico, the largest Guatemalan city outside of Guatemala, and the largest Iranian city outside of Iran. San Francisco is the largest Chinese city outside of Asia.

Tourism in Anglo North America

Following World War II, tourism in North America grew quickly. The continent today is one of the largest tourism receiving and generating regions of the world, together with Western Europe. The United States and Canada (as well as Mexico) are regularly ranked by the World Tourism Organization (UNWTO) in the world's top twenty destinations. Furthermore, the United States has been the largest tourism earner for many years. Five primary characteristics account for North America's global tourism position. The first is its sheer size. The continent extends over dozens of physiographic, climatic, and botanical zones, which provides a wide range of climates and weather patterns, landforms, flora and fauna, natural landscapes, cultures, and patterns of human habitation. This varied environment is the foundation for the growth of much of North America's tourism sector.

The second factor is rapid advances in travel innovations. Post-World War II air travel improvements and larger transportation networks (including an expanded highway system) have facilitated higher levels and more efficient forms of travel and opened up new destinations. Similarly, computer-based technology has put travel planning in the hands of individuals, who had in the past relied more heavily on travel agents and tour operators. Approximately half of all online dollars spent in the US are for travel and tourism products and services. Fourth, since the 1950s, the economies of Canada and the United States have grown rapidly, with a relatively low level of unemployment and inflation, enabling many more people to travel than before.

NAFTA

North America has been a fertile laboratory for cross-border alliances. In 1989, the Canada-United States Free Trade Agreement (FTA) was launched to start reducing trade barriers for goods and services between the two countries. This coalition was instrumental for tourism because it addressed tourism in detail. It effected various regulations pertaining to air travel, collaborative marketing efforts, increased cross-border travel, and eliminated restrictions on the value of services that may be purchased in the neighboring country. In 1989 and 1990, additional bilateral treaties were signed between Canada and Mexico and the United States and Mexico that pertained to tourism, facilitating cross-border travel, cultural exchanges, binational human resource education, common promotional efforts, and mutual collaboration in achieving UN World Tourism Organization (UNWTO) standards and practices. On January 1, 1994, the FTA was replaced by the North American Free Trade Agreement (NAFTA), a tripartite accord between Canada, Mexico and the United States. Its primary objectives were to eliminate duties and other trade tariffs in stages over the next two decades. Unlike the FTA, tourism was not an explicit concern of NAFTA, but it did deal with issues affecting tourism, such as temporary entry, trade in services, monetary investments and telecommunications.

Sport is another foundation for tourism in Canada and the United States. Baseball, football, basketball and hockey are the most watched and played sports in the United States and Canada. Soccer/football is most popular in Mexico, as are bullfighting, charreads, and jai alai. The traditionally narrow scope of sport following in Canada and the US has recently been supplanted in part by motorsports in terms of attendance and fanship. Stock car racing (NASCAR), for instance, has grown to achieve a substantial following during the 1990s and early 2000s.

Shopping

Like sport, shopping has emerged as a significant tourist activity in North America, focusing largely on outlet shopping centers, mega-malls and shops in border regions. Cross-border shopping is important in the Canada-United States and Mexico-United States borderlands. During the past 15 years, several shopping centers have been built in Mexico near the US border in an effort to disuade Mexicans from out shopping to the United States. Outlet centers became popular during the 1980s and 1990s to cater to more budget-minded consumers, who can often find brand-name products in factory-direct outlets at discount prices.

Malls have popped up all over North America and the world in the past half century. The first mega-mall and the largest mall in North America, the West Edmonton Mall in Edmonton, Alberta, Canada, was built in the 1980s and expanded in the 1990s. Following suit in the 1990s, the Mall of America was constructed in Minneapolis, Minnesota, and is North America's second largest mall. These centers are tourist destinations in their own right, offering playgrounds and theme parks, zoos, restaurants, bowling alleys and skating arenas, travel agencies, car rentals, hotel accommodations, currency exchange booths, cinemas and swimming pools, as well as other recreational and financial services. In Japan and Europe, West Edmonton Mall and Mall of America package tours are offered in which shopping enthusiasts fly into Edmonton or Minneapolis, spend two or three nights at the mall and return to London or Tokyo. Malls and other shopping centers in North America no longer serve only a utilitarian function; they have become entertainment and holiday complexes.

North America's national park systems are among the most inclusive and expansive in the world. Yellowstone National Park was the world's first national park (in 1872) and a precursor to the US National Park Service (NPS). Parks Canada and the US NPS and their precursors have owned and operated hundreds of natural and cultural sites in their respective countries. Most of these sites in the east focus on maritime history and the colonial past, while western properties tend to spotlight the cultural pasts of Native Canadians and mountain environments. National Park Service properties in the United States fall under several categories, including battlefields, battlefield parks, battlefield sites, historic parks, historic sites, lakeshores, memorials, military parks, monuments, parks, parkways, preserves, recreation areas, reserves, rivers, scenic trails, seashores, and wild and scenic rivers. Each has its own definitional criteria. Mexico has a complex system of approximately 123 national parks and protected natural areas under the administration of several national level conservation agencies.

TOURISM ISSUES AND INSIGHTS
URBAN IMAGING

A major feature of Canadian and American cities is urban imaging. Contemporary imaging strategies are typically policy responses to the social and economic problems associated with changing nature of cities as a result of globalization and economic restructuring. Issues include de-industrialization, urban renewal, increased gaps between haves and have-nots, multi-culturalism, and social integration and control. The principal aims of imaging strategies are to:

- attract tourism expenditure;
- generate employment in the tourist and related industries;
- foster positive images for potential investors in the region, often by *reimaging* previous negative perceptions;
- provide an environment which will attract and retain the interest of professionals and white-collar workers, particularly in *clean* service industries such as tourism and communications;
- increase public spirit by making communities feel good about themselves.

In urban areas imaging processes are characterized by some or all of the following:

- the development of a critical mass of visitor attractions and facilities, including new buildings/prestige/flagship centers (e.g., shopping centers, stadia, sports complexes and indoor arenas, convention centers, and casino development);

Continued

United States of America

Native American cultures play an important role in US tourism product. However, a recent trend has in many ways superseded this cultural function: Indian reservation gaming. According to treaty, federally controlled American Indian reservations are *sovereign nations* and not legally part of the state in which they are located. With this as the legal framework, the Indian Gaming Regulatory Act (IGRA) was passed by the United States Congress in 1988 to allow various forms of gambling, including high-stakes casinos, to be developed on Native American lands that are under the control of the federal Bureau of Indian Affairs. Casinos could be developed on federal reservations (not state reservations) within the boundaries of states where any form of gambling was already allowed. Thus, several states that permitted lotteries or sports betting, suddenly became hosts to Native American casinos. Since 1990, hundreds of casinos have been built on Indian reservations in all parts of the country, except for Utah – the only state where all forms of betting and gambling are illegal. Foxwoods and the Mohegan Sun, two of the world's largest casinos, are located on two small Indian reservations in the state of Connecticut.

Since the 2001 terrorist attacks on New York and Washington DC, there has been a tightening of controls on the US-Canada and US-Mexico borders for fear of terrorism. Canada and Mexico are seen by the United States as having more relaxed immigration policies, and the United States has set out to protect itself from potential threats via the north and south. On September 11, 2001, immediately following the attacks, all travel into and out of the United States was halted, both United States borders were sealed and all airports and harbors were closed. This immediate sealing of the border had a critical impact on Canada and Mexico, and the intensification of border controls has created additional economic pressures for both neighbors, who are heavily dependent on US trade and tourism for their economic well being.

The most recent policy to affect Canadian and Mexican inbound tourism was the change in the US government's passport regulations, known as the Western Hemisphere Travel Initiative (WHTI). Previously, Canadians and Americans have not required a passport to visit one another's country, and Americans have not required a passport to visit or return from Mexico or to take in Caribbean cruises. As of January 2007, however, all travelers who fly into or out of the US must possess a valid passport. Travel to US overseas territories (American Samoa, Guam, Northern Marianas, Puerto Rico and the United States Virgin Islands) is not considered international, and passports are not required. The WHTI designates 2009, as the date extending the requirements for people traveling to the United States by car, boat and foot, to present a valid passport at ports and border crossings.

The Northeastern United States

The eastern United States is perhaps best known for large cities. New York City, Boston, Washington, Philadelphia and Baltimore are important international gateways and are favored destinations for domestic tourists. New York City is America's definitive city. A major transportation hub, gateway, and destination in its own right, New York is known for glamorous shopping, ethnic foods and neighborhoods, city skyline, and theater district. The most devastating terrorist attack on US soil took place in downtown Manhattan on September 11, 2001. While this event essentially annihilated tourism in New York, and virtually the entire United States, for some time, the industry has somewhat recovered, and Ground Zero, the site of the World Trade Center's twin towers, has become a major tourist destination.

Boston is an old city and home to many places of historical significance in the American Revolution and the years leading up to it. It has one of the nation's most visible urban heritage trails and has an important maritime history. The United States capital, Washington DC, is a unique political destination popular among Americans who desire to visit their nation's political history. Between the 1960s and 1980s, Baltimore's old waterfront was redeveloped into a thriving tourism, service, and recreational area. Today, it has one of the most well-known waterfront attractions in the country and is used as a model for other cities around the world who are revitalizing their derelict waterfronts. Philadelphia is home to many patriotic icons including the Liberty Bell and Independence Hall which contribute to its heritage appeal for American tourists.

Most of the nation's colonial heritage is located in the eastern US, and many of the earliest settlements have become important attractions, including reconstructed living heri-tage villages, such as Old Sturbridge Village, Plimouth Plantation, Mystic Seaport and Colonial Williamsburg. In the New England states, maritime heritage overshadows other types of patrimony. Lobster and cod fishing are synonymous with Maine. Shipyards, fishing villages, and marine aquariums are important in the tourist milieu, as are the *quaint* villages with churches and autumn colors. Skiing dominates some mountainous communities in New York, Vermont and New Hampshire. The famed witch trials of Salem, Massachusetts, and cranberry agriculture on Cape Cod are important regional heritage icons as well.

Source: Lauren A. Hall-Lew

Outside cities, the coastline and mountains are the backdrop for most recreational and tourist activities. The rugged coast of Maine in the north, and the beaches further south, in Massachusetts, Connecticut, New York, New Jersey, Virginia, Delaware, Pennsylvania and Maryland, have long been important destinations. The early 1800s nascent popularity of eastern seaboard resorts, such as Coney Island, New York; Atlantic City, New Jersey; and Ocean City, Maryland, were made even more popular and accessible in the mid-1800s by the expanding rail lines, attests to the coastline's importance. The Appalachian Mountain chain, is a focal point for much nature-based and recreational tourism. Several national parks and recreation areas are located in the Appalachians, but most obvious is the famed Appalachian Trail, which extends 3,500 km from northern Georgia to northern Maine, traversing through fourteen states. Thousands of people every year hike the trail or portions of it, spending anywhere from a single afternoon to several months.

The South
The South is a popular destination region, known for slave heritage, civil war battlefields, beaches, business travel and amusement parks. Florida is the region's most popular destination for tourists and the second most visited state in the country. Florida is home to sandy beaches, a semi-tropical climate, interesting wildlife, swamp lands, and Disneyworld and dozens of other mega theme parks. Miami is a major international gateway for flights from the Caribbean and Latin America, and

is home to a large transnational Spanish-speaking population. Most of the US-based Caribbean cruises depart from Florida.

New Orleans, Louisiana, is another important urban destination that has heritage appeal. The city is known for its music, festival (Mardi Gras), and spiritual and slave-related traditions. The New Orleans area is still a stronghold of old French Acadian culture (Cajun) with its culinary, musical and mystico-religious connotations. The city is also an important cruise destination and point of departure. In August 2005, Hurricane Katrina hit land in New Orleans, destroying thousands of homes and public buildings, killing nearly 2,000 people, and resulting in tens of billions of dollars in damage. Thousands of residents were relocated as thousands more outsiders were mobilized to assist in recovery efforts. It was the costliest and second deadliest hurricane in United States history, and as would be expected, devastated the area's tourism industry, along with most other industries. Since 2005, the old historic quarter has recovered and tourists are once again arriving, though the city has a long way to go in reconstructing residential housing and public buildings.

Plantation and slave heritage, together with the Civil War legacy in the southern states, has received a great deal of attention in recent years among scholars and tourists, particularly African-Americans, as plantations, slave cabins, museums, and the homes of prominent African-Americans have been restored and promoted as tourist attractions. In the past these sites have kept hidden the true conditions under which slaves lived and worked, but public cries for truth in heritage interpretation have begun to effect more realistic portrayals of slave life and death. Although the United States is embarrassed by its slave past, it is beginning to come to terms with it through history, story-telling, heritage management and site interpretation. Thus, the *whitewashed* south is seen as becoming more balanced in its treatment of history. Hundreds of thousands of Civil War enthusiasts, not all of them Americans, travel to the south to involve themselves in battle re-enactments or simply to visit the battlefields and other sites associated with this 1860s conflict.

The southeastern coasts are home to many beach and golf resort developments and vacation homes. Offshore gambling, also known as casino cruises, have become popular in southeastern states where high-stakes gaming typically is not allowed. These casino cruises embark from ports in Georgia and Florida, travel just outside United States territorial waters (12 nautical miles) and float as passengers enjoy an afternoon or evening of gaming.

The Midwest

The middle portion of the United States possesses the largest and most voluminous rivers and lakes in the country. The tourism and recreational role of these water bodies is clear. Sailing, fishing, water skiing and jet skiing are popular pastimes on the Great Lakes of the upper Midwest. Several of America's largest and most important industrial cities developed on the shores of the Great Lakes, including Chicago, Detroit and Cleveland, owing to the navigability of the lakes in relation to the St. Lawrence River and the transportation of industrial products. These cities are all important international air gateways, airline hubs, and highway and railroad exchanges. The region's great rivers (Mississippi, Missouri, Ohio) have played a vital role in the history of United States industrial growth and transportation.

Previously an important method of transportation, river boats on the Mississippi and Ohio Rivers have become attractions, not just for their nostalgic value, but for their role in the gambling sector. Several states do not permit gaming on land, but they do on water. Once the river boats leave dock, the casinos open their tables and slots, navigate up and down the rivers, and close up shop before returning to the riverbank. Indian gaming is also important on reservations in the Midwest, and several of the Indian reservations in places like Minnesota were among the first to establish casinos following the passing of the IGRA.

Because the upper Midwest states have a long history of heavy industry, the region has become known for its industrial heritage. This sub-theme within heritage tourism focuses on factories, waterfronts and dockyards, mines, canals, and other infrastructure and enterprises associated with the history of manufacturing or resource extraction. This region is best known for steel mills and automobile assembly plants, and associated museums, such as the Henry Ford Museum and Greenfield Village in Michigan.

Among the most prominent elements of human geography in the midwest is agriculture. The agricultural heritage includes dairy products, corn, wheat, oats, soybeans, pork, beef, cotton, fruits and vegetables. Like wineries in Northern California, the cheese factories of the upper Midwest attract many people to visit the farm, observe the production process, and sample and purchase the final product. The ethnic heritage of the Midwest includes Swedes, Finns, Norwegians, Dutch, Germans, Czechs, Poles and Irish who arrive throughout the 19th and early 20th centuries.

These two heritages, agriculture and ethnic migration, have resulted in a vast array of food-based and ethnically oriented festivals and events. The Turkey Festival, National Cherry Festival, Strawberry Days, Watermelon Festival, Pork Days, Platteville Dairy Days, Sparta Butterfest and the Great Wisconsin Cheese Festival are only a few examples of the hundreds of annual community events that commemorate the region's agricultural importance. Similarly, from a cultural perspective, Tulip Time, the Wilber Czech Festival, Finnfest, German Folk Fest, St. Patrick's Day Parade and Pub Crawl, Høstfest, Midsommar Festival Swedish Days and Polish Fest are an important part of the immigrant landscape that draws visitors from around the US and Canada, as well as from the homelands of these diasporic peoples. Nearly every city, town, and other settlement, no matter how small, boasts some kind of agricultural fair or ethnic festival to increase its tourism potential and assert its heritage identity.

The Mountain West and Southwest

The western and southwestern regions of the US are endowed with high mountains, grasslands, and barren deserts. This varying physiography has laid the foundation for the highest concentration of national parks and monuments in the United States. Over 67 percent of the territory of the state of Utah, for example, is owned by the federal government, much of it in national parks and other protected uses. Bryce Canyon, Carlsbad Caverns, Glacier, Grand Canyon, Grand Teton, Joshua Tree, Rocky Mountain, Saguaro, Yellowstone, Yosemite and Zion are among the most popular national parks in the US and located in this western region. Likewise, tucked in the Rocky Mountains system are many of the country's finest ski resorts and exclusive mountain getaways, especially in Colorado, Utah and Idaho are the most famous prominent ski destinations in the country.

The themes of most cultural attractions in this region are Native American lifestyles and archeology, cattle ranches, cowboys, mines and ghost towns, and the Spanish-American borderlands. Indian ruins are featured prominently in many National Park Service properties, and several reservations today invite tourists to their dances,

PHOTO 5.7

Telluride ski resort in the rocky mountains of Colorado. The old mining town of Telluride is located in the valley below the ski area

Source: Alan A. Lew

foodways and music. The region's ranching traditions have given rise to numerous dude ranches and guest-oriented cattle drives, wherein visitors are permitted to assist in feeding and caring for animals and working on large farms. Ranching, cowboys, mining and ghost towns are all inter-related heritage features of the west. Mining locations, such as Tombstone, Arizona, and Virginia City, Nevada, epitomize old stereotypes where cowboys and outlaws ruled the Wild West. These communities have based their tourism industries on their Wild West cowboy image, although their degree of authenticity has often been questioned and resulted in significant public debates in recent years.

In addition to defunct mines, active mines in Arizona, Colorado, Montana, Nevada, Utah and Wyoming, have become salient industrial heritage attractions, offering guided tours and souvenir shops, which are merely incidental to the mines' primary function and are seen as a public-relations tool to demonstrate to the public the important role of mining in everyday life and to show how they are not negatively affecting the environment.

A distinctive form of heritage tourism is religious tourism. Hundreds of Native American sites and natural places in the western states have been identified as important New Age spiritual attractions, where nature worshippers and other animists travel to experience the powers of Mother Earth. Most notable of these is Sedona, Arizona, known to some worshippers as the New Age capital of the world. Several holy sites associated with the Catholic Church have become significant religious destinations in

Arizona and New Mexico, and Salt Lake City, Utah, is the headquarters of the Church of Jesus Christ of Latter-day Saints and a chief destination for the church's 12 million strong global population.

The southwest, particularly southern Utah, Arizona, southern New Mexico and western Texas, has become a highly desirable winter destination for *snowbirds* from the north – retirees who spend the warm summer months in the north and the cold winter months in the southwest. The population of the greater Phoenix region of Arizona, for example, swells by approximately 300,000 between December and March each year. Spending by these temporary residents is estimated to inject over a billion dollars in the local Arizona economy each winter. Snowbirds in Arizona and Texas often travel to nearby Mexican border towns for medications, dentures, dental services, and physician care that are a fraction of their cost in the US. Other travelers appreciate the warm winters of the southwest, which has become a haven for golfers and sun, sea and sand tourists, minus the sea, but with mega-resort development.

The Pacific Coast

This region includes California, Oregon, Washington, Alaska and Hawaii. Contrary to most people's images of Alaska and Hawaii, people can snow ski in Hawaii and lay on the warm beaches of southern Alaska. Alaska's main draw is its wild and remote setting, separated from the rest of the United States by Canada. It is possible to drive from the mainland United States to Alaska through British Columbia and the Yukon, but the majority of people arrive by air and cruiseship. The state's unique selling propositions are its arctic climate, glaciers, abundant wildlife, scenic mountain parks, and unique native cultures. Dog sled races, skiing, ice fishing and snowmobile racing are popular winter activities, and the state's cities – Juneau, Fairbanks, and Anchorage – are becoming more popular business travel and special events destinations.

Hawaii, while not in the top 10 destination states, is a mysterious place in the minds of most Americans and a desirable destination. The newest state in the union, it is one of the country's favored wedding and honeymoon destinations, owing to its tropical climate, beaches, lush rainforest and many resorts. In addition to domestic visitors, Hawaii is a favorite destination for Japanese and Korean tourists, whose primary goal on the island is to shop. From an academic perspective, Hawaii is often cited as an example of how tourism (beginning with early explorers, traders, missionaries and whale hunters) can change a destination in both positive and negative ways. Waterfalls, volcanoes, vegetation and dramatic coastlines are natural foundations of the tourism sector, while World War II heritage is appealing to most Japanese and American visitors, especially veterans of that war. Agritourism is important in Hawaii, as visitors tour pineapple plantations and banana farms.

As already noted with Alaska and Hawaii, nature plays a critical role in tourism in the far western United States. Volcanic activity, including the destructive 1980 Mount St. Helens eruption, is a fact of life along America's Pacific Rim. Many mountains and craters through Washington and Oregon are volcanic in origin and play a major role in tourism as hiking venues, ski resorts and parklands. The countless islands in Washington's Puget Sound are focal points for recreational second homes. The entire coast from British Columbia to central California is an important linear attraction for people traveling along its length. This is an important corridor for camping trips and scenic drives.

California

California is the country's most visited state, and tourist expenditures are highest there. Amusement parks are a trademark of southern California, with Disneyland leading the way since its opening in 1995. The creation and success of Disneyland has spurred the development of theme parks, especially Disney theme parks around the world. While European colonization was taking place on the east coast, Spanish explorers and missionaries were penetrating deep into the territory that is today Northern California. Historic missions and churches are what remains from these explorer days. Other heritage resources include mining ghost towns and Hollywood studios where many movies and television shows have been filmed. Film-induced tourism is important for the Los Angeles region; it includes studio tours, famous film locations and tours to stars' homes. Near San Francisco, Sonoma Valley and Napa Valley are world-renown wine-growing regions, and their products have been distributed throughout the world for many years. This heritage of viticulture forms the backdrop for a thriving culinary and wine tourism sector in northern California.

California's largest cities are important international ports of entry for air and sea travelers. Many cruises along Mexico's west coast originate in Los Angeles or San Diego, and San Francisco is a major port of departure for cruises to western Canada and Alaska. Los Angeles, the second largest city in the US, is a major conference center, shopping venue and urban destination. The San Diego suburb, San Ysidro, abuts the Mexican border town of Tijuana. Tijuana and San Diego are closely linked by history, culture, economics and modern transportation. San Diego's promotional literature includes cross-border visits to Tijuana, expressing the role of the Mexican city in *greater San Diego*. Sea World and the San Diego Zoo are San Diego's most visible icons. As the spiritual capital of the *Left Coast*, San Francisco has a distinguished itself as a significant gay and lesbian tourist destination. The city hosts many of the word's best attended gay events, including the annual San Francisco Pride Event. Chinatown is also a salient feature of San Francisco. It is one of the earliest and largest Chinatowns in North America and is popular for its food selection, shops and interesting cultural landscape.

Canada

As already noted in this section, North America is a vast territory that transects many climatic, topographic and vegetative zones. Canada, geographically the second largest country in the world, exemplifies this pattern. The diverse physical and human geographies of Canada give the country its tourist appeal. In the west, tourism is based largely on mountains, aboriginal cultures and European settlement. In the mid-portion of Canada, tourism focuses on indigenous people and agriculture-based heritage. Ontario and Quebec are seen as the heartland and original points of European *discovery* and settlement, and are well established cultural heritage destinations, especially pertaining to Canadian national heritage and Franco-Canadian identity. East of Quebec, in the Atlantic Provinces, tourism is largely oriented toward the Atlantic Ocean and its resources, such as fishing, and the cultural landscapes created by maritime trade, fishing villages, rugged coastal and forest scenery, and European settlement. The far north is home to vast expanses of arctic wilderness, giving it a significant nature-based tourism appeal.

Like its southern neighbor, Canada faces many aboriginal (First Nations) issues in relation to tourism. Gaming on First Nations lands has been a focal point of tourism development in recent years, and aboriginal land rights have been a primary focus in legislation within and outside of tourism debates.

Canada and the United States have long been major trading partners and traditionally have had interdependent economies. One aspect of this has been the phenomenon of cross-border trade and shopping. For decades, Canadians have crossed into the United States to shop, but in the early 1990s, when the Canadian dollar gained significant strength against the US dollar, the phenomenon grew to incredible heights, with some 60 million Canadians visiting American border communities in 1991 for the express purpose of shopping. Reasons for this growth among Canadians were favorable exchange rates, lower taxes in the United States, a wider variety of products south of the border, and higher-quality goods and services. American border towns thrived on this deluge of people and money coming from the north, and new retail landscapes were created to cater to their northern neighbors' desires.

However, by the mid-1990s, the Canadian dollar lost much of its competitive value, making it more expensive to shop abroad. However, with this turn, a reverse pattern occurred as Americans began shopping north of the border for items that became a better value with the strength of the US dollar. A primary form of United States-Canada border tourism is pharmaceutical purchasing, where Americans cross to buy prescription medications for a fraction of their cost in the United States. Meanwhile, the weakening of the US dollar in the late 2000s has once again reversed the shopping migration in favor of the Canadian shoppers coming to the US.

British Columbia

Canada's westernmost province is British Columbia (BC), which possesses some of the most notable mountain scenery in North America. There are many national and provincial parks in British Columbia that attract millions of visitors each year. Skiing is especially popular, and many world-class resorts have been built since the 1960s. The Okanagan Valley is also growing in significance as a wine and food tourism destination, as is Vancouver Island and the Gulf Islands that lie between Vancouver Island and the mainland. Canadian native culture is an important tourist draw on Vancouver Island, along with the rainforests that the native had depended on for centuries.

Urban tourism is concentrated in Vancouver, the province's largest city, and Victoria, its capital. Both cities are noted for the quality of their lifestyle. Regular ferries ply between Vancouver Island and the mainland, and the populated southwest corner of British Columbia is in many ways more connected to the United States than to the rest of Canada. Tourism in BC's sparsely populated far north is based on natural areas with their accompanying fishing and hunting. British Columbia is also an important cruise destination. Many west coast cruises from San Francisco and Seattle stop in Victoria or Vancouver on their way to Alaska.

The Prairie Provinces

Alberta, Manitoba, and Saskatchewan comprise the prairie provinces of Canada, although the westernmost portion of Alberta lies in the Rocky Mountains. These provinces are the breadbasket of Canada, producing most of the grains and other agricultural products for the entire country and for export abroad. There is also a unique migration history, particularly from Ukraine and other Eastern European

PHOTO 5.8

A walk across the capilano suspension bridge is a popular tourist experience in Vancouver, British Columbia

Source: Alan A. Lew

countries, that has left its footprint on the social and physical environment of the region. Like the US Midwest, these ethnic and agricultural heritages have led to the growth of many ethnic and food-based festivals. Likewise Parks Canada and the individual provinces maintain a large number of cultural sites that highlight the human past of the region. Native Canadians still live in reservations in the region and have begun utilizing their heritage as a tourism product and capitalizing on Canada's gaming laws that allow casinos on First Nations reservations. Cattle ranching history also plays an important role in the region's tourism industry; the Calgary Stampede, for instance, was first held in 1912 and has since become the largest rodeo in the world.

The Prairie Provinces reach from the United States border northward into the sub-arctic and taiga northlands, including the vast Canadian Shield. The northern half of the provinces is sparsely populated and strewn with lakes, rivers and vast forests, providing many outdoor opportunities for recreational fishers and hunters. Some of the world's largest national parks lie in northern Canada. The far north has little by way of road and transportation infrastructure, although it is possible to drive the entire length of Alberta and into the Northwest Territories. Many of the water bodies are favored by recreationists because of their relative isolation; floatplanes are the most commonly used mode of long-distance transportation.

Several international attractions lie astride the United States-Canada border in this region. The International Peace Garden on the border of Manitoba and North Dakota (USA) is a botanical park divided by the international border but united as a monument to peaceful relations between the two countries. It is one of the most popular attractions in Manitoba. Against the Saskatchewan–North Dakota border are a few provincial parks and other protected areas. On the border of Alberta and Montana (USA) is located the Waterton-Glacier International Peace Park, comprised of Glacier National Park, in the US, and Waterton Lakes National Park, Canada.

Ontario

Ontario is the home of Canada's capital, Ottawa, and its largest city, Toronto. The cities are the hallmark of Ontario's tourism industry, with thriving business and stock market exchanges, theaters and arts, and ethnic communities. Toronto is home to strong Chinese, Italian, Greek and Portuguese ethnic communities that add appeal to the city with food, festivals and culture. The outbreak of SARS (severe acute respiratory syndrome) had a drastic impact on Toronto's tourism sector in 2003, when dozens of cases were reported in the city, leading to thousands of canceled bookings and an estimated loss of half a billion dollars in tourism revenue. Even though the situation was largely under control and the outbreaks were limited to hospitals, the situation was exacerbated by the World Health Organization's release of a worldwide warning against non-essential travel to Toronto.

Ontario's vast rural areas have become trendy destinations as well, especially former agricultural villages in the southwest that have been transformed into popular tourist-shopping villages. St. Jacobs is one of the most notable. It is the center of Mennonite Country, where old-order Mennonites still dress, farm, drive carriages, and perform their traditional religion, language and agricultural practices. Another notable rural activity in Ontario is wine tourism, which is mostly concentrated in the Niagara Falls region. Famous for its unique ice wines, the Niagara wine country has become popular for winery and vineyard tours, and its products are exported all over the world.

Second home ownership is a salient phenomenon in various parts of the province, particularly on lakeshores around Georgian Bay and Muskoka. Canadians from all over country and even Americans when their dollar is strong, come to the region to purchase vacation properties in the woodlands and lakeshores of Ontario. The rural, agricultural landscape of the area is an important part of heritage as well, which comes in many forms. War of 1812 battle sites along the Niagara and St. Lawrence Rivers appeal to history buffs, while colonial and indigenous heritages are exemplified in outdoor living museums. Canadian national heritage is preserved in an array of museums and monuments in Ottawa and Toronto.

Niagara Falls is probably the province's best-known landmark. The United States-Canada border bisects the falls, with nearly all of Horseshoe Falls being located in Canada. The town of Niagara Falls, Ontario, is one of Canada's premier destinations, and has been the subject of much geographical inquiry into how tourist destinations develop into measurable zones of intensity. By all accounts, Niagara Falls, Ontario, is more appealing to tourists than its cross-border counterpart, Niagara Falls, New York. The US side of the falls has been described by several observers as a *backdoor* to the United States, where power plants, factories and heavy industry dominate, and the community is old and in a state of disrepair. The Canadian side, however, is seen as Canada's *front door*, which is reflected in the falls and riverfront being designated a provincial park, well groomed, and more inviting than its US neighbor. In spite of this, the Ontario town is often criticized by academics as being too touristy and overdeveloped with souvenir shops, cheap restaurants, and tacky museums and other peripheral attractions.

Quebec

Since the mid-20th century, there has been a movement in the Canadian province of Quebec to separate itself from Canada and become an independent country. Through the 1960s, 1970s and 1980s, this movement gained momentum as more and more French-speaking Canadians became interested in sovereignty for their *homeland*, because they felt their unique language and culture were not receiving the recognition and prioritization they deserved in the federal model of Canada. Several referenda have been held over the years wherein the public have been able to voice their vote on whether or not to secede from Canada. While there has yet to be a majority yes vote in favor of secession, support appears to be growing with each successive referendum, which might mean that in future efforts, a majority vote could lead the province to declare independence from Canada. If the separation ever comes to fruition, it will have important implications for tourism. Namely, questions about whether or not Quebec will continue to use the Canadian dollar and the Canadian national banking system will need to be addressed. Citizenship, passports, and the right to cross borders into Canada and the US will also be salient points of negotiation. Likewise, the establishment of customs and immigration posts on Quebec's new international boundaries and its potential membership in NAFTA would need to be addressed. These are only a few of the many issues that would need to be addressed, and that reflect directly on tourism, if Quebec were to go its own way from Canada.

Montreal and Quebec City are the two centers of tourism in the province. Quebec City, the provincial capital, is one of the oldest European settlements in North America, and its old town (*Vieux-Québec*) was inscribed on the UNESCO World Heritage List in 1985. Heritage is a major resource in Quebec City; many of its buildings date from the 17th century, and the city has a distinct European ambiance. Its position on the St. Lawrence River has facilitated economic growth for hundreds of years and today allows cruise ships to visit. Montreal is Canada's second largest city and an important heritage destination. The old town, harbourfront, and Olympic Park are important components of Montreal tourism. Scenic French-Canadian rural landscapes, where little English is spoken, contribute to the appeal of the province as a destination. Skiing is a popular winter pastime, primarily for domestic tourists, near Quebec City in the Laurentian Mountains.

The Atlantic Provinces

While the four Atlantic provinces of Canada (Nova Scotia, New Brunswick, Prince Edward Island and Newfoundland and Labrador) are among the least affluent areas of Canada, they are among the most scenic, culturally rich and desirable destinations in the country. Rugged coastlines, thick forests, lakes and rivers, lighthouses, and small fishing villages are trademarks of the region. Newfoundland and Labrador is the easternmost province and home to several unique national parks. Iceberg sighting and whale watching are popular tourist activities, and the UNESCO-designated L'Anse aux Meadows, the site of the first European (Viking) landing and settlement in the Americas, typically draws some 30,000 people a year.

Prince Edward Island (PEI) is a good example of a literary heritage destination in North America. The province, located off the coast of New Brunswick and Nova Scotia, is known as the location of the Anne of Green Gables books and television series. It is especially popular among Japanese, Canadian, American and European tourists. Until the mid-1990s, the only way to arrive in PEI was by boat or air. However, in 1996, the 13-km long Confederation Bridge was finished to link PEI with New Brunswick and the rest of Canada. As another alternative means of travel the new bridge has resulted in a growth in visitation levels since its completion. PEI markets itself as North America's *Island Experience*, and offers biking and hiking trails, national park walks and picnics, windsurfing and lighthouses.

Nova Scotia and New Brunswick are perhaps Canada's best examples of maritime and fishing heritage. Small fishing villages, many of which have been the settings for TV series and motion pictures, attract visitors to their dockyards and shipyards, shopping zones, seafood restaurants and lighthouses. Many of the historic communities still survive largely on fishing and tourism. Nova Scotia is also a hub of genealogy and family history research, for the area was one of the primary immigration points in Canada and all of North America. The province estimates that approximately 25 million North Americans can trace their roots back to Nova Scotia since the 16th century. The province is home to Scottish, Acadian (French Canadian), and indigenous Mi'kmaq cultures that are still manifest in everyday life and form the foundation of heritage tourism. Ethnic festivals, music, food, dance, and folklore are important components of tourism in these provinces, and New Brunswick is endowed with thick forests and rivers that have become a focal area for scenic drives and historic routes.

The Northern Territories

In addition to its ten provinces, Canada is home to three territories: Nunavut, the Northwest Territories and the Yukon Territory. Most of the area's population is located in a few medium-size towns and cities (e.g., Iqaluit, Yellowknife, and Whitehorse) that serve as territorial capitals and regional trade centers. The rural population is scattered throughout the north in small, isolated villages, where travel is done exclusively by airplane, and where residents supplement their grocery stores with seal, walrus, polar bear and caribou hunting. Owing to physical limitations and lack of demand, few roads exist, most of them extending only a few kilometers outside of regional towns. Travel in the far north is extremely expensive, with even short flights often costing thousands of dollars. As a result, most northern travel is done by residents themselves, who sometimes receive government travel assistance, and affluent tourists who desire to experience the vast arctic national parks, indigenous Inuit culture, or fishing and hunting. Inuit (Eskimo) culture is appealing to many people,

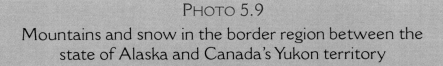

Source: Alan A. Lew

and winter guests can enjoy dog-sledding and snowmobiling tours, as well as igloo stays. In the Yukon Territory around Dawson, gold rush heritage is heavily promoted, and people travel there to try their own hand at gold panning.

Other Countries in North America

Most people are unaware that there are other countries located within the geographical reaches of North America. Saint Pierre et Miquelon (population 7,000), a territory (overseas territorial collectivity) of France is a small group of islands off the coast of Newfoundland and is the last remnant of France's North American possessions. Cod fishing has traditionally been the economic mainstay of the islands, but with the forced reduction in fishing activity in the 1990s Cod Wars with the US, the islands have become more dependent on tourism. As part of France in North America, Saint Pierre et Miquelon is becoming a more popular cruise stopover and shopping destination. Canadians are the islands' biggest market; they come to purchase French products (e.g., perfumes), French food, and French lifestyle without having to travel to Europe.

Greenland, *the world's largest island*, is located off the northeast coast of Canada. The island is a self-governing territory of Denmark and is home to a large Inuit population that still depends on fishing and hunting for much of its subsistence. Most travel to Greenland is undertaken by Danes, although new air connections to the United States are expected to increase American arrivals. The island also has close air links with Iceland, and many visitors arrive in east Greenland on short trips from there. Cruise ships visit Greenland's western communities along with Canada's Arctic islands.

Most of Greenlands is an impenetrable ice cap, with the population occupying the green coastal zones. Passenger ships ply coastal waters, and most remote communities are serviced by regularly scheduled flights. In the winter, visitors can sleep in a hotel constructed completely of snow and ice, play winter ice golf, and tour by dog sled. During the non-winter months, tourists tour the fjords and small coastal islands, and gaze at migrating whales and icebergs. Viking archeological sites and Inuit culture are the basis of Greenland's cultural heritage.

Although Bermuda is not officially part of North America (it is better classified as a mid-Atlantic island), it is often considered part of North America, being 620 miles (1,000 km) off the US coast. It is better connected to the US than Europe. Bermuda (a territory of the United Kingdom) is an expensive destination and geared toward an affluent clientele who stay in apartments, bed and breakfasts, or beachfront resorts. To reduce tourism's ecological and social impacts, there are no rental cars on the island, so local transportation must be done by scooter, taxi, or horse-drawn carriage. Bermuda resembles its British colonial cousins in the Caribbean in terms of architecture, population, culture, and festivals, and it has become a popular port of call for cruises from the United States.

5.2   LATIN NORTH AMERICA

Physical Geography of Latin North America

Latin North America consists of three major geographic subregions: (1) the country of Mexico, (2) Central America (also known as Meso-America) and (3) the Caribbean Sea (also known as the West Indies). Central America includes the countries of Guatemala, Belize, Honduras, El Salvador, Nicaragua, Costa Rica and Panama. As noted in the introduction to this section, physical geography transcends the boundary between Anglo and Latin North America, so there is some overlap of the discussion of Latin North America's physical geography with that in the previous section. In particular, the subregions of Latin North America share many of the physical geography characteristic of the southern portions of Anglo North America. The two major physiographic regions of Latin North America are (Figure 5.4):

1. The Mountains and Basins, which extend south from Anglo North America's Rocky Mountains and Basins and Plateaus and
2. The Caribbean Sea and Gulf of Mexico, including the large islands of the Greater Antilles and the smaller islands of the Lesser Antilles, which together are known as the West Indies.

The mountains of Mexico and Central America are closely related to the Rocky Mountains, being formed by the collision of the North American continent with several plates that make up the Pacific Ocean floor in this region. Mexico's Sierra Madre Occidental (west) and Sierra Madre Oriental (east) are extensions of the

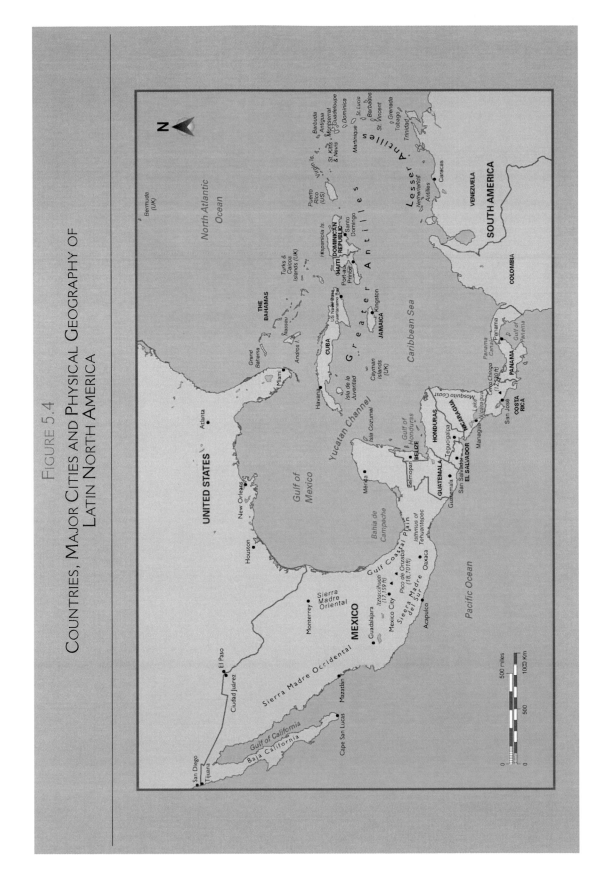

FIGURE 5.4

COUNTRIES, MAJOR CITIES AND PHYSICAL GEOGRAPHY OF LATIN NORTH AMERICA

Rocky Mountains into Mexico, while the Sierra Madre Del Sur (south) transitions to the highlands of Central America, and then down to the Andes Mountains in South America. The Sierra Madre Occidental and Oriental are heavily folded (like the Appalachians), while the Sierra Madre Del Sur is mostly igneous (volcanic). All of these mountain ranges are part of the Alpine Orogeny, which is the current geologic period of mountain building, starting about 80 millions years ago. The islands of the Caribbean, from southeast Cuba and Hispaniola southward, are also part of this Alpine Orogeny and are geologically connected to the highlands of Central America and the northern Andes in South America.

The northern Mexico portion of the North American continent is sliding laterally against the Pacific Ocean Plate, similar to the situation in California. The major difference here, however, is that Baja California, which is on the Pacific Ocean Plate, along with the city of Los Angeles in the United States, is slowly breaking away from North America as it moves northward. Some models predict that it will completely break away from the North America mainland in the geologic future. South of Baja California there is a separate ocean plate, the Cocos Plate, that is subducting directly under southern Mexico and the entire Central America region. This is similar to the Juan de Fuca Plate in the United States Pacific Northwest, except that the number of active volcanoes and frequency of earthquake activity is much greater on the south west coast of Mexico and Central America than in Oregon and Washington.

The Basin and Range landscape of Nevada and Arizona extends into northern Mexico with its high-elevation plateaus, older mountains that have eroded into low-lying hills, and internal drainage basins with sand dunes and flat playas. This area between the Sierra Madre Occidental and Sierra Madre Oriental is known as the *Mexican Plateau* as it increases in elevation toward central Mexico, around Mexico City. The Mexican Plateau is the heart of Mexico. It is about 700 miles (1,130 km) long and ranges from 4000 to 8000 ft (1220 to 2440 m) in elevation. Most of the Mexican Plateau is arid, with climatic conditions similar to the US Southwest. Rainfall, however, increases further south toward Central America, where the summer rains from the equatorial intertropical convergence zone (ITCZ) are more pronounced.

Like the Great Basin to the north, most of the drainage basins on the Mexican Plateau drain internally and have no outlet to the sea. Mexico City, one of the world's largest cities (over 22 million people), is located in one of these basins. A few large rivers drain from the plateau into the Gulf of Mexico in the east and the Gulf of California in the west. A chain of extinct volcanoes is located in the vicinity of Mexico City, including Citlaltepétl (also known as Orizaba) which, at 18,700 ft (5,700 m), is the highest peak in Mexico. South of Mexico City, the Sierra Madre Occidental and Sierra Madre Oriental converge in a jumbled mass of mountains called the Sierra Madre del Sur.

South of the Sierra Madre del Sur is a break in the mountains known as the Istmo de Tehuantepec. This isthmus is 135 miles across and is used by some to define the boundary between Mexico and *Central America*, because the climate, geology and culture of the region to the south is distinct from that of both Mexico and Anglo North America to the north. Here, the Mexican state of Chiapas, with its large Mayan Indian population, borders the country of Guatemala. The highlands of Central America share the west-to-east trending mountain system that created the Greater Antilles islands in the Caribbean Sea (Cuba, Hispaniola and Puerto Rico). These mountains of folded sedimentary rock, uplifted by the collision of South America and North America, extend along the southern coast of the Yucatan Peninsula, then under the Caribbean Sea and over to the Greater Antilles and then down the Lesser Antilles islands.

The Caribbean

The Caribbean islands, also known as the West Indies, stretch in an arch from Cuba and the Bahamas to the north coast of South America. They are divided into the larger islands to the north and west, known as the Greater Antilles, and the smaller, more volcanic islands to the southeast, known as the Lesser Antilles. This chain of islands separates the Caribbean Sea from the Atlantic Ocean. Northwest of the Caribbean Sea is the Gulf of Mexico, which is enclosed by Mexico's Yucatan Peninsula, the island of Cuba, and the Florida Peninsula. The Gulf of Mexico is an extension of the North American Interior Lowlands and Gulf Coast Plain, which includes much of northeastern Mexico, Mexico's Yucatan Peninsula, most of Cuba, the Bahama Islands, and Florida. All of these areas have very low elevations and, along with the lower-elevation islands, are seriously threatened by rising sea levels due to global warming.

The Caribbean islands were formed by the complex collision of several small ocean floor tectonic plates that were pushed together by the northward movement of South America into North America starting about 70 million years ago. Some of the islands are former sea beds, while others are volcanic in origin. Earthquakes and volcanic activity remain a frequent occurrence in the region, which occasionally result in major disasters.

The islands of the Greater Antilles were once a single mountain range that was forced upward by plate tectonics and was connected to the highlands of Guatemala and Honduras in Central America. Today, it includes the islands of Cuba (the largest island in the Caribbean), Jamaica, Hispaniola (containing the countries of Haiti and the Dominican Republic), Puerto Rico (a commonwealth territory of the United States), and the Virgin Islands (which are divided between a British part and an American part). The highest elevation in the Caribbean is Duarte Peak, in the Dominican Republic, at 10,400 ft (3,170 m). All of the Greater Antilles islands have mountainous centers that are surrounded by relatively broad coastal plains. Coral reefs are also common off the coasts of these large islands. The valleys of the ancient mountain range are now submerged below sea level, with the deepest place in the Caribbean being the Cayman Trench (25,200 ft; 7680 m deep) between Cuba and Jamaica.

The Lesser Antilles lie to the southeast of the Greater Antilles and generally mark the outer edge of the North American continental shelf. The Lesser Antilles have two types of islands. An inner, western ring of larger islands (from Saint Kitts and Montserrat in the north to St. Vincent and Grenada in the south) are more mountainous and volcanic (known as *high islands*). An outer, eastern ring (including Anguilla, St. Martin, Barbuda and Antigua in the north, and Barbados in the south) consists of *low islands* that are mostly limestone sitting atop the stubs of eroded volcanoes and other rocks. The Lesser Antilles are also divided into the Leeward (meaning downwind) Islands in the north and the Windward Islands in the south and facing closer to the ITCZ rains. The Lesser Antilles are more volcanic because they area located in a subduction zone facing the Atlantic Ocean.

Other islands are also considered part of the Caribbean, but are not part of the Antilles. These include the Bahamas (which are low-lying limestone and coral reef islands on the continental shelf to the southeast of Florida), Trinidad and Tobago and the Netherlands Antilles (which are geologically part of South America), and Bermuda (a British territory that is actually a mid-Atlantic island) and was discussed in the Anglo North America section.

Climate of Latin North America

Throughout Latin North America the predominant wind movement is from east (Atlantic Ocean) to west, which is the opposite of the predominant pattern in Anglo North America. The major influence on the region is the ITCZ which is a belt of low pressure and rainy weather that roughly follows the equator around the globe. The ITCZ moves northward, following the sun, in North America's summer months, bringing more rain throughout Latin North America, as well as hurricanes. In the winter months, the ITCZ moves southward toward the Amazon Basin in South America. This is the dry season for all of Mexico. Central America and the Caribbean receive less rain at this time of the year, though some precipitation still occurs throughout the season, and temperatures remain very warm producing rainforest vegetation. In addition, many of the taller and larger islands of the Caribbean are affected by altitudinal zonation and rain shadow effects, with cooler peaks, more rain on their windward sides and arid conditions on their leeward side. These conditions make the winter season in the Caribbean and Central America ideal for holiday makers in the northern latitudes of Anglo North America and Europe who are looking for warmer weather.

In the far north of Latin North America, northern Mexico has dry and desert-like conditions throughout the year, with cooler winter temperatures, similar to the border areas of the United States. The high elevation and low latitude of the Mexican Plateau gives Mexico City mild weather conditions throughout the year. In the far south of Latin North America, the tropical rainforests are more dense, though much of them have been cut for forestry products. Precipitation is also more common throughout the year on the southernmost Caribbean islands, close to South America.

Hurricanes

Starting in June each year, the collision of warm air masses off the coast of West Africa in the Atlantic Ocean gives rise to low pressure air systems that move toward the Caribbean Sea. About one hundred of these swirls become *tropical disturbances*, and about a dozen of those become *tropical storms*. When the winds in these storms reach 74 miles per hour (119 km per hour) they are classified as Category 1 hurricanes. (The same phenomenon in several other parts of the world is called a *typhoons* and *cyclones*.) When a hurricane hits land it quickly looses its source of energy – the warm waters of the tropical and subtropical ocean and seas – and dies out, though winds can remain quite strong far inland. The hurricane season lasts through the end of November, when the warm air masses shift further southward.

Hurricane Alley is the name given to the Caribbean region just south of the Greater Antilles and up through the Gulf of Mexico that receives more tropical summer storms and hurricanes than anywhere else in the Americas. At least six hurricanes a year take this path, typically affecting the Yucatan Peninsula and making landfall in Texas or Louisiana, though they could also land in Mexico or Florida. Alternatively, some hurricanes approach North America to the north of the Greater Antilles and then turn up the east coast of Florida, sometimes making landfall as far north as New York City.

A large hurricane can have devastating impacts on human settlements and the natural flora and fauna of the places in its path. Because of the nearness of South America to Africa, only the northernmost portions of that continent is ever affected by hurricanes (which are called *cyclones* in South America). Unfortunately, the hurricane season occurs during the summer holiday season for North Americans, which can cause trip cancellations when inclement weather is forecast. Hurricanes are also found in the Pacific Ocean side of North America, and on rare occasions they hit Hawaii and bring strong winds and rains to Baja California in Mexico and southern California.

Human Geography and Tourism of Latin North America

Mexico

The country of Mexico is officially known as Estados Unidos Mexicanos (United Mexican States). It has a population of 105 million (July 2004), more than half of whom live in the center of the country on the Mexican Plateau. The more arid north and the tropical south are sparsely settled, except for several large cities on the United States-Mexican border. In recent decades, Mexico has experiences a large migration from the countryside to the cities. Two out of three Mexicans now live in cities, and while some agriculture is still practiced, the petroleum industry and tourism have become the country's two most important economic sectors. The name *Mexico* comes from *Mexica*, which was an alternative name for the Aztecs. Prior to European contact, Mexico City was the center of the Aztec civilization, one of the most advanced in the New World. The Aztec culture dominated central Mexico from the 14th to 16th centuries. The Aztecs had a complex culture in which feudal-like lords paid tribute to a central authority, often referred to as the Aztec emperor.

Like many early civilizations, the central rulers were spiritually responsible for the predictability and success of the annual agricultural cycle. To do this, the Aztecs developed a very precise calendar, which had 365 days in a year, combined with a 260-day ritual cycle. Together, these two cycles created a 52 year cycle that was similar to a century in the modern calendar. The Aztec cities demonstrated highly advanced architectural design, irrigation technology and social organization. Their capital city, of Tenochtitlan, was built on islands in Lake Texcoco. Today, the lake is gone and the valley is the site of Mexico City.

Hernan Cortes landed in Mexico in 1517 and named it New Spain. Montezuma II, the Aztec emperor at the time that Cortes landed, thought that Cortes was the god-king, Quetzalcoatl. Cortes used this confusion to overthrow Montezuma and conquer the Aztecs. The Spanish brought smallpox and other communicable diseases to Mexico, which killed up to 90 percent of the estimated 25 to 30 million Indians who inhabited Mexico and Central America at the time of European contact. For the next 300 years, New Spain was ruled by Spain. In 1810, Mexico declared independence from Spain, and after a long war, finally gained its full independence in 1821. At that time, all of the southwestern United States from Texas to California was part of Mexico. Growing United States migration into these areas prompted the US government to try to purchase them from Mexico, which Mexico refused. The United States then instigated the Mexican–American War (1846–1848), which resulted in Mexico's loss of about a third of its territory to the United States.

In addition to the Aztecs, there were a large number of other Indian groups living throughout Mexico at the time of Spanish arrival. Remnants of the Maya civilization (which peaked in the 7th century CE in Guatemala) are prominent to this day on Mexico's Yucatan Peninsula and in the southern state of Chiapas, and Zapotec Indian communities abound in the Oaxaca area and in the remote Sierra Madre del Sur mountains south of Mexico City. Unlike Anglo North America, racial mixing was much more commonplace between the Spanish and Indians in Mexico. The resulting mestizo racial group today forms the bulk of Mexico's population. Mestizos in Mexico tend to have much more Indian blood than European blood because of the comparatively large numbers of Indians who lived there at the time of European contact.

Today, Mexico is considered one of the more successful countries in the developing world, and in comparison to the countries further south in Central America. However, in comparison to its neighbors to the north, Mexico remains poor and large numbers of Mexicans leave the country each year both legally and illegally to seek their fortunes in the United States and Canada. The number of illegal crossers who are apprehended by United States border officials ranges from 1 to 1.7 million a year. It is difficult to know how many illegal crossers are not apprehended. Within Mexico, the most traditional lifestyles tend to continue in isolated rural areas and in Indian peasant societies. Smaller Spanish colonial towns are rich in their historic architecture, and some have become major tourist attractions, such as Oaxaca and Talaquepaque. The large urban centers of Mexico City, Guadalajara, Monterrey and Ciudad Juárez are modern metropolitan regions, each with over two million people. The result is a wide range in incomes, lifestyles, wealth and poverty, on top of a tremendous cultural and environmental diversity.

Tourism in Mexico

Most of Mexico's international tourists come from the United States and Canada, but many also visit from Europe, Asia and other parts of Latin America. Mexico is best known for beach resort-based tourism on the west and east coasts, particularly in the resort destination of Cancun (a purpose-built resort community) and Cozumel in the east and Los Cabos, Mazatlan, Acapulco and Puerto Vallarta on the Pacific Coast. Cruise tourism is also a vital component of the tourism industry in Mexico. Cruises on the west coast, typically leaving from Los Angeles or San Diego on 3–7 day trips along Baja California and reaching as far south as Acapulco and Puerto Vallarta. On the Caribbean side, cruises frequently call in Cancun and Cozumel.

Another form of tourism that has become more popular in Mexico is nature-based tourism, particularly in the rainforests of the southern states, where a large variety of endemic species of plants and animals can be found and where large tracts of rainforests still dominate much of the natural landscape. Most images of *ecotourism*, or nature-based tourism, are geared toward tropical regions with rainforest trekking as the major activity. However, in Mexico, a significant level of nature-oriented tourist activities also take place in the mountains, canyons and desert areas of the central and northern regions, focusing primarily on the country's widespread system of national parks and nature preserves.

Cultural heritage tourism is also a popular niche in the Mexican tourism industry. This specialized form of tourism is based primarily on the built heritage of Mexico's rich indigenous and colonial past. Many of the largest cities of Mexico are home to important built heritage areas, of historic zones, where centuries-old Spanish colonial architecture stands among modern skyscrapers and busy streets in the form of churches, government buildings, and stately homes.

The country's indigenous heritage is known worldwide for ancient cities and archeological sites. As mentioned above, the Aztecs built large cities in Mexico's central region, and Mayan ruins and cities dominate in the south. Many of these sites have been designated UNESCO World Heritage Sites and are among the country's most salient tourist attractions. Chichén Itzá, the best-known ancient Mayan city, recently was elected onto the list of the New Seven Wonders of the World, which will likely result in increased visitation. Another important form of cultural heritage that receives considerable tourist attention is Mexican cuisine. The food is the highlight of many trips, and Mexican culinary heritage has spread to other countries and influenced some of the largest fast food chains in the world.

PHOTO 5.10

Resort at Cabo San Lucas at the southern tip of the
Baja Peninsula in Mexico

Source: Alan A. Lew

In spite of the importance of tourism in Mexico's coastal regions, large cities, natural areas, and heritage places, the country's most significant tourist region in terms of total visitor arrivals and money spent is its northern border with the United States. Mexico's border towns are in statistical terms its most important tourism asset. In fact, the Tijuana-San Ysidro port of entry is the busiest border crossing in the world. These communities, most of which were originally cattle trading centers, became popular tourist destinations in the early 1900s beginning with the prohibition of alcohol and its production and consumption in the United States. Unable to purchase and consume alcohol at home, many Americans began traveling to Mexican border towns to drink where it was legal. As this phenomenon grew so did other exotic vices, including prostitution and gambling. Some of these activities have become less important among visitors to the border towns (e.g., prostitution), but others continue to thrive. Today, the most important border tourism activities on Mexico's northern frontier include drinking, gambling, purchasing pharmaceutical items, and buying the services of dentists and physicians. These last two activities have become more popular in recent years with the high cost of medicine and health care in the United States. All of these activities have grown as a result of legal and pricing differences on opposite sides of the border.

Throughout the 20th century, the reputation of Mexico's border towns as lude and dirty places grew. In an effort to change the public view of the border towns, the Mexican federal government started a border development program in the early 1960s, in an effort to stimulate tourism and expand the borderland economies. As part of this measure, border towns were cleaned up, old buildings razed, sidewalks poured, shops remodeled, and parks and welcome archways were built. Additionally, the Mexican government created a special economic zone near the border to entice foreign-owned industries to set up shop just inside Mexico. Assembly plants and factories (maquiladoras) were built by US automobile manufacturers, small appliance companies, and clothing manufacturers. By locating just inside Mexico (typically between 50 ft and a few miles), foreign-owned companies could pay lower wages to Mexican workers, and the national government provided many tax and location incentives.

Today, these maquiladoras are among the largest employers in northern Mexico, and people from around the country often give up rural life to head for the booming border cities to work in manufacturing, where they earn as much as two or three times what they would make in the interior of Mexico. This phenomenon has resulted in waves of relatively affluent Mexicans traveling across the United States border to shop on same-day or overnight trips.

In 2006 there were 28 million Americans of Mexican decent and direct migrants from Mexico living in the United States. One of their preferred tourist activities is to travel back to Mexico to visit relatives. Mexicans are socially connected by strong family ties, which often determine where they will take their vacations. Visiting friends and relatives (VFR) tourism is therefore one of the most significant forms of tourism to Mexico.

Because of its widespread appeal and diverse resources, Mexico is one of the most important tourist destination countries in the world, regularly ranking in the UNWTO's top 20 list, but history has not always been kind to Mexico. In 1994, NAFTA took effect and started the process of eliminating trade barriers between the United States, Canada and Mexico. NAFTA was an unpopular treaty among many of Mexico's southern indigenous people, who still eked out a living from traditional forms of agriculture, because it meant that they would have to compete with more efficient and inexpensive farm products from the United States and Canada. As a result, on January 1, 1994, an indigenous uprising broke out, supported by the Zapatista National Liberation Army, against the national government and its military forces. Thousands of people were displaced and many were killed. A ceasefire was later signed, and today the Zapatistas have moved toward more peaceful means of negotiation. This event dramatically affected tourism to all parts of Mexico, particularly the south, and placed the country on travel warning lists of its major markets. While relations between the Mayas and the government are normalized, the conflict still lingers in the tourism image of Mexico, and there is still a military presence that has an effect on tourism.

Also affecting tourism has been drug-related murders in Mexico near the northern border, which along with crimes against tourists, has prompted the US State Department to issue warnings on travel to the region. The result has been a significant decline in American tourists in cities such as Tijuana.

Central America

Central America Comprises the southern tip of North America, between Mexico and South America. As mentioned above, there is some logic to placing the northern boundary of Central America at the Isthmus of Tehuantepec in Mexico, because of the tropical climate and Mayan cultural influences that roughly start there. Excluding Mexico, the countries of Central America include Guatemala, Belize, El Salvador, Honduras, Nicaragua, Costa Rica and Panama. Together, the land area of these seven countries is about one-fourth the size of Mexico to the north, and about half the size of Colombia to the south. Sometimes Panama is included in South America instead of Central America because it used to belong to Colombia.

Central America separates the Pacific Ocean from the Caribbean Sea and the Atlantic Ocean. Costa Rica and Panama form an isthmus, which at its narrowest point in Panama is only about 30 miles (50 km) wide. All of the countries of Central America are close to one or both of these large water bodies. The Caribbean coastal lowlands of Central America are closely tied to the Caribbean Sea and share many cultural similarities with the Greater and Lesser Antilles. A major characteristic that they share is the almost complete extinction of native populations and the dominance of immigrant peoples from Europe and Africa. One major exception to this is on the Mosquito Coast, which still has native Indian groups who live very traditional lifestyles. However, much of the Caribbean east coast of Central America has very low population densities and is thickly covered with tropical rainforests.

Tropical rainforests and high mountains are found throughout Central America, though the forests have been heavily cut or burned for agriculture. These conditions have created many isolated and remote areas within this relatively small geographic territory. The interior mountains and the western coast of Central America still maintain strong Indian and Spanish colonial influences, much like southern Mexico. It is here where the majority of the Central American population lives. Because the mountains are cooler, the higher slopes are the preferred places to live, with most the major cities lying between 3000 ft (900 m) and 8000 ft (2400 m) in elevation. Overall, the east coast of Central America is very lightly populated, the West Coast is moderately populated, and the interior highlands are heavily populated, and even overpopulated in some parts.

For Central America overall, about 20 percent are pure Indian, while 60 percent are mestizo (European-Indian mix, also called *ladinos* in Guatemala). Mulattos (Black and European) make up 5 percent of the population, and zambos (Indians and Blacks) make up 1 percent. Pure European ancestry is claimed by 12 percent of the people in Central America. Costa Rica is the only country in Central America with a majority of its population claiming white European ancestry. It had a very small Indian population to begin with, and was not of particular interest to the Spanish. Most of its population was attracted to the country in the 19th and 20th centuries, as Costa Rica appeared to have a more stable government and economy than the rest of Central America. Even today, Costa Rica is often recommended as an inexpensive *retirement haven* for Anglo North Americans. Blacks are proportionally greater in Belize, which was a British Colony until 1981, and in Panama, where many West Indians were brought to construct the Panama Canal (1850–1855).

In 1821, the colonies of Central America declared their independence from Spain, and with Mexico's support they gained full independence in 1823. In that year they formed the United Provinces of Central America, which was a federal, democratic republic, much like the United States. This union, however, collapsed by 1840, when countries sought different policies on trade and governance. (However, the flags for four of the countries of Central America still share the colors and stripes from the original federal republic.) Many other attempts at union have been made since 1840, but none has been successful. A Central American Parliament was established in 1991 and continues to meet, though it only has advisory status. The Dominican Republic is part of the Parliament, but Costa Rica has so far refused to join.

Central America has suffered significant economic problems since the countries gained their independence from Spain. Their primary export is fruit and they have been highly dependent on trade with the United States, as well as on US development assistance and private investment. Poverty remains widespread, and wealth isolated in the hands of a small few. Insurgencies and civil wars have been a problem in Guatemala, Honduras, El Salvador and Nicaragua. Civil unrest has calmed down in recent years, allowing the countries to develop their significant eco-tourism potential. The quieter country of Costa Rica has long been one of the leading ecotourism destinations in the world, and Belize is developing a similar reputation.

Tourism in Central America

Although the countries of Central America have considerable potential for tourism development, only about half have experienced notable tourism growth. In addition to many issues related to underdevelopment, one of the primary reasons for this has been political conflict and security problems. The most successful tourism destination countries in this region are Belize, Costa Rica and Panama, with Guatemala and Honduras having seen some success recently as well. El Salvador, Guatemala and Nicaragua have been plagued by political and security problems (i.e., civil wars) for the past quarter century, although these have calmed down considerably in recent years. Nonetheless, these countries have had a difficult time recovering from their tainted images of fighting guerillas and military conflicts.

The countries of Central America have similar tourism products: rainforests, colorful cultures and beachfront developments. Mayan ruins and the lifestyles of indigenous people today form the basis for much of the region's tourism. Mayan civilizations in the northernmost countries of the region appeal to throngs of outsiders each year. In countries such as Panama and Costa Rica, the success of indigenous involvement in tourism has been cited throughout the world as being among the most sustainable, where the natives have a strong voice in, and benefit from, the development of tourism. Nature provides another important resource for the industry, primarily rainforests, beaches and volcanoes. Because of the combination of these cultural and natural elements, more and more Caribbean cruise itineraries have begun to include stops in Central America, such as Belize City, Roatan (Honduras), Puerto Limón (Costa Rica), and the Panama Canal.

There are several supranational alliances that also focus on Central America, such as the Central American Economic Integration (SIECA, members include Costa Rica, El Salvador, Guatemala, Honduras and Nicaragua), the System of Central American Integration (SICA) (formerly the Organization of Central American States), and SICA's related Central American Commission of Directors of Migration (OCAM). Like other free trade agreements, SIECA aims to improve trade between member countries and facilitate the transport of goods across national boundaries, and eventually the establishment of a customs union between its five member states. SICA's goals include regional economic development, the promotion of democracy, environmental protection, establishing a common customs union (trading block) to enhance trade with other non-party countries, and the protection of human rights.

Together these two organizations, comprised of all seven Central American countries, work together to ease border crossings for people from within the region. For non-Central American tourists, however, border crossings have not been streamlined as they have for locals, although the two organizations jointly issue a common immigration card for foreigners arriving in any of the member states. While tourism is not openly a significant priority in these agreements, many of their other priorities, such as environmental protection, border-crossing formality alleviation, free trade and transportation, have a significant bearing on tourism.

Another issue of significance in this region is transportation. In 1923, an agreement was reached at the Conference of American States to build a single transportation corridor (Pan-American Highway) that would link all of the Americas from Alaska in the north to Argentina and Chile in the south, some 16,000 miles (25,800 km). This goal has been met, except for a nearly 60 miles (100 km) break in eastern Panama and northern Colombia known as the Darien Gap – a swampy, rainforest-covered region that is under the control of dangerous drug smugglers and rebel guerrillas. The area's physical features have long prevented this last stretch of *Interamericana* from being developed, and now that adequate technology exists to overcome these barriers, precarious security conditions continue to inhibit the project. The countries of Central America have good and comprehensive bus transportation systems. Nearly all cities and towns, and many rural areas, are served by coach routes and minivan services. Unique to this region is the international company, TICA Bus, with routes from southern Mexico through all countries, except Belize, as far south as Panama City.

Belize

One of the most developed countries in Central America, in terms of tourism, is Belize. It has a well-established tourism image, particularly among the American, Canadian and Western European markets. One of the appeals of Belize is its population's ability to speak English, owing to its political history as a former British colony (known then as British Honduras). It gained independence as recently as 1981 and has flourished since then as an important destination, despite strained relations with neighboring Guatemala over their common border. Belize is home to the Belize Barrier Reef (also known as the Great Maya Reef or the Mesoamerican Reef), the second largest barrier reef system in the world after Australia's Great Barrier Reef. In 1996, the Belize Barrier Reef was inscribed as a UNESCO World Heritage Site. The reef also extends into Mexico in the north and Honduras in the south. This natural resource is home to thousands of aquatic plant and animal species and provides much of the appeal of Belize as a tourist destination. Small islands on and near the reef (e.g., Caye Caulker and Ambergris Caye) are the center of the country's resort facilities and diving operations. Many of the smaller islands are rented out for honeymoons and other significant events.

Mainland-based tourism focuses on the remnants of ancient Mayan civilizations, such as Altun Han and Lamanai, and on ecotreks through the rainforests of the country's southern and western regions. Most of the Mayan ruins in Belize have yet to be fully excavated. Belize City, the country's primary international gateway, is now a regular stopover on Caribbean cruises. Ecotourism and archeology-based heritage tourism, as well as limited diving and snorkeling, are among the most popular onshore cruise excursions. Despite the importance of tourism in the national economy, and although many of the lodging establishments and souvenir shops are owned by expatriates, Belize has been quite successful in withstanding pressures to welcome the establishment of large, foreign-owned and brand-name lodging and fast food services. In the remote south, Belize has also been noted as being a socially and ecologically

PHOTO 5.11
Ancient Mayan pyramids in Guatemala

Source: Dallen J. Timothy

friendly tourist destination with the development of village-based and community-operated lodging and tour services.

Guatemala

Civil war plagued Guatemala from 1960 to 1996 and still has salient repercussions for the country's economy and society today. In spite of the country's 1996 peace accord, between 2000 and 2006 there were several reports of foreign tourists being raped, murdered, carjacked or robbed. These images have been accentuated by media reports and have been a significant impediment for tourism development in Guatemala. Nonetheless, the country has potential for tourism growth. Its primary appeal lies in indigenous (Maya) heritage, both living and ancient. Languages, handicrafts, folklife, mixed Mayan and Catholic religious celebrations, costumes and food are an important part of the cultural product today, with several towns and regions in the highlands of Guatemala having become significant cultural destinations, including the famed Maya market towns of Chichicastenango, Panajachel and Santiago Atitlán.

Built heritage is an important part of tourism in the country. Tikal in the northeast is an important national park and is one of the best examples in Central America of pre-Columbian Mayan civilization. Antigua and Quetzaltenango are important towns for many reasons in Guatemala, but their tourism value lies in their exemplary Spanish colonial influence. In addition to cultural heritage, Guatemala has a rich and diverse natural heritage, which it is beginning to exploit for tourism purposes by offering rain-forest-based nature tours and adventure activities. It lags behind its neighbors Mexico, Belize, Costa Rica and Panama in the area of *ecotourism*, in part because some of the most pristine areas of the country have also been bastions of conflict between guerilla fighters and the military, and many of those areas are still risky to visit.

Honduras, El Salvador and Nicaragua

While it has not experienced the degree of political conflict its adjacent neighbors have gone through, Honduras suffers from an under-exposed image in the world of tourism. In common with Belize, Mexico and Guatemala, Honduras has a rich Mayan past that forms the basis of much of the country's heritage tourism product. Honduras also has several national parks and protected areas where nature-based tourism is beginning to develop. Perhaps the most popular region of Honduras for tourism today, however, is the Bay Islands off the Caribbean coast of the country, particularly Roatan, which attracts water-loving tourists to its growing beach-based resorts and accommodations.

Like Guatemala, El Salvador and Nicaragua have seen a good share of political conflict and instability in recent decades, which has hampered their efforts to develop tourism. Efforts are under way by both countries to develop tourism, but the world, particularly their main potential market (i.e., the United States), is still a bit reluctant. In 2006, Nicaragua held national elections wherein Daniel Ortega, a former adversary of the United States was re-elected president. In the 1970s, he was a leader of rebel guerillas who overthrew the government, and after coming into power adopted a Marxist-socialist form of government, which the United States opposed. In fact, the United States funded efforts by Contra rebels to oppose the Ortega (Sandanista) government. In 1990, he was ousted from office but returned again as president in November 2006. Since his recent re-election, Ortega has met with some foes of the

United States, including Iran, and declared his hostility toward the United States. After years of economic recovery and growth, the future of tourism in Nicaragua will no doubt be affected by inter-American politics.

Costa Rica

Like Belize, Costa Rica has a well-developed tourism sector and a positive image abroad. Costa Rica has experienced the least degree of political turmoil in Central America and is one of the most affluent countries of the region. This has assisted in establishing a successful tourism industry that is well-known throughout the world and is commonly cited as an example of the congruent relationship between sustainable development and tourism, particularly among the native inhabitants of the mountains and rainforests. Forest-based ecotourism is the country's primary tourism product, focusing on numerous cloud forests and volcanoes in the Central and Guanacaste regions. Between San Jose and the Panamanian border are a series of less-accessible national parks that are popular among wilderness adventurers. Puerto Limón on Costa Rica's Caribbean coast is becoming an ever more popular cruise port city, and beach resorts are well established on both the Caribbean and Pacific coasts. Like the rest of Central America, Costa Rica is seen as a good value for North Americans in that airfares and accommodations are relatively inexpensive, and the country is well connected with transportation options.

Panama

Panama as a destination is growing in popularity. Since the 1990s there has been considerable growth in the number of beach resorts on the Caribbean and Pacific coasts, to supplement the already popular San Blas Islands. Many tourism service providers are still small scale and locally owned and operated, but the country has seen the growth of expatriate ownership of small hotels, guesthouses, restaurants, and souvenir shops, as has happened in Costa Rica and Belize. There is also a movement toward large-scale resorts, many of which are and will be owned and operated by large multinational corporations. Of all the countries of Central America, Panama has the highest level of rainforest cover (ca 40 percent), and is dotted with amazing volcanoes. These forests and mountain regions are home to a vast array of flora and fauna. Based on these resources Panama has become a destination for nature buffs with a notable growth in nature-based/ecotourism since the late 1980s. Several national parks exist in the northern and southern portions of the country, including the UNESCO-listed World Heritage Area of La Amistad – an international park comprised of two adjacent parks in Panama and Costa Rica.

Panama is also home to thousands of indigenous Amerindians, who also have a significant stake in tourism enterprises. Their material and non-material culture is an important base for Panama's tourism product, although there have been significant conflicts in recent years between the indigenous people and the government in the utilization of natural resources or their conservation. The best-known tourism feature of Panama, however, is undoubtedly its famous Canal, built by the French and Americans in the early 20th century. The Panama Canal and the adjacent Canal Zone functioned as part of the United States until it was gifted back to Pamana by President Carter and returned to Panamanian control in 1999. It is estimated that more than 14,000 ships pass through the canal each year, including cargo ships and cruise ships. Many cruises in the eastern Caribbean include the Panama Canal on their itineraries.

The Caribbean Sea and Gulf of Mexico

The islands of the Caribbean Sea (or West Indies) include 25 separate political entities, including sovereign countries, overseas departments (French provinces) or colonies, and territorial dependencies. The largest island and country is Cuba, with more than 10 million people. Many other islands are very small, and some are uninhabited. Some islands are independent, while others are still governed by colonial rulers. They all share in common their insularity (they are islands), a colonial heritage, a former plantation economy (mostly sugar), and a history of African slavery.

Spain, France, Britain, the Netherlands, Denmark and the United States have all fought for control of various islands in the Caribbean Sea in the 17th, 18th and 19th centuries. Islands would be captured during wars and traded during peace negotiations. Because they belonged to different colonial rulers, there has never developed a strong sense of cohesion among the islands, as there was in Mexico and to a degree in Central America. The official languages of the islands tended to be that of their colonial rulers, and economic ties were often stronger with the colonial homeland than with neighboring islands. Today, the Spanish-speaking territories (such as the Dominican Republic) have closer ties to the other Spanish-speaking countries of Latin America, but the other islands and territories do not.

At the time that Columbus arrived in the Caribbean, there were perhaps 500,000 to 1 million Indians living there, with the main tribes being the Ciboney, the Taino and the Carib. Of these, only a couple hundred Carib survive in the Caribbean region today, though there are some Ciboney in Florida. The main cause of their death were the diseases brought by the Spanish. Common English language words that are of Carib origin include *hammock, iguana, hurricane* (after the Carib god of evil), and *maize.* To replace the native population, large numbers of African slaves were brought to the Caribbean to work on the sugar plantations that the Europeans established there. Today, approximately half the population of the Caribbean is of African descent, and about half is of European descent. The number of mulatto (mixed Black and white) is very small, although they comprise 75 percent of the population of the Dominican Republic. On Cuba and on Puerto Rico, 80 percent of the population is of white European descent. Elsewhere, Blacks form the largest racial group.

Although slavery ended more than 150 years ago, society in the Caribbean continues to be highly stratified based on race and culture (African vs. European). This is especially true in the Spanish-speaking islands. On the English, French and Dutch islands, mulatto and black leaders have been more likely to hold political power. Jamaica (formerly British) has been a country where a strong black national identity has formed and has fostered a multi-racial society. Neighboring Haiti (formerly French) is a country that has had a much more difficult time fostering racial equality under its Black leadership. (The United States has invaded Haiti several times in the 20th century to enforce peace in the country.) Trinidad and Tobago also has a large Asian Indian population, brought there by the British, who have made demands for greater political participation.

Today, sugar plantations are almost completely gone, except for in Cuba. The mainstays of the Caribbean economy are tourism and some mining, oil and natural gas drilling. The Caribbean is home to the largest cruise ship tourism industry in the world, and luxury beach resorts there cater to Anglo North Americans and Europeans. These often stand in stark contrast to impoverished local residential areas. Most Caribbean islands are too small to develop diversified economies and are dependent on only one or a few export products. They are also highly depended on subsidies and aid from their current or former colonial rulers. Because the islands are so dependent on imports for almost everything they have, the cost of living is very high and subsistence lifestyles are difficult. Puerto Rico, a United States commonwealth territory, is the wealthiest entity in the Caribbean, though its per capita income is well below that of the mainland United States.

Tourism in the Caribbean

The Caribbean basin is one of the most popular tourism regions in the world. It is especially popular among Americans, Canadians and Europeans for its warm climate, beautiful beaches, and seaside resorts. It is the most popular cruise destination in the world with many ships plying its waters everyday. Because of the region's varied colonial history, led by the British, French, Spanish and Dutch, the islands are rich in cultures that are a patchwork of African and European celebrations, foods, music, religions and languages. Many of the islands have become independent countries, while others are still under colonial rule from the United Kingdom, France and the Netherlands. Nearly all of the islands have well-developed tourism industries, with most of them being heavily dependent on tourism for their economic livelihoods. Some, in fact, are dangerously over dependent on tourism, which creates economic hardships when hurricanes blow through, or when economic conditions in their market areas decline. Hurricanes are a major threat to the entire Caribbean region, and every year, at least some of the islands are negatively affected by these tropical storms and their aftermath, sometimes wiping out an island's economy in one storm. In these cases, it is important for government leaders and other decision makers to try, inasmuch as possible, to diversify the local economies, such as through agriculture, manufacturing or other service industries aside from tourism.

Several supranational alliances have also formed in the Caribbean, but unlike the situation in North, Central and South America, the Caribbean treaties are more concerned with tourism. The Caribbean Community (CARICOM), the Organization of Eastern Caribbean States (OECS), and the Association of Caribbean States (ACS) are the most significant of these and include most of the region's independent countries and several members from Latin America as well. In tourism terms these trade alliances particularly deal with air transportation, facilitating inter-island flows of people, trade in goods and services, economic growth, and human resource development. The ACS has the highest number of member countries and is deeply involved in tourism-oriented treaties that deal with sustainability, air transportation, and regional marketing. The OECS also has adopted a common currency (East Caribbean Dollar) among its member nations (Anguilla, Antigua and Barbuda, the British Virgin Islands (BVI uses the United States dollar), Dominica, Grenada, Montserrat, St. Kitts and Nevis, St. Lucia, and St. Vincent and the Grenadines) to simplify inter-island transactions.

While not a supranational alliance in the strictest sense, because it is not imbued with political power to legislate, the Caribbean Tourism Organization was formed in 1989 as a non-political international development agency with offices in the Caribbean and North America. It works closely with the ACS and is responsible for marketing, human resource development, tourism research and information management, statistics collection, technical assistance, product development, and consulting services through the entire region. Although the tourism product is at one level fairly uniform throughout the entire region, the following sections attempt to elucidate the uniqueness of each island and country and highlight its commonalities with other islands.

Bahamas Turk and Caicos, and the Cayman Islands

While the Bahamas and Turks and Caicos border the Caribbean Sea, they are officially located in the Atlantic Ocean. Nonetheless, the two archipelagos are culturally and environmentally very similar to their Caribbean brothers and sisters, and in general terms and for most tourism purposes they are classified as Caribbean islands. The Bahamas, Turks and Caicos, and the Cayman Islands have a very similar product – sun, sea and sand, and all three island groups are heavily dependent on tourism. In the Bahamas, tourism employs over half the workforce directly and much more indirectly (e.g., through construction for tourism) and makes up some 60 percent of the country's gross domestic product (GDP). The Caymans depend heavily on tourism for nearly three quarters of their GDP and foreign exchange earnings. Nearly 50 percent of the Turks and Caicos workforce is involved in tourism and other services, and tourism is a significant portion of the local economy. All three entities are havens for offshore banking and insurance, and all three produce small amounts of fruit and fish for local consumption and export. In 2003, there were more than 68,000 companies registered in the Cayman Islands alone, many of which were banks, mutual funds and insurance agencies. In these islands, the banking and insurance industries stimulate a great deal of business travel as well.

Historical evidence suggests that Christopher Columbus first set foot in the New World on San Salvador Island in the Bahamas. A monument has been erected to commemorate the event, and the Bahamas Ministry of Tourism has worked hard to promote the site as one of the country's pre-eminent heritage locations. Cruise tourism is especially important in the Bahamas and Cayman Islands, the Bahamas being one of the heaviest cruised archipelagos in the world, while the focus of tourism in the Turks and Caicos is beach resorts. The Bahamas lies only 160 miles (100 km) off the coast of Florida and has become a convenient, yet foreign, destination for Americans who desire a quick trip overseas but not far from home. Many beach resorts have been built on Grand Bahama, New Providence, Andros, and Great Abaco to cater to this specific niche.

Cuba

Cuba is perhaps among the most interesting island situations in the Caribbean. Until the late 1950s, Cuba was a major destination for Americans and Canadians. However, as a result of the island's socialist revolution in the mid-20th century, which resulted in the eventual placement of a communist government in power, relations with the United States soured, while relations with the USSR improved. To have a communist country in such close proximity to the United States was a threatening proposition for the Americans, and the situation escalated nearly to the brink of war on a few occasions in the 1960s. Nonetheless, a non-armored approach was eventually taken, and in an effort to try to overthrow Fidel Castro and his state-socialist system, the United States enacted strict economic sanctions against Cuba, which are still in effect today. These sanctions translate into embargos against the purchase and use of Cuban products by Americans and travel by United States citizens to Cuba. The exceptions to the travel ban are journalists, sport teams, religious service missionaries, and occasionally Cuban-Americans being allowed to visit relatives on the island, although even this last function was severely curtailed by the Bush administration in 2004.

Despite the travel ban, tens of thousands of Americans travel to Cuba each year to enjoy the island's rich Latin culture and natural landscapes. Historic Old Havana is a significant tourist destination and was listed by UNESCO as a World Heritage Site in 1982. In addition, the island boasts many luxury coastal resorts with tours to the rainforest interior. Cuba is a popular destination for Canadian, Mexican, and Spanish tourists, and while their own government prohibits visits to the island, Americans are welcomed by Cubans with open arms, as they tend to be big spenders. However, as there are no direct commercial flights or ferry services between the United States and Cuba, people must travel via a third country, such as Canada, the Bahamas, Jamaica or Mexico. If caught visiting Cuba, United States citizens can be fined thousands of dollars and jailed, although this is rare.

Jamaica

The population of Jamaica, like most Caribbean islands, is primarily of African origin, reflecting the former thriving slave trade on the island and in the region. Jamaica's slavery was based mostly on sugarcane plantations, but with the abolition of slavery there in 1834, the slaves were freed and many of them became small farmers. The island's independence from the United Kingdom in 1962 furthered the self-determination of the people and paved the way for Jamaica to become one of the most successful tourism destinations in the Caribbean. Jamaica, unlike several of its regional counterparts, is not overly dependent on tourism. While tourism is a very salient part of the economy, the island has a more diverse economy than many of its neighbors. Activities such as gypsum, limestone and bauxite (aluminum) mining, rum production, agriculture (tropical fruit, vegetables, sugarcane, coffee), and cement and chemical production lend considerable diversity to the Jamaican economy.

An extremely popular cruise and all-inclusive resort destination, Jamaica depends heavily on visitation from the United States, Canada, and Western Europe. Kingston, the capital, is not the central focus of tourism, but is one of the country's two primary air hubs, the other being Montego Bay. Jamaica is unlike most of the other islands as well in its diversity of attractions. While sun, sea and sand are the principle appeal, slavery-related historic sites, Christopher Columbus monuments, colonial architecture, music and food form a solid foundation for cultural heritage tourism as well. In addition, Jamaica has capitalized on recent growing demand for agritourism, wherein people visit agricultural landscapes, plantations, farms, and processing plants. Several large papaya and banana plantations are involved in tourism, together with rum (made from sugarcane) estates where visitors can taste and see the production process. Likewise, coffee plantations are a growing element of agritourism in Jamaica, and the island's Blue Mountain coffee has become a popular drink among visitors and an essential export item. River cruises complete with crocodile sightings, jungle walks, and waterfall climbs are the most typical nature-based products of Jamaica.

Hispaniola

The island of Hispaniola is home to two countries: the Dominican Republic (DR) and Haiti. Haiti, one of the poorest countries in the world, has significant potential for tourism development; however, it has experienced some notable political problems in recent years that have prevented the successful growth of the industry. Coups d'etats have been a common occurrence, with successive governments being put into power (sometimes with United States assistance) and systematically removed by the military. Likewise, in 2005, political unrest in a few provincial towns led to even more decreases in tourist arrivals and the placement of Haiti on several countries' travel warning lists. Most tourism in Haiti today is comprised of cruise stopovers in Port au Prince and Labadee, as well as cross-border day visits from resort areas in the Dominican Republic.

Haiti's neighbor, the Dominican Republic, is among the best holiday values in the Caribbean and appeals foremost, like most islands in the region, to American and Canadian tourists, although it also receives considerable numbers of arrivals from Europe and other parts of Latin America. It has not experienced the same turmoil as its neighbor, resulting in a more stable tourism economy, which has grown considerably in the past quarter century. Most tourism in the Dominican Republic centers on beach resorts in the areas of Puerto Plata, Sosúa and Santo Domingo, which is supplemented by cruise ship stopovers on the north coast. The country is also attempting to capitalize on its Spanish colonial heritage to supplement its traditional sun, sea and sand product.

United States Caribbean Territories

The United States has three territories in the Caribbean: Puerto Rico, the United States Virgin Islands (USVI), and Navassa Island (uninhabited). While Guantanamo Bay is occupied and controlled by the United States military, it is still under Cuban sovereignty and therefore part of that nation's territory. Tourism flourishes in Puerto Rico and the USVI, but obviously not on Navassa Island or in Guantanamo Bay. Both Puerto Rico and the USVI are unincorporated territories, which means that they belong to the US, and their residents are United States citizens, but not all the rights set out in the constitution apply to them (e.g., voting in certain elections). They are able to elect representatives in the United States Congress, however, and enjoy most of the benefits of all other United States citizens.

The USVI were purchased from Denmark in 1917 as part of an effort to prevent German submarines from taking over the islands in World War I. Since that time, tourism has thrived on the islands, and many luxury resorts have been built to service the needs of a primarily American market. The United States government now requires passports for all travelers traveling to and from the Caribbean. However, the USVI and Puerto Rico are exempt from these requirements since they are part of the United States. Both territories emphasize this fact in their promotional literature and websites. Some observers believe this new regulation will grow tourism in the two territories since non-passport bearing Americans will divert their Caribbean vacations from other islands in the region to USVI and Puerto Rico. St. Croix, St. Thomas and St. John have become popular USVI destinations, especially for cruise and beach resort tourism. Water-based activities and honeymoons are especially popular forms of tourism in the USVI and gaining popularity. Virgin Islands National Park on St. John is a popular attraction for nature enthusiasts, and the USVI holds the unique distinction of being the only place in the United States where driving is done on the left side of the road.

Photo 5.12
Isla verde beach resort in San Juan, Puerto Rico

Source: Alan A. Lew

The United States gained possession of Puerto Rico in 1898 from Spain during the Spanish-American War. There is a political movement in Puerto Rico toward independence from the United States, led by the nationalist Puerto Rican Independence Party, through a peaceful electoral process. Other groups have lobbied to achieve full statehood as America's fifty-first state; the third movement is to keep the status quo – the Commonwealth of Puerto Rico, an unincorporated organized territory of the United States. Puerto Rico is an integral part of Caribbean tourism, and many cruises embark from the Port of San Juan. Spanish colonial heritage (forts, government buildings, plantation mansions) form a significant part of the island's heritage base, together with a rich tradition of Latin food, music and dance. Because of its large size (by Caribbean standards), the island is endowed with a rich variety of landscapes that have long formed the basis for tourism – white sandy beaches, rainforests, mountains and historic cities.

Anglo Eastern Caribbean

Tourism generates nearly half of the total economy of the British Virgin Island (BVI), although services in general comprise over 90 percent of the islands' GDP. The BVI is perhaps best known for sailing and diving. Most people fly into Tortola, the main island, rent boats and sail casually through the BVI's 36-plus green islands. Like BVI, Anguilla is still a colony of the United Kingdom and best known for white sandy beaches. The island caters to an upscale market, but it is not accessible directly from

PHOTO 5.13

Cruise ships at St. Thomas in the United States
Virgin Islands in the Caribbean

North America or Europe, which adds a sense of secludedness that simultaneously attracts and wards off potential travelers. Connections by air are only from nearby islands (e.g., Sint Maarten, Puerto Rico, Antigua, St. Kitts and USVI) and boat services from St. Martin. Antigua and Barbuda, and St. Kitts and Nevis are both independent countries in the eastern Caribbean and both provide similar tourist experiences. They are fundamentally resort-based tropical destinations where tourism focuses on the beaches, diving, golf and honeymoons, with a little exploring and colonial heritage mixed in. Uncommon for the Caribbean, St. Kitts and Nevis, while both part of the same country, each has its own separate tourism authority.

The British colony of Montserrat was a rather successful, if low key, tourist destination that boasted of beautiful coral reefs and a fascinating volcano. In 1995 and 1997, however, the Soufriere Hills Volcano erupted twice, killing at least 20 people and forcing the evacuation of nearly 8,000 residents to other islands. The eruption essentially buried the capital, Plymouth, and resulted in the designation of the southern half of the island a *volcanic exclusion zone*, which is inaccessible to everyone but scientists. These disasters essentially ruined tourism in Montserrat, but since that time the industry has started to recover. Many residents have returned, and the Tourist Board is once again actively promoting the island. Capital city functions and the tourism industry have been relocated to the northern end of the island out of immediate danger. While snorkeling and scuba diving are still the foundation of Montserrat's tourism industry, the volcanic eruptions have also resulted in a new product – disaster tourism – wherein people visit the island to see the volcano and its destruction from safe distance lookout points.

Dominica is unique in the eastern Caribbean and differs from its neighbors in three fundamental ways. First, it is the only island with a remaining indigenous population. There are approximately 3,000 Carib Indians still living in Dominica. Second, tourism and other services amount to less than 50 percent of the GDP; Dominica's economy depends more on agriculture and manufacturing than it does on tourism. Finally, the focus of Ministry of Tourism, Industry and Private Sector Relations efforts is heritage (indigenous and colonial) and ecotourism. Unlike other Caribbean islands, most of Dominica is still covered by rainforest, which provides an important backdrop for trekking trails, waterfalls and river walking.

Like several of their Leeward and Windward Island neighbors, St. Lucia and St. Vincent and the Grenadines are volcanic islands with green mountains and hills that lend themselves well to nature-based tourism. Both countries specialize in diving and water sports, yachting, beaches and eco-adventures. The Creole culture, a mix of African and European cultural traditions, such as music, language, food and religion, are also an important part of tourism. Although both countries rely heavily on tourism, agriculture is an important economic mainstay.

In addition to bananas, cocoa, spices, citrus, avocados, sugarcane and vegetables, Grenada's economy is nearly three quarters dependent on diving, boating, cruises and wedding/honeymoon tourism. This dependence has placed the country in a vulnerable position, especially given its location in the Windward chain of islands. Grenada has seen a larger number of tourism ups and downs than most other islands in the region. In 1979, for example, a series of coups by the leftist Maurice Bishop and the New Jewel Movement overthrew the young country's government and established a socialist system that thrived on improving standards of living, health care, education and self-reliance. The new government did, however, have a Marxist slant; it supported many Soviet policies and established close ties with Cuba and other socialist states. Under Bishop's regime, opposition media were censored and free elections were canceled, which swiftly caught the attention of the United States.

On October 19, 1983, hardline Marxists in the New Jewel Movement led another coup that ousted and executed Bishop and his advisors. With the hardline communist government in control for only 6 days, the United States, with assistance from Jamaica, Barbados and a handful of other Caribbean countries, invaded Grenada on October 25, 1983, overthrowing the Marxist-socialists, and establishing free elections. This significant event in the history of the Caribbean had serious consequences for tourism in the short term, although the industry has since recovered, and Grenada has turned this dark period of history into a national holiday and tourist attraction. Another major blow to Grenada's tourism occurred in 2004 with the passing of Hurricane Ivan, which was especially destructive for Grenada and its neighbors. Dozens of people were killed, some 90 percent of all homes were destroyed or heavily damaged, and much of the tourism infrastructure, including the cruise ship port, was destroyed. While not as powerful as Ivan, Hurricane Emily hit Grenada the following year, doing additional damage to an island already struggling to recover. Tropical storms are a significant threat throughout the entire region, but Grenada has paid a heavy cost in recent years.

Barbados is a low-lying Windward Island and one of the few in the Caribbean with petroleum and natural gas resources. In addition to sugar, rum, cotton and vegetable production, tourism forms a significant part of the economy based on festivals, culture, sport, cruises and golf resorts. Although Barbados remains a popular destination for leisure travel, in an effort to boost sluggish growth in tourism, the Barbados Tourism Authority actively markets itself as a meetings and conferences (MICE) destination, complete with good access, beautiful weather and scenery, first-class facilities, and quality hospitality.

With the emancipation of slaves in 1834, South Asian laborers were brought to Trinidad and Tobago by the British colonialists to work the sugarcane industry, which traditionally has formed the backbone of the nation's economy. As a result of this late 19th and early 20th century labor migration, the population of Trinidad and Tobago remains predominantly Indian/South Asian. Petroleum and chemical products account for approximately half of the GDP, followed by tourism and agriculture. Trinidad and Tobago is the largest producer of oil in the Caribbean and as a result also has one of the highest standards of living and per capita incomes in the region.

Trinidad and Tobago are faced with a unique situation, shared with St. Kitts and Nevis, and Antigua and Barbuda in the Caribbean Basin – the notion of twin-island states. Scholars and other observers have commented recently about conditions of twin-island states, although Tobago has received the majority of attention given its separatist desires that have made world headlines. Tobago, Barbuda and Nevis argue that they are treated by their larger national partners as second-rate regions, lacking in political power and public representation at the national level, and being ignored in economic development efforts, particularly in tourism. This has resulted in strained relations between the larger islands and the smaller islands and a growth of independence movements in all three of the smaller island partners. While separatist lobbies exist in Barbuda and Tobago, they are more subtle than the movement in Nevis. In 1998, a Nevis referendum vote to separate from St. Kitts fell short of the two-thirds majority needed, although many supporters of independence for tiny Nevis continue their support of these efforts. While Trinidad and Tobago are seen by many as a model of successful twin-island states, others suggest that the system is highly flawed and unbalanced.

The French West Indies

The French West Indies are comprised of Guadeloupe, Martinique, St. Barts (Barthelemy) and St. Martin – all important tourist destinations. St. Martin is unique in that it shares a small island with its Dutch counterpart, Sint Maarten. While the French-Dutch border is well marked and is part of the tourist appeal of the island, there are no customs or passport controls between the two entities, and there never have been. However, in the mid-1980s when France began requiring visas of nationalities that had not previously needed them (e.g., the United States of America and Canada), the French government considered erecting border checkpoints on the small island. Local Dutch and French authorities, cruise companies, and airlines fought the measure because of the damage it would have done to tourism; the primary international gateway to French St. Martin is via Dutch Sint Maarten's Princess Juliana International Airport. Given the need to acquire a French visa, tourists to the island would inevitably choose to stay in the south. Eventually the proposal was defeated.

The French side of the island is nearly twice the size of the Dutch portion and is conspicuously French in its language, religious landscape, architecture, foodways,

music, relaxed atmosphere, and more conservative values. Beaches and resorts are the primary basis of tourism. St. Barts is an upscale destination with white sand beaches, lush green hills and a yacht harbor. Tourism in Martinique and Guadeloupe thrives on beachfront development, shopping, cruises, sailing, golf and diving. All of the islands in the French West Indies are markedly French, which gives them a unique array of cuisines and French imported products that are popular among tourists.

Aruba and the Netherlands Antilles

Aruba belonged the Netherlands Antilles until 1986 when, as part of its preparations for full independence, it separated from the Antilles and became an autonomous part of the Kingdom of the Netherlands. The island has stopped short of being fully independent, but future plans still include separation from the Netherlands. Aside from tourism, Aruba has a thriving oil refining industry and some offshore banking. Aruba is one of the most popular destinations in the region, although its tourism was noticeably affected by the terror attacks of September 11, 2001. Likewise, the island experiences a tourism blow in May 2005, when an American teenager went missing on the island and was feared dead. The news of her disappearance hit hard as Americans canceled or re-routed their travel plans. By 2008 the young woman still had not been found, which has not boded well for an island that depends on tourism for its economic survival.

As noted earlier, the island of St. Martin is shared by two countries: France and the Netherlands. The Dutch portion (south), Sint Maarten, is a popular cruise destination and shopping haven, because it is, like many Caribbean islands, a duty-free port. Gambling is allowed only on the Dutch side of the island, so casinos and bordello

Organizers of international cricket's showpiece event in one of the world's dream tourist destinations were left facing many empty seats inside stadiums and poor business with vacant hotel rooms outside them. The seven-week Cricket World Cup in the West Indies in 2007, which was eventually won by Australia, was promoted as the perfect sports tourism package, sun-drenched beaches, Caribbean hospitality and the chance to watch the sport's elite contest its premier one-day tournament.

However, organizers, governments and the tourism industry for the nine Caribbean nations that staged World Cup matches and warm-up games for the event (Jamaica, St. Kitts and Nevis, Antigua and Barbuda, St. Vincent and the Grenadines, Saint Lucia, Barbados, Grenada, trinidad and Tobago and Guyana) are extremely disappointed after only a fraction of the tens of thousands of fans expected actually took up the expensive trip.

A number of reasons have been put forward for problems associated with the event. In sporting terms the shock first-round elimination of India and Pakistan, with the Indian team having the world's biggest fan base, meant that Indian supporters went home early. The host team the West Indies' poor form did not help either as they did not qualify for the semi-finals. However, the event was regarded by many as being too long, as it can be difficult for fans to secure seven weeks of holidays. Furthermore, the nature of the event meant that although the locations of matches in later stages of the competition was known, the teams that would be competing was not. Therefore, fans had to *second guess* the results of games in order to pre-book flights, accommodation and book tickets. The unpredictable nature of sport meant that teams did not perform as expected therefore you had situations in which fans had tickets to games but could not get flights between the islands to see them.

Visa requirements were also altered for the event. A special CARICOM visa was introduced for some visitors to Dominica and the nine host countries for the period February 1 to May 15, 2007 supposedly on the grounds of security and ease of movement, as visitors with the special visa were able to move freely between the host countries without further immigration formalities. Unfortunately, the visa was introduced quite late in the lead up to the event with some fans already having purchased flights to the event. However, more confusing was that nationals from some countries did not need a CARICOM special visa: Canada, France and overseas territories, Germany, Ireland, Italy, Japan, the Netherlands and overseas territories, United Kingdom and Dependent Territories, South Africa, Spain, United States and Dependent Territories, and nationals and residents of CARICOM Member States (Except Haiti). Yet this meant that nationals of some of the potentially biggest markets for the event: Australia, Bangladesh, India, Pakistan, New Zealand and Sri Lanka, did require such visas.

Other issues included the relative high cost of accommodation for nationals of most of the counties that were participating as well as the high entrance prices. The situation contrasted with major sports events in other parts of the world, such as the soccer or rugby world cups, which budget tourists can usually afford to attend. Ticket prices were also high because regional governments wanted to recover the large sums spent on infrastructure. For example, the Jamaican Government spent US$81 million via a loan from China for refurbishing the Sabina Park ground and constructing a new multi-purpose facility in Trelawny. Another US$20 million was budgeted for *off-the-pitch* expenses, putting the total at more

Continued

than US$100 million or JM$7 billion. The total amount of money spent on all the stadiums was estimated at over US$301 million.

Unfortunately, while there was substantial pre-tournament ticket sales, actual attendance was approximately 40 percent less than what would have been expected, primarily as a result of the loss of Pakistan and India from later rounds and difficulties in fans being able to get to venues via the Caribbean's airline system. This meant that returns to the hotel sector, food and beverage suppliers, were well below what was expected. Furthermore, it appeared that some hotels actually had rooms available during what would normally be the peak holiday season leading up to Easter as a result of some potential visitors not coming to the Caribbean because of the event. The World Cup therefore highlights the difficulties for developing countries with a limited financial base running such large events.

bars have become popular attractions for tourists staying on both sides of the island. Nude beaches and luxury resorts dot the coastline of Sint Maarten, and slave- and plantation-related historic sites are becoming fashionable attractions on both sides of the border.

Bonaire and Curacao are both known for their petroleum refineries and trans-shipping facilities, primarily with oil connections to Venezuela. Tourism is a very significant part of their economies as well, as it is for St. Eustatius and Saba, the two smallest islands of the Netherlands Antilles. Saba is a well-known honeymoon destination owing to its small physical size and relatively secluded location. St. Eastatius is a trendy destination for hikers and divers.

5.3   SOUTH AMERICA

South America is the fourth largest continent in the world. It makes up 12 percent of the Earth's land area, but only 6 percent of the planet's population. The Andes mountain range and the vast Amazon Basin rainforest limit the potential settlement areas of the continent. Along with North America, South America is part of the Western Hemisphere. The Western Hemisphere is also referred to as the New World, in comparison to all of the other continents that comprise the Old World. The term *the Americas* is also used to refer to both North and South America together. The name, America, comes from the Italian navigator Amerigo Vespucci who was one of the first to sail and map the coastline of northeastern South America (early 1500s). He was also one of the first to propose that the Americas were not to part of Asia but were a separate continent (a *new world*). Using information from his sailings, by 1507 Spanish and German cartographers had applied the name *America* to South America. Soon thereafter it was applied to North America, as well.

Physical Geography of South America

South America shares some features in common with Africa, to which it was attached some 245 million years ago. It is a very compact continent with few large peninsulas, seas or bays. There are also very few islands associated with South America. The islands that do exist are mostly at the very southern tip of the peninsula, including the Falkland Islands (also known as the Malvinas), and Tierra del Fuego. The country of Trinidad and Tobago, which are islands off the north coast of South America, and the Galapagos Islands off the coast of Ecuador are the two other significant island groupings of South America.

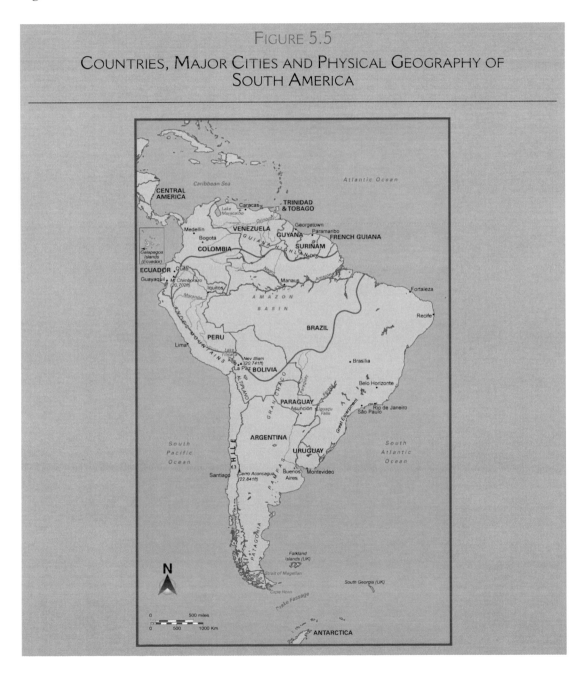

FIGURE 5.5

COUNTRIES, MAJOR CITIES AND PHYSICAL GEOGRAPHY OF
SOUTH AMERICA

Like Africa, South America's geologic structure is mostly comprised of large highland massifs separated by major drainage basins. There are two major highland regions that were once part of the core of the ancient continent, Gondwana, along with much of the continent of Africa. These are the Guiana Highlands to the north of the Amazon River, and the Brazilian Highlands to the south of the Amazon. The Guiana Highlands are much smaller and have an average elevation of about 1000 ft (305 m), though their highest peak is 9000 ft (2743 m). The Brazilian Highlands are also known as the Brazilian Plateau and have an average elevation of about 3000 ft (914 m), with their highest peak over 9000 ft. Patagonia is a third tableland area of ancient rock located in the very southern part of Argentina, south of the Negro River.

The major basins of South America include the Orinoco River Basin, the Amazon Depression, the Paraguay River Basin, and the Pampas of Argentina. The Orinoco River Basin is north of the Guiana Highlands and southeast of the Andes Mountain Range. It is mostly in the countries of Venezuela and Columbia and is a grassland region also known as the *Llanos*. The Paraguay River Basin is situated between the Andes Mountains and the southern part of the Brazilian Highlands. The Paraguay River, South America's second largest river, enters the Atlantic Ocean at the city of the Buenos Aires, Argentina. South of Buenos Aires is the *Pampas*, which is a vast outwash plain of the Andes Mountains (Figure 5.5).

The Amazon

The Amazon Depression (also known as the Amazon Basin) is the world's largest river basin. The Guiana Highlands form its northern boundary, the Andes Mountains form its western boundary, and the Brazilian Highlands form its southern boundary. It is very flat reaching an elevation of only 385 ft (117 m) in Iquitos, Peru, on the eastern slopes of the Andes Mountains. The elevation of Manaus, Brazil, in a very center of the Amazon basin, is only 144 ft (44 m). The Amazon River is about 4000 miles (6,400 km) long. Only the Nile River in Africa and the combined Missouri and Mississippi Rivers in North America are longer. The Amazon, however, contains 20 percent of all the river waters of the world and its outflow is 10 times greater than that of the Mississippi/Missouri River. The Amazon has more than 1000 tributaries, several of which are over 1000 miles (1609 m) long.

The Amazon rainforest is the largest rainforest area in the world, and possibly contains the earth's oldest forested areas. Some of its trees are more than 300 ft (91 m) high, and hover over an incredible diversity of species of plants and animals. Unfortunately, human activity has been transforming the rainforest. Hundreds of square miles of tropical rainforests are cut annually to make way for large-scale agriculture.

The Andes Mountain Range

One major difference between South America and Africa is the Andes Mountain Range, which forms a spine along the entire continent on its western edge. The Andes were formed by the movement of the South American continental plate over the Pacific Ocean plate. The Pacific plate slides under the South American plate in a process known as *subduction*. Material from the Pacific Ocean plate, as well as sediments scraped from the South American plate, are heated as they slide deeper into the earth's crust. The more volatile of these materials melt and then float upward pushing the land area above into high mountains and creating earthquakes and volcanic activity. The entire western coastline of South America is dotted with active volcanoes and is subject to frequent earthquakes.

The Andes are actually a very young mountain range, having risen in only the last 66 million years. They are 5500 miles (8851 km) long and second only to the Himalayas in average elevation. Several large rift valleys exist within the Andes. These valleys are formed by faulting and the spreading apart of mountains, rather than by erosion. One of these large rift valleys is the Magdalena River Valley in Colombia. The most famous, however, is the Altiplano (high plain) of Bolivia and southern Peru. This valley has a base elevation of 12,000 to 15,000 ft (3658 to 4572 m) and is as wide as 125 miles (201 km). Only in Tibet are similar conditions found. Several internal drainage basins are scattered across the Altiplano, containing marshes and lakes, the largest of which is Lake Titicaca on the border between Peru and Bolivia.

The highest peak in South America is Mount Aconcagua in Argentina on the border with Chile, a little north of Santiago. At 22,831 ft (6959 m), it is the highest peak in the Western Hemisphere. (Although, when measured from the distance out from the very center of the earth, the highest peak in the world is actually Mount Chimborazzo 20,702 ft (6310 m) in Ecuador, which sits close to the equator.) In the southern portion of the Andes the mountain valleys are submerged below sea level and the peaks form a vast region of islands. Because of the high precipitation in this area, glaciers are also widespread.

Photo 5.15
Ruins of the Incan city of Machu Picchu in the Andes mountains of Peru

Climate

The equator runs just north of the Amazon River through the Amazon Basin, the intertropical convergence zone (ITCZ) extends roughly along the equator around the entire earth and directly through the Amazon region as already noted. The ITCZ is an area where air from the northern and southern hemispheres come together and rise into the upper atmosphere. In doing so it creates a band of low pressure and brings moisture from ground level to higher altitudes where condensation occurs, followed by rain. Along the ITCZ rain falls all year long and on a frequent basis. Temperatures are hot and the air is humid. Tropical rainforests are the dominant vegetation under such conditions, and is the natural vegetation throughout the Amazon Basin.

North and south of the ITCZ are regions dominated by high pressure. For South America there is a large high-pressure system located most of the year off the coast of Chile, as well as high-pressure systems in the North Atlantic and South Atlantic. High-pressure systems are characterized by air descending from the upper atmosphere that is dry and cloud free. The biggest impact of these high-pressure systems is on the west coast of South America, in the area from northern Chile through Peru where desert climate conditions exist. Desert-like conditions also extend into southern Argentina, which lies in the rain shadow of the southern Andes Mountains. The southern Andes extends further south toward Antarctica than any other land mass. This places them in the high southern latitudes where an intense Marine West Coast climate brings heavy rain and snow to their west coast side.

The high-pressure systems and ITCZ low-pressure belt migrate north and south following the sun through the year. January is the southern hemisphere summer when these air masses migrate southward. In July the ITCZ moves northward, as do the high-pressure systems off the coasts of South America, and the low-pressure Marine West Coast storms in the far south.

Human Geography of South America

There are basically four major groups that have shaped the human geography of South America. These include American Indians, the Spanish and Portuguese who conquered the Indians starting in the 1500s, Black Africans who were mostly brought to South America as slaves, and immigrants from Europe and Asia who came to South America after its countries gained their independence from colonial rule.

The earliest humans to settle in South America most likely arrived from North America after crossing from the Asian continent some time between 45,000 and 12,000 years ago. It is quite certain that human groups lived in Chile 11,000 years ago. By 3,000 years ago a village-based civilization existed in the valleys and coastal areas of Ecuador and Colombia where they built temple mound complexes, created fine ceramics and cultivated many crops including maize (corn). Their culture spread to Peru and Chile where new technologies and innovations appeared.

Cultures in the central Andes built some of the most elaborate stonewalled terraces and irrigation canals of their time. Growing populations, especially in the Andes, led to the development of tribal chieftains, early cities, and the first empires of South America. The best known of these empires was that of the Inca (Inka). The Inca state expanded out of northern Peru to the north and south through the Andes Mountains starting about 1100 CE, though it never encompassed all of the advanced agricultural societies of its time. Its expansion was only stopped by the arrival of the Spanish in 1532.

At the height of the Inca period, it is estimated that there were 10 to 20 million human inhabitants of South America, half of whom lived in the central and northern Andes. In some areas up to 95 percent of the indigenous population died of diseases that were brought by the Europeans. Today the major Indian regions are the Amazon and Orinoco basins, Paraguay, north and central Chile, and the Andean Highlands of Venezuela, Colombia, Ecuador, Peru, and Bolivia. These were all areas of major Indian societies prior to European contact. The diversity of languages that were traditionally spoken among different Indian groups was immense. More than 100 different linguistic families once existed in South America. Many were very localized and only spoken by a small group of people, and many have become extinct in modern times due to Indian acculturation into European languages.

European Colonization

In the early 1500s, the two most powerful countries of Europe were Spain and Portugal. Spain and Portugal were at the vanguard of European overseas colonial expansion. In 1494, the two countries signed the Treaty of Tordesillas, which divided the world in half between them, based on a line drawn down the middle of the Atlantic Ocean. Spain received the western half of that line and Portugal was granted everything to the east of that line. This line was intended to give all of the New World to Spain and all of the uncolonized Old World to Portugal. However the line ended up giving a large chunk of South America to Portugal, which became the Portuguese colony of Brazil.

Spain and Portugal both had policies to keep out all other Europeans from their territories. It is estimated that fewer than 150,000 Spaniards actually migrated to South America. Up to one million Portuguese migrated to Brazil, drawn by the gold rush there in the 1700s. Manyy of these migrants eventually returned to their homeland. Although their numbers were not large, Spanish and Portuguese political and religious domination of the continent had a significant impact on the culture that has developed in Latin America in modern times.

A major impact of the Iberian invaders of South America was the introduction of Roman Catholicism. Well over 80 percent of the people in South America consider themselves Catholics. Catholicism, however, is often combined with more traditional and local religious beliefs. Shaman practices are common among Indian populations, while African influences are widespread among Black populations. Protestantism has increased considerably in the late 20th century.

As was discussed in the Sub-Saharan Africa reading, the Portuguese were the first Europeans to import African slaves to work on their colonies in the New World. Starting in the early 1600s, large numbers of African slaves were brought to both the Portuguese and Spanish areas of South America. It is estimated that some 4 million Africans were brought to Brazil, and 3 million were brought to Spanish South America (which includes the modern day countries of Venezuela, Colombia, coastal Ecuador and Peru, and northern Argentina). Large numbers of Africans were also brought to British Guyana, Dutch Guyana (Suriname), and French Guiana. The major Black regions of South America today include the coastal areas of the three

Guyanas, Venezuela, Colombia, Ecuador, Peru, most of eastern Brazil, and north-western Argentina. Africans have contributed much to the culture and food of South America, especially in these regions.

Although the social customs that South America inherited from Spain and Portugal emphasize a separation of race and class, much intermixing among the indigenous people and the immigrants to South America took place. Important designations have been developed to describe these interracial offspring, even if they are very simplistic. *Mestizo* refers to those who have a mix of European and Indian blood, *caboclo* is the term used in Brazil for those who have a mix of Portuguese and Indian blood, *mulatto* refers to those of mixed European and African blood, *zambo* is the term for a mix of African and Indian blood, and *cholo* has the same meaning as mestizo, though it also refers to those of Indian blood who aspire to the higher social status of the dominant European social classes.

Most of the countries in South America gained their independence from colonial rule in the early 1800s. Independence allowed the countries of South America to allow immigration from other regions of the world besides the Iberian Peninsula. Large-scale immigration started in around 1850, reaching its peak in the late 1800s, and decreasing considerably in the 1930s. (This period of migration roughly paralleled the era of large European migration to the United States.) During this time some 11 to 12 million people migrated to South America, over half of whom went to Argentina and about one-third to Brazil. The largest numbers were from Italy, Spain and Portugal. Chinese laborers came in the 1800s to help build railroads and created Chinatowns in South America, much as they did in North America. South Asians and Indonesians migrated to the three Guyanas, where they were invited as laborers.

After World War II large numbers of Koreans were invited to migrate to Argentina, while large numbers of Japanese settled in Brazil, Bolivia and Argentina. Together these three countries have the largest Japanese population outside of Japan. Today the region of South America that is the most dominated by Europeans and other relatively recent immigrants extends from southern Chile and Argentina to southeastern Brazil. In these areas commercial agriculture predominates, including wheat and dairy farms and cattle and sheep ranches.

South American Tourism

Tourism is an important part of the social and economic environment of several South American countries, although the region as a whole is one of the least visited (after Africa) in terms of arrivals from outside the region. Growth has been slow in the past, but recent data suggest that South America is experiencing a renewed annual growth in regional and extra-regional tourist arrivals. The continent of South America has a varied image, ranging from beautiful beaches, Amazon jungles, and snow-peaked mountains on the pleasant end of the spectrum to dangers associated with corruption, violence and narcotics-related guerilla warfare on the other end. Several countries in the region appear regularly in the global media as hotspots for violent crime and drug trafficking. Travel warnings issued by many western, developed countries, such as the United States, Canada and the United Kingdom, feature countries of South America.

Culturally and ecologically, South America is very diverse. The continent has a rich variety of native peoples, whose cultures are prominently on display for tourists, and

PHOTO 5.16

Rio de Janeiro, Brazil, is famous for its spectacular natural
setting, as well as its carnival celebration, beaches,
and low-income shanty towns

an extensive colonial heritage of Spanish, Portuguese, French, British and Dutch influences. It is a large region extending from equatorial tropics in the north and central areas to a cold, polar climate in the far southern reaches of Chile and Argentina, with several more-temperate climatic zones in between. Tourism is unevenly spread; Brazil, Venezuela, Ecuador, Peru, Chile and Argentina are the most visited countries of the region, with Colombia, the three Guianas (French Guiana, Suriname and Guyana), Bolivia, Paraguay and Uruguay being secondary destinations.

The Guianas

The Guianas is a generic term that refers to the two countries of Guyana and Suriname, and the French department of Guiana (Guyane). These three countries/territories demonstrate the diversity of colonial influences in South America aside from Spanish and Portuguese rule. Guyana was a British colony. Suriname is a former Dutch colony, and Guiana is still a French overseas department. Although they have some of the most dramatic natural scenery in all of South America, Guyana, Suriname and French Guiana comprise one of the least visited areas of the continent. The tourism industry in all three lands ranks below gold and bauxite mining, timber, fishing, and petroleum in economic importance. Tourist offerings in all three countries are very similar, focusing on trekking in rainforest nature preserves, wildlife viewing, river boat tours, waterfalls (Guyana is said to have some 300 waterfalls), capital cities and some Amerindian culture. Most of the region is comprised of uninhabited rainforests, rivers, and swamps, with few interior roads to facilitate travel and the spread of tourism, which tends to be primarily located in the coastal cities and towns.

Tourism has been significantly affected by ongoing border disputes between Guyana and its neighbors, Venezuela and Suriname. Although relations have improved since the mid-1990s, territorial disagreements still hinder normalized and neighborly relations. More than 50 percent of Guyana's territory is claimed by Venezuela, and the far southeastern corner of the country is claimed by Suriname. Guyana's maritime boundaries with the two countries are also contested in a region that has considerable offshore petroleum potential. These conflicts have contributed to a lack of cross-border tourism between Guyana and its neighbors. In fact, there are no official border crossings (or bridges) between Venezuela and Guyana, although indigenous people commonly cross by canoe for trade and apparently illicit drugs and gold mining. Nonetheless, for tourism, there are no cross-border connections between the two countries, and even air travel must be done via a third country such as Brazil or Trinidad and Tobago.

There has been talk since 2005 of building road links between Venezuela, Guyana and Suriname, with official border-crossing points, but this has yet to come to fruition. Suriname has a road link with Guyana, which facilitates some cross-border travel, but strained relations between the two countries and poor infrastructure still prevent the development of larger-scale tourism. There is also a car-carrying river boat between Suriname and French Guiana. Political relations aside, building roads and bridges between Guyana and Venezuela and Suriname and French Guiana would create a logistics frenzy, because driving in Venezuela and French Guiana is on the right, while in Guyana and Suriname it is on the left. This is one of only a few borderlands in the world that face this situation.

Brazil

Brazil, the largest and most populous nation in South America, is one of the most tourist-friendly countries on the continent. Brazil's economy is the strongest in South America, and although tourism is an important sector, it falls far behind agriculture and heavy industry in relation to total GDP. Brazil gained independence from Portugal in 1822 and since then has thrived economically on timber products, coffee, sugarcane, beef, wheat, cocoa, shoe and textile manufacturing, mining, and chemical and steel production.

Brazil has an extensive transportation infrastructure with good air and land links throughout the entire country. The primary exception to this is the jungle interior region, where most travel is undertaken by boat on the Amazon River and its tributaries. The Amazon Basin, with its capital, Manaus, and numerous national parks, is at the center of the country's ecotourism activities, where people travel by boat, visit indigenous villages, and hike in the rainforest. Some of the country's wealthy class have begun investing in boats to offer public transportation and tours through the rivers and jungles. Dozens of eco-lodges have been built and are managed by natives with only cursory interference from state and national governments, and academic researchers have begun examining the role of Brazilian natives as vital stakeholders in rural tourism development. Part of Brazil's recent promotional efforts to cultivate rural tourism has

Photo 5.17

Cruise ship makes its way on Brazil's Amazon river

been an emphasis on agrotourism, where domestic urbanites and foreigners visit sugar-cane, cocoa, tropical fruit, and coffee plantations and spend time on cattle ranches in the country's interior. Of all the countries in South America, Brazil has by far the most diverse tourism industry, with nearly every sector and activity being represented.

Rio de Janeiro is perhaps Brazil's best-known destination owing to its bounteous beaches, lively culture, active nightlife, accessible location, international gateway status, and world-renowned media image. Carnival is Brazil's most notorious festival and is celebrated all over the country, although Rio's event tends to draw the most international visitors. Rio de Janeiro's Copacabana Beach is one of the best-known beaches in the world and is the center for tourism in this city of over six million inhabitants. São Paulo is one of the largest cities in the world (population 12.6 million) and best known for its cosmopolitan atmosphere and famous art galleries and shows. The city is best known among homosexual travelers for hosting what is said to be the world's largest annual gay gathering, São Paulo Pride. Other important urban coastal destinations include Recife, Porto Alegre, Salvador de Bahia, and Fortaleza. Salvador de Bahia is Brazil's center for African culture, a remnant of the Portuguese sugarcane slave trade. The city is known as a center for Afro-Brazilian music, food and culture. Fortaleza and Recife are well established beach and urban destinations with many historic buildings, famous nightlife, and a wide variety of entertainment and recreational options.

Brazil is also a hub for heritage tourism, and the country has more UNESCO-designated World Heritage Sites than any other country in Latin America outside of Mexico. Most of the heritage product derives from historic cities and towns (e.g., Salvador de Bahia, Ouro Preto, Olinda and Goiás) with an emphasis on the colonial past. As already noted, indigenous cultural heritage is also an important part of tourism, but it does not receive the same level of attention by government officials, tourism developers, or tourists that the coastal and interior historic towns receive.

Another important part of the European heritage of Brazil is found in this southern reaches, in and near the city of Porto Alegre. Beginning in the late 1800s, the southernmost states of Brazil saw heavy waves of immigrants from Germany, Italy, Poland and other parts of Europe and Asia. Many of their original settlements still resemble transplanted European villages. The German architecture, food, festivals, handicrafts and the physical characteristics of blue eyes and blonde among the Itajaí Valley population appeal to Brazilian travelers, as a kind of European getaway; the region is also trendy for travelers from Germany who visit to see how their diasporic kin have fared across the Atlantic.

The Southern Group

South America's southernmost countries, Argentina, Chile and Uruguay, offer tourists a variety of mountain, flatland, and coastal scenery, with small towns and arctic climates in the south, and larger colonial cities in the north. Southern Chile and Argentina's Patagonia region feature high mountains with permanent glaciers and alpine scenery in dozens of national parks and preserves. Most Antarctic cruises depart from Ushuaia, Argentina, or Punta Arenas, Chile, both on the island of Tierra del Fuego, which is in its own right a significant tourist destination with glaciers, parklands and rural villages.

One of Argentina's most spectacular attractions is the renowned Iguazu Falls, which lies on the border of Argentina and Brazil, and only a few kilometers from the tripoint with Paraguay. Iguazu is one of the world's most spectacular falls, descending 230 ft (70 m) over a span of 1.7 miles (2.7 km). The falls with its surrounding Iguazu National Park (Argentina) and Iguaçu National Park (Brazil) has been inscribed on UNESCO's list of World Heritage and is an important tourist destination in both countries. Argentina's Route 40 is a favored corridor among tourists; it runs the length of the country from north to south and passes through some of Argentina's most vivid cultural and natural landscapes. Argentinian and Chilean wines have become favorites among wine connoisseurs in recent years. Viticulture has grown considerably in response, and several wine routes have been developed in both countries, which include visits to vineyards, wineries, and sales shops. Like southern Brazil, the Patagonia region also saw large numbers of immigrants arriving from Europe in the early and mid-20th century, particularly from Wales and Germany. The communities they established also bear a strong resemblance to their European landscapes, and family names and traditions reflect a strong European heritage. The urban heritage of Buenos Aires and other large cities is typical of Latin American colonial pasts in terms of architecture, layout, and population. Health, sport, and meetings and conventions are now a primary thrust of the Tourism Secretariat to complement the more traditional culture- and nature-based activities that have long defined Argentinian tourism.

Santiago, Chile, is one of South America's key gateways with many flights fanning out to other cities. The city is a major center of commerce for the continent and as a result hosts many business travelers each year. The country's largest cities are located in the central region, and the long, slender shape of the country means that one can travel from the coast to the upper reaches of the snow-capped Andes within a short distance. Glaciers and ski resorts appeal to mountain enthusiasts, while the country also is

Photo 5.18

Iguazu Falls on the border of Brazil and Argentina consists of 275 falls along a 1.67 mile/2.7 km stretch of the Iguazu river as it flows into the Parana River. It is one of the largest waterfall areas in the world, rivaled only by Victoria Falls in Southern Africa

home to beach resorts. Fishing, golf, hiking, birding, sea kayaking, and other outdoor adventures are heavily promoted by the Chilean Tourism Promotion Corporation. Chile's Easter Island is one of the earth's most remote islands – more than 2,000 miles (3,200 km) from South America – and one of the most mysterious. Nobody is quite sure about the origins of the island's Moai sculptures, but they are the foundation of tourism to the island. The sculptures and entire island are protected as Rapa Nui National Park, which has become a center for New Age travelers who believe in the mystical earth powers of the island and its former inhabitants.

Uruguay's agricultural export economy is quite affluent, trading mostly with Brazil, Argentina, the United States, and China. On a global scale, Uruguay is one of the least tourism-oriented economies in South America, although it has considerable potential for growth. Like its neighbors, Uruguay's tourism focus is cultural heritage, rural tourism, and ecotourism, although recent promotional efforts have spotlighted beach resorts and thermal springs and spas.

Peru

The official languages of Peru are Spanish and Quechua, the latter reflecting the importance of indigenous people in the country's socio-ethnic composition and their relative power. Much of Peru's tourism industry is based on ancient remnants of the Incas, as well as the living cultures of their descendants today. Machu Picchu, near Cusco in southern Peru, is a UNESCO World Heritage Site (since 1983) and one of the most recognizable sites in the world. In 2007, the New7Wonders organization elected Machu Picchu one of the new seven wonders of the world because it embodies global heritage at its best. The location is visited by thousands of tourists each year and is growing in popularity among New Age tourists and other nature spiritualists as a worship site owing to what some believe was the site's possible role as an ancient Inca place of worship.

Although cultural heritage dominates Peru's tourism image, the country also promotes itself as a nature and adventure destination with river rafting, birdwatching, and mountain climbing. Volunteer tourism has gained a strong foothold in Peru and other parts of South America, as people travel on short-term health and hygiene service missions from the United States and Canada to work among the poor of Peru. In the southeastern corner of the nation, Lake Titicaca has become a mythical destination for people who have read about the mystique of the floating islands and interesting cultures. Titicaca, the earth's highest navigable lake, is home to the unique culture of the Uro Indians, who build homes on floating islands they construct from reeds and other plant materials.

Unfortunately, Peru's tourism industry has suffered during the past quarter century from media-led images of Shining Path communist guerilla kidnappings of Peruvians and foreign aid workers, crimes against tourists in Lima, and harassment of tourists by narcotics gangs. The northeast border region is considered dangerous because of possible incursions by Colombian drug gangs and armed insurgents. While most of Peru is relatively safe, suffering from the same ailments that other countries in the region face, these images keep many less-adventuresome tourists from visiting. Despite these representations by the media and official government travel warnings, tourism has become a salient economic sector in Peru.

Ecuador and the Galapagos Islands

For tourism promotion purposes, Ecuador is divided into five regions: Amazon, northern Andes, southern Andes, Coast and Galapagos Islands. Tourism in the hot and humid Amazon region centers around ecotourism, adventure and Amazon natives. The Northern Andes region is home to the capital, Quito, and the town of Otavalo, where indigenous people attract tourists by living much the way they have for centuries. Quito is located in an Andean valley, some 9350 ft (2,850 m) above sea level, which gives the town a cooler climate than lower elevations so close to the equator. Old Quito itself has been listed by UNESCO as a World Heritage Site and is home to much colonial architecture, and the city is a major trading crossroads for Ecuador's many indigenous people. As a result, the city is recognized for its markets, cultural attractions, and handicraft centers. The Northern Andes is also home to growing adventure and sport tourism outside of Quito with a focus on kayaking, hiking, trekking, windsurfing and horseback riding. Nature-based/ecotourism, agritourism, archeological sites, and indigenous markets and culture are the foundations of tourism in the south Andes area. The Coast is known best for beach resorts, ecotourism, whale watching, arts and crafts, and culture.

The Galapagos Islands are almost 620 miles (1,000 km) off the coast of South America, but they are still one of Ecuador's most sought-after tourist destinations. The islands are especially well known as the place that inspired Charles Darwin to conceptualize his Theory of Evolution. While there is some beach-based and intra-island cruise tourism, the Galapagos is ranked by avid nature enthusiasts worldwide as the ultimate ecotourism destination, not only for its diverse nature, but also because of its connections to Darwin. The islands are somewhat protected as a national park, but researchers have recently voiced concern that the masses of tourists traveling to the Galapagos in the name of ecotourism have begun to exceed carrying capacity and are resulting in negative impacts. These islands are one of the few places in the world that are promoted by the government ministry (Ministry of Tourism of Ecuador) as a *scientific tourism* destination. Scientists from around the world are consistently working in the Galapagos on issues related to preserving reptile, bird and plant species, developing water-based agriculture, preserving marine life and developing educational programs.

Columbia and Venezuela

Colombia, like Peru, has suffered an image problem owing to unsafe conditions for foreign travelers. Several Colombian terrorist organizations involved in illicit drug trafficking have waged attacks against the country's infrastructure, public places, modes of transportation and civilian targets. Foreign aid workers, missionaries, and tourists have been kidnapped and murdered in recent years. This has led to travel bans by several North American and European countries. Rebel occupation of national parks and protected areas has prevented domestic and international tourists from visiting them. Several parks have fallen into guerilla control, and visitors are charged to enter, not by official park management but by rebel groups.

In spite of these problems, Colombia has some tourism potential. One of the strongest and most notable forms of tourism is VFR. Colombians living throughout the world travel often to their homeland to visit family members and friends. This, in addition to their remittances from overseas to those remaining in Colombia, are important to the economy. The Tourism Promotion Fund of Colombia is attempting to look through the instability in the area to develop ecotourism, heritage, urban and beachfront tourism, and recent guidebooks suggest that it is relatively easy to avoid the country's trouble areas. If the situation changes in the future visitors will find that Colombia has some very desirable cultural and natural assets.

Colombia's criminal activity has spilled over into the Venezuelan borderlands, negatively affecting an otherwise desirable and potential ecotourism destination. Approximately 90 percent of Venezuela's export earnings come from oil, but tourism and agriculture are an important part of the economy as well. Margarita Island, off Venezuela's Caribbean coast, is a popular cruise port of call and otherwise desirable sun, sea and sand destination. Together with Lima, Peru, Caracas has become one of the least expensive gateways to South America, not only to Venezuela. The country's many national parks, beaches and Amazon rainforests attract many tourists each year.

The Landlocked States

Bolivia and Paraguay are the only two countries in South America without access to the sea. Some observers believe this to be one of the reasons they have lagged behind other countries on the continent in terms of economic development and prosperity. Most tourist activity in Bolivia concentrates on indigenous culture, which is appropriate for a country where approximately half the population still practices traditional lifestyles and cultural customs. Bolivia has several of these unparalleled distinctions. For example, it is the highest and most inaccessible country on the continent, which adds to its tourist appeal and is one of the reasons for its ability to preserve native cultures. It is sometimes referred to as the *other Tibet*. It is also one of the few countries on earth that has two capital cities – La Paz and Sucre. Likewise, as noted above, Bolivia shares the world's highest navigable lake, Titicaca, with Peru, and La Paz is one of the highest cities in the world at 11,750 ft (3,580 m). The Titicaca region is among the most visited parts of Bolivia, often on side trips from Puno, Peru. La Paz and Sucre, despite being the twin capitals, are attractive towns that feature traditional architecture and unique urban landscapes.

Paraguay is possibly the least tourism-oriented country in all of South America. It has an adequate transportation system and accommodations, but it lacks an appealing image abroad. Most tourism in Paraguay occurs in the southern portion of the country in the capital, Asunción, with its colonial architecture and city squares lining the Paraguay River. Secondary foci are the central city of Concepción, the Jesuit Missions of La Santísima Trinidad de Paraná and Jesús de Tavarangue World Heritage Site, and a handful of national parks and nature preserves scattered around the country.

The Falkland Islands

Since 1833, these islands off the coast of Argentina have been controlled by the British as an overseas territory, and Falkland Islanders are United Kingdom citizens. However, Argentina also lays claim to the islands which it refers to as Islas Malvinas. On April 2, 1982, the Argentinian military dictatorship then in government asserted its claim over the Falklands and invaded, in what it argued was a re-establishment of its legal rights over the islands. The timing of the invasion appeared to be as much for domestic political reasons as the dictatorship was becoming increasingly unpopular and the invasion of the islands was seen as a potentially popular measure. The Argentinian military did not believe that Britain would seek to retain control of the islands. The United Kingdom, however, saw this as an act of aggression on its sovereign territory and responded with military force, resulting in the Argentinians surrendering on June 14, although Argentina still has not given up its claim to the islands.

While the battle was devastating, and many lives were lost on both sides, it put the Falkland Islands on the tourist map. Most of the world's population had never heard of the Falklands until the altercation, and once the hostilities ended, tourism began to boom as people from Europe, the United Kingdom, and North America began to visit. Today, fishing and sheep farming are the primary industries (95 percent) with tourism becoming a more important sector since the 1980s. Much of the islands' tourism product focuses on ecotourism and environmental history. It was visited by Charles Darwin as part of the voyage of the Beagle and played a crucial role along with the Galapagos Islands and southwestern Australia in the development of his evolutionary theories. War history with battlefield tours is also among its more popular activities.

TOURISM ISSUES AND INSIGHTS
WHALE WATCHING

Since the growth of the international environmental conservation movement in the 1960s and the *Save the Whale* movements of the early 1970s whales have been regarded as representative of a country's overall marine conservation policy. Whales have become an international conservation icon species that are also referred to as charismatic mega fauna, examples include elephants, pandas, and harp seal pups, which possess considerable emotive potential. The public appeal of whales, particularly in the Western world, has been sustained through a proliferation of books, magazines, films (e.g., *Free Willy*), television shows, music and works of art.

Related to the media interest in whales has been a growing fascination with observing whales and dolphins in their natural environment. With the worldwide ban on commercial whaling, with the exception of Japan which undertakes so-called *scientific* whaling, there has been a shift from the consumptive use to the non-consumptive utilization of whales. This has resulted in financially viable businesses based on taking tourists to watch whales in the open sea and a rapid worldwide growth in marine mammal-based tourism. Whale watching has become an important economic, educational and recreational activity. Organized whale watching appears to have begun in the United States in the 1950s on small, isolated scales in Hawaii and California. It grew slowly at first with the concept not reaching Europe, Australia and New Zealand until the mid-1980s. The whale watching industry is a significant contributor to many coastal communities, particularly in more peripheral coastal and maritime areas. Nevertheless, the overwhelming growth in the whale watching industry has stirred some serious concerns over planning and management issues.

Whale watching can provide both benefits and costs to animals and humans. Much work is needed to develop techniques to quantify both the biological risks and ethical values of whale watching. Management must confront both human demands and the impact it has on the animals. Indeed, management officials often find it difficult to come up with ways to insure both tourist satisfaction and the continued success of marine mammal programs. In relation to whales and dolphins, management concerns range from maintenance of the whale's habitat, harassment of the whales and dolphins by commercial and private vessels, and defining and enforcing the policies that affect both tourists and whales.

One of the objectives of ecotourism is to change the tourists' behavior and lifestyle so that their actions become more environmentally responsible both during the tourism experience and in the longer term. Opportunities to view whales may therefore provide an important platform for public education regarding the natural environment. It has even been argued that any negative impacts on populations of marine mammals that are constantly pressured by tourist boats and viewers may be counterbalanced by the education and awareness that whale watchers receive. If clear and concise this education may increase a whale watchers overall environmental awareness, and benefit all cetacean species. However, if inadequate education is provided, and the operator is instead simply exploiting a natural resource, then such operations may need to be extensively reviewed.

	Population 2006 (1,000)	World population share 2006 (%)	International tourist arrivals (1,000)		Change since 1990 (%)	World market share 2004 (%)
			1990*	2004		
WORLD	**6525170**	**100.0**	**436757**	**776837**	**77.9**	**100.0**
The Americas	**892411**	**13.7**	**92803**	**124688**	**34.4**	**16.1**
Anglo North America	331672	5.1	54572	65237	19.5	8.4
Latin North America	185294	2.8	30509	43397	42.2	5.6
South America	375445	5.8	7722	16054	107.9	2.1
Top 10 Destination Countries						
1　United States of America	298444	4.6	39363	46085	17.1	5.9
2　Mexico	107450	1.6	17172	20617	20.1	2.7
3　Canada	33099	0.5	15209	19152	25.9	2.5
4　Brazil	188078	2.9	1091	4794	339.4	0.6
5　Puerto Rico	3927	0.1	2560	3541	38.3	0.5
6　Dominican Republic	9184	0.1	1305	3450	164.4	0.4
7　Argentina	39922	0.6	1930	3353	73.7	0.4
8　Cuba	11383	0.2	327	2017	516.8	0.3
9　Chile	16134	0.2	943	1785	89.3	0.2
10　Uruguay*	3432	0.1	2000	1756	−12.2	0.2

*Uruguay International Tourist Arrivals estimated for 1990.
Sources: World Tourism Organization (UNWTO), 2007, Facts and figures; GeoHive. 2007, The population of continents, regions and countries (July 1, 2006)

APPENDIX

SUBREGION COUNTRIES AND TERRITORIES

EAST ASIA
China
China, Hong Kong SAR
China, Macao SAR
Japan
Korea, North
Korea, South
Mongolia
Taiwan

SOUTH ASIA
Bangladesh
Bhutan
India
Maldives
Nepal
Pakistan
Sri Lanka

CENTRAL ASIA
Afghanistan
Kazakhstan
Kyrgyzstan
Tajikistan
Turkmenistan
Uzbekistan

SOUTHWEST ASIA AND
NORTH AFRICA
Iran
Azerbaijan
Bahrain
Iraq
Israel
Jordan

Kuwait
Lebanon
Occupied Palestinian Territory
Oman
Qatar
Saudi Arabia
Syria
Turkey
United Arab Emirates
Yemen
Algeria
Egypt
Libya
Morocco
Sudan
Tunisia
Western Sahara

SOUTHEAST ASIA
Brunei
Cambodia
Indonesia
Laos
Malaysia
Myanmar
Philippines
Singapore
Thailand
Timor-Leste (East-Timor)
Vietnam

SUB-SAHARAN AFRICA
Burundi
Comoros

Djibouti
Eritrea
Ethiopia
Kenya
Madagascar
Malawi
Mauritius
Mayotte
Mozambique
Rwanda
Seychelles
Somalia
Tanzania
Uganda
Zambia
Zimbabwe
Angola
Cameroon
Central African Republic
Chad
Congo, Democratic Republic of the
Congo, Republic of the
Equatorial Guinea
Gabon
Sao Tome and Principe
Botswana
Lesotho
Namibia
South Africa
Swaziland
Benin
Burkina Faso
Cape Verde
Cote d'Ivoire
Gambia, The
Ghana
Guinea
Guinea-Bissau
Liberia
Mali
Mauritania
Niger
Nigeria
Saint Helena
Senegal
Sierra Leone
Togo

ANGLO NORTH AMERICA

Bermuda
Canada
Greenland
Saint Pierre and Miquelon
United States of America

LATIN AMERICA AND THE CARIBBEAN

Anguilla
Antigua and Barbuda
Aruba
Bahamas, The
Barbados
British Virgin Islands
Cayman Islands
Cuba
Dominica
Dominican Republic
Grenada
Haiti
Jamaica
Mexico
Montserrat
Netherlands Antilles
Puerto Rico
Saint Barthelemy
Saint Kitts and Nevis
Saint Lucia
Saint Martin
Saint Vincent and the Grenadines
Trinidad and Tobago
Turks and Caicos Islands
Virgin Islands, United States
Belize
Costa Rica
El Salvador
Guatemala
Honduras
Nicaragua
Panama

SOUTH AMERICA

Argentina
Bolivia
Brazil
Chile

Colombia
Ecuador
Falkland Islands (Islas Malvinas)
Guyana
Paraguay
Peru
Suriname
Uruguay
Venezuela

EASTERN EUROPE AND EURASIA
Armenia
Georgia
Belarus
Bulgaria
Czech Republic
Hungary
Moldova
Poland
Romania
Russia
Slovakia
Ukraine
Albania
Bosnia and Herzegovina
Croatia
Macedonia
Montenegro
Serbia
Slovenia

NORDIC EUROPE
Denmark
Estonia
Faroe Islands
Finland
Iceland
Norway
Svalbard
Sweden

NORTHERN EUROPE
Ireland
Jersey
Latvia
Guernsey
Lithuania
Man Isle of
United Kingdom

Austria
Belgium
Germany
Liechtenstein
Luxembourg

SOUTHERN EUROPE
Cyprus
Andorra
Gibraltar
Greece
Holy See (Vatican City)
Italy
Malta
Portugal
San Marino
Spain
France
Monaco
Netherlands
Switzerland

OCEANIA
Australia
New Zealand
Norfolk Island
Fiji
New Caledonia
Papua New Guinea
Solomon Islands
Vanuatu
Guam
Kiribati
Marshall Islands
Micronesia, Federated States of
Nauru
Northern Mariana Islands
Palau
American Samoa
Cook Islands
French Polynesia
Niue
Pitcairn Islands
Samoa
Tokelau
Tonga
Tuvalu
Wallis and Futuna

INDEX